Oxford Studies in Normative Ethics

Oxford Studies in Normative Ethics

Volume 2

EDITED BY

MARK TIMMONS

OXFORD

UNIVERSITY PRESS

OXFORD
UNIVERSITY PRESS

Great Clarendon Street, Oxford, OX2 6DP,
United Kingdom

Oxford University Press is a department of the University of Oxford.
It furthers the University's objective of excellence in research, scholarship,
and education by publishing worldwide. Oxford is a registered trade mark of
Oxford University Press in the UK and in certain other countries

First Edition published in 2012

Impression: 1

British Library Cataloguing in Publication Data

Data available

Library of Congress Cataloging in Publication Data

Data available

ISBN 978–0–19–966295–1 (Hbk)
978–0–19–966296–8 (Pbk)

Printed in Great Britain by
MPG Books Group, Bodmin and King's Lynn

Contents

Contents

Acknowledgments

Versions of the articles in this collection were presented at the second annual Arizona Workshop on Normative Ethics that took place in Tucson, Arizona on January 6–8, 2011. I would like to thank the Freedom Center and the Department of Philosophy at the University of Arizona for their generous financial support of the Workshop. Michael Bukoski assisted with Workshop details, and he and Brandon Warmke prepared the volume's index. Thanks to Michael and Brandon for their help. I would also like to express my sincere thanks to the following philosophers for serving as de facto program referees: Matt Bedke, Ulrike Heuer, Robert Johnson, Sam Kerstein, Doug Portmore, Holly Smith, and David Sobel. Matt Bedke and two referees, who wish to remain anonymous, generously commented on penultimate versions of the papers which helped to make a strong batch of papers even stronger. Thanks finally to Peter Momtchiloff, my OUP editor, for his continuing support and good advice.

Mark Timmons

Contributors

Robert Audi is John A. O'Brien Professor of Philosophy at the University of Notre Dame

Christian Coons is Assistant Professor of Philosophy at Bowling Green State University

Julia Driver is Professor of Philosophy at Washington University in St. Louis

William J. FitzPatrick is Associate Professor of Philosophy at the University of Rochester

Thomas Hurka is Jackman Distinguished Chair in Philosophical Studies at the University of Toronto

Daniel Jacobson is Professor of Philosophy at the University of Michigan

Elinor Mason is Lecturer in Philosophy at the University of Edinburgh

Michael Nelson is Assistant Professor of Philosophy at the University of California, Riverside

Luke Robinson is Associate Professor of Philosophy at Southern Methodist University

Jacob Ross is Assistant Professor of Philosophy at University of Southern California

Andrew Sepielli is Assistant Professor of Philosophy at the University of Toronto

Esther Shubert is a graduate student in Philosophy at Yale University

Cynthia A. Stark is Associate Professor of Philosophy at the University of Utah

Introduction

MARK TIMMONS

Oxford Studies in Normative Ethics aims to provide, on an annual basis, some of the best contemporary work in the field of normative ethical theory. This second volume features twelve essays that contribute to our understanding of a wide range of issues and positions in normative ethics and that I am proud to present as exemplary of some of the best work being done in this field.

One of the ways in which common-sense morality is seemingly at odds with versions of impartial consequentialism is that it recognizes permissions to sometimes act for one's own lesser good instead of for the greater good of others (agent-favoring permissions) and to sometimes act for the lesser good of others at the expense of one's greater good (agent-sacrificing permissions). In "Permissions To Do Less Than the Best: A Moving Band," **Thomas Hurka** and **Esther Shubert** seek an explanation for such permissions. They reject explanations in terms of competing types of reason for action, and propose instead recognition of fundamental underivative permissions: an agent-favoring permission and an agent-sacrificing permission. After setting forth and defending their basic proposal, the authors turn to various details and implications of their view. Of particular interest are issues about the comparative strengths of the two types of permission, including the degree to which one is permitted to favor oneself or others. The "band of permission" (the *extent* to which one is permitted to either self-sacrifice or self-favor) is, they argue, sensitive to and thus varies ("moves") according to one's relationship with others. So, for instance, on their account, the more intimate one's relationship with someone, the less one is permitted to self-favor and more one is permitted to self-sacrifice. They further suggest that the degree of self-sacrifice one is permitted in relation to close intimates is less than the degree of self-favoring one is permitted in relation to strangers, though (as Hurka and Shubert admit) this leaves them with the problem of reconciling this intuition with their explanation of the movement of the band.

It is standard to distinguish objective versions of consequentialism from subjective versions. Objective versions make the deontic status of an action depend entirely on the actual or on the objectively probable outcomes of actions. By contrast, subjective versions either make the deontic status depend on an agent's actual psychological states at the time of action (her beliefs and/or desires) or make the deontic status sensitive to an agent's epistemic situation at the time of action. Some subjective views combine reference to an agent's psychological and epistemic situation. Arguments for one or other subjective version over their objective counterparts often turn on such worries as the apparent failure of objective versions to provide action guidance or the fact that objective versions make performing a right action often a matter of good luck. Various subjective versions are meant to deal with some type of failure. In "What the Objective Standard is Good For," **Julia Driver** defends the claim that an objective consequentialist standard enjoys evaluative and thus explanatory priority over the various subjective standards that have been proposed. On her view, an objective standard can be used to generate taxonomy of different types of failure—motivational and epistemic—that can be used to evaluate the relative success of subjective standards that are meant to deal with such failures. Viewed in this way, an objectivist standard enjoys evaluative primacy over subjectivist standards.

It is widely thought that under conditions of uncertainty, one needs to guide one's behavior by one or another subjective norm—ought-norms that are appropriately related to the agent's perspective. **Andrew Sepielli's** "Subjective Normativity and Action Guidance" offers an explanation of why this claim is true. A number of issues need to be addressed in providing an adequate explanation, including: an account of subjective norms and how they relate to objective norms, the conditions under which subjective norms become necessary for action guidance, and an explanation of why they are needed. In addressing the first question, Sepielli offers an account of subjective normativity (of the concept of what subjectively one ought to do) in terms of one's *best try* at doing what is objectively valuable. The conditions under which use of subjective norms are indispensable are those in which the agent is consciously uncertain of what he or she objectively ought to do—this is the condition under which one will need to act under the description, "trying to do A." What, then, explains why subjective norms are needed under this condition? Sepielli rejects certain proposed explanations, including the widely accepted view that says we need subjective norms in cases of uncertainty because we need norms that advert to what is internal to, or within the agent's grasp. After explaining why this sort of "inside the agent" explanation is tempting and why it should be resisted, Sepielli offers his own explanation in terms of the "multidirectional" phenomenology that he argues is constitutive of conscious uncertainty.

Jacob Ross's "Actualism, Possibilism, and Beyond," tackles the question of how what one morally ought to do is related to the question of what an agent ought to prefer that she do. According to *actualism*, an agent ought to Φ if and only if she ought to prefer Φ-ing to what she would do otherwise. Opposed to versions of actualism are versions of *possibilism*, which maintain that an agent ought to Φ if and only if he ought to prefer the prospect of some "maximally specific option that involves his Φ-ing to the prospect of any maximally specific option that does not involve his Φ-ing." As Ross explains, versions of actualism imply that an agent ought to prefer doing terrible things in cases where doing such things is less bad than what the agent actually does, and so such views imply that one ought to do such terrible things, even in cases where intuitively there is some morally acceptable alternative available action that the agent clearly ought to perform. Possibilism, which admits of various specific formulations, including certain forms of what is called *securitism*, also founders in having unacceptable implications in a range of cases. After explaining the problems these views confront, and diagnosing why these views fail, Ross goes on to propose a theory of obligation that he calls *momentwise wide-scope securitism*.

According to the doctrine of double effect (DDE) considerations of intention are crucial in the determination of the moral permissibility of actions. The doctrine is typically understood (especially by its critics, but by supporters as well) as tying the permissibility of an agent's act to that agent's actual intentions, and this leaves DDE vulnerable to many well-known counterexamples. Critics claim that DDE susceptible considerations that bear on the permissibility of action with considerations that bear on a person's character: a person's intentions may reflect on the moral quality of that person's character, but are not directly relevant (in the way DDE seems to suppose) to the permissibility of what the person does (or refrains from doing). **William J. FitzPatrick** in his "Intention, Permissibility, and Double Effect," challenges the key assumption upon which critics seize in objecting to DDE, namely, that the doctrine is best interpreted as making permissibility depend on an agent's *actual intentions*. According to FitzPatrick's interpretation, what matters is not an agent's actual intentions, but rather the question of whether with regard to a proposed justification of the action in question, "an otherwise good moral agent *could* perform the action *because* of that justification *without* engaging in any illegitimate intentions and acting badly." In the standard case of the evil terrorist bomber who (unlike the non-evil tactical bomber) intends to kill the innocent people whose lives will be lost as a result of bombing an enemy military installation, her bad intentions do not suffice to make what she does impermissible: in this case there is a morally legitimate justification available to an otherwise morally good agent, just as in the case of the tactical bomber. Hence, DDE so understood does not have the implausible implication in the terrorist bomber cases (and related cases) to which critics appeal. Intention still plays a fundamental role in DDE in the way it figures in the structure of moral justification represented by this doctrine. After arguing for this interpretation, FitzPatrick proceeds to defend the importance of appealing to the central idea of intending harm as a means or as an end as especially morally problematic against those who might hold that even if DDE can be understood so as to avoid standard counterexamples, there is no need for this central idea in explaining the difference between permissible and impermissible acts.

Two common objections to Rossian pluralism (intuitionism) is that it lacks a way of unifying the principles of prima facie obligation, and that the view lacks adequate resources for adjudicating conflicts among prima facie obligations. In "Kantian Intuitionism as a Framework for the Justification of Moral Judgments," **Robert Audi** addresses these objections, employing the resources of his Kantian intuitionism—an ethical theory that aims to integrate a Ross-style pluralism with an understanding of Kant's formula of humanity. According to Audi, the negative standard of avoiding merely instrumental treatment and the positive standard of aiming at treatment of persons as ends in themselves—the two central aspects of the formula of humanity—are more comprehensive than Rossian duties, and one or both can be understood as involved in fulfilling the more specific duties. More precisely, Kant's formula provides unification to what otherwise might seem a mere hodge-podge by serving as a "justificatory rationale" of the Rossian obligations (though such a justificatory route is compatible with the self-evidence of principles expressing these obligations). As for the problem of resolving conflicts among competing grounds (or reasons) as represented by Rossian principles of obligation, Audi formulates a series of generalizations—weighting principles—that aim to facilitate the rational adjudication of such conflicts.

Moral rationalism is the view that all rational agents have sufficient reason to conform their behavior to moral requirements, and that therefore immoral action is contrary to reason. Kantian versions of moral rationalism attempt to secure the rational authority of moral requirements by grounding their authority in a conception of practical agency. But can any such conception serve to underwrite this form of rationalism? J. David Velleman, for example, holds that the constitutive aim of practical reason is self-understanding—an understanding that one seeks through one's conception of oneself as an individual with commitments and concerns that define one's practical identity. It is one's practical identity, then, that is the source of particular reasons one has for action. However, because for Velleman the commitments and concerns in question are contingent, it is a contingent matter whether an individual has most reason to comply with moral requirements. The committed Mafioso may, for example, have most reason to break the fingers of the person delinquent in his loan payments to the mafia, despite the immorality of doing so. On Velleman's compromised Kantian view, even if having a Mafioso practical identity is itself contrary to reason, nevertheless, given the Mafioso's practical identity, he may not have most reason to comply with moral requirements, and if not, then not all immoral action is contrary to reason. In his "An Uncompromising Connection Between Practical Reason and Morality," **Michael Nelson** defends an orthodox Kantian version of moral rationalism. He agrees with Velleman's conception of practical reason as having the aim of self-understanding, but he proceeds to argue that Velleman fails to recognize the kind of constitutive connection that exists between acting autonomously and the aim of self-understanding—a connection that requires being able to provide a complete explanation of one's behavior on the basis of reasons that the agent is able to fully endorse and thereby make sense of oneself as a self-governing being. Nelson argues that this conception of the aim of self-understanding imposes on agents the requirement that they act only on principles that they can will as universal law—that they are bound by Kant's Categorical Imperative. And granting that Kant's principle grounds moral requirements, the upshot is that autonomous agents are subject to moral requirements that enjoy rational authority over any competing non-moral reasons grounded in one's particular practical identity. If Nelson is right, then one need not settle for the sort of compromised Kantian view we find in Velleman; an uncompromised connection between practical reason and morality can be vindicated.

In "Coercion and Integrity" **Elinor Mason** develops a response to the so-called integrity challenge to utilitarianism famously raised by Bernard Williams. Williams argued that utilitarianism (as a form of consequentialism), because it is focused exclusively on outcomes of actions, cannot make sense of the idea that agents are especially morally responsible for what they do, rather than for what other people do. In one of Williams's well-known examples, Jim the innocent botanist happens upon a situation in which he is given the option of killing one of twenty captives and thereby saving the lives of the remaining nineteen, otherwise the Captain, who is holding the twenty as hostages, will kill them all. The disturbing idea is that according to utilitarianism the evil project of the Captain shapes Jim's options in a way that represents an attack on Jim's integrity. According to Mason, consequentialism (and thus utilitarianism) can be saved from this sort of objection by defending an account of coercion that relieves one of being fully morally responsible (in the sense of being accountable) for the outcomes of coerced actions. On Mason's "reasons responsiveness" account of moral responsibility, a key aspect of Jim's situation is that the Captain dominates Jim's options by providing him with a very strong reason to kill one of the captives—an action which, before this intervention, Jim had strong reason not to perform and indeed believed was wrong. Thus, if Jim does kill the one native then, because he was coerced by the Captain into doing something he believed to be wrong, the Captain bears full moral responsibility for the bad outcome of what Jim does. Furthermore, as Mason explains, not only can consequentialists hold that agents are not fully responsible when coerced, they can make sense of the idea that coercion is an attack on an agent's integrity.

Welfarism is the view that (1) welfare is the sole fundamental value of moral relevance (axiological monism), (2) it alone explains the deontic status of actions and practices (priority of the good), and (3) considerations of welfare provide agent-neutral reasons to aim at its preservation and production (agent-neutrality). **Christian Coons** explains in his "The Best Expression of Welfarism," that despite the strong attractions of welfarism, the approach requires a plausible theory of beneficence—a theory of how to rank states of affairs with respect to welfare value. Unfortunately for welfarists, since Parfit's *Reasons and Persons*, the existence of any such theory has been in doubt. For instance, it has been argued that no plausible theory of beneficence can, at once, avoid the well-known "repugnant conclusion" and the "non-identity" problem while retaining transitivity of the better-than relation. Rather than abandon welfarism, Coons argues that the best way around these problems is to hold that under certain conditions, we do not have agent-neutral reasons to promote welfare—that welfare, despite its foundational role in ethics, is only conditionally valuable. Defense of this position requires explaining in a principled way when welfare is valuable and when it is not. Following an idea defended by Elizabeth Anderson, Stephen Darwall, and David Velleman, Coons proposes that an individual's welfare has instrinsic value only when that individual merits care. Coons develops this idea in terms of an "Ideal Carer" view according to which (roughly) the goods that constitute welfare and their comparative ranking are reliably indicated by preferences of a properly characterized ideal carer—an ideally informed and formally rational agent who cares for welfare subjects. The repugnant conclusion is avoided, because an ideal carer has no reason to endorse policies that involve preferring more people. And the non-identity problem is met by understanding care as a *de dicto* attitude—caring for individuals as being welfare subjects. After spelling out how appeal to an ideal carer's preferences helps characterize the welfarist's axiological theory, Coons explains how the concept of an ideal carer can be used to characterize different moral concepts, including the morally optimal, the morally required, the supererogatory, and the permissible. He concludes by addressing how and to what extent his ideal carer theory can be of practical use.

The notion of self-respect plays an important role in John Rawls's theory of justice. According to Rawls, it is one of the primary social goods which, along with wealth, liberties, and opportunities, serve as necessary conditions for citizens to achieve their ends. He also argues that his principles of justice are justified partly because they promote the self-respect of citizens. But as **Cynthia A. Stark** explains in her "Rawlsian Self-Respect," Rawls's argument based on self-respect apparently rests on a well-known equivocation: the conception of self-respect Rawls identifies as a primary social good is that of *believing one's conception of the good to have value*, while the conception that his principles promote is that of *having a secure belief in one's equal standing as a citizen*. This equivocation undermines—so it is argued—Rawls's attempt to show that his principles ensure that citizens will have a good essential to the pursuit of their ends, namely the valuing by individual citizens of his or her conception of the good. The problem appears to resist a neat solution because the attitude that Rawls shows to be supported by his principles is not a primary social good; one need not have a secure belief in one's own equal standing as a citizen in order to successfully pursue one's goals. Moreover, the ideal of self-respect as valuing one's conception of the good is not plausibly supported by Rawls's principles. One of Stark's aims is to defend an interpretation of Rawls according to which the sort of self-assessment that constitutes a primary social good and that is also supported by his principles of justice is a univocal notion of self-respect, understood as a belief in the *legitimacy* of one's ends—the belief that one's pursuit of her ends matter in what they contribute to a system of social cooperation. Such an interpretation, argues Stark, overcomes the alleged equivocation. But Stark does think that Rawls's position contains an apparent tension between construing self-respect qua primary social good as of mere instrumental value while also, qua something the principles of justice help secure, as an intrinsic good. A second aim of Stark's essay is to explain how this apparent tension in Rawls's thought can be avoided. She argues that Rawls's main interest in the importance of self-respect is to explain how his conception of justice can counter the unfavorable effects of market economies on economically lower class citizens. Viewed in this way, Rawls's view takes self-respect to be of intrinsic value.

In cases where there are competing morally relevant considerations, some of them favoring the performance of an action and some of them disfavoring that same action, how do these factors figure in a determination of the overall moral status of the action? One response to this question is what is called "the simple model," which makes two assumptions. First, according to atomism, each of the relevant factors carries a particular normative valence and weight that is unaffected by the presence of other morally relevant factors. Second, the moral status of the action is determined by the "net balance" of the various morally relevant factors. This is the *additivity thesis*. This simple model that embraces both atomism and additivity has been forcefully criticized by Shelly Kagan who argues that it is not normatively neutral because it cannot accommodate certain very plausible moral convictions about certain cases. For instance, normally the difference between doing harm and allowing harm exerts a great influence on the moral status of an action. However, in cases of permissible self-defense the doing/allowing distinction seems to make no moral difference; the fact that the case is one of self-defense negates the typical moral effect of this distinction. In this case (and others like it), morally relevant factors arguably combine and interact in complex ways that the simple model rules out. One way to accommodate such cases is to reject atomism in favor of *holism*, and so allow that morally relevant factors in a particular case can affect the valence and weight of each other. Indeed, such examples are often used to motivate rejecting atomism in favor of holism. But another possible option, one suggested by Kagan, would be to retain atomism and accommodate the kinds of cases in question by rejecting additivity. **Luke Robinson** in his "Exploring Alternatives to the Simple Model: Is There an Atomistic Option?" examines this latter option and the particular challenge it faces, namely, developing a conception of the kind of non-additive contribution a factor can make to the overall moral status of an action that is consistent with the commitments of atomism. In addressing this question, Robinson considers the resources of Ross's atomistic pluralism, which, as he notes, is the *locus classicus* for the idea of a contributory right-making feature. He argues that Ross's view cannot meet the challenge. And its failure to do so casts doubt on the project of developing a coherent position that combines atomism and non-additivity. So, it may well be that Rossian pluralists are well advised to abandon atomism in favor of holism.

Psychologist Jonathan Haidt and colleagues have devised experiments in which subjects are asked to respond to various hypothetical scenarios, some of them that presumably do not involve harm (including most famously, a case of consensual incest among adults), and others described as "taboo violations," and still others as "offensive yet harmless." In these experiments, many subjects react to the hypothetical scenarios by firmly claiming that the action in question is morally wrong even when they are not able to provide good reasons to support their moral judgment. These subjects are said to be dumbfounded, and this phenomenon has been used by Haidt and others in support of the descriptive claim that, in general, reasons and reasoning play little role in generating people's moral judgments, and also in support of normative views that deny that there are good reasons for the judgments made by subjects in the various studies. In "Moral Dumbfounding and Moral Stupefaction," **Daniel Jacobson** challenges both the descriptive and normative claims in question. The scenario involving incest as well as a particular case involving cannibalism are put forward by Haidt as cases in which the actions in question do not involve the production of harm. Hence, one implication would seem to be that moral theories that take harm as the wrong-making reason are not able to condemn these cases of incest and cannibalism; on these views no good moral reason supports the verdict that such actions are wrong. But contrary to this claim, Jacobson argues that plausible action-guiding theories that feature harm as a wrong-making moral reason—including subjective act consequentialism and rule consequentialism—can and should invoke a notion of harm that reveals the harms done in the incest and cannibal scenarios. Thus, Haidt's examples do not work on their own terms; they do involve harms. As for the taboo violation and harmless offense cases, Jacobson argues that there are reasons that support the wrongness verdicts in these cases that have to do with the expressive nature of actions—a kind of reason completely overlooked by Haidt and others. According to Jacobson, then, there are good (even if not conclusive) moral reasons in support of the wrongness judgments in the various hypothetical scenarios featured in Haidt's studies. Hence, the main normative claim that dumbfounding is supposed to support is highly questionable. As for the descriptive claim, Jacobson argues that in light of the fact that there do seem to be good reasons that support the wrongness judgments made by subjects in Haidt's experiments, Haidt's work fails to distinguish genuine moral dumbfounding from moral inarticulateness. Dumbfounding involves cases in which (at a time) one holds a particular moral view without (at that time) having reasons that one is able to cite in defense of the view. Inarticulateness is where (at some time) one does have supporting reasons for one's moral view, but one is not able to articulate them (at that time). Even if people are sometimes morally dumbfounded, there are likely to be cases in which people are responsive to good reasons for their judgments but which, perhaps owing to the pressures of a controlled experiment, they are not able to articulate.

I

Permissions To Do Less Than the Best: A Moving Band[1]

THOMAS HURKA AND ESTHER SHUBERT

Our topic in this paper is moral permissions, in particular permissions not to do what will have the best outcome impartially considered. We'll discuss the basis of these permissions and how they relate to other moral ideas such as your special duties to people who are close to you, such as your family and friends. Our main positive suggestion will be that the strength of the permissions, compared both to each other and to the duty to promote another's good, isn't constant but varies with the affected person's closeness to you. If there's a band within which you're permitted to make certain choices, that band moves.

We'll discuss two main types of permission, of which the first are agent-favouring permissions, or permissions to favour yourself. If you can give either one unit of happiness to yourself or five units to another person, impartial consequentialism says you must give the five units to the other person. But common-sense morality disagrees. It says that while you do nothing wrong if you give the five units to the other, you also do nothing wrong if you give the one unit to yourself. That's because you're permitted, at least up to a point, to prefer your own lesser to another's greater good, for example, your own lesser to her greater happiness.[2] This agent-favouring permission underlies the

---

[1] For helpful comments and suggestions we are grateful to Sergio Tenenbaum, Holly Smith, Shelly Kagan, Luke Roelofs, Tom Donaldson, Guy Fletcher, and audiences at the University of Toronto, Rutgers University, the University of Delaware, and the Arizona Normative Ethics Workshop.
[2] Early discussions of this permission are in Derek Parfit, "Innumerate Ethics", *Philosophy and Public Affairs* 7 (1977–8): 285–301; Nancy Davis, "Utilitarianism and Responsibility", *Ratio* 22 (1980): 15–35; and, most extensively, Samuel Scheffler, *The Rejection of Consequentialism* (Oxford: Clarendon Press, 1982).

common-sense idea that some acts are supererogatory, or beyond the call of duty. It would certainly be commendable of you to give the five units to the other person, but it's supererogatory rather than something you're morally required to do. And the reason it's supererogatory is that you're permitted to care somewhat more about yourself.

But there are also agent-sacrificing permissions, or permissions to care less about yourself. If you can give either two units of happiness to yourself or one unit to another person, impartial consequentialism says you must give the two units to yourself, because that will result in the most happiness. Common sense again disagrees, saying you do nothing wrong if you give the one unit to the other person. You don't have a duty to do this, since you likewise do nothing wrong if you prefer your own two units. But you're not required to maximize happiness impartially. You have another permission not to do what will have the best outcome, now an agent-sacrificing permission to produce somewhat less good for another rather than somewhat more for yourself.[3]

So common sense gives you both permissions to care more about your own good than about another's and permissions to care less. Assuming it's right to do so, what is the basis of these permissions? We start with the more familiar case of agent-favouring permissions. If you're permitted to prefer your own lesser to another's greater good, why is this so?

I. AGENT-FAVOURING PERMISSIONS

Many philosophical accounts of agent-favouring permissions ground them in a conflict between two types of reason. On one side are impersonal or moral reasons to promote the good of all people impartially; on the other are personal or prudential reasons to care disproportionately about your own. The clash between these types of reasons, it's then said, yields agent-favouring permissions. Samuel Scheffler's appeal to "the independence of the personal point of view" is one account of this type. According to Scheffler we aren't just impartial maximizers but have a special attachment to our own projects

---

[3] That common-sense morality grants agent-sacrificing permissions is noted in Michael Slote, *Common-Sense Morality and Consequentialism* (London: Routledge & Kegan Paul, 1985), ch. 1.

and interests, with each of these standpoints generating or recognizing a distinct type of reason. Granting an agent-favouring permission rather than requiring us to maximize impartially recognizes this duality in our motivational structure, by letting sometimes one and sometimes the other win out.[4]

But these reason-based accounts, as we'll call them, either don't yield sufficiently broad agent-favouring permissions or give them the wrong rationale. The permissions common sense grants are fairly extensive. If you're permitted to prefer one unit of your own happiness to five units for another person, you may also be permitted to prefer one of your own to six or seven for another, and you're certainly permitted to prefer it to four, three, or two units for another.

But imagine, as is perfectly consistent with reason-based accounts, that impersonal and personal reasons can be weighed precisely against each other. Imagine, for example, that while impersonal reasons count everyone's happiness equally, your personal reasons count your own happiness ten times as much as other people's, and the two types of reason have exactly equal weight. Then weighing them against each other will result in a ranking that splits the difference between them and is equivalent to a single ranking counting your own happiness five times as much as other people's. And while this ranking lets you choose either one unit of happiness for yourself or five units for another, it requires you to prefer six units for another to one for yourself and also requires you to prefer one unit for yourself to four, three, or two for another. Given full comparability between reasons or points of view, their duality yields no broader a permission than does impartial consequentialism. The permission may involve a precise 1:5 rather than 1:1 ratio, but it's no more extensive.[5]

A reason-based account can avoid this result by denying that the conflicting reasons can be precisely compared. Derek Parfit takes this line. He says that if you can give either one unit of happiness to yourself or a thousand units to another, your impersonal reason outweighs your personal one and you should prefer the thousand. But if your choice is

[4] Scheffler, *The Rejection of Consequentialism*, ch. 2.
[5] This objection is made in Shelly Kagan, "Defending Options", *Ethics* 104 (1994): 333–51, pp. 338–9; and Douglas Portmore, "Position-Relative Consequentialism, Agent-Centered Options, and Supererogation", *Ethics* 113 (2003): 303–32, pp. 306–7.

between one for yourself and five for another, it may be that neither reason outweighs the other nor that they're exactly equal in weight; likewise if you have a choice between one for yourself and six, four, or three for another. When reasons can't be determinately compared, however, you're free to act on either. So given a broad band within which reasons aren't precisely comparable, there's an equally broad band of agent-favouring permissions.[6]

But this account gives the resulting permissions the wrong rationale. For it makes it a necessary condition for their existence, and therefore for the existence of supererogation, that reasons not be completely comparable. But surely when common sense holds that some acts are beyond the call of duty it isn't thinking about the comparability of reasons; it has no view about so *recherché* a topic. And surely it need have no such view. It's simply a persuasive idea in itself that morality doesn't demand large sacrifices of you to give only slightly greater benefits to others—if it did, it would be unreasonable.

It may be replied on Parfit's behalf that we could never weigh impersonal and personal reasons precisely, and this is true at least epistemically. But the fact that *we* can't assign precise weights to reasons is consistent with there being, metaphysically, completely determinate truths about what those weights are. And the common-sense view isn't that supererogation is a merely epistemic phenomenon. It's not just that we have to act as if two choices are both permitted because we can't know which is required; it's that the choices are in fact both permitted. For that metaphysical view to be justified in Parfit's way the weights of reasons would have to be in fact only partly determinate, and our belief in supererogation surely doesn't depend on that abstruse metaphysical claim.

There are other reason-based accounts of agent-favouring permissions, but they have other objectionable features.[7] And we think this

---

[6] Derek Parfit, *On What Matters* (Oxford: Oxford University Press, 2011), Vol. 1, pp. 137–41; see also Joseph Raz, *Engaging Reason: On the Theory of Value and Action* (Oxford: Oxford University Press, 1999), p. 243. Unlike Scheffler's, Parfit's view is not about specifically moral permissibility, but it can be turned into one that is if the reasons it weighs are all called "moral".

[7] Elaborating a suggestion of Slote's, Portmore argues that in supererogation cases your prudential reason to promote your own lesser happiness outweighs your moral reason to promote the other's happiness, so you're rationally required to prefer your lesser happiness. But you're morally permitted to prefer the other's greater happiness, because you're always

whole approach is misguided. It tries to derive the permissions from more basic normative factors that aren't themselves permissions but count positively in favour of an act, such as a reason or an "ought other things equal" to do it. And we don't think the relevant "may" can be derived in the right way from just "oughts". A successful account must start with moral factors some of which are themselves permissive. We now propose an account of this sort, formulated using language derived from W. D. Ross.[8]

This account generates agent-favouring permissions by positing an independent and underivative permission to pursue your own good. More specifically, it holds that alongside a prima facie duty, or duty other things equal, to promote everyone's happiness impartially, you have a prima facie permission to promote your own happiness. This permission has to be weighed against the impartial duty and in some cases will lose to it. If you can produce either one unit of happiness for yourself or a thousand units for another person, your duty outweighs your permission and what's true all things considered is that you ought to produce the thousand. But if you can produce either one unit for yourself or five for another, the permission outweighs the duty and you're permitted all things considered to favour yourself.[9]

Unlike the two accounts discussed above, this one yields broad agent-favouring permissions even if all normative factors can be precisely compared. Let's say your prima facie permission outweighs your prima facie duty up to but not beyond the point where the ratio of

---

morally permitted both to do what's best supported by all your reasons and to do what's best supported just by your moral reasons; see Slote, "Shelly Kagan's *The Limits of Morality*", *Philosophy and Phenomenological Research* 51 (1991): 915–17, and Portmore, "Position-Relative Consequentialism, Agent-Centered Options, and Supererogation". As Kagan objected to Slote, however, this view implies that supererogatory acts are irrational, which is neither plausible nor the view of common sense-morality (Kagan, "Replies to My Critics", *Philosophy and Phenomenological Research* 4 (1991): 919–28, pp. 927–8). Portmore replies that this objection applies to all accounts of supererogation and so doesn't count specially against his own (p. 328), but it does not apply to the account we defend below.

[8] W. D. Ross, *The Right and the Good* (Oxford: Clarendon Press, 1930), pp. 19–20.

[9] Accounts that likewise posit underivatively permissive factors are given by Joseph Raz and Joshua Gert. See Raz, "Permissions and Supererogation", *American Philosophical Quarterly* 12 (1975): 161–8, and *Practical Reason and Norms* (London: Hutchinson, 1975), pp. 89–97; and Gert, *Brute Rationality: Normativity and Human Action* (Cambridge: Cambridge University Press, 2004). We find our Ross-inspired account simpler and more perspicuous than these two, but the basic idea is the same.

benefits to you and the other is exactly 1:5. Then you're permitted to prefer one unit of your own happiness to five for the other, though not to six for the other. But you're also permitted to prefer one unit of your own happiness to four, three, or two units for the other, because a permission that outweighs a four-unit gain in happiness also outweighs a three-unit, two-unit, or one-unit gain. The resulting all-things-considered permission is therefore broad even if the moral truth is completely determinate, and it's also only a permission, involving no duty to prefer your one unit. The prima facie duty to promote happiness impartially that weighs against it implies a prima facie permission to do so, and since nothing conflicts with that permission, you're also permitted all things considered to prefer the other's five. As common sense holds, in a one-for-you vs. five-for-another case you may make either choice.

Some may resist the idea that there are underivative permissions, saying that if an act is permitted there must be some deeper explanation why. If this objection is based on the more general view that no normative truths can be underivative, it raises metaethical issues beyond the scope of this paper. But many, including Scheffler and Parfit, think there can be underivative truths about reasons or oughts. If asked why we have reason or ought other things equal to promote happiness impartially, they'll say there's no explanation: we just do. But the concepts of ought and permission are interdefinable. You ought to do an act when you're not permitted not to do it, and you're permitted to do it when it's not the case that you ought not to. But then there's no reason why, if claims using one of these concepts can be underivatively true, claims using the other cannot. If it can be a primitive truth that you're other things equal not permitted not to do something such as pursue your happiness, surely it can also be a primitive truth that you *are* permitted to do it.

Others may object to the idea that permissions can have weights. We understand what it is for one prima facie duty to be stronger than another, they may say, but talk of a permission's weight is meaningless.

Again, however, we see no force in this objection. What exactly is the strength of a prima facie duty? We think it's just that duty's tendency, in competition with other duties and perhaps permissions, to make some act your all-things-considered duty. One duty is therefore stronger than another if it has more of that tendency, so a prima facie duty to do

X is stronger than a prima facie duty not to do X if, taking the two together, what's true on balance is that you ought to do X. Just as one physical force is stronger than another if, when they conflict, it does more to determine the physical outcome, so one prima facie duty is stronger than another if it does more to determine a normative outcome, by making the act it favours simply your duty.[10]

But the same analysis can be applied to permissions: the strength of a prima facie permission is again its tendency to determine a normative outcome, now by making an act all things considered permitted. We don't need this concept in order to weigh permissions directly against each other, because they don't conflict. A prima facie permission to do X and a prima facie permission not to do X don't oppose each other, since it can be true both that you're permitted all things considered to do X and that you're permitted all things considered not to; you can have the option to choose either. But we do need the concept to weigh prima facie permissions against duties. A prima facie permission to do X and a prima facie duty not to do X do conflict, and we have to decide which is stronger. If the permission is stronger, you're all things considered permitted to do X; if the duty is stronger, X is all things considered forbidden. As was the case with duties, a permission's weight is just its capacity to determine, in competition with other factors, an all-things-considered normative outcome, though now a permission rather than a duty. And once we've weighed permissions against duties in this way, we can use the result to weigh them indirectly against each other. If the permission to do X outweighs some duties that the permission to do Y does not but the opposite never occurs, the permission to do X is stronger. Though it doesn't win in direct conflicts with the permission to do Y, it wins other conflicts that the permission to do Y does not.

It may be objected to this analysis that we can make sense of weighing one prima facie duty against another because, like conflicting physical forces, they are items of the same kind; but we cannot meaningfully weigh a duty against a permission because they are of different kinds.[11] But while a force pushing an object in one direction can conflict with

---

[10] Ross explicates the concept of prima facie duty by analogy with physical forces in *The Right and the Good*, pp. 28–9.
[11] We are grateful to a referee for this objection.

a force pushing it in a contrary direction, it can also conflict with friction, which resists the object's moving in any direction. Analogously, a prima facie duty tending to make an act right can conflict not only with one tending to make it wrong, but also with a prima facie permission tending to make it neither right nor wrong. Just as we can weigh a force causing motion against one resisting it, so we can weigh a prima facie duty against a prima facie permission.

We therefore see no sound objections to positing an underivative permission to pursue your own good, and an account that does so may have the further advantage of allowing a more complete account of supererogation.

The concept of supererogation has two sides. On one side, a super-erogatory act isn't morally required; on the other side, it's somehow better than its alternative, or "beyond" duty in a sense that connotes superiority. A complete account of the concept must capture this second side, explaining how supererogatory acts are better even though not strictly your duty.

We could attempt this by noting that supererogatory acts have better consequences than their alternatives, for example, five units of happiness rather than one. But this isn't a specifically moral property of the acts, since it can be shared by purely physical facts such as sunny weather and good food. We could also note that supererogatory acts are usually done from a more virtuous motive, such as an altruistic desire for another's five units of happiness rather than a selfish desire for your one. But this isn't an essential feature of supererogation. If you see Warren Buffet drowning and try to save him at significant risk to your life but do so only because you think he'll give you a large reward if you succeed, your act is still supererogatory, in the sense of beyond the call of duty, even though your motive is entirely selfish.[12] As Holly Smith has remarked,[13] the concept of supererogation is a deontic one, in the same family as right and wrong, rather than one from the theory of moral virtue or of moral credit and blame. Its superiority must therefore be accounted for in purely deontic terms.

---

[12] See Paul McNamara, "Supererogation, Inside and Out: Toward an Adequate Scheme for Common-Sense Morality", in Mark Timmons (ed.), *Oxford Studies in Normative Ethics*, Vol. 1 (2011), pp. 202–35.
[13] In conversation.

This is again something reason-based accounts can't do. If you choose another person's five units of happiness over your own one, your act is impersonally or morally better. But if you choose the one for yourself, that's personally or prudentially better. And on these accounts there's no ground to prefer one kind of betterness, the impersonal or the personal, to the other, or to say that either act is unqualifiedly better. At the all-things-considered level, the two acts are on a par.

But the permission-based account may be able to do better. According to it, each of your choices is supported by prima facie moral factors: the prima facie permission to pursue your own happiness on one side, and the prima facie duty to pursue happiness impartially, which implies a prima facie permission to do so, on the other. Whichever choice you make you exercise a prima facie permission, but if you give the five units to the other you also fulfil a prima facie duty, and this may explain that act's superiority. It is deontically higher-ranked because while equally permitted they are also prima facie required. A key feature of prima facie duties is that they don't disappear when they're outweighed. They remain as part of the moral situation and can leave what Robert Nozick calls "moral traces".[14] One of these is the appropriateness of your feeling, if not quite guilt, then what Ross called "compunction" about not fulfilling an outweighed duty;[15] another can be a duty to compensate the person to whom the duty was owed. A third trace, we are now suggesting, may be to explain why supererogatory acts are superior: though no more permissible than their alternatives, they fulfil a prima facie duty that the alternatives don't and are therefore on balance better. The prima facie permission opposing them makes them not required, but the prima facie duty favouring them makes them deontically higher-ranked.

The permission-based account therefore has several advantages over reason-based ones, but it also requires a complication. A plausible moral view can't grant agent-favouring permissions without also imposing deontological constraints such as one against killing the innocent. Otherwise the same permission that lets you save your own life rather than save the lives of five others will permit you to kill five others if that's

---

[14] Robert Nozick, "Moral Complications and Moral Structures", *Natural Law Forum* 13 (1968): 1–50.

[15] Ross, *The Right and the Good*, p. 28.

necessary to save your life, for example, if you need their organs for transplant to yourself. If there's no intrinsic difference between killing and allowing to die, you'll be permitted to prefer your life to theirs in both cases—a result that's even farther from common sense than impartial consequentialism is.[16] But not only must the permissions be accompanied by deontological constraints, they can have no special weight against these constraints. Surely if it's wrong to kill one innocent person to save two others, as deontological moralities hold, it's also and equally wrong when one of the two is you: your agent-favouring permission has no bearing on this case. So the prima facie permission to pursue your own good must have more weight against the duty to promote the good than it does against deontological constraints, and that leads to a more complex structure than if the permission had the same weight against all duties. But the complication is needed in any account of agent-favouring permissions: a reason-based account too must say the reason to promote your own good has more weight against an impersonal reason than it does against deontological ones if it's to forbid killing one to save two who include yourself.

2. AGENT-SACRIFICING PERMISSIONS

Given this account of agent-favouring permissions we now turn to agent-sacrificing ones. And here there's a further difficulty for reason-based views such as Scheffler's and Parfit's, for it's not clear that they even allow these permissions. If you can give either two units of happiness to yourself or one to another person, your personal reason favours giving the two to yourself but so does your impersonal reason, since this will produce the most happiness. But if both types of reason favour the same act, that act should surely be required and the alternative of giving one unit to the other person should be all things considered forbidden.[17]

A permission-based view has no such difficulty. It can generate agent-sacrificing permissions by positing another underivative prima facie

---

[16] Shelly Kagan, *The Limits of Morality* (Oxford: Clarendon Press, 1989), pp. 19–24.

[17] In his initial discussion of agent-sacrificing permissions, Slote argued that they don't fit Scheffler's justification of agent-favouring permissions and therefore tell against that justification; see *Common-Sense Morality and Consequentialism*, ch. 1.

permission, now one *not* to pursue your own good. If you can give either two units of happiness to yourself or one unit to another person, you have on one side a prima facie duty to produce the most happiness, which favours giving yourself the two. But you also have a prima facie permission not to pursue your happiness, and if this permission out-weighs the duty, you're all things considered permitted to prefer the other's one unit. You're not required to do this, because your prima facie duty to produce the most happiness implies a prima facie permission to do so, and that permission is undefeated. But by positing a second underivative permission we can explain agent-sacrificing as well as agent-favouring permissions. You're permitted other things equal not to do what will give you happiness, and are therefore some-times permitted on balance to prefer another's lesser to your greater happiness.

This second underivative permission connects with a striking view of Ross's while also giving it a more persuasive rationale. Ross held that though there's a moral duty to pursue other people's happiness, there's no duty of any kind to pursue your own; you ought to seek knowledge and virtue in yourself, but are under no obligation to seek your happi-ness.[18] But he stated this view in a problematic way.

Like the reason-based theorists discussed above, Ross assumed that the basic normative factors must all be positive or favouring ones, which in his case meant they must be prima facie duties rather than permissions. But imagine that you can give either a thousand units of happiness to yourself or one unit to another person. Ross's view implies that you're required to give the one unit to the other person. This act is supported by the prima facie duty to promote the happiness of others, while the alternative is supported by no duty and therefore by nothing. So you're required to prefer the other's vastly smaller happiness. But surely you do nothing wrong if you prefer your own vastly greater happiness.[19]

---

[18] Ross, *The Right and the Good*, pp. 21, 24–6, 151; and *Foundations of Ethics* (Oxford: Clarendon Press, 1939), pp. 72–5, 129–30, 272–4, 284.

[19] This objection to Ross is made in A. C. Ewing, "A Suggested Non-Naturalistic Analysis of Good", *Mind* 48 (1939): 1–22, p. 20, and Michael Stocker, "Agent and Other: Against Ethical Universalism", *Australasian Journal of Philosophy* 54 (1976): 206–20, p. 208.

We can avoid this implication if we supplement Ross's view with some prima facie permissions. A permission to pursue your own happiness will make room for supererogatory acts, which Ross himself did not recognize; he thought that when doing so won't violate any deontological constraint, you're required to maximize the good.[20] And a permission not to pursue your happiness will often yield his view that you have no duty to pursue your happiness without making it wrong for you to do so. You'll be permitted to prefer one unit for another to two for yourself without that being your duty, and you'll also be permitted to forgo two units of happiness when taking them wouldn't affect anyone else. How far the resulting all-things-considered permissions go will depend on what duty this prima facie permission is weighed against. If this is only the duty to promote other people's happiness, as in Ross's view, the resulting permission will be unlimited and you'll also be permitted to prefer another's one unit to a thousand for yourself and to simply forgo a thousand when no one else will be affected. But if the opposed duty is to promote happiness impartially, as we think is more plausible, the prima facie permission will eventually be outweighed and forgoing a thousand units in these cases will be wrong. Just as there is excessive agent-favouring, so some agent-sacrifice will then be excessive and forbidden.

3. A BAND OF PERMISSIONS

Positing two prima facie permissions yields an even broader range of all-things-considered permissions, some agent-favouring and some agent-sacrificing, and this range can be helpfully represented in a diagram. In Figure 1 the vertical line represents different ratios between your own and another's good, with agent-favouring ratios like 1:10 above the 1:1 midpoint and agent-sacrificing ones like 10:1 below it. The shaded band includes all those ratios that permit you all things considered to choose either your own or another's good, and the fact that this band extends

---

[20] Ross, *The Right and the Good*, p. 39.

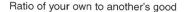

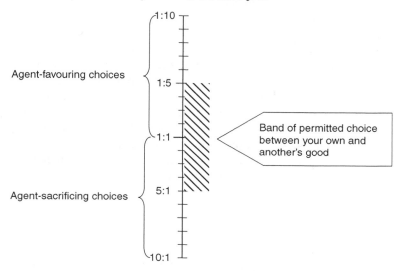

Figure 1

around the midpoint shows that you have both kinds of permission, agent-sacrificing as well as agent-favouring. You're permitted to choose either your own or the other's good both when it's one unit for you or two for her, and when it's two units for you or one for her. Moreover, the size and location of the band reflect views about how strong the prima facie permissions are. In Figure 1 the band stretches from the 1:5 ratio to 5:1, so you're permitted to prefer one unit of your own happiness to as many as five for another person, and one unit for another to as many as five for yourself. This treats the two permissions as moderately strong compared to the duty to promote happiness impartially: if the band were wider, running, say, from 1:10 to 10:1, they'd be stronger compared to this duty, whereas if it were narrower they'd be weaker. Figure 1 also treats the two permissions as of equal strength—note that the band is symmetrical around the 1:1 point—and that too isn't necessary. We may, for example, think the permission to pursue your own good is stronger than the permission not to, so the band should extend farther above the 1:1 point than it does below it, and we anticipated that possibility when we introduced the two kinds of permission. Our initial example of an agent-favouring permission had you choose one unit of happiness for yourself over five for another person, whereas for agent-sacrifice we had you choose one for another over two for yourself. This reflected our belief that, when the two are stated abstractly, the agent-favouring permission is intuitively more extensive, which demands an asymmetrical diagram, as in Figure 2. With more of the shaded band above the midpoint, there's here more self-favouring allowed than self-sacrifice, or more extreme ratios permitted for the former than for the latter. But the opposite view is also in principle possible, with a band that extends further below the 1:1 point than it does above it. And the extreme of either view recognizes only agent-favouring or only agent-sacrificing permissions; this requires a diagram whose band starts at 1:1 and goes only up or only down.

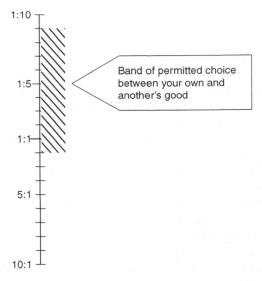

Ratio of your own to another's good

1:10

1:5

1:1

5:1

10:1

Band of permitted choice between your own and another's good

Figure 2

So far we've formulated the permissions in terms of ratios, so you're allowed to prefer your own or another's good up to a certain ratio but not beyond. But it may be wondered whether your permissions should instead depend, either wholly or in part, on the absolute size of the gap between your and the other's good. Imagine that you give one unit of happiness to yourself rather than ten units to another person. Can what matters here be not that you cared ten times more about your happiness but that you preferred happiness of yours that was nine units smaller? Can the latter be what determines whether your act was permitted?

We don't think your permissions can depend only on the absolute gap between your own and another's good. Then if it was wrong to prefer one unit of happiness for yourself to ten for another, it would be equally wrong to prefer a million and one units for yourself to a million and ten for another. That's surely implausible: at the million level a nine-unit gap is trivial. But more moderate views count both the absolute size and the ratio, saying the maximum ratios for permitted favouring and sacrifice are different given different-sized totals. Is some view of this type preferable to one that looks only at ratios?

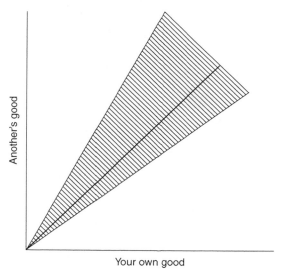

Figure 3

These alternative views require a more complex diagram, as in Figure 3. Here the vertical axis represents the other's good and the horizontal axis your own, while the 1:1 ratio is now a 45-degree ray going out from the origin and the band of permissions has become a cone surrounding that ray. If your permissions depend only on the ratio between your and the other's good, the rays bounding this cone are straight, as in Figure 3. (And note how the cone's asymmetrical placement again allows more agent-favouring than agent-sacrifice.) But we can imagine other views. One allows greater ratios of favouring and sacrifice at greater absolute levels; this generates rays that bend out, as in Figure 4. Another, represented in Figure 5, allows smaller ratios at higher levels and has rays that bend in. Given this latter view, a degree of self-favouring that's permitted when dividing small benefits may not be permitted when dividing large ones.

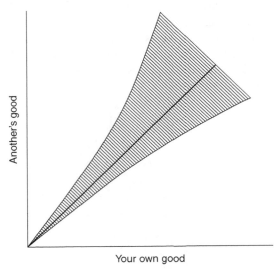

Figure 4

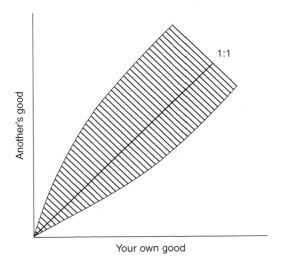

Figure 5

We think these views, and especially the last, have some intuitive appeal. But they all face what can be called a "batch" problem. Imagine that the view in Figure 5 allows you to favour yourself up to a 1:10 ratio when ten units of happiness are being divided but only up to 1:8 when there are a hundred. Then if, when forced to divide a hundred units between yourself and another in one go, you give yourself ninety, you act wrongly, whereas if you could divide the hundred into ten lots and give yourself nine units from each you could reach the same outcome permissibly. But surely it can't make a moral difference whether you reach a ninety–ten division in one step or many, and since a version of this problem arises for any view that counts absolute size as well as ratios, we'll stick from here on to the simpler view that looks only at ratios.[21]

Though in one sense straightforward, adding a second prima facie permission creates a problem for our account of supererogation. That account says that supererogatory acts are superior because, as well as exercising a prima facie permission, they fulfil a prima facie duty. But consider the case where you can produce either two units of happiness for yourself or one for another person. Here each of your options is supported by a prima facie permission, but if there's a prima facie duty to promote happiness impartially, giving yourself the two units also fulfils that duty and should therefore be preferable in the same way that supererogation is: it has more prima facie factors on its side. But this doesn't seem true: preferring your own greater happiness in this case *doesn't* seem better. The alternative of preferring the other's lesser happiness also doesn't seem better; your two options seem to be on a par. So our account of supererogation seems to have a counterintuitive implication when extended to agent-sacrifice.

There are several ways to avoid this implication. One is to say that, while the outweighed duty to promote happiness impartially does leave a trace in agent-favouring cases, it doesn't in agent-sacrificing ones. This move isn't completely impossible, since sometimes an outweighed duty doesn't leave traces. If you let five patients who need transplants die because the only way to save them is to kill another innocent person, you shouldn't feel compunction about your choice to let the five die and

---

[21] We are grateful to Luke Roelofs for suggesting these alternative views to us and to Tom Donaldson for the batch objection against them.

don't owe anyone compensation. Still, having the very same outweighed duty make a maximizing option superior in one kind of case but not another does seem to us worryingly ad hoc. Another possibility is to hold, as Ross did, that the competing duty is one to promote happiness not impartially but only in other people. Then the outweighed duty won't count in favour of the two units for yourself in agent-sacrificing cases and giving them to yourself won't be preferable. But now the alternative of giving the one to the other will be preferable, and that too seems wrong; as we said, your two options seem on a par. In addition, the Rossian view implies that agent-sacrificing permissions never run out, so you're permitted to prefer one unit of happiness for another to a thousand or a million for yourself, which we find implausible. We're therefore not sure how to respond to this problem and will have to leave it unresolved. An initially promising account of supererogation seems to have counterintuitive implications when extended to agent-sacrifice, and while there are ways to avoid these implications, none is entirely satisfactory.[22]

4. A MOVING BAND

We've suggested that agent-sacrificing permissions are less extensive than agent-favouring ones, and the intuitive case for them may also be less compelling. But some may go further and reject that case entirely, saying that while you're permitted to prefer your own lesser to another's greater good, you're never permitted to do the opposite. To sacrifice your own greater for another's lesser happiness is wrong.

In taking this line they may appeal to a Kantian duty of self-respect, or duty not to act in ways inconsistent with respecting yourself as

---

[22] Does this problem remove the permission-based account's advantage over reason-based accounts, which we criticized for not being able to explain why supererogatory acts are superior? It does not. Our account does give an explanation that covers cases of supererogation as such; it only has problematic implications in certain other cases. And though none of the devices that would remove these implications is entirely satisfactory, several are available. By contrast, reason-based accounts can give no explanation whatever of the superiority, in an unqualified sense, of supererogatory acts. In addition, the permission-based account retains its other advantages: that it can generate extensive agent-favouring permissions without assuming that reasons aren't precisely comparable, and that it allows, as reason-based accounts cannot, agent-sacrificing permissions.

equal in status to other persons and having the same rights and duties.[23] One aspect of this duty, they may say, is a requirement to treat your own good as equally important to other people's and therefore never to subordinate it to theirs. But you do subordinate it if you prefer their lesser to your greater happiness.[24]

We don't find this argument persuasive. If self-respect involves properly honouring your status, rights, and duties, it presupposes an independent account of what those are and can't determine their content. If you don't have an independent permission to prefer others' lesser happiness, your doing so may well show self-disrespect. But imagine that you do have such a permission, sacrifice no further than it allows, and have the following beliefs: that you're only permitted to prefer another's lesser happiness but have no duty to do so; that you're also permitted to prefer your own lesser happiness, and even to do so to a greater extent; and that your mix of permissions and duties is exactly the same as everyone else's. If you then make a free choice to prefer another's lesser happiness, knowing that it's a free choice and in no way required, you surely violate no duty of self-respect.

This leaves the bare claim that you're not permitted to prefer another's lesser good, which we again find unpersuasive. But we think there's something to be learned from a more restricted version of it suggested to us by Sergio Tenenbaum.[25] He notes, rightly in our view, that the most intuitively compelling cases of permitted agent-sacrifice involve someone closely related to you, such as a spouse, child, or friend. If we're asked to imagine a case where preferring another's lesser happiness is allowed, we naturally think first of ones where the other is some kind of intimate. As a partial sceptic about agent-sacrifice, Tenenbaum concludes that it's permitted only with people who are close to you and not at all with strangers. While not condemning all such sacrifice, he does condemn it outside a specified area.

We're not persuaded even by this weaker anti-sacrifice view; we think you're permitted to prefer the slightly lesser happiness of someone

---

[23] A classic discussion of self-respect is Thomas E. Hill, Jr., "Servility and Self-Respect", in his *Autonomy and Self-Respect* (Cambridge: Cambridge University Press, 1991).

[24] An argument of this kind is given by Jean Hampton in "Selflessness and the Loss of Self", *Social Philosophy and Policy* 10/1 (Winter 1993): 135–65, and "The Wisdom of the Egoist", *Social Philosophy and Policy* 14/1 (Winter 1997): 21–51.

[25] In conversation.

you've never met, for example by continuing to contribute to charity a little beyond the point where the benefit to others becomes less than the cost to you. But we think there's truth in a generalization of Tenenbaum's view, namely that the degree of agent-sacrifice you're permitted is greater the closer another person is to you, so the gap between your greater and her lesser happiness can be larger with a spouse or child than it can be with a stranger. It can be all things considered permissible to give up a very enjoyable night out to comfort a child with a mild illness, whereas it wouldn't be permissible to make the same sacrifice for a stranger. It can be permissible to forgo the opportunity for major career success to allow a smaller career success for your spouse, but not for someone you haven't met. While some degree of agent-sacrifice is permitted with strangers, it's significantly less than with intimates.

We also accept a complementary view: that the degree of agent-favouring you're permitted is smaller the closer someone is to you. With a stranger you're permitted to prefer your own lesser to his significantly greater good. On some views you're permitted to prefer keeping $1000 to saving the life of someone starving on the other side of the world, but surely no one thinks it's permissible to prefer keeping $1000 to saving the life of a close friend, and it would be appalling to prefer keeping $1000 to saving the life of your child. In these cases the duty to save the other clearly outweighs the permission to seek your own happiness. So whereas the degree of agent-sacrifice you're permitted increases the closer someone is to you, the degree of agent-favouring you're permitted decreases.

These two views have a combined effect: in our diagrams the band of permissions no longer has a fixed position, as it did in Figures 1 and 2, but moves down as the person whose happiness you can promote gets closer to you. If she's a stranger, the band comes fairly far up the diagram, with its top much farther above the 1:1 midpoint than its bottom is below it. If she's a friend, the band is lower down; maybe now it's symmetrical around the midpoint, with as much self-sacrifice allowed as self-preference. And if she's a spouse or child, the band is even lower, with its bottom farther below the midpoint than its top is above it. A sequence of diagrams with these features is given in Figure 6, where the diagram on the left represents your permissions concerning strangers, the one in the middle those for friends, and the one on the right those for a spouse or child. As the person you can benefit becomes more of an intimate the whole band moves down, allowing less agent-favouring and more agent-sacrifice.

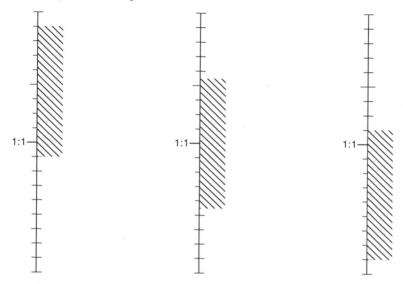

Figure 6

We find this idea intuitively attractive, and it also has a natural explanation, one that reverses that for the locations of the bands in Figures 1 and 2. In those diagrams we assumed that there's just one prima facie duty, to promote everyone's happiness impartially, and saw what results when that duty is weighed against prima facie permissions with different strengths compared to each other. If the permission to pursue your own good is stronger than the permission not to, the band of permissions stretches farther above the 1:1 point than it does below it, as in Figure 2; if the permission not to pursue your good is stronger, the opposite is true.

But common-sense morality doesn't think there's just one duty to promote happiness impartially. It accepts what C. D. Broad called "self-referential altruism", the view that you have stronger duties to promote the good of people who are closer to you, so you're required to show some degree of partiality toward those who are close.[26] If you can give

[26] C. D. Broad, "Self and Others", in D. Cheney (ed.), *Broad's Critical Essays in Moral Philosophy* (London: George Allen & Unwin, 1971), pp. 279–80.

either two units of happiness to a stranger or one to a friend, you ought to give the one to your friend because he's closer; if you can give either two units to a friend or one to your child, you should for the same reason favour your child. But then we can see the movement of the band in Figure 6 as resulting when prima facie permissions of constant strength are weighed against duties of differing strengths. Consider first agent-favouring. If you can give either less happiness to yourself or more happiness to a stranger, your duty to benefit the stranger is, because he's a stranger, comparatively weak. It will therefore often be outweighed by your permission to pursue your own happiness, making your all-things-considered permission to favour yourself fairly extensive. But if the other is a friend or spouse, the opposing duty is stronger and the resulting permission will run out more quickly: favouring that would be permitted with a stranger is not permitted here. Something similar happens with agent-sacrifice. Here your duty to promote the other's happiness positively supports your permission not to promote your own, since the more you ought to benefit her, the more you're permitted to prefer hers to yours. But with a stranger this duty is comparatively weak, and only weakly supports the permission against the duty to pursue your happiness that comes, say, from the duty to promote happiness impartially; the result is only a limited permission to prefer the other's good. But as she becomes closer, your duty to promote her good gets stronger and the resulting all-things-considered permission becomes more extensive. Weighing your two prima facie permissions against duties of increasing strength leads to less extensive permissions to favour yourself and more extensive ones to favour her.

5. THE MOVING BAND: FURTHER QUESTIONS

There are therefore theoretical as well as intuitive reasons to believe the band of permissions moves, but there are also more detailed questions about this view. In Figure 6 the majority of the diagrams are asymmetrical, allowing either more agent-favouring or more agent-sacrifice. But the sequence of diagrams embodies a kind of symmetry, since it ends with an agent-sacrificing permission that's exactly as extensive as the agent-favouring one with which it begins; while asymmetrical at particular points, it's symmetrical as a whole. And the same symmetry can be a feature of other sequences, which start either higher or lower on the scale but also end the same distance below the 1:1 point as they began above it.

But though this kind of symmetry is possible, we don't find it most plausible. We think the degree of agent-sacrifice you're permitted with your closest intimates is less than the degree of agent-favouring you're permitted with strangers, so that even at the extremes your agent-sacrificing permissions extend less far. We've said that on some views you're permitted to prefer keeping $1000 to saving the life of a distant stranger, but it's surely not permissible—it's beyond the threshold of permissible agent-sacrifice—to sacrifice your life to save $1000 for your spouse or child. That would be wildly unreasonable.[27] You may be permitted to watch a favourite TV show rather than help a stranger achieve a major career success, but it would be excessive to forgo a major success for yourself to allow your child a night of TV. For us a plausible sequence of permissions must start with a band that extends farther above the 1:1 point than its final band extends below it, so you can prefer yourself more to strangers than you can sacrifice yourself to your closest intimates. A view of this kind is represented in Figure 7, and it sustains the priority we initially gave to agent-favouring permissions. Though with your closest intimates you're permitted more agent-sacrifice than agent-favouring, with people in general you're permitted more agent-favouring, because the greatest self-preference you're ever permitted is greater than your greatest allowed self-sacrifice.

---

[27] We owe this example to Shelly Kagan. It may be said that the reason it would be wrong to sacrifice your life in these cases is that your spouse or child would lose more by your death than they would gain from the $1000. But, first, this is not the only or even the main reason the sacrifice is intuitively wrong; it would also be excessive in itself. Second, we can imagine cases where there would not be this loss, for example, because your child does not know of your existence; here too the sacrifice would be excessive.

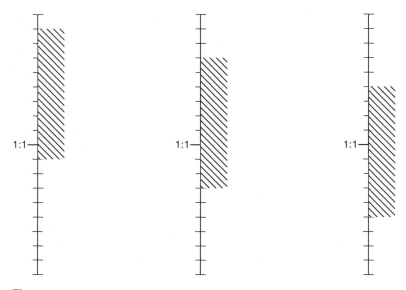

Figure 7

There's a further issue to consider. In Figures 6 and 7 the band of permissions stays the same width as it moves down the graph, so that with all people the gap between your greatest allowed self-favouring and greatest allowed self-sacrifice is the same. A natural question is whether this is necessary. Must the band always be the same width, or can it either narrow or widen as the person you can benefit becomes closer to you? Can there be a bigger or a smaller gap between your maximum permissions for intimates than there is for strangers, or is the gap always the same size?

There's an intuitive limit on any possible changes in width. We've said both that your agent-favouring permissions are less extensive with intimates and that your agent-sacrificing ones are broader, so the ends of the band should move in the same direction. But consistent with this, there's an intuitive case for its narrowing as it moves down.

We've said that on some views you're permitted to keep $1000 rather than save a distant stranger. If this is right, then the maximum permitted ratio for agent-favouring with strangers is considerably more than 1:10, and that's so even if you need to have $10,000 at stake to be permitted not to save a stranger. Let's say, somewhat arbitrarily, that the top of the band of permissions for strangers is at the ratio 1:20. And let's add that the maximum permitted ratio for agent-sacrifice with strangers is just 2:1. This makes the band for strangers quite wide, running from 1:20 at the top to 2:1 at the bottom. But though more agent-sacrifice is permitted with a spouse or child than with a stranger, we think there are fairly strict limits on this sacrifice, so you're not permitted to prefer her much lesser good. Let's say the maximum ratio for sacrifice with an intimate is 5:1, which is just modestly greater than for a stranger. This means that for the band to stay the same width as it moves down, the maximum agent-favouring permitted with intimates must be by the same modest amount less; more specifically, it must be the same three units down from the maximum for strangers, that is, it must be 1:20 minus 1:3 equals 1:17 for intimates. We find that highly counter-intuitive. We think you're only permitted some slight self-favouring with a spouse or child, if you're permitted any at all, and you're certainly not permitted to care seventeen times as much about yourself as about a spouse or child. So it seems that the top of the band must move down much more than the bottom does, resulting in a band of permissions that narrows, as in Figure 8.

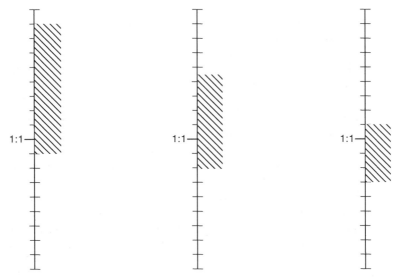

Figure 8

This point can be put more abstractly. With strangers, it's intuitive that you're permitted a significant amount of agent-favouring but only a small amount of agent-sacrifice. With intimates you're permitted only a small amount of agent-favouring but also only a modest amount of agent-sacrifice—remember that you may not sacrifice your life to save $1000 or even $10,000 for your child. So the overall extent of your permissions is less with intimates, and the band that represents them should be narrower.

Unfortunately, it's hard to reconcile these intuitions with the explanation we gave of why the band moves down. That explanation weighs prima facie permissions of constant weight against prima facie duties of differing weights: as the duty to benefit another gets stronger, it tells more against the permission to favour yourself and more for the permission to favour her, reducing the one and extending the other. But then it's hard to see how the width of the band can change. Shouldn't the same change in the strength of a duty have the same effect on both permissions, so the resulting reduction and extension are the same size and the band's top and bottom move the same distance? How can the same alteration in a factor that weighs against two permissions not yield the same result against both?

There seems then to be a conflict between some intuitive judgements about the width of the band of permissions and a natural explanation of why the band moves. We could avoid this conflict by rejecting some of the intuitive judgements, saying either that your agent-favouring permissions with strangers are less extensive than we thought—maybe you're not permitted to keep $1000 rather than save a stranger—or that your agent-sacrificing ones with intimates are more so. Alternatively, we could say that strengthening the duty to promote another's happiness has more effect against the permission to pursue your happiness than against the permission not to, so the reduction in your agent-favouring permission is greater than the expansion in your agent-sacrificing one. This is again in principle possible. Just as your permission to pursue your happiness can have more weight against one kind of duty than against another, so perhaps a duty to benefit can have more weight against one permission than against another. But this idea still seems worryingly ad hoc. If the two permissions are of the same type but just have contrary contents, shouldn't the same duty interact with them in the same way?

We have no satisfying solution to this conflict, though perhaps others will propose one. But we hope to have raised some new issues in this paper. There's been considerable philosophical discussion of permissions to produce less than the best outcome impartially considered, though perhaps more of agent-favouring than of agent-sacrificing ones. But we know of no discussion that asks how the two types of permission relate to each other and which, if either, is more extensive. There's also been discussion of self-referential altruism, the view that you have stronger duties to people who are closer to you. But again we know of no discussion that relates this view to the two types of permission. Here we've argued that as someone gets closer to you your permissions concerning her change, getting less extensive on the agent-favouring side and more extensive on the agent-sacrificing one. You can favour yourself less over intimates than over strangers, and you can favour them over yourself more. There's a band within which you're permitted to choose either your own or another's good, and that band moves down.

2

What the Objective Standard is Good For

JULIA DRIVER

A recent spate of articles has reinvigorated discussion of objective versus subjective standards of "rightness" and "rationality." In a recent work I defended an objective standard of 'right' in consequentialist moral theory, by holding that the objective standard is prior to the subjective standard. However, the objective standard has been criticized as setting an unrealistic standard, one that, in effect, conflates rightness with good moral luck. What good is a standard of right that we cannot—and, in some cases, should not try to—live up to? This worry, on my view, is traceable to the assumption that the work "right" does—indeed, the only work it does—is as a mode of evaluation in holding people responsible for what they do. However, I believe a case can be made for the practical significance of the objective standard in that *acceptance of* such a standard offers a way of measuring success. The objective standard allows for a very natural taxonomy of how our actions go morally wrong, a taxonomy that does, indirectly, provide guidance.

THE ACCOUNT

What counts as an *objective* standard? Typically, objectivity is understood as holding regardless of an agent's psychological states—regardless of her beliefs, desires, and so forth. But this underdetermines the contrast between the objective and subjective consequentialists, as I have argued elsewhere.[1] Another characterization is that the standard, to be objective, is not in any way evidence-sensitive. This is distinct from the previous way of carving the distinction since evidence might bear on an agent's beliefs, though the agent is not at all aware of the

---

[1] *Consequentialism* (London: Routledge, 2012).

evidence. For example, Peter Graham has recently defined an objective moral theory in contrast with an evidence-subjective theory:

A moral theory *T*, is *evidence-subjective=def.* according to *T*, necessarily, a person has the moral obligations that she has at a time solely in virtue of facts about her evidential situation at (or prior to) that time.

A moral theory *T*, is *objective=def.* it is not the case that *T* is evidence-sensitive.[2]

Graham is not discussing consequentialist theory *per se*, but the distinction would apply.

Often, evidence-subjectivity, or evidence-sensitivity, includes the agent's actual belief and/or desire states, either present beliefs or merely dispositional ones, but it need not. A person, for example, who thought that the right action was the action that the agent ought to believe maximizes the good, given the evidence available at the time, is proposing an evidence-sensitive standard that does not appeal to the agent's *actual* beliefs. Indeed, what makes the action right is not recoverable at all from the agent's own psychology at the time of action. For this reason, I have argued elsewhere that such "subjective" theories do not solve a major problem that subjective theories are supposed to solve—the action ownership problem discussed by Frank Jackson, and many other writers who argue in favor of a subjective standard.[3] However, Jackson, in his own account of a subjective standard of "right" does appeal to the agent's actual beliefs, though he idealizes the agent's valuing: a right action on his view involves appeals to the agent's beliefs and what the agent ought to desire at the time of action.[4] An agent with the wrong desire set may end up viewing the wrong action as the right one. But, on his view, as long as her desires are in the right place, her action is right as long as it is what she would believe maximizes the good given her other beliefs. Technically, Jackson's account is not evidence-sensitive in the way that Graham spells out: it is possible for

---

[2] "In Defense of Objectivism about Moral Obligation," *Ethics* 121 (2010), 89. Graham later modifies the subjective account by noting that most who are subjectivists also hold the view that it must be "ability constrained" as well as evidence-sensitive. This builds into the account the intuition that "ought" implies "can." He acknowledges, however, that this additional constraint is inadequately motivated.

[3] *Consequentialism*, see chapters 5 and 6.

[4] "Decision-theoretic Consequentialism and the Nearest and Dearest Objection," *Ethics* 101 (April 1981), 461–82.

someone to hold beliefs against the evidence, and yet, on Jackson's view, still do the right thing. Her "evidential situation" dictates one set of beliefs, and yet she is insensitive to her evidential situation. Perhaps self-deceptive people are like this.

In any case, depending on what problem one is primarily worried about, the subjective account can be spelled out in a variety of ways.

A standard of moral evaluation, S, is *evidence-sensitive* when the evaluation (according to S) is made relative to either the evidence the agent has at the time of action, is available to her at the time of action, or she is aware of at the time of action.

The evidence-sensitive approach may or may not involve the agent's psychology, depending on how the evidence-sensitivity is spelled out. If the standard is spelled out so that the requisite evidence is something the agent is aware of, then psychology is brought in. If, however, the evidence-sensitivity is understood in terms of evidence the agent should be aware of (though she may not be), then it is not brought to bear in the standard. A different subjective standard more explicitly cites the agent's psychology.

A standard of moral evaluation, S, is *psychological state-sensitive* when the evaluation (according to S) is made relative to the agent's psychology, that is, the beliefs and/or desires she has (either consciously, or recoverably).

Given this type of standard, with respect to "right," we could hold that an action is right iff the agent believes the action will produce the best results. Or, more plausibly, given what the agent believes, the action in question would produce the best results. Thus, if Melissa believes that suffering is bad, if she believes that alleviating suffering is morally good, and if she believes that the best way to alleviate suffering is to give to famine relief, then the right action (for her to perform) is to give to famine relief (even if she fails to put these all together herself).

Why make this distinction? The distinction is important in that one can isolate discrete problems for the objective approach if one understands what different people are attracted to in the subjective approach. In the case of the psychology-sensitive standard, the problem it seeks to avoid is the agent-ownership problem: on the objective view an action's rightness is independent of the agent's psychology at the time of action, and this is deemed "alienating." For the agent to be truly responsible, so the criticism goes, the agent needs to "own" the action in terms of justification. The conditions of justification cannot be alien to the agent, rather, those conditions need to be present in some way in the agent's psychology.[5] Peter Railton tried to solve this problem by arguing that one can be committed to the objective standard without it dominating each decision one makes, that was his attempt to solve the alienation problem.[6] The commitment to, and identification with, the right set of values as a regulative ideal is compatible with developing dispositions to act in ways that don't explicitly appeal to those values at the time of acting on the disposition. On Railton's view, this is the way that the sophisticated consequentialist proceeds. It is an elegant solution, though attacked by Frank Jackson, among others, as failing to lead to the right answers in certain cases. Another strategy—compatible with Railton's, but in principle, separable—is to simply divorce a standard of right from a standard of praise and blame and hold that the standard of praise and blame is psychology-sensitive. We will return to this suggestion.

The evidence-sensitivity standard is concerned to avoid another problem. That is the problem of moral luck in justification. A fully objective standard of right seems to be unfair in that it seems to hold people responsible for something they have no control over. If the evidence that a course of action would prove disastrous is unavailable to me, then how can I be held responsible in performing that action? Writers such as Frances Howard-Snyder and Elinor Mason are concerned that the objective standard thus, in effect, violates the most morally compelling formulation of "'ought' implies 'can'" since it holds that the right thing will be beyond the *practical* means of the agent.[7] It may be logically and physically possible to do the right thing, but due to epistemic limitations, not psychologically possible.[8] Again,

---

[5] This line of criticism was famously developed by Michael Stocker in "The Schizophrenia of Modern Ethical Theory," *Journal of Philosophy* 73 (1976), 453–66, and also picked up on in Jackson, "Consequentialism and the Nearest and Dearest Objection."

[6] "Alienation, Consequentialism, and the Demands of Morality," *Philosophy & Public Affairs* 13 (1984), 134–71.

[7] Frances Howard-Snyder, "It's the Thought that Counts," *Utilitas* 17 (2005), 265–81; Elinor Mason, "Consequentialism and the 'Ought'-implies-'Can' Principle," *American Philosophical Quarterly* 40 (2003), 319–31.

[8] Of course, much hinges on what is meant by "psychologically" possible. I discuss this in *Consequentialism*, chapter 5.

this problem is addressed by the objective consequentialist by distinguishing the standard of right from the standard of praise and blame. The different subjective standards highlight different ways in which actions can go morally wrong and deviate from the objective. This indicates an important role a commitment to the objective standard plays in providing a *taxonomy* of moral mistakes for the responsible agent to be sensitive to.

It is important to keep track of this distinction. While many people hold the subjective view to be the same as the evidence-sensitive view, this isn't always the case. Donald Regan defines the objective view, in opposition to the subjective view, as one in which ". . . the agent's beliefs about his obligation or about the state of the world do not determine what he should do . . ."[9] This is clearly a psychology-sensitive standard. On the other hand, those who opt for a "foreseeable consequences" standard are opting for one that is evidence-sensitive.[10] What is foreseeable may not be actually foreseen by the agent, but it will also not count as "foreseeable" unless the evidence available supports it.

There is some disagreement in the consequentialism literature that centers on which way to understand, at the very least, praiseworthiness and blameworthiness—is it tied to what is recoverable from the agent's psychology, or from what the agent "ought" to believe on the basis of available evidence? But even granting a distinction between "right" and "praiseworthy" there is an attack on the objective account of right that focuses on its *pointlessness* or failure to do anything. It is this worry I would like to address.

Carving the space can be even more complicated when we factor in the different psychological states an agent can have. For example, it isn't merely beliefs that factor into what an agent decides to do; the agent's desires provide the motivational impetus. If the agent's desires are fundamentally very bad desires, if the agent wants to do things he ought not want to do, then this can render the subjective standard of right quite dubious—that is, if the standard is understood by appeal to the agent's *actual* beliefs and desires. This is one reason Frank Jackson has articulated a standard which appeals to the agent's actual beliefs and

---

[9] *Utilitarianism and Cooperation* (Oxford University Press, 1980), 12.
[10] See, for example, Bart Gruzalski's "Foreseeable Consequence Utilitarianism," *Australasian Journal of Philosophy* 59 (June 1981), 163–76.

what the agent *ought* to desire, given the right value function. But the standard is only subjective part way—it is evidence-sensitive, but not fully psychology-sensitive.

Persons who advocate a purely psychology sensitive standard of right (or "ought") hold that an agent acts rightly if she does what she believes is best, even when her understanding of "best" is based on false value claims.[11] The intuition here is that if an agent is functioning properly as an agent, she will display the correct *formal* features in her deliberation. So, for example, if Bob believes that perfecting human nature is our proper moral goal, and that this perfection requires that we suppress all emotion, then he *ought* to work to suppress emotion; this would be the right thing for him to do, even if his view of value was completely mistaken and leads to what is, objectively speaking, a defective sort of motivation. This is because the failure to do what one believes to be best (and here I am indifferent about how "best" is understood), is a failure in one's abilities as an agent. It is a failure that denotes a severe structural flaw in agency itself, when that agency is not guided by the agent's beliefs and values. There is something to this intuition that if someone acts in ways that don't reflect her beliefs and desires, there is something seriously wrong with the person. Indeed, one might even wonder if the person is *acting* at all. This is too radical. A person can, loosely speaking, be weak willed and act in ways she disapproves of. But to limit wrongness, or even blameworthiness, to these sorts of cases is much *too* limiting. A person's own critical practices have application beyond what she presently believes and desires. A person—to borrow an example from Mark Twain—may look back on her life and be ashamed of her heartless youth, judging herself to have been morally mistaken. We can't account for that sense of moral error without appealing to a standard that is *at least* not psychology-sensitive.

But the subjectivist will concede this point, perhaps, and instead opt for one of the evidence-sensitive approaches, or even a mixed approach. If one holds that the right action is the one that the agent would perform given she is well motivated and has all available information, the standard is evidence-sensitive but not psychology-sensitive. Bob is not acting rightly given this standard. But this intermediate between the

[11] Brian Hedden articulates such a view of "ought" in "Options and the Subjective "Ought"," *Philosophical Studies*, forthcoming.

fully subjective and objective strikes me as an unhappy compromise if what we are considering is the standard by which we measure moral success. Better to keep to the classic distinction between "right" and "praiseworthy" and note varying degrees of "praiseworthy" as deviations from the standard are realized.

Again, even granting a distinction between "right" and "praiseworthy" there is an attack on the objective account of right that focuses on its pointlessness or failure to be of any practical use. I find the criticism odd, since the standard is intended as one of evaluation. However, I also find it false given what we are talking about is a *commitment* to the standard.[12]

As an example, the following offers a basic rendering of an objective consequentialist standard of right.

(SR) the right action is the one that produces the best *results* amongst the action options open to the agent at the time of action; it is the action that the well-motivated, fully informed agent would perform in those circumstances.[13]

First, there are very many different forms the standard can take when spelled out in more detail: one can hold that best is understood in terms of what promotes objective probability of the maximally good outcome; or one can hold that best is understood in terms of what a risk-averse agent would do in avoiding the worst outcome. There are many possibilities. What is key about a pure objective standard? The following: (1) right is understood independent of the agent's actual psychology and/or (2) right is not "evidence-sensitive" in the ways discussed above.

Second, it is important that this is understood as a standard, and not as a decision procedure, though a decision procedure may well be extractable. This was Peter Railton's view when he argued that what counts as a good decision procedure given this standard will be an empirical issue. As a standard, it sets the success condition for **rightness.** Of course, there are serious epistemological difficulties associated with success when that is understood objectively. It may be difficult to know if and when one has actually performed an action that is "right." This

---

[12] I discuss this more fully in *Consequentialism*, particularly in chapters 5 and 6.

[13] There is some debate on whether or not "full information" should be included in the objective standard. Indeed, I am skeptical, but that particular issue is orthogonal to the project of this discussion. If not "full" information, then substitute "all relevant" information.

limitation is what led W. D. Ross to note that the right action is the "fortunate" action:

> If we cannot be certain that it is right, it is our good fortune if the act we do is the right act. This consideration, does not, however, make the doing of our duty a mere matter of chance. There is a parallel here between the doing of duty and the doing of what will be to our personal advantage. We never *know* what act will in the long run be to our advantage. Yet it is certain that we are more likely in general to secure our advantage if we estimate to the best of our ability the probable tendencies of our actions in this respect than if we act on caprice.[14]

In my view, Ross' views here are quite instructive. Indeed, some of his insights have been clarified and expanded in the service of arguing that there is a legitimate objective standard of "right." Ross is implicitly, note, appealing to a distinction between doing what is "right" and doing one's duty. There is the right action, and then there is doing the best one can in trying to get there. It is one's duty to do the best one can. In setting a success condition, then, as Railton has noted, one can extract decision procedures that one has empirical evidence will help one get closer to reaching the goal. And, further, those decision procedures themselves, whatever they happen to be, will be assessable by reference to how closely they allow us to reach success, and successfully reach success. They are evaluated in terms of relative success. Thus, the best procedure is the more accurate one. Some procedures will be better or worse in terms of meeting the standard. Since the standard is what is used to evaluate other standards of evaluation, as well as the decision procedures people employ in actual practice, the standard has *evaluative* primacy relative to those procedures.

In seeing how this works an analogy with another standard might help. Suppose that Marissa is an architect in charge of building a new theatre, and the theatre owners are striving for the most comfortable seats, given certain efficiency or cost constraints. Let us also suppose that the greatest comfort—given those constraints—is achieved by allowing for exactly 12 inches between seats in the theatre. How well the standard is met in any given case is an objective matter, and it may, in practice, be difficult to measure exactly 12 inches between seats. But whatever method is employed by the workers to measure the distance between

---

[14] *The Right and the Good* (Oxford University Press, 1930), 31–2.

seats, the adequacy, the goodness, of that measure is dependent on how close such a method gets one to the objective standard. The methods or procedures themselves are assessed, and assessed in terms of evidence regarding how close they get to the standard.

Other writers have drawn analogies between moral evaluation and other sorts of *normative* evaluation. So, for example, if one judges the aim of belief to be truth, then simply a person's believing that the belief she holds is true is not sufficient for epistemic success. Of course, there are subjectivist counterparts in epistemology—these are persons who hold that epistemic success is achieved through justification alone, and then one can have more or less demanding standards of justification, as one sees in the literature on moral evaluation. In some of Roderick Chisholm's writings he seems to adopt the view that we ought, *epistemically*, believe reasonably and avoid believing unreasonably.[15] The latter stipulation is important to note. Responsibility involves avoiding mistakes as well as achieving successes in absolute terms.

On the view that I have been sketching so far, the objective standard is the standard by which we understand the normative import of yet other standards, such as that of **praiseworthiness**. Here is an example that incorporates both evidence-sensitive and psychology-sensitive elements.

(SP) the praiseworthy action is the action that the agent (reasonably) expects will produce the best results amongst the options she perceives to be open to her at the time of action.

"Reasonably" appeals to evidence-sensitivity; "expects" and "perceives" are the psychology-sensitive elements. There are numerous ways to combine these elements in a standard of praiseworthiness. My view is the appropriateness of standards like (SP) is a function of pragmatics— what best serves utility in the long run. Thus, the objective standard of right guides both the selection of standards of praiseworthiness as well as, ultimately, the appropriateness of decision procedures for agents to follow.

Many of those—at least, in the consequentialism literature—who object to (SR) believe that something like (SP) is the standard not only

---

[15] He makes this claim in "The Place of Epistemic Justification," *Philosophical Topics* (Spring 1986), 85–92.

of praiseworthiness, but also of rightness. Extracting a plausible moral guide from such a standard seems quite intuitive. This is because success is reached via reasonable attempts. Thus, one can recommend that people try, for example, to get the best information possible relevant to the decision at hand, and then act on what they expect given that information will produce the best results. This has the supposed advantage of reducing the impact of luck on rightness. Again, in the consequentialist literature, for the objective consequentialists these two standards come apart. Note, also, that the decision procedures extracted from (SR) and (SP) could, in principle, be the same. Whether the decision procedures diverge will again be an empirical issue.

The more difficult claim to defend is the one that something like (SR) has evaluative primacy with respect to (SP). Indeed, a set of problems for the evaluative primacy of the objective has developed over the years. What unites these problems is the idea that there will be situations in which agents ought not pursue the best option; that pursuing the best option runs a significant risk of leading to the worst outcome. Thus, one *ought* to pursue a suboptimal outcome that has less, or even no risk, of leading to the worst outcome. But the key factor is that, though (SR) still provides the standard of right, there are practical worries about successfully meeting such a success condition. The practical worries, having to do in this particular case with the epistemic limitations we often labor under, may imply that a sophisticated consequentialist not try to do what has any chance at all of the best outcome, because the chance is small relative to the chance of generating a relative disaster. This would mean that (SP) is not *the* standard of praiseworthiness, at least, not without significant modification. One such modification would be to include consideration of avoiding disaster.

Frank Jackson presented a case such as this in his argument for a (somewhat) subjective standard of right. He builds up to the crucial case by tweaking our intuitions about standard uncertainty cases. The case involves Jill, a doctor, and her patient, John who is suffering from a non-fatal skin condition. Jill needs to decide how best to treat John:

She has three drugs to choose from: drug A, drug B, and drug C. Careful consideration of the literature has led her to the following opinions. Drug A is very likely to relieve the condition, but will not completely cure it. One of the drugs B and C will completely cure the skin condition; the other though will kill the patient, and there is no way that she can tell which of the two is the perfect cure and which the killer drug.[16]

Jackson goes on to note that clearly Jill should prescribe A, even though A is clearly not the best option, where that is understood as the option which maximizes the good. Thus, it looks like Jill ought to do what she knows is wrong. This is very odd, and in cases such as this can be iterated so that a policy of acting wrongly (on the objective view) can seem to be morally best as well. This case has other parallels in the literature, most notably Derek Parfit's mine-shaft case. In this example, Parfit asks us to consider:

Mine shafts: A hundred miners are trapped underground, with flood waters rising. We are rescuers on the surface who are trying to save these men. We know that all of these men are in one of two mine shafts, but we don't know which. There are three flood-gates that we could close by remote control. The results would be these:

		The miners are in	
		Shaft A	Shaft B
	Gate 1	We save 100 lives	We save no lives
We close	Gate 2	We save no lives	We save 100 lives
	Gate 3	We save 90 lives	We save 90 lives[17]

Clearly what we ought to do in the ordinary dominant sense of "ought" is to close Gate 3, thereby doing what in the objective sense we know to be wrong, and yet also picking the option with the least overall down side. We avoid the disaster of losing 100.

Parfit's case is based on an example presented by Donald Regan:[18]

		Poof	
		Push	Not-Push
	Push	10	0
Whiff	Not-push	0	10
	Override	9	9

---

[16] "Consequentialism and the Nearest and Dearest Objection," 463.
[17] *On What Matters* (Oxford University Press, 2011), Vol. I, 159.
[18] *Utilitarianism and Cooperation*, 264–5, fn. 1.

Regan presents this as a variation on a standard Whiff/Poof case. In such cases the moral universe consists of just two persons, Whiff and Poof. The case is presented as one in which each of these persons has a button that she may or may not press, and:

> Suppose that from Whiff's point of view the subjective probabilities are that Poof is equally likely to push or not-push. It is clear that subjective AU [Act Utilitarianism] requires Whiff to override (producing a subjective expected value, and indeed a certain value, of 9 units) instead of either pushing or not-pushing (each with a subjective value of 5 units), even though overriding cannot possibly be the best act in the circumstances . . . [19]

This case is much less dramatic than the doctor case and the mine-shaft case. We are not worried about anyone dying. Instead, what is at stake is a small loss of utility. And yet it still seems true that the agent "ought" to "override" for a guarantee of 9 units instead of a 50% chance at 10 units. The agent ought to do what the objectivist views as the wrong thing to do, it seems, even when the losses are fairly small.

In Jackson's version of the case, the judgment that Jill ought to opt for A, that this is the right thing for her to do, is a problem for the objective consequentialist because, according to Jackson, the objective consequentialist such as Railton is committed to a decision procedure, based on the standard of rightness, which involves the agent ". . . setting . . . the goal of doing what is objectively right—the action that has in fact the best consequences—and then performing the action which the empirical evidence suggests is most likely to have this property."[20] I have argued elsewhere that this is a very uncharitable reading of Railton's suggestion.[21] The more natural way to view the objective consequentialst's remarks on decision procedures is to separate out two different issues: the *standard* of praise and blame is one issue, and the recommended decision procedure another. What the objective consequentialist is best regarded as holding is the view that the standard of praise and blame is to be explained in terms of the standard of right— that there is an explanatory and evaluative primacy to the standard of right. Then, what decision procedures help us to arrive at the best

---

[19] Regan, *Utilitarianism and Cooperation*, 265.
[20] Jackson, "Consequentialism and the Nearest and Dearest Objection," 467.
[21] See my discussion in *Consequentialism*.

overall outcome is to be determined based on what standard we are seeking to satisfy. But, ultimately, the evaluative standard is fully objective.

Also, the Whiff/Poof case, Jill, and the mine-shaft case pose a supposed problem for the objective standard of right because it sounds odd to say—as the objective theorist should in these cases—that "He ought to do an action that is wrong." But on the objective view the oddity does not translate into inconsistency. There is nothing at all incoherent in this claim. The objective theorist gives a perfectly coherent account of both why the suboptimal option is wrong, and yet why one ought, nevertheless to do it. Further, there are numerous other cases in the literature demonstrating that this oddity is not escapable by subjective consequentialists. Satisficers have argued that there are cases—at least, imaginable cases—in which there is no best outcome. One such case is suggested in the writings of Michael Slote.[22] Imagine that one is a heroine in a fairy story. One has found a genie bottle, uncorked it, and the genie grants one a wish: as much money as one names! How much does one ask for? A million dollars? But wouldn't that be irrational, since one could ask for more, such as a million and one dollars? Indeed (assuming that one would be able to translate the money into some other good), where does one draw the line in picking a number to ask for? Satisficers invoke such cases to try to show that maximizing versions of consequentialism are wrong because there are cases where there is no maximum, and it is perfectly rational (and moral) to fall somewhere short, as long as it's good enough. I am not a satisficer, but the case does plausibly demonstrate a situation in which there is no right answer so whatever one does one acts wrongly. In this case it is also true that "He ought to do the action that is wrong" whether or not one is an objectivist or a subjectivist. A subjectivist is stuck with the odd locution in any case.

Jackson himself opts for a standard that *seems* to be a mixture of the evidence-sensitive and the psychology-sensitive. The right action is a function of the agent's actual beliefs and what the agent ought to desire (or value). Given how I have specified the two distinct forms of

---

[22] This is not exactly Slote's case, but is similar to one he presents on p. 147 in his section of "Satisficing Consequentialism," written with Philip Pettit, *Proceedings of the Aristotelian Society, Supplementary Volume* 58 (1984), 139–63.

sensitivity that seem to figure into subjective standards, Jackson's standard is psychology-sensitive in that it appeals to the agent's actual beliefs,
but (perhaps) evidence-sensitive in that it also appeals to what the agent
ought to value. But the latter will be an evidence-sensitive factor only if
we view the value as something there is evidence for. Since this seems
like a plausible assumption to make, I view Jackson's standard as one
that mixes the two sorts of sensitivity.

Peter Graham has argued that one objectivist strategy to undermining Jackson's counterexample is to deny certain assumptions that he
makes.[23] Namely, most importantly, the assumption that the morally
conscientious person is solely focused on doing the right thing. Graham
points out that she must also be concerned with avoidance of wrongdoing. This, then, leads to a potential conflict that occurs in cases like
Jackson's. Further, in the case of wrongdoing, we can look at the
seriousness of the wrong to be avoided—there will be greater moral
pressure to avoid worse outcomes, for example. Thus, as Graham notes,
the morally conscientious person not only tries to do what is right, but
also tries to avoid doing what is wrong, and what is really, really, wrong
in particular. This seems quite clear in the cases the literature has tended
to focus on, Jackson's doctor case and Parfit's mine-shaft cases. The
Whiff and Poof case illustrates that the avoidance of disutility is
important even when the disutility is relatively small.

Thus, one way for the objective consequentialist to respond is to note
that there is the best, which I cannot be confident of, and there is what
seems on balance best, given my own awareness of my serious epistemic
limitations. One can then keep the standard of right, but to accommodate Jackson style cases, modify the standard of praiseworthiness to
something like the following:

(**SP***) An action is praiseworthy if the well-motivated agent performing the
action would judge it to be, on balance, best amongst her alternatives at the
time of action.

"On balance" is then unpacked to account for *risk aversion* of the
rational agent. One's ignorance—glaringly apparent in the Jackson
and Parfit style cases—is something the epistemically responsible
agent should be sensitive to. This, then, ought to be factored into the

---

[23] "In Defense of Objectivism about Moral Obligation," 95 ff.

standard of praiseworthiness. We need to worry about things going badly, just as we need to worry about things going well.

Someone guided by a desire to do the best he can will also use the same criteria that establish what counts as best in guiding his choice about how to act. With regard to praise and blame, risk is very important, and the responsible agent considers what happens if he *fails*. But success is determined relative to the standard, not relative to the agent's *attempt* to meet the standard. The role of the objective standard of "right" is to set a comprehensive standard for moral success by which other standards measure, or define themselves.

Thus, the competing standards point to the fact that different things go wrong in the performance of the morally right, as well as the morally praiseworthy actions, and that we are not measuring success—even an action's success—along a single parameter.

To see this more clearly, we can create a taxonomy of moral failure that appeals to this standard (Table 1). An agent might know what to do, but not care; or might have all the information she needs to determine the best course of action, but some misguided set of values. These lead to motivational failures. The other failures are epistemic. Lack of all relevant information leads to errors; lack of information that is available to the agent leads to errors; and, most unforgivingly of all, lack of utililization of the information one actually has in one's possession.

On the objective view, an agent fails to perform the right action due to numerous factors—failure to be properly motivated, failure to have all the relevant information, failure to have the available information, and failure to properly utilize the information one has. There is also clumsiness and ineptitude. Further, and this is what strikes many as

Table 1: Taxonomy

Relevant factors	Motivation/ desire	Full information	Available evidence	Evidence agent is aware of	Agent's actual psychology
Objective right	x	x			
Praiseworthy 1	x		x		
Praiseworthy 2	x			x	
Praiseworthy 3	x				x

absurd—the failure can also be due to sheer accident, and sheer bad luck. On Jackson's view the only way an action counts as a moral failure is when the agent lacks the appropriate motivation and fails to utilize the information she has. If an agent intends well, and acts on what she believes (even if more or better information was available to her) she has acted rightly, and in a morally praiseworthy manner.

Why think that failures of information, will, and sheer accident are *moral* failures? They are moral in the sense that they are morally relevant. It matters to how things turn out. There is an empirical assumption being made. One is that willing the good is at least correlated with good outcomes; that information improves the level of control we exert over the world, and thus over the effects of what we do. These are entirely reasonable assumptions, as is the following:

(**MRel**) If factor f is a factor that one ought to take into consideration in performing an action, then it is morally relevant.

and

If a factor is morally relevant then the objective moral standard is sensitive to it.

Consider the appropriate response to such a failure: imagine that Jackson's doctor, Jill, failed to attend a vital seminar—to which she was invited—that would have provided information about the skin condition that would have enabled her to have treated the patient more effectively. That she lacks such information does reflect badly on her. What guides the standard of praise brought to bear in a given case reflects our justifiable expectations regarding how a person should be held responsible in the service of promoting the good. The overarching standard is thus the objective standard of "right." What makes it a mistake—a morally significant mistake—that the doctor did not go the seminar? If she had gone the outcome would likely have been much better for the patient. What is it to be *better for* the patient? Closer to the best, *really* best, outcome for the patient. The aim of morality, including practical morality, is to achieve the good, not to achieve what one just happens to believe to be good.

It may be that what is behind the view that certain mistakes, while making achievement of the good less likely, are nevertheless not morally relevant, is the view that the well-motivated agent, the agent whose *desires* are guided by the right sorts of value commitments, has fulfilled whatever is demanded of her morally already, and that the content of her (non-moral) beliefs is not something that can affect that. On this view, however, an agent can do no wrong no matter how ill-informed, as long as she wants to act rightly. If this is understood Jackson's way, as being only partially psychology-sensitive—then it is much more plausible than the purely subjective view. However, it still seems quite implausible in that if such a standard is the standard of right that is primary—against which the others are compared—then there is no room for moral improvement. Yet arriving at better outcomes, and taking pains to acquire information that makes sure one arrives at better outcomes, does constitute moral improvement. Thus, the purely objective standard is the primary standard.

3

Subjective Normativity and Action Guidance[1]

ANDREW SEPIELLI

It's often claimed that when we are uncertain about what's the case, we cannot guide our actions by[2] objective norms (e.g. objective utilitarianism) and must instead avail ourselves of subjective norms (e.g. subjective utilitarianism). I agree with this claim, once it is appropriately restricted. But I don't think anyone has satisfactorily explained why it is true.

Equipped with only unsatisfactory explanations, we risk seriously distorting our understanding of the notions implicated in the debate about subjective normativity and action guidance—to wit, the notions of a subject, of normativity, of action, and of guidance.[3] In this paper, then, I want to take the first steps towards an explanation of why subjective norms are uniquely suited to play the action-guiding

---

[1] Thanks to Adam Arico, Ruth Chang, Kelin Emmett, Benj Hellie, Tom Hurka, Leon Lukic, Christopher Maloney, Elinor Mason, Jennifer Nagel, Devlin Russell, Holly Smith, Mark Timmons, and two anonymous referees for helpful comments and discussions.

[2] It is natural to say, "Ms. X guided her action by such-and-such a norm," and also to say "Ms. X guided her action by such-and-such a belief state." "Guided by . . . " seems clearly to be equivocal. The sense in which I guide my action "by" a mental state is not the sense in which I guide my action "by" the content of a mental state. Cf. Turri 2009. To reinforce this distinction, then, I will say that one guides one's actions *by* the contents of one's beliefs, and *with* the beliefs themselves.

[3] Hewing to the wrong explanation will also imperil our ability to solve more specific problems. For my own part, I'd like to defend a theory of how we ought to behave when we must act under *normative uncertainty*—that is, uncertainty about the reasons, "oughts," requirements, etc. provided by the non-normative facts. (Uncertainty among *moral theories* is a notable type of normative uncertainty.) Any such theory faces a nasty regress problem— "what if you're uncertain about which theory of what to do under normative uncertainty is correct?"—that we'll be unable to solve without having in hand the correct account of the role subjective norms play in the guidance of action. For more on normative uncertainty and the regress problem, see Sepielli 2010.

role they do. In other work, I present my positive proposal in detail.[4] My aim here is simply to lay the groundwork for this positive view by presenting a conceptual framework within which candidate explanations should operate, showing how certain of these explanations fail, and drawing some lessons from their failure.

I'll begin with a characterization of subjective normativity and its relation to objective normativity. Then, I'll clarify and restrict the claim about action guidance the truth of which I seek to explain. After that, I'll argue against four candidate explanations. I'll conclude by providing the beginnings of my own explanation.

OBJECTIVE AND SUBJECTIVE NORMATIVITY

Let us suppose that a pill will kill James if he takes it, but that James reasonably believes that the pill will cure some illness of his. I might say of James that he ought not to take the pill, on the grounds that it will kill him. You might say of James that he ought to take the pill, on the grounds that he reasonably believes that it will cure his illness. It is an assumption of this paper that we may both be right. I am right insofar as I am employing the objective sense of "ought"; you are right insofar as you are employing one of the subjective senses of "ought." Now, parties might disagree about which of these senses is more important, or about the role(s) played by each sense, or about which sense the ordinary, natural-language "ought" is identified with in this context or that. But I'll assume throughout that in employing our respective "oughts," we are not having a straightforward substantive disagreement about what someone in James's situation ought to do. That is, ours is not a disagreement of the sort the utilitarian and the deontologist are having when they argue about whether one ought to push the large man in front of the trolley.

There are different ways of spelling out the thesis that there are multiple "senses" of "ought." One possibility is that they express different OUGHT concepts;[5] there is the objective OUGHT concept,

---

[4] See Sepielli (work in progress-a).

[5] Following Jerry Fodor, I use words or phrases in all capital letters to refer to concepts. See Fodor 1998. I use words or phrases in quotation marks to refer to words or phrases that express those concepts. I'll shift back and forth between speaking of different senses of "ought"

and at least one subjective OUGHT concept. Another possibility is that, rather than there being separate objective OUGHT and subjective OUGHT concepts, OUGHT concepts contain a *parameter* that is set by context, assessor's information, speaker's intention, or something else.[6] Whether "ought" in some use is objective or subjective depends on how the parameter of the concept it expresses is filled in at the time of expression. I want to remain neutral between these spellings-out. I can say what I want to in this paper without endorsing either of them over the other.

Several people have suggested to me that there's no way of understanding the subjective sense(s) of "ought" in terms of any objective normative notion(s). No doubt this skepticism has been engendered by the history of failed attempts at doing so. Nonetheless, I'd like to make an attempt of my own. I'll begin with a rough "first pass" proposal; then I'll refine it into the view I wish to defend.

We should allow that the objective OUGHT may depend for its proper application on any feature of the world whatsoever. Some authors say that the objective OUGHT's proper application may depend on any feature of the world *except* the agent's beliefs, or the evidence available to the agent, presumably because these are the things upon which the proper application of the subjective OUGHT(s) depend. But this is a mistake. First, there are cases where what I objectively ought to do seems to depend on my beliefs. I ought not to say "P" if it would be a lie, but whether it is a lie depends on whether I believe that P. Second, as a methodological matter, we will want to leave open as a conceptual possibility that what I objectively ought to do may depend on anything whatsoever.[7]

Subjective OUGHTs depend for their proper application on the agent's beliefs or degrees of belief, or on the agent's evidence, or on the probabilities *regarding the features of the world upon which the proper application of the objective OUGHT depends.* So if it turns out that the utilitarian is right, and what one objectively ought to do depends on how much utility each of one's candidate actions would produce,

---

(referring to the word), and different senses of OUGHT (referring to the concept or family of concepts).

  [6] See Dowell (work in progress); and Kolodny and MacFarlane (work in progress).
  [7] On these points, see also Smith 2010.

then what one subjectively ought to do will depend on one's beliefs or degrees of belief about how much utility each action will produce, or on the evidence or the probabilities regarding the same.

There are different subjective OUGHTs because beliefs/degrees of belief, evidence, and various sorts of probability are all different things, and there is a subjective OUGHT that depends for its proper application on each. Following Derek Parfit, we may speak of the *belief-relative* sense of "ought," the *reasonable-belief-relative* sense, the *degree-of-belief-relative* (or *credence-relative*, or *subjective-probability-relative*) sense, the *evidence-relative* sense, and the *objective-probability-relative* sense, each of which depends for its proper application on the feature mentioned in its label.[8] We could ramify even further. There are, for example, different "interpretations" of objective probability—the long-run frequency interpretation, the propensity interpretation, the logical interpretation, etc.—and there could be an OUGHT corresponding to each interpretation.

Finally, there is a subjective OUGHT that I call the *minimal-probability-relative* OUGHT. As far as I know, nobody in moral philosophy has discussed this sense before. This is unfortunate, for it is, I believe, the sense most crucial for action guidance. What's more, as we'll see later, we'll be tempted into confusion when we ask other subjective senses—specifically, the credence-relative and evidence-relative senses—to play the role most naturally occupied by the minimal-probability-relative sense. Let me take a moment to explain what minimal probability is, and the category of norm that is relative to it.

One *reports* one's belief that P by saying, "I believe that P." One *expresses* one's belief that P by saying, simply, "P." Just as one can report a belief, one can report a degree of belief, or credence. One does this by saying, e.g., "I have a credence of .6 that P," or, less precisely, "I'm slightly more confident than not that P." But how does one *express* a credence? Not with a sentence like the ones just mentioned; that would elide the distinction between reporting and expressing. And not by saying, "There's a .6 objective probability that P." That would be expressing a full belief about objective probabilities. And not by saying, "The evidence supports a credence of .6 that P," or "There's evidence of

---

[8] Parfit 2011.

'degree .6' that P." These would be expressions of full beliefs about evidence.

I will call the statements we use to express, rather than report, our degrees of belief "minimal probability" statements. Those with "minimal probability" in their vocabulary might express a .6 credence that P by saying, "There's a .6 minimal probability that P." But of course this term is a neologism. I suspect, however, that ordinary people express the same thing with statements like: "Frank's probably already at the party"; or "Five-to-one odds Koopmans ain't even gonna show." I also suspect that most uses of "I'm not sure the bank is open on Saturdays" and the like are non-literal; someone who says this is typically not reporting her credence that the bank is open on Saturdays (in the same way she might report her friend's credence by saying, "My friend is not sure the bank is open on Saturdays"). Rather, she is expressing her credence in what, to us sticklers, is a grammatically misleading way. All of these quotidian statements are ways of expressing the same thing we might more precisely express using the language of minimal probabilities.

So what *are* minimal probabilities? Of particular concern is whether they are features of the world to which we commit ourselves whenever we express our credences, in the way that we commit ourselves to objective probabilities when we make statements about objective probabilities. That'd be strange. If I can express a full belief that there are ostriches without committing myself to any non-ostrich entities or properties, I should be able to express a credence that there are ostriches without committing myself to any non-ostrich entities or properties.

We can avoid the strange result by assigning semantic values to minimal probability statements, in part, *expressivistically*. Rather than explaining the semantic features of the "probably" in statements like "Frank's probably already at the party" by appeal to minimal probability properties in the world, we explain their semantic features by the mental states they're used to express—namely, credences. So suppose we want to explain why "There's a .8 minimal probability that P" and "There's a .8 minimal probability that ~P" are inconsistent. We would do that by saying that the former expresses a credence of .8 that P, the latter expresses a .8 credence that ~P, and these are credences that it's not rational to hold together.[9]

There is a sense of OUGHT that is minimal-probability-relative. It is the sense one typically expresses when one says to oneself, "Hmmm, it's probably gonna rain. If it's probably gonna rain, I ought to bring an umbrella. So yeah, I'll bring an umbrella." In other words, "minimal-probability-relative" is just an unfamiliar label for a sense of OUGHT that, I contend, couldn't be more familiar or primordial for agents like us. We'll see later on that understanding this primordial sense of OUGHT is very helpful theoretically.

It will be helpful to draw one last distinction: between "oughts" relative to different *subsets* of beliefs or probabilities. Sticking with belief-relative normativity for a moment, we may distinguish between an "ought" that is belief-relative only with regard to one's *non-normative beliefs*; one that is belief-relative only with regard to one's *normative beliefs*; and one that is belief-relative with regard to all of one's beliefs.[10] Moral theories like subjective utilitarianism are belief-relative in the first sense. What one ought to do according to subjective utilitarianism is independent of one's beliefs about utilitarianism itself and its competitors. Theories of "what to do when you don't know what to do" (i.e. under uncertainty among normative theories), like those offered by Ted Lockhart,[11] Jacob Ross,[12] and myself,[13] are belief-relative in the second sense. What one ought to do according to such theories *does* depend on one's degrees of belief in utilitarianism, contractualism, and all the rest.

---

[9]　My expressivist treatment of minimal probability is similar to Seth Yalcin's expressivist treatment of epistemic probability. See, e.g., Yalcin 2011. I explain the differences in my (work in progress-c).

[10]　This is just one way of carving one's set of beliefs "at the joints." We might, for example, also have an "ought" that is relative to one's beliefs about *a priori* matters only, and another that is relative to one's beliefs about *a posteriori* matters only. We could also carve up belief-sets less naturally—with an "ought" that is belief-relative only with regard to one's beliefs about rodents, say.

[11]　Lockhart 2000.

[12]　Ross 2006.

[13]　Sepielli 2009.

SUBJECTIVE NORMATIVITY AND TRYING

As I noted in the last section, this "first pass" characterization of the relationship between objective and subjective normativity isn't exactly right. Again, the proposal has been: subjective OUGHTs depend for their proper application on the (degrees of) belief/evidence/probabilities regarding the features upon which the proper application of the objective OUGHT depends.

This characterization fails because it is inadequately specific. For while the proper application of the subjective OUGHT does indeed depend upon these beliefs, probabilities, and so on, so does the proper application of the subjective FORBIDDEN, the subjective OUGHT *NOT*, the subjective LESS REASON TO ... THAN TO ..., and so forth. They depend in different ways, and we want to be able to say which way corresponds to the subjective OUGHT. We want to define the subjective OUGHT in such a manner that our definition picks out that very subjective normative notion, rather than any of the others.

We don't want to get *too* specific though. For example, we can't define what I subjectively ought to do as whatever maximizes expected objective value (hereafter: "EOV"), relative to some probability distribution or other.[14] I myself think it's very plausible that this *is* what we subjectively ought to do,[15] but it's a bad definition, for it rules out by fiat all other theories thereof. Notably, it rules out alternative views about how to respond to uncertainty or risk-maximin, risk-aversion or risk-seeking, the view that I subjectively ought to do what's most likely what I objectively ought to do, etc.

Instead, I offer as a basic proposal:

What I subjectively ought to do =*df.* the *best try* for me at doing what's objectively valuable.

This will require some unpacking. We are all acquainted with the concept TRYING; as agents of limited abilities, our most primordial use of it is in action. In acting under the description "trying to do A,"

---

[14] By "value," here, I simply mean "strength of reasons," however those reasons are determined. So considerations other than, say, the consequences of actions could determine actions' "values," as I'm using the term.

[15] For arguments, see Sepielli 2010, chs. 2–3.

I aim at doing A just as I do when I act under the description "doing A."[16] As Benj Hellie puts it, both trying to do A and doing A involve a "strand of agency working towards having done" A.[17] What it is to aim at doing A, or for there to be such a strand of agency, is difficult to explicate, but for present purposes I want to assume the reader's understanding of this "highest common factor" of trying and doing.

The difference between trying and doing is essentially this: When I act under the description "trying to do A," I am consciously uncertain that I will succeed in doing A; but when I act under the simple description "doing A," I am not consciously uncertain that I will succeed in doing A. I can simply do A without doing something *else* that I conceive of as an attempt or a try. The distinction between conscious uncertainty and uncertainty that is not conscious will be important later on, so it's worth getting clearer on:

Conscious uncertainty is a conscious representational attitude that, necessarily, has a phenomenal character that includes a feeling of unsurety (or as we'll call it later, a "multidirectional" phenomenology). (By contrast, *conscious certainty* is a conscious representational attitude that, necessarily, has a phenomenal character that includes a feeling of surety (or as we'll call it later, a "unidirectional" phenomenology.)

Non-conscious uncertainty is a non-conscious representational attitude that, necessarily, has a functional profile characteristic of uncertainty. (By contrast, *non-conscious certainty* is a non-conscious representational attitude that, necessarily, has a functional profile characteristic of certainty.)[18]

I leave it open what the functional profile of non-conscious uncertainty is. Perhaps it is a set of dispositions to act or reason in certain ways; perhaps it is a disposition to feel *consciously* uncertain in response to some cue; perhaps it is something else. I take it that most of us are non-consciously uncertain about *most* propositions, insofar as we would not admit upon questioning to a credence of 1 in them, or would not, say, stake our lives on them for a payout of a single chocolate chip.

---

[16] On the notion of action under a description, see Anscombe 1957, section 11; as well as Anscombe 1979.

[17] Hellie (forthcoming).

[18] I am using "conscious," then, to mean what Ned Block has called "phenomenally conscious" rather than what he has called "access conscious." See Block 1995.

It would be wrong, then, to say that one who aims to do A, but is uncertain whether he will succeed, must consign himself to merely trying to do A. For one may do A under non-conscious uncertainty without employing the TRYING concept, so long as he is not consciously uncertain. There are two ways to be non-consciously uncertain of a proposition without being consciously uncertain of it. One way is to have no conscious doxastic attitude at all regarding it. We sometimes call this "taking something for granted." Another way is to be consciously certain about it. Both of these situations are common. I am non-consciously uncertain whether the door knob will stay on the door when I turn it, and yet I take for granted that it will. I am non-consciously uncertain that the morning bus will leave at 6:55, and yet in running through the day's plans in my head, I am consciously certain that it will.[19]

I may do without trying if either I take for granted my success or I am consciously certain of it. For example, I can simply act under the description "saying my mother's name." I do not have to conceive of myself as merely saying the name that is most likely my mother's, and then praying that I am correct. Unless we see this crucial point, we will end up with a psychologically unrealistic picture of human action—one on which we see ourselves as "rolling the dice" with our every movement.[20]

Now on to the second part of the formulation: "... at doing what's objectively valuable." It is very important that we state things this way rather than saying "... at doing what's objectively best." For the feature of being the best is a *non-scalar* feature, and so the best try at doing what has this feature is simply the action with the greatest chance of having the feature. But it is highly implausible that one subjectively ought to do the action that is mostly likely to be objectively best. Suppose action

[19] On the effects of what I'm calling "deliberative context" on conscious (un)certainty, see Gollwitzer 1990; and Kruglanski and Webster 1996. For a helpful philosophical discussion of these psychological phenomena, see Holton 2009. Thanks to Jennifer Nagel for showing me around the psychological literature.

[20] So I'm rejecting the old-fashioned picture on which (a) there are a small class of actions that are "basic" for every agent in every situation, and (b) we do everything else *by* doing one of these basic actions. My preferred picture accords with the psychological literature cited in fn. 18 *supra*, and with Candlish 1984; John McDowell's discussion of Chuck Knoblauch in McDowell 2009; and Hellie (forthcoming).

A has a .51 chance of having a value of 100 and a .49 chance of having a value of −1,000,000, and action B is certain to have a value of 99. A is more likely than B to be objectively best, but surely B is what one subjectively ought to do. At the very least, we will not want to enshrine it as a definitional truth that one subjectively ought to do what is most likely to be objectively best.

The feature of being valuable, though, is a *scalar* one. It comes in degrees. And the best try at doing what has a scalar feature needn't simply be the action that is most likely to have the highest degree of the feature. (For example, the best try at making money on the stock market is not simply to throw all of one's initial investment into high-risk, high-return penny stocks.) Rather, it need only be an action that maximizes some function of the degrees of the scalar feature and the action's probability of having each of those degrees, respectively. It is an open, substantive question exactly what such a function should look like. But on what seem like the only plausible answers, action B will come out as the best try at doing what's objectively valuable in our example.

A definition of the subjective OUGHT in terms of trying and some scalar objective normative feature seems, then, to be the best way to avoid both underspecificity (i.e. a definition that fails to pick out the subjective OUGHT uniquely) and overspecificity (i.e. a definition that rules out what should be live theories of what one subjectively ought to do).

Now, we noted earlier that there are different senses of OUGHT that we might call "subjective"—the belief-relative sense, the minimal-probability-relative sense, and so forth. The present account of subjective OUGHTs in terms of TRYING can capture this, because there are, correspondingly, different senses of TRY, GOOD TRY, and so on. There are senses of TRY that are relative to our beliefs, and senses that are relative to each of the different types of probability, respectively.

As saw earlier, we use TRY in its most primordial sense when we ourselves act under "trying..." descriptions—that is, when we are consciously uncertain that we will succeed in our aims. This is the sense of TRY we can use to define whichever kind of subjective OUGHT that is most fundamental to action guidance under uncertainty. This sense of TRY is, I shall claim, relative to minimal probabilities, and so we may use it to define the minimal-probability-relative OUGHT:

What I minimal-probability-relative ought to do=*df.* the best minimal-probability-relative try for me at doing what's objectively valuable.

But we also use the language of "trying" in a more third-personal way, to describe the behavior of others (or of our past or future selves) who may not be consciously uncertain of their success, but whose probability of success is, on some interpretation of probability, less than 1. Suppose James is consciously certain that he will succeed at some ball-involving carnival game. Then he will not, in playing the game, token the concept TRY. But unbeknownst to him, the game is actually very difficult. Then we might speak of him as trying—and perhaps of his try as "good" or "poor"—despite his own conscious attitudes regarding his success.

For suppose that the publicly available evidence suggests that, say, bouncing the ball off of the side wall is the surest strategy for winning the game. Then we might rightly say that James's bouncing the ball off of the side wall is a good try. But suppose that James believes that the ball is completely inelastic, and correspondingly believes that the surest strategy is, say, throwing the ball straight at the hole. If he expresses this credence to us, we might then say that, given his credence, throwing the ball straight at the hole is a good try. A good try, in the former sense, at doing what is objectively valuable is what one ought in the evidence-relative sense to do. A good try, in the latter sense, at doing is what is objectively valuable is what one ought in the credence-relative sense to do.

THE EXPLANANDUM, IN LIGHT OF THE FOREGOING

This understanding of subjective normativity will allow us to state our explanandum more precisely.

For consider action under *certainty*. Suppose a millionaire tells me that he will donate $1000 to a cause of my choosing. If I am certain that I have most (objective) reason to choose Oxfam, then I may simply guide my choosing Oxfam with this belief. Not only needn't I employ a subjective norm; it would be downright *weird* to. Imagine asking oneself, "What subjectively ought I to do given that it's certainly the case that I objectively ought to do A?"

Now consider an otherwise similar description of action under *uncertainty*. I have some credence that I have very strong (objective) reasons to choose Oxfam, slightly weaker reasons to choose Greenpeace, and substantially weaker reasons to choose PlanUSA; I also have some credence that I have very weak reasons to choose Oxfam, stronger reasons to choose Greenpeace, and substantially stronger reasons to choose PlanUSA. In other words, I have a credence distribution over "objective reason"-propositions. I cannot move straight from this uncertainty to an action or to an intention to act such that my action would count as guided with this credence distribution. If I wish to guide my behavior with a doxastic attitude toward a normative proposition, I will have to form a conclusion about what I subjectively ought to do when confronted with these branching possibilities.

When objective normative propositions are placed in the "content box" of a full belief or certainty, we have an actionable belief state, but when they are placed in the content boxes of intermediate credences, we end up with this set of belief states that is impotent in guiding action, and need to avail ourselves of subjective norms—norms about "what to do when you don't know what to do." This is what I seek to explain.

Now, I said at the outset that this explanandum is true only if it is "appropriately restricted." The restriction I have in mind is that the uncertainty in question must be conscious. For I do not need to employ subjective norms when I am non-consciously uncertain, so long as, at the conscious level, I either take the relevant objective normative proposition(s) for granted or am consciously certain of them. I need only resort to subjective norms when I am consciously uncertain of them.[21]

---

[21] A referee suggested that since a phenomenal zombie would "need action guidance under uncertainty," but would have no use for a subjective OUGHT defined in terms of phenomenology, the subjective OUGHT I am discussing cannot be the one relevant to the guidance of action under uncertainty. I am unsure why phenomenal zombies call for a different treatment than those who I labeled as "taking for granted" the propositional contents of their non-conscious uncertainty, since both types of agents combine non-conscious uncertainty in these propositions with the lack of *any* conscious doxastic attitude towards them. In response to the referee's example, though: Consider a case where a phenomenal zombie's non-conscious uncertainty regarding objective normative propositions causes a bit of behavior. In keeping with what I said about cases of "taking for granted," I would want to say that this zombie guided her behavior with this uncertainty. Denying this, it seems to me, would commit us to denying the possibility of action guidance except in the very rare instance where an agent is utterly certain, in this non-conscious, dispositional sense, of some objective or subjective norm. (We saw earlier why this would be rare, and I discuss it again in the conclusion.) The latter denial strikes me as utterly implausible. However, if we do wish to say that the zombie cannot guide her behavior by her uncertainty, but could for some reason guide her behavior by a state of non-conscious certainty in a subjective norm, then I would question the propriety of the

This follows from our earlier analysis of "what I subjectively ought to do" as "the best try for me at acting in accordance with objective normativity," along with our distinction between "trying to do A" and "doing A" in terms of *conscious* uncertainty specifically. We said that I can act under the description "doing A" (rather than "trying to do A") so long as I am not consciously uncertain that I will succeed in doing A (even if I am non-consciously uncertain that I will succeed). So it follows that I can act under the description "doing what I objectively ought to do" even if I am non-consciously uncertain that I will succeed. I'll need to act under the description "trying to do A" only if I am consciously uncertain that I will succeed in doing A. So it follows that I will need to employ a subjective norm only if I am consciously uncertain about the objective normative status of my action.

THE "METACOGNITIVE SIGNAL" EXPLANATION

With our conceptual framework on the table, and a clearer idea of what we seek to explain, let's have a look at some candidate explanations.

One draws inspiration from some recent work in empirical psychology, and the uptake of this work by a few philosophers. We might interpret the characteristic feeling of conscious uncertainty as a sort of "metacognitive signal"—a feeling that delivers information about the functioning of our own cognitive processes.[22] On this explanation, the feeling of unsurety is plausibly construed as a warning that, if we simply act on our uncertainty without forming a separate belief about *how* to act under that uncertainty, we are likely to act in a way that is improperly responsive to that uncertainty—that is irrational. We have

---

locution "*need* action guidance." For I would wonder what, on this conception of guidance, was the import of the contrast between guided and unguided action such that the former could be said to be "needed."

[22] See Alter et al. 2007. Peter Railton stresses the role of such signals in "shaping and guiding . . . coordinate suites of thought and action." See Railton 2009: 106. Railton discusses the example of a driver, Christine, whose fluent driving is interrupted when she notices an older driver ahead puttering along and decides to slow down to avoid startling him. He says, "In Christine, the negative affect generated by her . . . simulation of the other driver's situation tend[s] to inhibit her current course of action (blasting ahead), refocus attention, and prompt thoughts of less aggressive alternatives." In recent work, Jennifer Nagel emphasizes the role of the "feeling of knowing" some fact in prompting attempts to remember that fact. See Nagel 2010.

difficulty transitioning from a credence distribution over objective normative propositions to an action because, were we to do so, we would be acting in the face of an indication that such a transition is likely irrational.

I don't wish to deny that the feeling of unsurety may serve as this sort of signal. But I deny that it is merely such a signal, and that its status as a signal is underivative of its other roles. For one thing, an unadorned "metacognitive signal" hypothesis leaves out half the phenomenology of conscious uncertainty. When I am consciously uncertain, it is not as though I see some action as the thing to do, but something in the back of my mind tells me that I have erred in so seeing it. Instead, there is a feeling of being unsettled, of not having enough to go on, of the contents of my divided credences failing to direct me towards doing one candidate action rather than the others. The phenomenology is not simply one of something holding me back; it is also one of nothing pushing me forward. Moreover, the feeling of being held back seems derivative of the feeling of not being pushed forward. Candidate actions strike me as risky *because* undirected. And this is something that the bare "metacognitive signal" hypothesis fails to capture.

Furthermore, and relatedly, the metacognitive signaling answer fails to explain why guiding one's actions with states of conscious uncertainty is *impossible* as opposed to merely unlikely. For we may deliberate and act—we may "push on"—despite the presence of inhibitory metacognitive signals. This happens often. Sometimes we ignore metacognitive signals because we deem them inaccurate. Suppose, for example, that you conclude that the answer to an exam question is "William Lyon MacKenzie King," but then immediately have the feeling of having misremembered. If you were to discover that you had been slipped a drug, the effect of which is to induce this feeling of misremembering, it seems that you could simply and safely ignore this feeling, and guide your writing this answer by your belief that it is correct. Or we may ignore metacognitive signals because we think the extra cognitive effort needed to silence them would be too costly. So if the metacognitive signaling hypothesis is true, it would be possible for us to guide our actions with conscious uncertainty. It might feel uncomfortable, but there would be no *in principle* bar to our doing it. But as I will suggest later on, guiding our actions with conscious uncertainty is impossible, for such uncertainty, as its phenomenology suggests, simply doesn't direct us toward a particular action to the exclusion of others. Suppose, for example, that you are consciously utterly uncertain what the correct answer to an exam question is. Learning that this feeling of unsurety was drug-induced wouldn't bring you any closer to writing an answer.

For all the "metacogntive signal" answer tells us, the phenomenology of conscious uncertainty could be anything. After all, the form a signal takes is irrelevant to its role as a signal, once we see what it's indeed a signal for. I could rig up my car so the gas gauge reads "empty" when the tank is full and "full" when the tank is empty; so long as I remembered that I did this, the ability of my gas gauge to serve a signal of my tank's fullness would be undisturbed. Similarly, a mere signal that I'm about to do something irrational could take the form of a painful sensation, a fearful sensation, a bubble-gummy taste in my mouth—anything. But the explanation for why I can't guide action with conscious uncertainty about what to do seems to inhere in that state's very particular phenomenology. As I suggest later and argue elsewhere,[23] this particular phenomenology is what *makes it the case* that I can't guide action with the state.

THE "INSIDE OF AN AGENT" EXPLANATION

A more widely endorsed explanation goes like this: We cannot guide our behavior by a state of uncertainty among objective normative propositions because such propositions advert to features that are in some sense outside the agent's grasp. We must instead guide our behavior by norms that advert to features *internal to the agent*, or at least *internal to the agent's ken.*

Frank Jackson suggests this explanation in a well-known discussion of objective consequentialism:

the fact that a course of action would have the best results is not in itself a guide to action, for a guide to action must in some appropriate sense be present to the agent's mind. We need, if you like, a story from the inside of an agent . . . and having the best consequences is a story from the outside.[24]

---

[23] See Sepielli (work in progress-a).

[24] Jackson 1991: 466–7. Elinor Mason suggested to me that there are ways to interpret Jackson other than the way I do in this section. This is a fair point, but ultimately I'm more

"Inside of an agent" explanations should be rejected. To see why, first imagine that I am certain what will have the best results. If I am a consequentialist, I will think to myself, "Doing A will have the best results. If doing A will have the best results, then I (objectively) ought to do A. So I (objectively) ought to do A." I may then guide my doing A by this conclusion. There is no need to employ a norm that adverts to one of my mental states, or to the evidence/information to which I have access.

But now note that "the fact that a course of action would have the best results" is no more "present to the agent's mind" when the agent is certain than it is when the agent is uncertain. Certainty is no guarantee that my beliefs about the world match the way the world actually is. Still it seems that, so long as we are certain about the relevant propositions, we may guide our conduct by norms that advert to mind-independent features of the world. We don't need a "story from the inside of an agent" in that case. So if we cannot guide our actions under conscious *un*certainty by objective norms, it cannot be because of some general fact that we can only guide our actions by norms that advert to features of our own minds. It's an utterly banal fact that the *vehicles* of our reasoning are our own mental states. But this does not imply that the *contents* of those vehicles must make reference to our mental states.

Unless we see that this explanation fails, we will be tempted into distorted pictures of human agency under uncertainty about what to do. Any view on which we must have access to the truth of P to use P as a premise in our practical reasoning is such a picture, and such views are widespread. But while there is a real problem of action guidance under uncertainty *qua* uncertainty, there is absolutely no problem of action guidance under ignorance *qua* ignorance. Action guidance is imperiled not by a bad connection between mind and world, but rather by a divided mind.

WHY THIS EXPLANATION MAY BE TEMPTING (AND HOW TO RESIST THE TEMPTATION)

So why have so many been tempted by this faulty explanation? I want to suggest one source of temptation both because I suspect it's very

---

concerned with whether this sort of explanation is "in the air" than with whether Jackson in particular endorses it. For another seeming endorsement of this explanation, see Gibbard 2005.

widespread, and because it can be cured using a piece of apparatus I introduced earlier. My speculation is that we first arrive, *via* an argument-by-elimination, at views about the sorts of norms we *must* use to guide our actions under uncertainty; then we *read off* from the contents of these norms the conclusion that we may only guide our actions under uncertainty by norms that advert to the contents of our own mental states or to features of the world to which we have access.

For suppose you are a utilitarian who is consciously uncertain about how much utility various actions will produce. Then you cannot guide your behavior by the objective norm: "One (objectively) ought to maximize (actual) utility." So which options are left? How about, "One ought (in the objective-probability-relative sense) to maximize the quantity Σ_i p(S$_i$) x u(A given S$_i$), where p(S$_i$) is the objective probability of state of affairs S$_i$ and u(A given S$_i$) is the utility produced by doing A, if S$_i$ obtains?" This seems unsatisfactory. Why? For reasons of ontological parsimony, you might not believe in such things as objective probabilities. Or you might not believe there are any objective probabilities other than zero and 1, in which case you will no more be able to guide your actions by this norm than by the objective norm. (After all, you will be just as uncertain about which state of affairs *has a probability 1 of obtaining* as you would be about which state of affairs *obtains*.) Even if you do believe in intermediate objective probabilities, you might be uncertain what they are, and consequently, uncertain whether A, or B, or C maximizes quantities like the aforementioned. In that case, you would presumably need another objective-probability-relative norm to guide your action under *this* uncertainty, another to guide your action under uncertainty regarding *that* norm, and so on. Finally, the objective probabilities you believe there are might not correspond to your credences, in which case you will be unable to guide your actions under uncertainty by norms that advert to objective probabilities. I am not imagining that, e.g., you believe there is an objective probability of .4 that P, but have a credence of .3 that P anyway. I'm thinking instead of cases involving disjunctive objective probabilities. Suppose a factory produces cubical boxes with side lengths in the interval o m < x ≤1 m. Let us suppose that if the next box produced has a surface area of >3 sq m, then a six-sided die will be tossed, and if it has a surface area of <3 sq m, then a twenty-sided die will be tossed." What is the objective probability of the next die roll yielding a "4"?

There are reasons for thinking the answer is: "either 1/6, or 1/20, and that's all we can say about it."[25] But one's credence cannot be: either 1/6 or 1/20, with no more to say. Rather, it may be some "fuzzy" credence, representable *via* an interval or a family of functions. This is the sort of case where objective probability and credence can come apart.

Given that objective norms and objective-probability-relative norms won't always help us guide our actions, it can seem that credence-relative or evidence-relative norms are the only other options. These norms advert to features that differ from objective probabilities in all of the crucial respects, namely: (1) there obviously are intermediate credences or degrees of evidence, (2) it's less plausible that one would be uncertain about one's own credences or the evidence to which one has access, as one might be uncertain about objective probabilities,[26] and (3) one's credences may not, of course, diverge from *themselves*, and one's accessible evidence will tend to line up with one's credences. The credence-relative version of utilitarianism, for example, says that one ought to maximize *expected utility*—or in other words, that one ought to maximize the quantity $\Sigma_i \ p(S_i) \times u(A \ \text{given} \ S_i)$, where $p(S_i)$ is the *subjective* probability of state of affairs S_i (i.e. the agent's credence that S_i will obtain).

But now that we think we must guide our actions under uncertainty by credence- or evidence-relative norms, it is only natural to think, "Well, obviously this is because of the one essential feature of credence- (evidence-) relative norms—that they advert to the agent's credences (evidence)!" And now it's natural to think, "Well, what separates credences or evidence, on the one hand, from objective probabilities and actual utility produced, on the other? Clearly it's that credences and evidence are inside the agent or accessible to the agent, and these other things are outside the agent! So the lesson to be drawn is that we must guide our behavior by norms that advert to features that are inside the agent, not outside."

This argument-by-elimination assumes that norms that advert to "inside of an agent('s ken)" features like beliefs and accessible evidence are our only alternatives to objective norms and objective-probability-relative norms. But we know from earlier that this is a

---

[25] See Hajek 2010, section on "Bertrand's Paradox."
[26] But see Smith 2010.

mistake. For it overlooks an important space on the conceptual chess-board—the one occupied by minimal-probability-relative norms. There are minimal probabilities other than zero and 1, just as there are credences other than zero and 1. Indeed, because "There's a minimal probability of X that P" stands to "I have a credence of X that P" in just the way "P" stands to "I believe that P" (the first statement of each pair expresses the mental state that the second statement of each pair reports), I cannot coherently hold that I have intermediate credences without also holding that there are intermediate minimal probabilities.

I suggest a picture on which minimal-probability-relative norms are the ones by which we *fundamentally* guide our actions, and that guidance by, say, credence-relative norms is more derivative and less primordial. For guidance by minimal-probability-relative norms is guidance by the informational content of one's credences about the situation;[27] guidance by credence-relative norms is, technically, guidance by the informational content of one's *beliefs about those credences.* But of course the general usability of the latter content in reasoning piggybacks entirely on the general usability of the former content. It's only if I can guide my behavior by *what I think* that I can guide my behavior (in a more self-alienated way) by *the fact that I think it.*

My preferred picture puts action guidance under uncertainty on all fours with action guidance under certainty. Under certainty: I express my belief that the plane will depart at 4 PM by saying, "The plane will depart at 4 PM." And when I consciously consider what to do, I say the following to myself (in "mentalese"): "The plane will depart at 4 PM. If the plane will depart at 4 PM, then I ought (objectively) to be at the airport at 3 PM. So I'll be at the airport at 3PM." And now under uncertainty: I express my reasonably high credence that the plane will depart at 4PM by saying, "The plane will probably depart [read: it has a high *minimal probability* of departing] at 4 PM." And when I consciously consider what to do, I say the following to myself (again, in "mentalese"): "The plane will probably depart at 4 PM. If the plane will probably depart at 4 PM, then I ought (in the minimal probability-relative sense) to be at the airport at 3 PM. So I'll

---

[27] By the "informational content" of a mental state, I simply mean the proposition stood for by an expression of that mental state.

Andrew Sepielli

be at the airport at 3 PM." In both cases, the premises in my practical reasoning are the mentalese expressions of the relevant mental states.

By contrast, the proposal that the fundamental form of action guidance under uncertainty is by credence- or evidence-relative norms yields a sharp break between reasoning under certainty and reasoning under uncertainty. It implies that, when I'm certain about, e.g., whether giving the patient a pill will kill him or cure him, I can employ norms that advert to the effect on the patient; but when I am uncertain about the same, I can only employ norms that advert to internal features like my own beliefs or the evidence that is presently available to me.[28] But why should the move from certainty to uncertainty occasion this change of focus from the outer to the inner?

"Inside of an agent" explanations of our explanandum lose their appeal once we reject this unnatural shoehorning of belief- and evidence-relative norms into the role that's played, most fundamentally, by minimal-probability-relative norms. For once we cast minimal-probability-relative norms in this role, we see that action under uncertainty is not typically guided by norms that advert to features "inside [] an agent."

THE EXPLANATION FROM "JACKSON CASES"

Another well-known explanation for why we cannot guide our behavior under uncertainty by objective norms is that these norms cannot deliver the right results in cases like those Jackson presents in his "Decision Theoretic Consequentialism and the Nearest-and-Dearest Objection."

Jackson takes as a jumping-off point this remark of Peter Railton's: "... objective consequentialism sets a definite and distinctive criterion of right action ... and it becomes an empirical question which modes of decision-making should be employed and when."[29] As Jackson characterizes Railton's idea: "... the moral decision problem should be approached by setting oneself the goal of doing what is objectively

---

[28] Of course, one way of discovering whether I believe P is by asking myself whether P. See Evans 1982, ch. 7. But this is not the *only* way to discover what I believe. There are third-personal ways as well—the same ways I'd use to discover what someone *else* believes—brain scans, observations of behavior, etc. And these ways seem offensively beside the point when a patient's life is on the line!

[29] Railton 1984: 117.

right—the action that has in fact the best consequences—and then performing the action which the empirical evidence suggests is most likely to have this property."[30]

Jackson argues that Railton's approach "gives the wrong answers" in cases like this one:

Jill is a physician who has to decide on the correct treatment for her patient, John, who has a minor but not trivial skin complaint. She has three drugs to choose from: drug A, drug B, and drug C. Careful consideration of the literature has led her to the following opinions. Drug A is very likely to relieve the condition but will not completely cure it. One of the drugs B and C will completely cure the skin condition; the other though will kill the patient, and there is no way that she can tell which of the two is the perfect cure and which the killer drug.[31]

And this one:

Jill has only two drugs, drug X and drug Y, at her disposal which have any chance of effecting a cure. Drug X has a 90% chance of curing the patient but also has a 10% chance of killing him; drug Y has a 50% chance of curing the patient but has no bad side effects.[32]

In the first case, Railton's proposal (as Jackson construes it) will counsel Jill to choose either drug B or drug C, since drug A has *no chance* of being what she objectively ought to do. In the second case, this proposal will counsel Jill to choose drug X, since that drug has a *higher* chance of being what she objectively ought to do than drug Y has.

But as Jackson points out, this seems like the wrong advice in both cases. A *morally conscientious agent* would choose drug A in the first case and drug Y in the second case. Therefore, Jackson concludes, the proposal that we guide our behavior under uncertainty by objective norms is flawed. We need to "go subjective" instead.

One might respond that I've changed the subject a bit in considering this point of Jackson's. We had been considering a *non-normative, purely psychological* problem for the proposal that one guide one's behavior under uncertainty by objective norms—namely, that it's impossible. But now it seems that we are considering a *normative*

---

[30] Jackson 1991: 467.   [31] Ibid.: 462–3.   [32] Ibid.: 467.

problem for this proposal—not that we *can't* guide our behavior under uncertainty by objective norms, but that doing so will lead us astray. And aren't these different problems? Isn't bad guidance still guidance?

Perhaps this response is right, and if so, read this part of the paper as an evaluation of an argument that subjective norms are essential for *morally conscientious* guided action under uncertainty, not for guided action under uncertainty, period. Such an argument, if successful, would still secure an important role for subjective normativity.

But I think this response a bit too quick, for the "psychological" and "normative" issues here are not so easily severable. The notion of action guidance is in part a normative notion. Here's why: As I suggest later and argue in other work, I guide my behavior with a conscious mental state only if that mental state renders my behavior intelligible from my perspective.[33] Rendering an action intelligible is a way of causally explaining it, but a mental state can causally explain an action without rendering it intelligible. Suppose, for example, that I am sure I ought to vote for Warren rather than for Brown, and that this state causes me in some aberrant case to vote for Brown. It is still not the case that this belief renders my vote intelligible from my perspective. Rather, a mental state can render something intelligible *only if* it *rationalizes* it—in other words, only if the behavior is right in the belief- or credence-relative sense, relative to that mental state.[34] So if, as in Jackson's cases, the action that is most likely to be objectively right given my credences is not *also* credence-relative right relative to these credences, then it cannot count as guided with these credences. So the normative problem Jackson alleges would, unless surmounted, end up imperiling the very guidedness of the action that in these cases of Jackson's is most likely to be objectively right.

But I am not convinced that Jackson has really scored a point against objective normativity or for subjective normativity. That's because it is

---

[33] Sepielli (work in progress-c).

[34] You may wonder whether guidance of an action, A, with a mental state, S, requires that A be *exactly* right relative to S. For can't I guide my doing A with S even if there's another possible action, B, that would be belief-relative better relative to S? As I argue in Sepielli (work in progress-b) and (work in progress-c), the answer is "no." In that case, S would at most *incompletely* intentionally explain my doing A, and thus my doing A would only be *partially* guided with S.

not obvious that the problem with the objective "ought" *qua* action-guide is with the "objective" part of it or with the "ought" part of it.

It's true that, if Jill does what she most likely objectively ought to do, she will fail to prescribe Drug A in the first case, and fail to prescribe Drug Y in the second case. But suppose that Jill believes in a form of objective consequentialism that specifies not only what she objectively ought to do, but also the strengths of objective reasons for various actions. Her belief in this scalar version of objective consequentialism gives Jill at least three other options.

Option #1: Consider Jackson's second case. Armed with her new, scalar form of consequentialism, Jill will have a credence of .9 that prescribing X has a fairly high value, and a credence of .1 that prescribing X has an extremely low value; she will also have a credence of .5 that prescribing Y has a fairly high value, and a credence of .5 that prescribing Y has a moderate value. Nothing that Jackson says forecloses the possibility that Jill may guide her prescribing drug Y *with this state of uncertainty*, without the need to form *any* further attitudes. If she does this, then she will have done the conscientious thing, without employing a subjective normative concept of any sort.

Option #2: Similarly, nothing that Jackson says forecloses the possibility of Jill's forming the *additional belief* that *prescribing Y has the highest expected objective value (EOV)*, and guiding her prescribing Y *with that belief*. Again, if she does this, she will have done what Jackson says is the morally conscientious thing, but without needing to employ a subjective norm. (To be clear about what's being envisaged: Jill is not guiding her action with the belief that she subjectively ought to do the action with the highest expected objective value; she is simply guiding it with the belief that prescribing Y has the highest expected objective value—no subjective normative concepts required.)

Option #3: Finally, nothing that Jackson says forecloses the possibility of Jill's forming the *additional belief* that *prescribing Y would be her best try, or best attempt, at doing what is objectively valuable*, and guiding her prescribing Y *with this belief*.[35]

---

[35] For a "scalar" response to Jackson, see Menzies and Oddie 1992. For more on scalar moral theories, see Norcross 2006.

Now, I don't think any of these options represents a way of success-fully denying the explanandum of this paper—but this isn't because of anything having to do with Jackson cases. Option #3 fails because it's not a way of denying the explanandum at all. As I explained earlier, "S subjectively ought to do A" simply *means* "A would be S's best try at doing what is objectively valuable."

Nor does Option #2 represent a way of denying the explanandum. If I guide my behavior with the full belief, or certainty, that some action has the highest expected objective value, I have not guided it with a state of uncertainty regarding the objective value of the action, but rather with a full belief that the action is the one that maximizes some quantity: EOV.

Option #2 also fails because we cannot generally guide an action with the belief that that action has the highest EOV. For it is an open question whether I ought, in any sense, to do the action with the highest EOV (why not be risk-averse instead?), just as it is an open question whether I ought to do the action that, say, yields the most equal distribution of resources (why not be a prioritarian instead?).[36] In other words, I can "step back" and sensibly wonder about the import of some action's having the highest EOV. I cannot, by contrast, sensibly wonder about the import of some action's being the one that I have most reason to do.

So far, we have no grounds for ruling out Option #1. As I've been claiming, this present argument of Jackson's does nothing to disparage it, because Jackson artificially restricts his focus to uncertainty among objective OUGHTs. And we've seen that neither the "metacognitive signal" nor the "inside of an agent" explanation seems to work. To rule out Option #1, we will need an alternative explanation. It's to such an explanation that I'll now briefly turn.

---

[36] In other work, I do argue that in selected "deliberative contexts," we can guide our behavior with beliefs about EOV, and even with beliefs with non-normative propositions as their content. See Sepielli (work in progress-a). We have no need in these contexts to appeal to beliefs with normative contents, or to desires understood as distinct mental entities. (See McDowell 1978 for a similar view, as well as the distinction between desires as distinct entities, and desires as ascribable *by courtesy* whenever motivation by beliefs occurs.) My point here is simply that we cannot *generally* do this. OUGHT-beliefs are, we might say, "deliberative-context-independent" guides to action. EOV-beliefs, EQUAL-DISTRIBUTION-OF-RESOURCES beliefs, and so on, are not.

TOWARDS A BETTER EXPLANATION

Why aren't objective norms sufficient for action-guidance under uncertainty? Why must we step back from uncertainty about objective reasons and form a judgment about what, subjectively, we ought to do relative to the probabilities represented in that uncertainty?

My view is that there is a certain sort of connection between action guidance and phenomenology: One cannot guide one's actions by conscious mental states with a "multidirectional" phenomenology, which, again, is the phenomenology constitutive of conscious uncertainty. This is a very weak claim, for it is compatible with denying many other alleged connections between guidance and phenomenology. For all I claim, there may be no phenomenology common to all mental states upon which one *may* guide one's action; some such states may have no phenomenal character at all. Specifically, as I've tried to emphasize throughout, it is no part of my position that one can only guide one's actions by a mental state with a "unidirectional" phenomenology.

An action cannot count as guided if it is prospectively unintelligible from the agent's perspective. Intelligibility from the agent's perspective is amenability to a particular sort of explanation—one that helps me understand my own action *as my action*. For a contemplated action to be unintelligible in this sense is compatible with its being explicable in all sorts of other ways. I might explain why I will do it by adverting to my nerves and neurons, to my upbringing, to my subconscious resolution of the Oedipal Complex, and even to the states of my mind characterized dispositionally. But all of these are distinctly third-personal sorts of explanation, and as such, none of them help me understand my action as such; hence, none of them render any of my contemplated actions intelligible in the sense I have in mind.

Insofar as one's conscious normative judgments regarding a contemplated action are multidirectional, that action will simply *feel* unintelligible. One will feel that that action does not make any more sense than any of the other contemplated actions towards which the multidirectional states "point." And I shall want to claim that, if an action of mine *feels* unintelligible, it *is* unintelligible from the agential perspective[37]—

---

[37] A referee suggests that it is implausible that if an action is intelligible, then it feels intelligible. I agree, and this accords with what I've been saying throughout. My claim is the

just as a visual state's having a partly "yellow" phenomenal character is sufficient for its representing something as being yellow, or a tactile sensation's being a hot feeling is sufficient for its representing the touched object as hot. This particular tight connection between feeling and being is a defining feature of the particular sort of intelligibility that is intelligibility from the agent's own perspective.[38] Were I to do the contemplated action in the face of conscious uncertainty, there would no doubt be some possible explanation I or others could give of it, but such an explanation would do nothing to dissolve its unintelligibility from the inside. And no action can be guided that is unintelligible from the inside.

Now, earlier, I said that a mental state renders an action intelligible only if it rationalizes that action. But the converse is not true. For a state of uncertainty over propositions about the objective values of actions might be sufficient for there to be an action with, say, the highest EOV. And if it turns out that, on the correct theory of rationality, the highest-EOV action is the rational one, then this uncertainty will be sufficient to rationalize the highest-EOV act. But it does not render this action intelligible from the agent's perspective. (As a parallel: Suppose that moral rationalism is true, and that it turns out—whether I believe it or not—that the correct moral theory is utilitarianism. This means that my belief that doing A maximizes utility will rationalize—render rational—my doing A. But this belief will not, all by itself, render intelligible my doing A.)

My account differs from the "Jackson cases" explanation in a way that the rationalizing/rendering-intelligible distinction helps to emphasize. I do not say that one cannot guide one's behavior with a state of uncertainty because such uncertainty will yield irrational action. Rather, I locate the inability of uncertainty to serve as an action guide elsewhere. My account differs from the "inside of an agent" explanation in that mine draws on the fact that states of uncertainty are states of a divided mind, while the "inside of an agent" explanation draws instead on the

very different one that if an action *feels un*intelligible, then it *is* unintelligible from the agent's own perspective.

[38] For more on the relationship between a state's phenomenal character and its intentional features, see Horgan and Tienson 2002; Kriegel 2003 and forthcoming; Pitt 2004; and Mendelovici 2010.

fact that states of uncertainty represent an imperfect connection between mind and world. Finally, my account differs from the "metacognitive signal" explanation in a more subtle way. Both accounts rely in some way on the phenomenology of conscious uncertainty. But I take this phenomenology to ground the unintelligibility-conferring features of this state, and in turn, the inability of the state to guide action. The "metacognitive signal" explanation is entirely silent on such features, and treats the phenomenology constitutive of conscious uncertainty as a mere signal of the normative "riskiness" of candidate actions—a signal that in another metaphysically possible world is played by, e.g., an itchy nose.

GOING FORWARD

Subjective norms are supposed to help us guide our actions when we are uncertain about what we objectively ought to do. But of course, we might be uncertain which of those subjective norms are correct. It is a perfectly good, substantive question whether we ought to maximize expected objective value, or be slightly risk-averse, or simply act on the most likely view about what we objectively ought to do, or do something else, under conditions of uncertainty. When we are unsure which subjective norms are correct, we might appeal to further, higher-order subjective norms in order to guide our actions. But again, we might be uncertain which of *these* norms is correct, and so on. Since there seems to be no principled stopping point to this uncertainty, it may seem mysterious how norm-guided action is possible at all.

I think this mystery and others like it can be dissolved, but not unless we think about subjective normativity and action guidance in the right way. We need a decent account of what subjective norms are, and how they relate to objective ones. We need a clear statement of the conditions under which subjective norms become necessary as guides to action. And we need the correct theory of *why* subjective norms become necessary under those conditions. I have tried to provide these things in this paper. I have given an account of subjective normativity that appeals to the notion of trying. I have said that subjective norms are necessary as action guides under uncertainty, but only when that uncertainty is of a phenomenally conscious sort. And I have suggested a theory of why subjective norms are necessary for this purpose, after rejecting some competing theories of the same. My hope is that, in doing so, I have put subjective normativity on slightly surer footing and helped to foster an appreciation of its importance.

REFERENCES

Alter, Adam L., Oppenheimer, Daniel M., Epley, Nicholas, and Eyre, Rebecca N. (2007) "Overcoming Intuition: Metacognitive Difficulty Activates Analytic Reasoning," *Journal of Experimental Psychology: General*, 136: 569–76.
Anscombe, G. E. M. (1957) *Intention* (Oxford: Blackwell).
——(1979) "Under a Description," *Noûs*, 13: 219–33.
Block, Ned (1995) "On a Confusion about a Function of Consciousness," *Behavioral and Brain Sciences*, 18: 227–87.
Candlish, Stewart (1984) "Inner and Outer Basic Action," *Proceedings of the Aristotelian Society*, 84: 83–102.
Dowell, Janice (work in progress) "Flexible Contextualism about 'Ought'."
Evans, Gareth (1982) *The Varieties of Reference* (Oxford: Clarendon Press).
Fodor, Jerry A. (1998) *Concepts: Where Cognitive Science Went Wrong* (New York: Oxford University Press).
Gibbard, Allan (2005) "Truth and Correct Belief," *Philosophical Issues*, 15: 338–50.
Gollwitzer, P. M. (1990) "Action Phases and Mindsets," in E. T. Higgins and R. M. Sorrentino (eds.), *Handbook of Motivation and Cognition*, Vol. 2 (New York: Guilford Press), 53–92.
Hajek, Alan (2010) "Interpretations of Probability," in E. N. Zalta (ed.), *The Stanford Encyclopedia of Philosophy*.
Hellie, Benj (forthcoming) *Conscious Life* (Oxford University Press).
Holton, Richard (2009) *Willing, Wanting, Waiting* (New York: Oxford University Press).
Horgan, Terence and Tienson, John (2002) "The Intentionality of Phenomenology and the Phenomenology of Intentionality," in D. Chalmers (ed.), *Philosophy of Mind: Classic and Contemporary Readings* (New York: Oxford University Press), 520–32.
Jackson, Frank (1991) "Decision-Theoretic Consequentialism and the Nearest and Dearest Objection," *Ethics*, 101: 461–82.
Kolodny, Niko and MacFarlane, John (work in progress) "Ought: Between Objective and Subjective."
Kriegel, Uriah (2003) "Is Intentionality Dependent on Consciousness?," *Philosophical Studies*, 116: 271–307.
——(forthcoming) "The Phenomenal Intentionality Research Program," in U. Kriegel (ed.), *Phenomenal Intentionality: New Essays* (New York: Oxford University Press).

Kruglanski, Arie W. and Webster, Donna M. (1996) "Motivated Closing of the Mind: 'Seizing' and 'Freezing'," *Psychological Review*, 103: 263–83.

Lockhart, Ted (2000) *Moral Uncertainty and its Consequences* (New York: Oxford University Press).

McDowell, John (1978) "Are Moral Requirements Hypothetical Imperatives?" *Proceedings of the Aristotelian Society, Supplementary Volume*, 52: 13–29.

——(2009) "What Myth?," in *The Engaged Intellect* (Cambridge, MA: Harvard University Press), 308–23.

Mendelovici, Angela (2010) "Mental Representation and Closely Conflated Topics" (Ph.D. Thesis, Princeton University).

Menzies, Peter and Oddie, Graham (1992) "An Objectivist's Guide to Subjective Moral Value," *Ethics*, 102: 512–33.

Nagel, Jennifer (2010) "Epistemic Anxiety and Adaptive Invariantism," *Philosophical Perspectives*, 24: 407–35.

Norcross, Alastair (2006) "Reasons Without Demands: Rethinking Rightness," in J. Dreier (ed.), *Contemporary Debates in Moral Theory* (Oxford: Blackwell), 38–54.

Parfit, Derek (2011) *On What Matters* (Oxford University Press).

Pitt, David (2004) "The Phenomenology of Cognition, or, 'What Is It Like to Think That P?'," *Philosophy and Phenomenological Research*, 69: 1–36.

Railton, Peter (1984) "Alienation, Consequentialism, and the Demands of Morality," *Philosophy and Public Affairs*, 13: 134–71.

——(2009) "Practical Competence and Fluent Agency," in D. Sobel and S. Wall (eds.), *Reasons for Action* (New York: Oxford University Press), 81–115.

Ross, Jacob (2006) "Rejecting Ethical Deflationism," *Ethics*, 116: 742–68.

Schroeder, Mark (2008) *Being For: Evaluating the Semantic Program of Expressivism* (New York: Oxford University Press).

Sepielli, Andrew (2009) "What to Do When You Don't Know What to Do," in R. Schafer-Landau (ed.), *Oxford Studies in Metaethics*, Vol. 4 (Oxford: Oxford University Press), 5–28.

——(2010) "Along an Imperfectly-Lighted Path" (Ph.D. Thesis, Rutgers University).

——(work in progress-a) "Why We Need Subjective Normativity."

——(work in progress-b) "Subjective Normativity, Action Guidance, and Regress."

——(work in progress-c) "What to Do When You Don't Know What to Do When You Don't Know What to Do."

Smith, Holly (2010) "Subjective Rightness," *Social Philosophy and Policy*, 27: 64–110.

Turri, John (2009) "The Ontology of Epistemic Reasons," *Noûs*, 43: 490–512.

Yalcin, Seth (2011) "Nonfactualism about Epistemic Modality," in A. Egan and B. Weatherson (eds.), *Epistemic Modality* (Oxford University Press), 295–332.

4

Actualism, Possibilism, and Beyond[1]

JACOB ROSS

How is what an agent ought to do related to what an agent ought to prefer that she does? More precisely, suppose we know what an agent's preference ordering ought to be over the outcomes of performing the various courses of action open to her. Can we infer from this information how she ought to act, and if so, how can we infer it? One view (which, for convenience, I will call "actualism") is that an agent ought to ϕ just in case she ought to prefer the outcome that would result from her ϕ-ing to the outcome of that would result from her not ϕ-ing.[2] Another view (which, for convenience, I will call "possibilism") is that an agent ought to ϕ just in case all of her options (in the relevant domain) with maximally preferable outcomes involve ϕ-ing. I will discuss actualism and possibilism in parts 1 and 2, respectively. I will argue, in part 1, that actualism is very far from the truth. And I will argue, in part 2, that while the standard version of possibilism faces significant problems, there are much better versions of possibilism that avoid the objections to the standard view. Ultimately, however, I will argue that even the best forms of possibilism are not acceptable. Then, in part 3, I will offer a diagnosis of why the existing theories fail, and I will offer an alternative theory that is neither actualist nor possibilist in form, and that avoids the difficulties with the other theories.

[1] I am very grateful to my colleagues Kenny Easwaran, Mark Schroeder, and Gideon Yaffe for many invaluable discussions concerning this paper. I owe a special debt to Shieva Kleinschmidt for extremely helpful comments on several earlier drafts. My greatest debt is to Doug Portmore. Many of the key ideas in this paper arose in the course of a correspondence I had with him during the summer of 2010. Had it not been for this correspondence, this paper could not have been written.
    [2] Examples of actualism are Sobel (1976) and Jackson and Pargetter (1986). Examples of possibilism are Feldman (1986) and Zimmerman (1996).

1.1 The absurdity of actualism

The main problem with actualism is that it's obviously false. This can be seen if we consider the following case:

> *Arsenic and Old Ace.* Absentminded Ace is looking after his three-year-old granddaughter Emily, who asks him for a glass of water. As a matter of fact, Ace is about to accidentally give Emily a glass containing an arsenic solution. When he does so, she will drink the contents of the glass and die. Ace has many options besides giving Emily the arsenic. He could instead give her a glass of water as she requested. Or he could give her a glass of Drano, or a glass of bleach, or a glass of ammonia. If he were to give her glass of water, she would drink it and be happy. If, on the other hand, he were to give her a glass of Drano, bleach, or ammonia, then while she would not drink enough of the liquid for it to be fatal, she would drink enough to suffer severe and irreversible damage to her mouth and esophagus.[3]

Of the options just described, it seems fairly obvious that there is only one that Ace ought to carry out: he ought to give Emily a glass of water. And there are many that he ought not to carry out: he ought not to give her arsenic, he ought not to give her Drano, he ought not to give her bleach, and he ought not to give her ammonia. The actualist, however, disagrees. The actualist says that, objectively speaking, Ace ought to give Emily Drano. For the nearest world in which Ace doesn't give Emily Drano is the actual world, where he gives her arsenic. Thus, Ace ought to prefer what would obtain if he gave her Drano (namely, that Emily is harmed but not killed) to what would obtain if he didn't give her Drano (namely, that Emily is killed). And so, objectively speaking, he ought to prefer the outcome of giving her Drano to the outcome of not giving her Drano, which implies, according to actualism, that he ought to give her Drano. For similar reasons, actualism implies that he ought to give her bleach, and it likewise implies that he ought to give her ammonia.

In this case, we can see two problems with actualism. First, there are many cases where it implies that agents ought to do really awful things:

---

[3] A similar counterexample to actualism is presented in Wedgwood 2009.

for any action ϕ, no matter how bad ϕ is, actualism entails that one ought to ϕ so long as ϕ-ing isn't quite as bad as what one actually does. In addition to implying that agents ought to do really awful things, there are simply too many things that actualism entails one ought to do. If there are a million options that are less bad than what one actually does, then actualism will entail, for each of these options, that one ought to do it. In the case just considered, we have seen that actualism entails, of each of three incompatible courses of action, that Ace ought to do it. But these aren't the only things it entails that Ace ought to do. Consider the course of action that consists in giving Emily Drano and then telling his boss where to go; or the course of action that consists in giving Emily Drano and then lighting the cat on fire; or the course of action that consists in giving Emily Drano and then spending the rest his one's life dressed as Napoleon Bonaparte. Each of these options is such that the outcome of carrying it out is preferable to the outcome of giving Emily the arsenic solution. And so actualism entails, for each of these courses of action, that Ace ought to do it. Thus, actualism leads to a deontic explosion of obligations to do terrible things.

1.2 *The contextualist response*

How might the actualist respond to this objection? One response, suggested by Jackson and Pargetter (1986), is to distinguish between two questions: the question of *whether* an agent ought to ϕ at t, and the question as to *what* the agent ought to do at t. On the Jackson–Pargetter view, *whether* x ought to ϕ at t depends on whether ϕ-ing at t is better than what x would do if x didn't ϕ at t. But *what* x ought to do at t is whichever option would have the best outcome, among the maximally relevantly specific options whose performance would occur at t. Assume that, in *Arsenic and Old Ace*, the time of action is noon. While Jackson and Pargetter are committed to saying that Ace ought to give Emily Drano at noon (since doing so is better than what he would do otherwise, namely give her arsenic), they are not committed to saying that what he ought to do at noon is give Emily Drano. Rather, on their view, there is only one correct answer to the question of what Ace ought to do at noon, namely, that he ought to give her a glass of water. For, among the maximally relevantly specific options that are available to Ace at noon, giving her a glass of water is maximally preferable, as it would have the best outcome. Perhaps, therefore, we can explain away our intuition that Ace ought not to give Emily Drano at noon, as a result of our conflating the two questions that Jackson and Pargetter distinguish. Perhaps we correctly judge that it is not the case that giving Emily Drano is what Ace ought to do at noon, and from this we fallaciously infer that Ace ought not to give Emily Drano at noon.

On the face of it, this solution does not appear coherent. If Ace ought to give Emily Drano at noon, then how could this fail to be (or to be part of) what he ought to do at noon? Jackson and Pargetter suggest a way of avoiding this charge of incoherence. The suggestion is that "ought" claims are implicitly relativized to sets of options. When we ask whether Ace ought to give Emily Drano, the relevant set of options consists of just two alternatives: {giving Emily Drano; not giving Emily Drano}. But when we ask what she ought to do at noon, the relevant set of options will be {giving Emily Drano; giving Emily bleach; giving Emily ammonia; giving Emily the arsenic solution; giving Emily water}. Thus, there is no conflict between the claim that Ace ought to give Emily Drano at noon and the claim that giving Emily Drano is no part of what Ace ought to do at noon. For the former claim is implicitly relativized to the first, more coarse-grained partition of options, whereas the latter claim is implicitly relativized to the second, more fine-grained partition of options.[4]

As I see it, however, this contextualist maneuver doesn't really solve the problem we discussed in the last section, for it retains the implausible implication that Ace ought to give his granddaughter Drano (or, in the formal mode, that utterances of the sentence "Ace ought to give his granddaughter Drano" are true). Further, even if it isn't strictly incoherent, is still fails to respect the intuitive connection between question of *whether to ϕ at t* and the question of *what to do at t*. Moreover, it introduces a further problem, which can be seen if we consider the following case.

> *President Muffley.* It is now noon. President Merkin Muffley has accidentally activated the Doomsday Machine. Before him are two buttons, A and B. At 12:01, he will have exactly three options: he can press button A, he can press button B, or he can press neither button. If and only if he presses

---

[4] For other views on which "ought" claims are relativized to sets of options, see Cariani (forthcoming) and Snedegar (forthcoming).

neither button at 12:01, at 12:02 he will have the opportunity to press button A. The outcomes for the various courses of action open to him are as follows:

- Press button A 12:01:   30% of the world destroyed
- Press button B at 12:01:   70% of the world destroyed
- Press neither button at 12:01; press
  button A at 12:02:   0% of the world destroyed
- Press neither button at either time: 100% of the world destroyed

Muffley knows that he himself will die right after 12:02, and he is indifferent to the fate of the world after his death. Thus, he has made up his mind about what to do by tossing coins. As a result, he will press neither button at either time, and what he does at 12:02 is causally independent of what he does at 12:01.

On Jackson and Pargetter's contextualist view, when we ask *whether Muffley ought to press only button B at 12:01*, the relevant options are *pressing only button B at 12:01* and *not pressing only button B at 12:01*. And since the former would result in 70%, rather than 100%, of the world being destroyed, the following claim is true:

(i) Muffley ought to press only button B at 12:01.

For similar reasons, if we ask whether Muffley ought to press only button A at 12:01, the answer will again be affirmative, so the following is true:

(ii) Muffley ought to press only button A at 12:01.

But now suppose we ask not *whether* Muffley ought to perform a given action, but rather *what* he ought to do at a given time. Suppose we ask, first, what he ought to do at 12:01. Here the relevant options will be all the maximally relevantly specific things he could do at 12:01, namely pressing button A, pressing button B, and pressing neither button. Among these, pressing button A is the option that would in fact have the best outcome, since it would result in only 30% of the world being destroyed, whereas pressing button B would result in 70% destruction, and pressing neither button would result in 100% destruction. And so the following claim is true.

(iii) What Muffley ought to do at 12:01 is press only button A.

Next, suppose we ask what Muffley ought to do at 12:02. Since, at 12:01, he won't press either button, he will have two options at 12:02, namely pressing only button A and pressing neither button. And, of these options, pressing button A would have the best outcome. And so the following is true:

(iv) What Muffley ought to do at 12:02 is press only button A.

Finally, suppose we ask not what Muffley ought to do at a particular time, but rather what he ought to do over the course of his life. In this case, the relevant options will be the four courses of action indicated in the description of the case. And, among these, the one with the best outcome consists in pressing neither button at 12:01, and then pressing button A and 12:02. And so the following will be true.

(v) What Muffley ought to do over the course of his life is press neither button at 12:01, and then press button A at 12:02.

Thus, we arrive at very different answers depending on which normative question we ask. What role, therefore, should the answers to these various questions play in deliberation?

It is generally agreed that rational agents intend to do what they believe they ought to do. As John Broome (1999 and forthcoming) puts the point,

> **Enkrasia:** Rationality requires, of every agent, that if she believes she ought to ϕ, and she believes that it's up to her whether she ϕs, then she intends to ϕ.

But if we accept the Jackson–Pargetter view, then we must reject this principle of Enkrasia. For on the Jackson–Pargetter view, if Muffley knows the facts of the case as we have described them, then he should believe both that he ought to press only button A at 12:01 and that he ought to press only button B at 12:01. It is hardly plausible, however, that rationality both requires him to intend to press only button A at 12:01 and requires him to intend to press only button B at 12:01. For then rationality would require him to have inconsistent intentions, and so rationality would require him to be irrational. Thus, anyone who accepts the Jackson–Pargetter view must deny that the principle of Enkrasia applies to our beliefs of concerning *whether we ought to act in certain ways*, such as Muffley's beliefs in (i) and (ii).

Nor can the principle of Enkrasia apply to our beliefs concerning *what we ought to do at a given time*, such as Muffley's beliefs in (iii) and (iv). For if this principle did apply to such beliefs, then it would imply that, if Muffley were aware of the relevant facts, then rationality would require him to press button A at 12:01, and rationality would also require him to intend to press button A at 12:02. But Muffley knows that if he presses button A at 12:01, then he won't have the option of pressing button A at 12:02. Thus, if the principle of enkrasia applied to such beliefs, then rationality would require Muffley to have intentions that he knows he can't jointly satisfy. And so rationality would require that Muffley be irrational.

It seems, therefore, that on the Jackson-Pargetter view, if the principle of Enkrasia applies at all, it can apply only to our beliefs about what we ought to do over the course of our lives, not to our ordinary beliefs about whether we ought to act in a given way, or about what we ought to do at a given time. Note, however, that as Jackson and Pargetter (1986) themselves admit (pp. 251–2), when it comes to the question of what an agent ought to do over the course of her life, their view has the exact same implications as the standard possibilist view. Thus, with respect to the only kinds of ought claims that satisfy the principle of Enkrasia, the Jackson–Pargetter view collapses into the standard form of possibilism. And, as I have argued elsewhere, following John Broome, it is precisely the "ought" claims that satisfy the principle of Enkrasia that are fundamentally normative, in the sense that they directly guide the deliberations of rational agents.[5] It follows, therefore, that with respect to the ought-claims that are fundamentally normative, the Jackson–Pargetter view collapses into the standard form of possibilism. It is to possibilism, therefore, that we should now turn.

2. POSSIBILISM

We have defined possibilism as the view that an agent ought to ϕ just in case all her maximally preferable options (within the relevant domain of options) involve ϕ-ing. Hence we can distinguish among different versions of possibilism, corresponding to different specifications of the relevant domain of options, as follows.

---

[5] See Ross (2010) and (unpublished) and Broome (unpublished).

Possibilism concerning a domain D of options is the view that, for any option ϕ in domain D, an agent x ought at t to ϕ just in case all the maximally preferable options among the options in D available to x at t involve ϕ-ing.

In the next three sections, we will consider three versions of possibilism corresponding to three alternative specifications of the relevant domain of options.

2.1 Possibilism concerning performable options

The standard form of possibilism involves a very broad conception of the relevant domain of options. On this conception, the relevant options are any options available to the agent, in the broadest sense of the term, or what we may call the *performable options*. How exactly the class of performable options is to be defined is a complicated matter that I will not pursue in detail, but to a first approximation, we may say that, at time t, an option ϕ is performable for x just in case there is some schedule of intentions, beginning at t, such that if x's intentions followed this schedule, then x would ϕ. Or, stated more simply, ϕ-ing is performable for x at t just in case, if x had the right intentions at the right times from t forward, then x would ϕ. (Note that, on this conception, an action can count as *performable* at t even if the performance of the action would occur long after t.)

Possibilism concerning performable options is the view x ought to ϕ just in case all of x's maximally preferable performable options involve ϕ-ing. While this view may be prima facie plausible, it seems to get the wrong results in certain cases in which an agent's future actions are not currently under her deliberative control. Consider, for example, the following case.

The Cabinet of Dr. Caligari: Ace's granddaughter Emily needs medicine. If she doesn't get her medicine, she will be very sick for a few days, and then she'll fully recover. However, the medicine she needs is in the cabinet, right next to the arsenic solution. And the cabinet is guarded by Dr. Caligari. Ace knows that if, and only if, he goes to the cabinet, Dr. Caligari will inject him with the dreaded Nepticide Serum. Anyone who is injected with this serum acquires a strong desire to kill his or her granddaughter. After being injected with this serum, one remains psychologically normal aside from this desire. One does not, for example, lose the psychological capacity to form or retain non-murderous intentions. However, if Ace were to go to the cabinet with the intention of giving Emily the medicine, then, as a matter of fact, he would change his mind after being injected with the serum, and he would end up giving Emily the arsenic solution, thereby killing her.

It seems clear that, in this case, Ace ought not to go to the cabinet. However, possibilism concerning performable options implies otherwise. For going to the cabinet and then giving Emily the medicine is a performable option for Ace—for if he had the right intentions at the right times (and, in particular, if he continued to intend to do so even after being injected with the serum) then he would do so. Moreover, this will be his maximally preferable performable option. And since this option involves going to the cabinet, it follows that all his maximally preferable performable options involve going to the cabinet. And so it follows from possibilism concerning performable options that Ace ought to go to the cabinet. And this result is very implausible.

2.2 *Simple securitism*

So what's going wrong in *The Cabinet of Dr. Caligari*? Possibilism says Ace should carry out the best performable option, which is to go to the cabinet and give Emily the medicine. This seems wrong, because it seems that, in the relevant sense, this option isn't now really open to Ace: even if he now fully intended to do it, he wouldn't do it, because he'd change his mind later. Perhaps, therefore, we ought to focus not on the domain of performable options, in the sense defined above, but rather on the narrower class of options that one would actually carry out if one were to intend, at the time under consideration, to carry them out. Inspired by Doug Portmore, I will call these the agent's *directly securable options*. More precisely, let us say that ϕ is a directly securable option for x at t just in case there is some set S of intentions such that,

(i)   If, *at t*, x had all the intentions in S, then x would carry out all these intentions;
(ii) Carrying out all the intentions in S would involve ϕ-ing;
(iii) At t, x has the psychological capacity to have the intentions in S.

Thus, while the options that are now *performable* for an agent at a time are the ones she would carry out if she had the right intentions *now and in the future*, the options that are now *directly securable* for an agent are the ones she would carry out if she had the right intentions *now*. We may now define *simple securitism* as the possibilist view as applied to directly securable options. That is, simple securitism is the view that, at t, x ought to φ just in case all the maximally preferable, directly securable options that are available to x at t involve φ-ing. A view of this kind was proposed by Holly Smith (then Holly Goldman) in her brilliant paper "Doing the Best One Can" (1978).

Simple securitism gets what are intuitively the right results in all the cases we have considered so far. In *Arsenic and Old Ace*, it implies that Ace ought to give his granddaughter water, and that he ought not to give her Drano (since all his maximally preferable, directly securable options involve giving her water and not giving her Drano). In *President Muffley*, it implies that Muffley ought to press neither button at 12:01, and that he ought to press button A at 12:02, since all his maximally preferable, directly securable options involve doing both these things. And in *The Cabinet of Dr. Caligari*, it implies that Ace ought not to go to the cabinet. However, there are some cases where it intuitively gets the wrong results. Here is one such case.

> *General Ripper*: Brigadier General Jack D. Ripper has accidentally activated the Doomsday Machine, and he's the only one who can deactivate it. It is now noon, and at 12:01 he will receive a prompt saying "Do you want to deactivate the Doomsday Machine?" If he presses the button to answer "yes," then at 12:02 he will receive a second prompt saying "Are you *sure* you want to deactivate the Doomsday Machine?" If Ripper proceeds to press the second button, thereby answering "yes" to the second prompt, then the Doomsday Machine will be deactivated, and the world will be saved. But if he fails to press both buttons, then the machine will not be deactivated, and the entire world will be destroyed. Furthermore, if he presses the first button but not the second, then, right before the world is destroyed, he will undergo a mild electric shock. It so happens that Ripper would prefer that the world be destroyed. Hence, even if he were now to intend to press both buttons, he would change his mind before 12:02, and so, while he might press the first button, he would not press the second.

It seems obvious, in this case, that Ripper is under a moral obligation to press both buttons. After all, it was he who accidentally activated the Doomsday device, he's the only one who can deactivate it, and pressing both buttons is only way he can deactivate it. Moreover, pressing both buttons is something he could easily do. It is highly implausible that the mere fact that he has a preference for the destruction of the world would get him off the hook from any obligation to save the world.

But simple securitism implies otherwise. For at noon, Ripper has no securable options that involve pressing both buttons, since, at noon, his intending to do so would not result in his doing so. And, among his directly securable options, those that involve pressing the first button would not have better outcomes than those that do not. It is not the case, therefore, that all his maximally preferable, directly securable options involve pressing the first button, and so simple securitism does not imply that he ought to do so. To the contrary, it implies that he ought to press *neither* button. For his only directly securable options involve either pressing neither button or pressing only the first button. And, among these options, it would be preferable for him to press neither button so as to avoid the electric shock.

It seems, therefore, that simple securitism has unacceptable implications in cases like *General Ripper*, where what would seem to be obligatory courses of action (such as pressing both buttons) are not directly securable because the agent has morally impermissible attitudes (such as preferring the destruction of the world).

2.3 Scrupulous securitism

In an early draft of his excellent book, *Commonsense Consequentialism: Wherein Morality Meets Rationality*, Portmore advocated a version of simple securitism. However, when I presented cases similar to *General Ripper*, he has revised his view. On his revised view—which we may call *scrupulous securitism*—what an agent ought to do is not whatever is involved in all her maximally preferable *directly securable* options, but rather whatever is involved in all her maximally preferable *scrupulously securable* options. He defines such options as follows:

> A set of actions a_j is, as of t_i, scrupulously securable by S if and only if there is a time t_j that either immediately follows t_i or is identical to t_i, a set of actions a_i (where a_i may, or may not, be identical to a_j), and a set of background attitudes B such that the following are all true: (1) S would perform a_j if S were to have at t_j both B and the intention to perform a_i; (2) S has at t_i the capacity to continue, or to come, to have at t_j both B and the intention to perform a_i; and (3) and S would continue, or come, to have at t_j B (and, where a_i is not identical to a_j, the intention to perform a_i as well) if S both were at t_i aware of all the reason-constituting facts and were to respond at t_j to these facts/reasons in all and only the ways that they prescribe, thereby coming to have at t_j all those attitudes

that she has decisive reason to have and only those attitudes that she has sufficient reason to have.

Given some plausible assumptions, scrupulous securitism gets the intuitively correct verdict in *General Ripper*. In particular, it implies that Ripper ought to press both buttons. For, while there is no *directly securable* option that involves pressing both buttons, there is plausibly a *scrupulously securable* option that involves pressing both buttons. This is true because, plausibly, there is a set of background attitudes B (which will include a preference for saving the world) such that (1) Ripper would press both buttons if he had B and intended to press both buttons, (2) Ripper has the capacity to have B and the intention to press both buttons, and (3) Ripper would have B if he were aware of, and appropriately responsive to, all the reasons for the attitudes in B. Since pressing both buttons is scrupulously securable for Ripper, and since doing so is the only way Ripper can save the world, we may infer that all of Ripper's maximally preferable, scrupulously securable options involve pressing both buttons. And so it will follow, from scrupulous securitism, that Ripper ought to press both buttons.

However, there are other cases in which Scrupulous Securitism gets what is intuitively the wrong result. Here's an example

> *Ice Cream of Doom:* Vanessa has been kidnapped by Martians, and is playing a high-stakes game called "ice cream of doom." She is asked which, out of chocolate or vanilla, is her preferred flavor of ice cream. If she successfully says either "chocolate is my preferred flavor" or "vanilla is my preferred flavor," then she will be released and given one million dollars, regardless of whether her answer is true. But if she fails to utter either sentence, then she and every other human being will be vaporized. Marvin the mindreading Martian is in attendance, and he hates liars. And so if she begins to utter a falsehood, he will paralyze her larynx, preventing her from completing her sentence, and thus ensuring the destruction of humanity.
>
> As a matter of fact, Vanessa prefers vanilla ice cream to chocolate ice cream. However, Vanessa could change her preference to chocolate ice cream. Moreover, Vanessa isn't very knowledgeable about ice cream, and if she became aware of all the relevant facts, then she would come to prefer chocolate ice cream. This reversal in her preferences, however, would be merely permissible. That is, it would be perfectly permissible for Vanessa, upon learning all the relevant facts, to continue to prefer

vanilla ice cream. For the objective reasons do not favor either ice cream preference over the other, and in light of these reasons, either preference would be permissible.

It seems obvious that Vanessa is under no obligation to utter, or to begin uttering, "chocolate is my preferred flavor." For, given her permissible preference for vanilla ice cream, her beginning to utter this sentence would result in the destruction of humanity. By contrast, her uttering "vanilla is my preferred flavor" would result in her receiving a million dollars. It seems, therefore, that it must be at least permissible, if not required, for Vanessa to utter the latter sentence. Scrupulous securitism, however, implies the opposite. For there is no scrupulously securable option in which Vanessa utters "vanilla is my preferred flavor." For it so happens that if Vanessa were aware of, and responded appropriately to, all the facts, then she would prefer chocolate ice cream, and if she had this preference and intended to say "vanilla is my preferred flavor," then she would be prevented from completing the sentence. By contrast, there *is* a scrupulously securable option in which Vanessa utters "chocolate is my preferred flavor." For if she were aware, and responded appropriately to, all the relevant facts, then she'd prefer chocolate ice cream, and with this preference, she could successfully utter "chocolate is my preferred flavor." Moreover, successfully uttering "chocolate is my preferred flavor" is her maximally preferable, scrupulously securable option, since it would result in her being released and receiving a million dollars. Thus, scrupulous securitism implies that Vanessa ought to utter "chocolate is my preferred flavor." And since uttering this sentence would involve beginning to utter this sentence, scrupulous securitism implies that Vanessa ought to begin to utter this sentence.

There would seem to be a natural way to solve this problem. All we need to do is substitute the word "could" for the word "would" in clause (3) of Portmore's definition of a scrupulously securable option, so that it reads "(3) and S *could* continue, or come, to have at tj . . ." On this revised conception, a scrupulously securable option is defined not as an option that would be directly securable given *the set of background attitudes the agent would actually have* if she responded appropriately to the relevant reasons; rather it is defined as an option that would be directly securable given *some set of background attitudes the agent could have* if she responded appropriately to the relevant reasons.

If we make this move, then Vanessa's uttering "vanilla is my preferred flavor" will count as scrupulously securable, and so we will avoid the implication that Vanessa ought to utter "chocolate is my preferred flavor." The problem will reemerge, however, if we consider a modified version of *Ice Cream of Doom*, in which Vanessa would receive a million dollars for saying "vanilla is my preferred flavor," but she would receive a million and one dollars for saying "chocolate is my preferred flavor." In this modified version of the case, the mere fact that Vanessa would receive one dollar more if she said "chocolate is my preferred flavor" would hardly seem to obligate her to prefer chocolate—it seems like a reason of the wrong kind to require preferring chocolate. So it seems Vanessa could permissibly prefer vanilla even in the modified case. And if she could permissibly prefer vanilla, then it seems she could permissibly answer "vanilla is my preferred flavor." But according to scrupulous securitism, even in the modified form we are now considering, Vanessa is obligated to answer "chocolate is my preferred flavor." For uttering this sentence is a scrupulously securable option, and its outcome is preferable to that of any other scrupulously securable option.

So far we have considered problems that arise for specific versions of securitism. *General Ripper* raises a special problem for simple securitism, and *Ice Cream of Doom* raises a special problem for scrupulous securitism. In the next section, we will consider a more general problem, the problem of *nonratifiability*, facing both simple and scrupulous securitism.

2.4 *The problem of nonratifiability*

The problem of nonratifiability is illustrated by the following case.

> *Satan's School for Girls*: It is now June 6, 2011. Sally is a fine, upstanding teenage girl whose moral character is impeccable. However, she is about to be kidnapped by Satanists, and brought up in Satan's School for Girls. As a result, her moral character will be severely corrupted, and she will come to desire, more than anything else, to sacrifice her firstborn child to the Prince of Darkness. At the appointed hour, on June 6, 2016, Sally will have the opportunity to kill her firstborn child, and will be able to do so either by cutting off the child's head with an axe, or by bludgeoning the child to death with a club. At that very moment, Child Services personnel will be arriving on the scene, and so if she refrains from killing her child, the child will be taken into protective custody and live happily ever after. If, on June

6, 2011, before being kidnapped by the Satanists, Sally were to intend to cut off the head of her firstborn child, then she would follow through with this intention five years later. And if she were to intend to bludgeon her child to death, then she would likewise follow through with this intention five years later. But if she were to intend not to kill her firstborn child, then she would change her mind after becoming a Satanist, and end up cutting off her child's head. The above three subjunctive conditionals are true not by any fault of Sally's, but purely in virtue of the fact that she is about to be kidnapped and brought up at Satan's School for Girls.

In this case, both forms of securitism have a very peculiar implication: they imply that on June 6, 2011, Sally ought to cut off the head of her firstborn child five years later, and yet they imply that, no matter what she may do in the meantime, it will be true five years later that she ought not to cut off the head of her firstborn child then. For on June 6, all of Sally's maximally preferable, *directly* securable options involve cutting off the head of her firstborn child. And it is likewise true that all of her maximally preferable, *scrupulously* securable options involve cutting off the head of her firstborn child. For, given that she's about to be brainwashed, there is no combination of intentions and background attitudes she could have that would prevent her from killing her first-born child five years later, and, among the two ways of killing her firstborn child, cutting off its head would cause less pain. Therefore, both simple securitism and scrupulous securitism imply that on June 6, 2011, Sally ought to cut off the head of her firstborn child five years later. However, on June 6, 2016, it will be true that all her maximally preferable, *directly* securable options involve *not* cutting off the head of her firstborn child. And it will likewise be true that all her maximally preferable, *scrupulously* securable options involve *not* cutting off the head of her firstborn child. For, at that time, refraining from killing her firstborn child will be both directly securable and scrupulously securable. And so simple securitism and scrupulous securitism both imply that, on June 6, 2016, Sally ought not to cut off the head of her firstborn child.

Thus, simple securitism and scrupulous securitism both imply that, prior to the time of action, it may be *obligatory* for an agent to act in a given way even though it will inevitably be *impermissible* for the agent to act in this way at the time of action. Thus, both theories make what we may call *nonratifiable prescriptions*: prior to the time of action, they make prescriptions which they will inevitably reverse at the time of action, regardless of what the agent does in the interim. It's hard to deny that this feature threatens the plausibility, if not the very coherence, of these theories.[6]

3. BEYOND

In this concluding part of the paper, I will begin, in section 3.1, by offering a diagnosis of why the theories we have considered thus far go wrong. I will then present an alternative theory of obligation that avoids these difficulties.

3.1 Diagnosis: why the existing theories fail

So far we have considered various theories of obligation that attempt to understand what an agent ought to do in terms of a preferability ordering over the outcomes of her options. We have seen that each of these theories faces serious problems. I will now offer a diagnosis. An adequate theory of obligation must capture the following intuition:

> **The Core Idea:** What is obligatory for an agent is that, at all times, she does the best she can do at that time, holding fixed what is not up to her at that time, but not holding fixed what is up to her at that time.

The various theories we have considered fail, because they fail to capture some aspect or other of this core idea. To see how this works, let's label the various aspects of the core idea.

> **The Core Idea Broken Down:** What is obligatory for an agent is that, (i) *at all times*, she does (ii) *the best she can do* at that time, (iii) *holding fixed what is not up to her at that time*, but (iv) *not holding fixed what is up to her* at that time.

Actualism fails because it fails to capture aspect (ii) of the Core Idea. Actualism does not identify what an agent ought to do with whatever is involved in doing the best she can do; rather, it identifies what an agent ought to do with whatever is preferable to what she would do otherwise. And as a result, actualism has horrific implications in cases such as *Arsenic and Old Ace*, where it implies that the agent ought to carry out the second worst option, no matter how bad it may be.

---

[6] The problem of nonratifiability is also faced by actualism. It is avoided by possibilism concerning performable options, as well as by the view presented in Goldman (1976).

The standard form of possibilism, what we have called *possibilism concerning performable options*, fails because it fails to capture aspect (iii) of the Core Idea. That is, in evaluating what an agent ought to do at a given time, it fails to hold fixed the facts that are not up to the agent at the time in question. In particular, in evaluating what an agent ought to be doing at a time t, it fails to hold fixed facts about what the agent will do at future times *irrespective* of the actions, intentions, and other attitudes of the agent at *t*. And so it fails to recognize that, in deciding how to act at a given time, there are sometimes facts about our future actions that we ought to treat as facts about the world rather than as objects of choice. As a result, possibilism concerning performable options gets the wrong result in *The Cabinet of Dr. Caligari*. In this case, it treats certain ends as realizable (namely, giving Emily the medicine) even though Ace would not realize these ends regardless of what his current actions and attitudes might be.

Simple securitism fails because it fails to capture aspect (iv) of the core idea. That is, in evaluating what an agent ought to do at a given time, it holds fixed facts that are up to the agent at the time in question. In particular, while it doesn't hold fixed facts about the agent's present intentions, it does hold fixed all the facts about the agent's other present attitudes that do not depend on her present intentions. As a result, it gets the wrong result in *General Ripper*. Here it holds fixed the fact that Ripper prefers the destruction of the world, and so it implies that he ought to press neither button, since pressing both is not securable given this preference. But it seems that Ripper's present preferences are no less up to Ripper than Ripper's present intentions. After all, Ripper *ought* to prefer that the world be saved, and so, in the sense of "can" that is relevant to normative evaluation, it seems to follow that Ripper *can* prefer that the world be saved. And if Ripper can prefer that the world be saved, it seems he must be able, in the relevant sense, to press both buttons. It seems, therefore, that simple securitism is wrong to exclude this course of action from consideration in evaluating what Ripper ought to do.

Finally, both simple securitism and scrupulous securitism fail because they fail to capture aspect (i) of the Core Idea. That is, they fail to capture the idea that we are obligated to do the best we can at all times. Since the maximally preferable securable option at a given time, t, may involve failing to do the best one can do at future times, both forms of securitism imply that, at t, one can be obligated to fail to do the best one can do at future times. As a result, they get the wrong result in *Satan's School for Girls*, where they imply that, on June 6, 2011, Sally is obligated to kill her firstborn child five years later.

3.2 *Toward an adequate theory of obligation*

I propose the following theory, which, for reasons that will become clear, I will call *momentwise wide-scope securitism* (MWSS).

> For any x and t, at t, x ought to be such that, for all t' from t forward, x satisfies the following conditional:
> For all ϕ, if whether x ϕs does not causally depend on the intentions x has after t', and if every maximally preferable option that is directly securable for x at t' involves ϕ-ing, then x ϕs.

Roughly, this principle states that, at any given time, an agent is obligated, at every future time, to be currently satisfying a wide-scope version of simple securitism. I will now illustrate this theory and argue that it captures each of the four aspects of the Core Idea. Recall that we stated this idea as follows.

> **The Core Idea Broken Down**: What is obligatory for an agent is that, (i) *at all times*, she does (ii) *the best she can do* at that time, (iii) *holding fixed what is not up to her at that time*, but (iv) *not holding fixed what is up to her* at that time.

To see how MWSS captures aspect (i), consider *Satan's School for Girls*, where the other forms of securitism fail to capture (i). The other forms of securitism imply that, on June 6, 2011, Sally is under an obligation to cut off the head of her firstborn child five years later, since, on June 6, 2011, all her maximally preferable, directly securable options involve so doing. MWSS avoids this implication. For what this theory implies is that, on June 6, 2011, Sally ought to be such that (if whether she cuts of the head of her firstborn child five years later does not depend on the intentions she will have *after* June 6, 2011, and if all her maximally preferable, directly securable options involve cutting off the head of her firstborn child five years later, then she cuts off the head of her firstborn child five years later). However, whether Sally cuts off the head of her firstborn child five years later clearly *does* depend on the intentions she will have after June 6, 2011, and so the antecedent of this conditional is not satisfied. Thus, Sally can satisfy the conditional without satisfying the consequent. And so MWSS does not imply that she is under any obligation satisfy the consequent by cutting off the head of her firstborn child.

To the contrary, MWSS implies that, on June 6, 2011, Sally is under an obligation to refrain from killing her firstborn child five years later. For MWSS implies that, on June 6, 2011, Sally ought to be such that, on June 6, 2016, she satisfies the conditional (if whether Sally refrains from killing her firstborn child on June 6, 2016 does not depend on her intentions after that time, and if every maximally preferable option that is directly securable for Sally on June 6, 2016 involves refraining from killing her firstborn child, then she refrains from killing her firstborn child). And, given the description of the case, come what may, Sally will satisfy the antecedent of this conditional. Thus, the only way Sally can satisfy this conditional is by refraining from killing her firstborn child on June 6, 2016. MWSS therefore implies that, on June 6, 2011, Sally is under an obligation to refrain from killing her firstborn child five years later. Thus, because of the manner in which MWSS quantifies over times—because, we might say, of its *momentwise* character—it captures aspect (i) of the Core Idea.

To see how MWSS captures aspect (ii), consider *Arsenic and Old Ace*, where actualism fails to capture (ii). In this case, MWSS correctly implies that Ace ought to now give his granddaughter water. For it implies that Ace ought to satisfy the following conditional (if whether Ace now gives his granddaughter water does not depend on his future intentions, and if all his *maximally* preferable, directly securable options involve now giving his granddaughter water, then he now gives his granddaughter water). And, given the description of the case, come what may he will satisfy the antecedent of this conditional.[7] And so he can satisfy the conditional only by giving his granddaughter water. The same does not hold, however, if we substitute "giving his granddaughter Drano" for "giving his granddaughter water"—for then Ace will permissibly satisfy the corresponding conditional by failing to

---

[7] Here, for the sake of simplicity, I am assuming that giving his granddaughter water is a basic action that Ace could do right away. We can get the same result if we understand it as a complex action involving a sequence of steps: we would simply need to consider each component of the action in turn, and then show how MWSS implies an obligation to perform each step.

satisfy the second conjunct of its antecedent: it is not the case that all his *maximally preferable*, directly securable options involve giving his granddaughter Drano. And so, unlike actualism, MWSS does not imply that Ace ought to give his granddaughter Drano. Thus, because of its *maximizing* character, MWSS captures aspect (ii) of the core idea.

To see how MWSS captures aspect (iii), consider *The Cabinet of Dr. Caligari*, where possibilism concerning performable options fails to capture (iii). Unlike the latter view, MWSS implies that Ace ought now to refrain from going to the cabinet. For it implies that he ought to satisfy the following conditional (if whether Ace now refrains from going to the cabinet does not depend on his future intentions, and if all his maximally preferable, *directly securable* options involve so refraining, then he so refrains). And since, given the description of the case, he cannot fail to satisfy the antecedent of this conditional, MWSS implies that he ought to *refrain from going to the cabinet*. The same does not hold, however, if we substitute "going to the cabinet" for "refraining from going to the cabinet"—for again Ace will permissibly satisfy the corresponding conditional by failing to satisfy the second conjunct of its antecedent: it is not the case that all his maximally preferable, *directly securable* options going to the cabinet. And so, MWSS does not imply that Ace ought to go to the cabinet. Thus, because of its *securitist* character, MWSS captures aspect (iii) of the core idea.

Finally, to see how MWSS captures aspect (iv), consider *General Ripper*, where simple securitism fails to capture (iv). Unlike simple securitism, MWSS implies that, at noon, Ripper is under an obligation to press both buttons. It implies that he is obligated to press the first button because it implies that he is obligated to satisfy the following conditional: (if, at 12:01, whether Ripper presses the first button does not depend on the intentions he has after 12:01, and if every maximally preferable option that is directly securable for Ripper at 12:01 involves pressing the first button, then he presses the first button). Now whether Ripper satisfies the antecedent of this conditional will depend on his background attitudes. For, on the one hand, if he prefers the destruction of the world, then pressing *both* buttons will not be directly securable for him, and so it will not be the case that all his maximally preferable, directly securable options involve pressing the *first* button. Hence, he will not satisfy the antecedent of the conditional. But, on the other hand, if he does *not* prefer the destruction of the world, then pressing both buttons *will* be directly securable for him, and so he will satisfy the antecedent of the conditional. Consequently, there are two ways in which Ripper could satisfy the entire conditional. First, he could prefer the destruction of the world, and hence fail to satisfy its antecedent. Or he could *not* prefer the destruction of the world, and press the first button, thereby satisfying both the antecedent and the consequent. But, of these two ways of satisfying the conditional, only the second is permissible, since (we may assume) it is impermissible for Ripper to prefer the destruction of the world. Thus, since MWSS implies that Ripper ought to satisfy this conditional, and since the only way he could permissibly satisfy this conditional is by pressing the first button, MWSS implies that Ripper ought to press the first button.

MWSS also implies that Ripper ought to press the second button. For it implies that he ought to satisfy the following conditional: (if, at 12:02, whether Ripper presses the second button does not depend on the intentions he has after 12:02, and if every maximally preferable option that is directly securable for Ripper at 12:02 involves pressing the second button, then he presses the second button). Now, so long as Ripper presses the first button at 12:01, he will satisfy the antecedent of this conditional. And we have just seen that, according to MWSS, Ripper ought to press the first button, and so he ought to satisfy the antecedent of this conditional. And so it follows that the only way he can permissibly satisfy the conditional is by satisfying the consequent, and hence by pressing the second button. Thus, unlike simple securitism, MWSS implies that Ripper ought to press both buttons, and hence that he ought to save the world.

Recall that *scrupulous* securitism likewise implies that Ripper ought to press both buttons. However, it does so at a cost. For, as we saw in section 2.3, the very features of scrupulous securitism that enable it to get the right result in *General Ripper* give rise to problematic implications in *Ice Cream of Doom*, such as the implication that Vanessa ought to begin uttering "chocolate is my preferred flavor." By contrast, MWSS avoids this implication. What MWSS implies is that Vanessa ought to satisfy the following conditional: (if whether Vanessa begins to utter "chocolate is my preferred flavor" does not depend on her future intentions, and if all her maximally preferable, scrupulously securable options involve beginning to utter "chocolate is my preferred flavor," then she begins to utter "chocolate is my preferred flavor"). However, since Vanessa permissibly prefers vanilla, she permissibly satisfies the conditional by failing to satisfy its antecedent. Hence, MWSS does not imply that she is under any obligation to satisfy the consequent.

In addition to avoiding the implication that Vanessa *ought* to begin uttering "chocolate is my preferred flavor," MWSS implies that it would be *impermissible* for Vanessa to begin uttering this sentence while simultaneously preferring vanilla. For in doing so she would fail to satisfy the conditional (if whether Vanessa begins to utter "vanilla is my preferred flavor" does not depend on her future intentions, and if all her maximally preferable, scrupulously securable options involve beginning to utter "vanilla is my preferred flavor," then she begins to utter "vanilla is my preferred flavor"). For in preferring vanilla, and beginning to utter "chocolate is my preferred flavor," she would satisfy the antecedent of this conditional but not its consequent.

Note that it is the *wide scope* character of MWSS that enables it to get the right results in *Ice Cream of Doom*. For, in this case, Vanessa could permissibly (prefer chocolate ice cream and begin uttering "chocolate is my preferred flavor"), just as she could permissibly (prefer vanilla ice cream and begin uttering "vanilla is my preferred flavor"). Thus, the reason why it is impermissible for her to (prefer vanilla ice cream and begin uttering "chocolate is my preferred flavor") is not that this would involve an impermissible action or an impermissible attitude, but rather because it would involve acting in a way that it is inappropriately related to one's attitudes. Consequently, the correct principle must concern not simply what actions we ought to perform, but rather how our actions ought to be related to our attitudes. The correct principle, therefore, cannot be one in which the "ought" takes narrow scope within a conditional—it cannot, e.g., state that *if* you have such and such attitudes, *then* you *ought* to act in such and such a way. Rather, it must be one in which the "ought" takes wide scope over any such conditional—it might, e.g., state that you *ought* to be such that (*if* you have such and such attitudes *then* you act in such and such a way). And MWSS has just this kind of form, as it states that one is obligated to satisfy certain conditionals, where the satisfaction of the antecedents of these conditionals depends on the agent's attitudes.

I conclude, therefore, that if we want a theory that captures all four aspects of the Core Idea, then we need a theory that (i) quantifies over all future times, (ii) requires maximization, (iii) concerns securable rather than performable options, and (iv) is wide scope in form. In short, we will need a theory along the lines I have proposed.

REFERENCES

Broome, John (1999) "Normative Requirements," *Ratio* 12: 398–419.
——(forthcoming) "Rationality Through Reasoning."
Cariani, Fabrizio (forthcoming) "'Ought' and Resolution Semantics," possibly forthcoming in *Noûs.*
Feldman, Fred (1986) *Doing the Best We Can: An Essay in Informal Deontic Logic* (Dordrecht: Riedel).
Goldman, Holly (1976) "Dated Rightness and Moral Imperfection," *Philosophical Review* 85(4): 449–87.
——(1978) "Doing the Best One Can," in A. I. Goldman and J. Kim (eds.), *Values and Morals* (Dordrecht: Reidel), 185–214.
Jackson, Frank and Robert Pargetter (1986) "Oughts, Options and Actualism," *Philosophical Review* 95: 233–55.
Portmore, Douglas (2011) *Commonsense Consequentialism: Wherein Morality Meets Rationality* (Oxford University Press).
Ross, Jacob (2010) "The Irreducibility of Personal Obligation," *Journal of Philosophical Logic* 39: 307–23.
——(unpublished) "Rationality, Normativity, and Commitment," possibly forthcoming in *Oxford Studies in Metaethics*, volume 7.
Snedegar, Justin (forthcoming) "Contrastive Semantics for Deontic Modals," possibly forthcoming in Martijn Blaauw (ed.), *Contrastivism in Philosophy* (London: Routledge).
Sobel, J. Howard (1976) "Utilitarianism and Past and Future Mistakes," *Noûs* 10(2): 195–219.
Wedgwood, Ralph (2009) "Against Actualism," *PEA Soup*, posted on September 11, 2009. <http://peasoup.typepad.com/peasoup/2009/09/against-actualism.html> (accessed March 28, 2011).
Zimmerman, Michel (1996) *The Concept of Moral Obligation* (Cambridge University Press).

5

Intention, Permissibility, and Double Effect[1]

WILLIAM J. FITZPATRICK

According to the doctrine of double effect (DDE), the intend/foresee distinction at least sometimes makes a difference to moral permissibility. The core claim is typically put as follows:

P: It is sometimes permissible to bring about as a *foreseen but unintended side-effect* of one's action some harm it would have been impermissible to *aim* at as a means or as an end, all else being equal.

Under the right conditions, for example, it may be permissible to carry out a tactical strike on a munitions plant during wartime despite foreseeable casualties for neighboring civilians, even where it would have been impermissible to aim at the deaths of the same number of civilians through a targeted strike on a village as a means to sow terror and demoralize the enemy. This is so even if the latter would equally have served to hasten a favorable end to the war. The DDE thus seems to capture the common intuition that there is an important moral distinction between terrorism and tactical strikes on military targets: while terroristic violence is never (or virtually never) justified, violence directed at military targets will often be justified despite foreseeable civilian casualties. According to the DDE, the source of this difference lies in a difference in *intention* and in the thought that there is something morally problematic about aiming at the deaths of innocent people as a means or as an end. This is what makes terrorism so deplorable even while other acts of violence with similar consequences for innocents may be permissible (McMahan 2009).

[1] I am grateful to participants of the 2011 Arizona Workshop on Normative Ethics, and to two OUP referees, for very helpful discussion and comments on an earlier draft of this paper.

There is, however, a problem lurking here. The formulation in P above makes it sound as if the DDE makes the permissibility of an act turn on the *actual* intentions of the *particular* agents involved. And critics, starting with James Rachels (1981), followed by Judith Jarvis Thomson (1999) and most recently Thomas Scanlon (2008), have seized upon this apparent feature of the DDE to raise an influential objection to it. The objection is that by linking moral permissibility to the actual intentions of particular agents in this way, the DDE implies that an otherwise permissible action can be rendered impermissible simply because of a particular agent's bad intentions, and that this is highly implausible, as can be seen using simple variants on the familiar cases. Rachels, Thomson, and Scanlon claim, then, that the DDE should be rejected on these grounds.

I shall argue, first of all, that the critics' construal of the DDE as primarily linking the permissibility of acts to the actual intentions of the particular agents involved—what I'll call the "actual intention" version of the DDE—is not in fact the best way to understand it. While some defenders of the DDE have accepted the actual intention version and tried to answer the critics' objection on these terms, accepting some of the implications critics attribute to the DDE but arguing that they are not absurd, there is an alternative way of understanding how the DDE relates intention to permissibility that (i) preserves everything that is attractive about the DDE in standard cases and (ii) does a better job of both answering the objection and dealing with the issues that defenders of the actual intention version raise in their own answer to the objection. After clarifying the critics' objection in section 1, I will therefore go on in section 2 to develop the proposed alternative version of the DDE, which I believe is actually how many of us implicitly understood it all along, despite often using the language in P as shorthand when not worrying about the objection in question, thus giving the misimpression of endorsing the actual intention version.

Once the alternative understanding of the DDE is explained and motivated, and we've seen how it avoids any absurd implications of the sort cited by critics, I will turn to consider the issues raised by defenders of the actual intention version of the DDE, who insist that the actual intentions of particular agents *can* directly affect permissibility after all but that there is nothing absurd about this. There is, in fact, some truth in these claims, but it is more limited than these defenders may recognize. I will therefore try to show, in section 3, how what is true here is handled at least as well or better within the alternative DDE framework I defend, which also brings out the limitations of the role of actual intentions in affecting permissibility. Getting more clear about this should help to avoid the temptation to think that the actual intention version of the DDE is the natural default. Finally, in section 4, I will argue that Scanlon's attempt to show that the DDE is in any case dispensable, because alternative principles that make no appeal to intention can handle all the cases for which the DDE has often been thought necessary, does not succeed. In the central cases we will consider, his alternative explanation for the relevant intuitions is in fact parasitic on the DDE for its deeper justification, and so isn't a genuine alternative after all. My conclusion is that the DDE remains a viable and plausible principle we have good reason to take seriously, and that this recurring but misguided objection to it should finally be put to rest.[2]

I. THE OBJECTION

What exactly is the objection that Rachels, Thomson, and Scanlon have raised against the DDE as they understand it—what I've called the actual intention version? Their strategy is to consider acts of the type usually favored by the DDE, such as tactical bombing, and to imagine that act done with the intention usually associated with the disfavored type of act, such as terror bombing. Suppose, for example, that the pilot selected to fly the sort of tactical bombing mission usually favored by defenders of the DDE turns out to harbor bad intentions of the sort usually associated with the disfavored kind of case: perhaps he hates the civilians in the neighboring village and delights in their foreseeable deaths from the fallout of the factory's destruction; or perhaps he privately doubts the significance of the munitions plant but sees the mission as worthwhile because it will kill nearby civilians and undermine popular support for the war. So he accepts the mission as a way

---

[2] Another common objection to the DDE is that the distinction between intended and merely foreseen harms is so arbitrary and vulnerable to manipulation that if the DDE can be used to help justify some things (such as tactical bombing) then it can equally be used to justify virtually anything (such as terror bombing). I develop an account to answer this objection in FitzPatrick (2006).

legally to kill some civilians: though he targets the munitions plant just like any other tactical bomber, he intends and welcomes the nearby civilian deaths as a means or as an end. Call this the "nasty munitions plant bomber" case.

The objection is that according to the actual intention version of the DDE, the bombing mission against the munitions plant is (implausibly) rendered *impermissible* by this pilot's bad intention: while it would have been permissible had he had appropriate intentions, it is impermissible given his bad intentions; he may not proceed with it, which means that if he is the only pilot available, the mission cannot permissibly be carried out (any more than a terror bombing mission could) and the war effort will have to do without it, despite its military importance.[3] But this, the objection goes, is absurd: if it is permissible to fly a bombing mission against this military target in the overall circumstances having to do with its proportional military value, then surely nothing that's going on inside any particular pilot's head can by itself make that mission impermissible. How could the permissibility of pursuing this bombing mission against the munitions plant be held hostage to a particular pilot's intentions, *independently* of what will actually be done in the world, such that the mission must be aborted unless another pilot turns up *who will not do anything differently apart from having better intentions* when he bombs the munitions plant?[4]

---

[3] See Scanlon (2008: 19–20), and compare Thomson, discussing a parallel case involving the injection of a pain-killing drug into a patient with a terminal and excruciating illness, where the dose required to control the pain will also lead to death: "According to [the DDE, at least when combined with the assumption that it remains impermissible to intend death even in these extreme circumstances], the question whether it is morally permissible for the doctor to inject a lethal drug turns on whether the doctor would be doing so intending death or only intending relief from pain … *If the only available doctor would inject to cause the patient's death*, or is incapable of becoming clear enough about her own intentions to conclude that what she intends is *only* to relieve the patient's pain, then—according to the [DDE]—the doctor may not proceed, *and the patient must therefore continue to suffer*. That cannot be right" (1999: 515–16, italics added to emphasize the parallel with the text above, i.e., that if the nasty bomber is the only available pilot then the war must therefore continue without the benefit of this mission against the munitions plant).

[4] We're assuming, of course, that the nasty pilot's bad intentions won't change his actions: he will fly exactly the same mission as the good pilot, but will simply have different intentions and feelings in doing so. If his bad intentions undermined his reliability in carrying out the munitions plant bombing according to his orders (e.g., making him likely to change plans mid-flight and target a city instead), then Scanlon would allow that it may be impermissible for him to fly the mission and for his commander to send him on it. But here the role of intention in affecting permissibility is *derivative*: it comes in merely in making the pilot unreliable and

The conclusion drawn by these critics is that it was a mistake to think that intention bears on permissibility in anything like the way suggested by the DDE. If it seems like it does, this is only because we're conflating different issues. The intention with which an agent acts does plausibly bear on the question whether she has *acted well,* or what sort of character she has, but this is distinct from permissibility (Thomson 1999: 517). If an act such as tactical bombing is otherwise permissible, then the fact that it would be done with a bad intention does not render it *impermissible,* but simply implies that the agent *will not be acting well* in doing this permissible thing: his concrete action may be bad (and it may reveal a defective character, though it needn't in all cases), but it remains true that the act-type in question—the bombing of the munitions plant—is permissible. We shouldn't conflate the two types of judgment. Scanlon puts this point in terms of distinguishing *critical* and *deliberative* uses of moral principles: only the critical use of principles, as when criticizing an agent for having acted badly by *failing to act on the right considerations,* is essentially sensitive to the agent's state of mind; by contrast, the deliberative use of principles, as in judging permissibility, is essentially concerned simply with *what counts for or against potential acts* (2008: 23).

Now I want to grant that this description is more or less correct (with qualifications to be noted later): the nasty munitions plant bomber's bad intention does not render the mission impermissible though it does mean that he will act badly in carrying it out, performing an act that is permissible but doing it badly by acting from the wrong considerations. The problem with the objection, though, is that the DDE is not best understood as claiming that an act's "permissibility depends on the agent's intention" (Scanlon 2008: 14). When the DDE is understood properly, the objection never even gets off the ground.

dangerous, which is what directly makes it impermissible for him to fly the mission (Scanlon 2008: 31–2). This is the focus of Alec Walen's (2006) "doctrine of illicit intentions," which, following Scanlon, rejects any direct or non-derivative role for intentions in affecting permissibility, as asserted by the DDE, but allows for this sort of indirect or derivative role.

2. A BETTER CONSTRUAL OF THE DDE

If the DDE does not link the permissibility of acts to the actual intentions of particular agents in the way critics have assumed, how *does* it relate intention to permissibility?[5] The central idea is this:

The DDE (in its prohibitive aspect, which is our focus here) is best understood as a *constraint on the justification of action*, having to do not with any particular agent's actual intentions but with the intentions that *would* be involved in performing a certain type of action for the reasons provided by a proposed justification.

Here is the argument for the DDE so conceived. We begin with a *condition of adequacy* for any proposed justification of an action as something permissible to do:

(i) A justification for an action is adequate only if a good and well-informed agent *could act well* (i.e., at least not act badly) in performing the action *because* of that justification for it.

I take this principle to be compelling regardless of the particular normative views one may hold: it is part of the concept of a practical *justification* for action that an adequate justification would be one that an otherwise good person could act on *without thereby acting badly*. If a proposed justification failed this condition, and its being taken seriously and acted upon would involve an otherwise good agent in something morally problematic enough that she will thereby be acting badly, then in what sense could it seriously be thought to be an adequate justification? The whole point of a practical justification is to show that the action in question is one that could legitimately be pursued for the reasons given in the justification. So whatever exactly is involved in a justification's being adequate—such as the citing of a good enough end, reasonably efficient means, and so on—it must also be the case that an agent could act on that justification, performing the act because of that justification, without thereby engaging in something morally problematic enough to constitute acting badly.[6]

---

[5] The material that follows in this section is a development and justification of the view briefly presented in FitzPatrick (2003).

[6] What about 'self-effacing' moral theories, according to which it is ultimately preferable that agents *not* generally act on the true justifications for actions (since, for example, employing certain rules of thumb instead—some of which may even involve moral fictions—best promotes utility)? Such theories claim that *it is contingently best* in terms of achieving the

Next comes the intuitive general claim that drives the DDE:

(ii) Intending significant harm toward innocents as a means or end is deeply morally problematic as such, which typically makes acting on such an intention constitute acting badly.[7]

This is a claim that even critics of the DDE can accept, and some (Thomson and Rachels) explicitly do, agreeing that the nasty munitions plant bomber, for example, has a defective character and *acts badly* by acting from bad intentions, motives, and desires. Their primary objection is to the idea that intention is relevant to *permissibility*, and premise (ii) says nothing yet about that: the implications for permissibility come later, as the upshot of the overall argument; nothing is being presupposed about permissibility at this point, the claim being only about the direct significance of bad intentions vis-à-vis acting badly (though we will need to explore some complications in this regard in section 3). So the claim in (ii) about morally problematic intentions and acting badly is prior to the claims about permissibility that are ultimately at issue and which we are still working toward.

Premise (ii) articulates the broadly appealing idea that there is something intrinsically inappropriate about entering into a relation with an innocent person such that one not only accepts harm to that person as a regrettable side effect of something important enough to justify it, but is positively *guided by* that undeserved harm, as Thomas Nagel puts it (1986: 181). This is obviously perverse when the person's harm is one's final end. Perhaps it isn't similarly perverse to pursue someone's harm as a means, but making an innocent person's harm one's strategic purpose in this way still puts one in an inherently objectionable relation to that person. Rather than merely tolerating some regretted harm and *remaining in solidarity* with the person at least to the extent of taking (or being prepared to take) all reasonable measures to avoid or minimize

---

relevant goal if people generally don't act on the true justifications, but this is consistent with the claim in (i) that an agent *could* nonetheless act well in acting on the true justification, performing the act for the reasons given in the justification *without thereby acting badly*. Thanks to Tom Hurka for raising this question.

[7] As explained shortly below, the qualification "typically" here and in the following steps of the argument is meant simply to allow for the possibility of threshold-based exceptions, for example; it is not meant to be doing the work in answering the objection from section 1.

it, one is instead *pursuing* that harm and adjusting (or being prepared
to adjust) one's actions as necessary to guarantee that it *does* occur.
As Nagel points out in his example of torturing a child to force his
grandmother to give us something needed for saving lives, if twisting his
arm one way doesn't make him scream, we have to twist it another way;
if that doesn't make him scream loudly enough, we have to twist it
further, until we get what we're after (Nagel 1986: 181–82). Instead
of being wholeheartedly repelled by this evil we are guided by it (even
if we regret "having" to inflict it), thus "swimming head-on against
the normative current" (182). This situation puts one radically at odds
with one's victim, abandoning even the basic solidarity still present in
the side-effect case and taking on a directly antithetical stance toward his
well-being.

The tactical bomber who destroys a military target *despite* the collateral harm to nearby civilians, fully regretting that harm and prepared
to do all he can to minimize it, maintains a certain connection to his
victims, sharing the aim of avoiding their harm and regretting it when it
occurs, despite having caused it; the terror bomber, by contrast, aban-
dons that aim and takes up a stance entirely opposed to it insofar as he is
deliberately seeking that harm. This difference matters not only from
the perspective of the agents involved, but also from that of the victims.
Harm is harm from the victims' perspective, one might be tempted to
say, so why should facts about the source make any difference to them?
But of course they can in many ways, and this is one of them. Victims of
collateral damage, if they could be made to understand the justification
of the act in terms of the importance of the end in question—such as
destroying a nearby military target as part of a just war—may quite
reasonably take a different attitude toward the agent of that harm than
they would have toward a terrorist who deliberately *targeted* them or
their children, apparently viewing them as *there to be used (to their
detriment) for his purposes* (Quinn 1993: 190). There is a distinct form
of disrespect and hostile interaction in the second case, meriting a
distinct form of resentment that is not present in the first case, however
unfortunate both harms may be.[8]

---

[8] The differences here will naturally diminish as the two kinds of case are brought closer
together. A tactical bomber who doesn't intend the deaths of innocents as a means but also
doesn't take steps to minimize them, using a blunt instrument that cannot literally be aimed at
the military target but not at the civilians, is likely to be resented in much the same way as a

Since our focus is on clarifying the basic structure of the DDE, perhaps this will suffice to motivate (ii), though there is certainly more to say about it in a more general argument for the DDE.[9] Continuing with the argument, then, from (i) and (ii) we now have:

(iii) So an adequate justification of action typically cannot be such that an agent who performed the action because of that justification would be engaging in the intention of significant harm toward innocents as a means or as an end.

In other words, an adequate justification for an action, showing it to be permissible, must be such that, among other things, an agent *could* perform the act in question *for the reasons given in the justification* without thereby intending harm toward innocents as a means or as an end (since otherwise the adequacy condition in (i) would be violated given (ii)). From this it follows that:

(iv) There is thus a constraint on the justification of action such that an action typically cannot be justified (shown to be permissible) by showing it to be an efficient means to a good end in cases where the action constitutes such a means precisely by virtue of being significantly harmful to innocents.

The qualification "typically" in (ii), (iii), and (iv) is meant to allow for exceptions where the harm in question is relatively minor and the end is sufficiently important, or where the harm is serious but a threshold has been crossed such that the end is of overwhelming importance and this overrides the considerations about intention, as in the case where one innocent person must deliberately be killed in order to avoid a

---

terror bomber. This is because his callousness manifests a similar level of disrespect toward his victims, though of a different kind.

[9] Obviously a fully adequate statement of this principle would require various qualifications. Intending harm as a means may be unobjectionable, for example, in cases of legitimate competition in zero sum situations, as in competition among businesses for customers or among political candidates for voters: one candidate's efforts to discredit and take votes from another needn't be objectionable (if done in an honorable fashion), even if this constitutes a harm to the other candidate and is aimed at as a means to winning the election. Presumably this is unproblematic because it is understood to be fair game in this sort of competition, and the parties consent to such rules of play in participating in it. Another exception involves aiming at lesser harms for someone's own greater good, with her consent, as with breaking a bone to set it properly.

cataclysm.[10] The crucial point for our purposes, however, is that apart from such exceptions the constraint on justification thus rules out candidate justifications that appeal to an act's being an efficient means to a good end where the act constitutes such a means by virtue of being harmful to innocents. And by ruling out candidate justifications in such cases, (iv) implies that unless some other, more adequate justification can be found for the action in question, it will be *impermissible*.[11]

We can illustrate how this works with the terror bombing case. Consider a proposed justification for terror bombing: *bombing the village is permissible because killing civilians will terrorize and demoralize the enemy and hasten their surrender, favorably ending the war.* This justification is ruled out by (iii) because it is impossible to act on that justification, performing the act in question (lethally targeting the village) for the reasons given in the justification (to terrorize and weaken the enemy through civilian massacres), without engaging in the intention to harm innocents as a means to one's end. This matters because, given (ii), this amounts to a failure to satisfy the basic adequacy condition for justification in (i): no agent could act well in acting on this justification, performing the act in question because of this justification. So assuming that there is no other candidate justification for bombing the village that does not share this structural feature, the action cannot be adequately justified: it is *impermissible*.

---

[10] The assumption here is that in cases where the threshold is crossed it becomes permissible to do what would have been impermissible below the threshold. An alternative approach would be to leave the principle unqualified and to maintain that such acts remain morally wrong or impermissible even above the threshold: they simply become the lesser of two evils. That would be a *moral dilemma construal* of threshold cases, as defended by Nagel (1979). Notice that on the first approach, step (ii) tells us that when the threshold is crossed in extreme cases it is no longer acting badly to intend the harm in question, though it remains morally problematic and there will still be "moral residue" from such actions: one is still violating a person in a way that is socially damaging.

[11] This move from lacking adequate justification to impermissibility might seem too fast: some actions, such as those done on a whim, might be permissible despite apparently lacking any adequate justification. But it's not clear that permissible whims lack adequate justifications: the fact that one just feels like skipping down the sidewalk may itself constitute sufficient justification for doing it, given that there's nothing wrong with it. Moreover, the crucial point for the argument is that the actions with which we are here concerned are all ones that involve harm to innocents, and so carry a presumptive burden of justification, unlike whims. The claim, then, is that if no adequate justification can be found for these harmful actions, then they are impermissible. Thanks to Houston Smit for raising this issue.

The DDE therefore condemns terror bombing the village, and equally condemns other actions the only plausible justifications for which appeal to the act's being an efficient means to a good end where the act constitutes such a means by virtue of being harmful to innocents (iv). By contrast, there is no similar problem with justification in the tactical bombing case, where the action's harmfulness to innocents is irrelevant to its instrumentality to the end. This is because in that case a good agent *could* perform the action *because* of the justification in question *and act well in doing so*, avoiding engaging in any morally problematic intentions. So if there is an otherwise sufficient justification for tactical bombing, in terms of proportionately important ends served by the destruction of the munitions plant, lack of reasonable alternatives, and so on, then the justification for tactical bombing will go through and it will be permissible, unlike terror bombing. The DDE thus both condemns terror bombing and allows tactical bombing, just as it should.

Now for the real test: what does the DDE have to say in connection with the objection from section 1? Consider our nasty munitions plant bomber again—the one who does everything a good tactical bomber would do but with bad intentions. Nothing in the DDE as laid out in the four steps above implies that the bombing of the munitions plant is rendered impermissible just because the actual pilot has bad intentions. What matters is simply that the (otherwise sound) proposed justification for bombing the plant passes the relevant test at the heart of the DDE: a good agent *could* perform the action *because* of that justification *without* engaging in any problematic intentions and acting badly. The actual intentions of particular agents are irrelevant to this, so the bombing of the munitions plant as such is permissible, period. We thus arrive at the correct judgment: while we criticize the nasty munitions plant bomber for acting badly, acting on inappropriate intentions and an inadequate justification (similar to the one the terror bomber acts on), we keep this judgment distinct from the judgment of the permissibility of the act in question, just as Scanlon insists we should. The act is permissible because various considerations (the ones the good tactical bomber takes into account) tell in favor of it in such a way as to constitute an adequate justification for the act—all independently of anything about this particular pilot's intentions.

Scanlon's objection, then, misses the mark when he portrays the defender of the DDE as being committed to the idea that permissibility depends on "what is intended by the agents involved," so that the Prime Minister, when asked by the air force commander whether he thinks a tactical bombing mission would be permissible, must reply: "Well, that depends on what your intentions would be in carrying it out. Would you be intending to kill the civilians, or would their deaths be merely an unintended but foreseeable (albeit beneficial) side-effect of the destruction of the plant?" (Scanlon 2008: 19–20).[12] The DDE implies no such thing. All the Prime Minister needs to worry about is whether there exists an otherwise sufficient justification for the mission that also respects the constraint in (iv), thus avoiding the problem described in (iii), thus meeting the adequacy condition on justification in (i). We needn't set about interviewing prospective pilots to determine that, and so the critics' objections are avoided.[13]

At this point Scanlon might object that the principle in (iv) makes no appeal to intentions at all: not only have we (appropriately) avoided appeal to the actual intentions of the particular agents, but we have factored out intention altogether, offering a constraint on justification having to do simply with a certain structural feature involving the causal role of harm to innocents. It might appear, then, that we have really abandoned the DDE, just as he thinks we should. This objection, however, misses the point of the above *derivation* of (iv): while it's true that (iv) does not itself make explicit reference to intention, the constraint on justification articulated in (iv) *is itself justified precisely by the claim about intention in (ii)*; we cannot simply focus on (iv) in isolation, forgetting how we arrived at it and what justifies it. This, then, is how intention comes in to the DDE: not as an appeal to the actual intentions of particular agents, but as a general claim about a certain kind of intentional stance that is specially morally problematic, thus

---

[12] Scanlon borrows this example from Thomson (1991: 293), who relies on the same construal of the DDE in her discussion of the euthanasia example in Thomson (1999), discussed in footnote 3 and further below.

[13] McMahan (2009) and Wedgwood (2011) offer their own, very plausible replies to this part of the objection, quite apart from the one I have developed above. The notion that the DDE implausibly instructs us to introspect and consult our intentions in the process of determining what it is permissible to do is perhaps the least compelling part of the critics' objection.

providing the rationale for the constraint on justification given in (iv). Intention thus plays a *fundamental* role here, not merely a derivative one of the sort Scanlon allows for (2008: 31–32). We have not watered down the role of intention in this understanding of the DDE: we've simply located it properly, and in doing so have shown how the DDE avoids any absurd implications arising from the idea that permissibility is a function of the actual intentions of particular agents. Intention can play a fundamental role in affecting permissibility without saddling us with the sorts of problems the critics have cited.[14]

How does this all connect up with ordinary, familiar talk about the DDE? When speaking loosely, proponents of the DDE will say that terror bombing may be impermissible while tactical bombing is permissible, where everything else is equal, 'because the terror bomber intends the deaths of civilians as a means whereas the tactical bomber does not'. This has misled critics into thinking that the DDE links permissibility to the actual intentions of particular agents, thus saddling us with implausible implications such as the need to abort a tactical bombing mission as impermissible if the pilot turns out to harbor nasty intentions. But the above claim, properly understood, does not have such implications: it is just convenient shorthand for the thoughts articulated in (i) through (iv). It's a simple way of indicating that a difference in permissibility is being traced to an asymmetry in the adequacy of available justifications for the two acts, based on structural differences in the justifications and the implications of those structural differences for the intentions that would have to be involved in acting on those justifications.

3. COMPLICATIONS

A. Having described what I take to be the proper understanding of the DDE and shown that it does not fall prey to the line of attack pursued by Rachels, Thomson, and Scanlon, let me turn now to an important

---

[14] This does not, of course, suffice to show that the appeal to intention in (ii) is the *only* possible way of arriving at the constraint on justification in (iv). Perhaps the support for (iv) is overdetermined and there is some other way of arriving at such a constraint that makes no reference to intention. I take this up in the critique of Scanlon's efforts along these lines, in section 4.

objection that is sure to arise in response. One might worry that I haven't after all escaped the critics' interpretation of the DDE as appealing to the actual intentions of particular agents, but am myself committed to it by my own principles. For if we say in step (ii) that it is deeply morally problematic to intend harm toward innocents as a means or as an end, then this implies that we *ought to avoid* doing so. But since the nasty munitions plant bomber would be acting with problematic intentions, this seems to imply that he *ought to refrain* from flying the mission, since presumably he ought to try to avoid acting badly and he would be acting badly in flying the mission with those nasty intentions. And if the pilot *ought to refrain* from flying the mission, this seems to imply that it is *impermissible* for him to fly it and that this mission therefore cannot permissibly be carried out if he is the only available pilot. But now we seem to be right back at the problematic, actual intention version of the DDE I earlier rejected!

The answer to this objection is that insofar as these claims about the pilot and the mission are implausible the version of the DDE on offer does not imply them, and insofar as there is some truth in some of the thoughts here the DDE helps to explain it; indeed, my version does so at least as well as, and likely better than, the actual intention version. To see this, we need to consider issues that arise in connection with different ways of describing *what is done* (depending on how much about intention is built into or left out of the description), different perspectives from which questions about permissibility arise (e.g., the pilot's vs. that of the commander responsible for launching or aborting the mission), and the weighting of the relevant normative considerations (e.g., the pilot's agent-relative reasons for avoiding acting badly vs. the importance of carrying out the mission). Once we clarify these issues, we may concede that the actual intentions of particular agents may sometimes play a limited role in permissibility after all. But this is not the implausible role critics have taken the DDE to imply, and the primary role for intention remains the more abstract one brought out by (i)–(iv).

To begin, then, consider two descriptions of what the nasty munitions plant bomber is doing:

(D1) bombing the munitions plant;
(D2) bombing the munitions plant with the intent of killing civilians, sowing terror and thus winning the war.

D1 is an example of what Wedgwood (2011) calls a *thin* act-type, while D2 is a *thick* act-type by virtue of building the intention into the description of what is done. If our question is about the permissibility of the thin act-type described in D1, then the version of the DDE I have defended answers it independently of any reference to any particular agent's actual intentions, just as the critics claim we ought to be able to do. We can determine that *it is permissible to bomb the munitions plant* in a certain set of objective circumstances without knowing anything about who the pilot will be, apart from matters of competence and reliability. By contrast, those who defend the *actual intention version* of the DDE (or something close to it) will claim that the DDE should be understood to be focused primarily on *thick* act-types rather than thin ones, so that the question about permissibility is really about D2; and they will claim that what is described in D2—bombing the munitions plant *with terroristic intentions*—is indeed plausibly impermissible, just as implied by the actual intention version of the DDE (McMahan 2009: 353f.; Wedgwood 2011).

Now although I reject the view that the DDE is primarily concerned with thick act-types, I grant that there is some truth in what is claimed by defenders of the actual intention version of the DDE regarding thick act-types. Even if one doubts that such thick act-types are generally the proper focus for questions about permissibility (and some action theorists will even reject the idea of thick act-types itself), one can certainly understand the question whether what is described in D2 is permissible. Or equivalently, one can understand questions not just about the permissibility of bombing the munitions plant (as in D1, without specifying an agent) but about the permissibility of *this pilot's* bombing the munitions plant (which is equivalent to *his instantiating the thick act-type* in question): is it permissible *for him* to bomb the munitions plant?[15] And defenders of the actual intention version of the DDE are certainly on to something here, which I too will have to accommodate.

[15] The questions here will arise whether we take D1 to be the proper description of the act itself and D2 to be something beyond that, or we instead regard D2 to be the proper description of the act or action, with D1 being an unhelpful abstraction. The fact remains that both D1 and D2 are natural ways of describing *what the nasty munitions plant bomber does*, and we should be able to say something about them in connection with claims about permissibility without having first to settle the larger debates in action theory, which I set to one side here. Thanks to Robert Audi for helpful comments here.

But the actual intention version may not get things quite right even here, at least if it moves too quickly and simply to the conclusion that what is described in D2 is impermissible or (equivalently) that it is impermissible for the nasty munitions plant bomber to proceed. Whether it is impermissible or not will in fact depend on further factors, and the version of the DDE I have defended provides a clear account of this.

The principle in step (ii) certainly tells us that the nasty munitions plant bomber should ideally drop his morally inappropriate intentions (and related desires and feelings) if he can, and that if he fails to do so and goes ahead and does what is described in D2 he will act badly. And insofar as we should all aim to avoid acting badly, it follows that there is *pro tanto* reason to avoid doing what is described in D2. Now suppose this pilot declines to make these psychological changes in himself, or he tries and fails, so that were he to fly the mission he would be doing what is described in D2. Then he will be acting badly if he flies the mission—killing innocents and delighting in it or at least welcoming it. In that case, since he would be acting badly in bombing the munitions plant, given his mental state, it follows that there is *pro tanto* reason for him to avoid flying the mission. It does not automatically follow, however, that it is impermissible for him to fly the mission. In some circumstances it will be, in others it won't be (even well *below* any plausible threshold).

Suppose all else is equal, and there are other capable pilots available to fly the mission instead. Then our nasty pilot surely ought to request to be reassigned to a different task. This is simply a consequence of the principle that we should aim to avoid acting badly. In these circumstances we might therefore say that given this moral aim and the easy availability of other satisfactory options, it would be *impermissible for this pilot* to neglect to request reassignment and to go ahead and fly the mission. This is not to back off of D1, but simply to supplement it with the recognition that doing this permissible thing (bombing the plant) would *not* be permissible for *this* particular pilot given his circumstances, since for him this would amount to *needlessly acting badly*, which he here has decisive reason to avoid, since he could easily find a replacement instead. So here we have a genuine example of a particular agent's actual intentions affecting the permissibility of his performing a certain action (of a permissible thin act-type), though only by way of (i) how the intention would bear on his acting well or badly, and (ii) the fact that the consideration about acting badly is not overridden by any other considerations here. (Contrast this with simply applying the actual intention version of the DDE to D2 and concluding straightaway that it is impermissible. Although the verdicts overlap here, they may diverge in other cases, as discussed below.)

Scanlon himself, in fact, suggests something very similar to this in the case of someone who, by virtue of harboring the wrong intentions, would be acting hypocritically in making a phone call to a sick relative—something that would otherwise be good to do, were it not for the poor intentions: one should *avoid hypocrisy*, Scanlon notes, so it might be wrong to do something knowing that it would involve hypocrisy (Scanlon 2008: 40, 59). My claim here is structurally similar, except that in my case I'm appealing not to avoiding hypocrisy but to avoiding acting badly (through acting on bad intentions, desires, and emotions), as in killing civilians where one would be welcoming it. The point, stemming from (ii), is that like acting with hypocrisy, acting with deeply problematic intentions makes for defective action, and so we should typically avoid it, just as Scanlon says we should avoid hypocrisy. Scanlon was willing to say what he does about the hypocrisy case because intentions are there coming in only *indirectly* or *derivatively* in influencing permissibility, while the avoidance of hypocrisy plays the direct role. By contrast, intentions come in directly for me in the bomber example, since relating to innocent people in this way, intending their harm as a means or as an end, is something I'm claiming we should equally avoid in itself, as claimed in step (ii). This, I think, is equally plausible, which means that we do after all have one limited way in which the bad intentions of particular agents *can* directly affect permissibility, and we are not here simply conflating critical and deliberative uses of principles (*contra* Scanlon 2008: 25–26, 30).

This is my small concession to the critics' interpretation of the DDE that I have mostly rejected as a misconstrual. It is important to emphasize, however, that this concession is very limited. First, it never commits us to saying that the permissibility of what is described in D1 depends on the actual intentions of particular agents—as if we can't judge the permissibility of D1 in abstraction from the actual intentions of particular pilots; the abstract judgment about permissibility has nothing to do with anyone's actual intentions. Second, insofar as actual intentions do have implications for permissibility in connection with a particular agent such as our flawed pilot, who would be doing D2, this is again only in very particular circumstances, as where acceptable alternatives are readily available and it would therefore be *impermissible for him* to decline to take them and thereby needlessly act badly.

Suppose now instead that the circumstances are different: there is no other pilot available and the mission is of great importance. In that case, the pilot's *pro tanto* reason to opt out of the mission to avoid acting badly will surely be *overridden* by the reasons in favor of flying the mission and not jeopardizing the war effort. Not only will it remain permissible for him to fly the mission in those circumstances, but it will likely be obligatory, despite the fact that he'll be tarnishing his moral record in carrying out his duty, given his mental state. His agent-relative reason to avoid acting badly doesn't translate into overall impermissibility in such circumstances, but is instead overridden by his duty to carry out legitimate and important orders. If no other pilot is available, then we simply have a case where it *remains permissible* or even obligatory *for this pilot* to fly the mission (just as for any other pilot) despite the fact that he will act badly in doing so. True, it would obviously be best for him to change himself psychologically in such a way that he could act well in carrying out the mission: that is what he should ideally be doing. But suppose he cannot, and will be stuck with acting badly if he acts; perhaps he just cannot convince himself that there is really any point to destroying the plant apart from the civilian deaths and their effects, doubting his superiors' judgment of the importance of the plant, or he cannot set aside his hatred sufficiently to avoid delighting in the deaths he causes. On my view, it is all things considered permissible and even obligatory for him to bomb the munitions plant (just as the critics insist).

This brings out a potential contrast with the actual intention version of the DDE. If proponents of such a view conclude straightaway that (barring threshold cases) D2 is impermissible—as Jeff McMahan (2009: 348, 353–55), does[16]—and then apply this to the present case, they will conclude that it remains impermissible for the nasty munitions plant bomber to proceed, despite the lack of any alternative pilot, inasmuch as

---

[16] "The proponents [of the DDE] then conclude that . . . it would be impermissible for him to act on the intention to kill children as a means of terrorizing the enemy" (348).

he will be engaging in D2. This, I have argued, is not quite right: where actual intentions make for impermissibility they do so only by way of making the agent's (otherwise permissible) action constitute acting badly, in circumstances where that is an overriding consideration; since the latter condition isn't met here, it is *not* after all impermissible for the agent to act here, all things considered: it is permissible and likely even required. Again, I agree that *ideally* he should *drop* his bad intentions by dropping his misconstrual of the reasons in play here, ceasing to see the civilian deaths as what justifies bombing the plant: then not only would his act be permissible, but he could act well in carrying it out. But if this is not a possibility for him, given his view of things, so that he will either do what is described in D2 or not fly the mission at all (not being able simply to will himself to see the considerations that in fact justify the action *as being* the genuine reasons in play), then it is permissible—even required—for him to act, despite the fact that he will act badly.[17]

Perhaps some construals of the actual intention view (or something close to it) can avoid having to deny this. Wedgwood (2011), for example, takes the DDE to claim here only that there are *stronger reasons* against the act-type *bombing with the intention of killing civilians* than against the act-type *bombing with the intention of destroying the munitions plant*, and to counsel us to adopt only the latter plan rather than the former. Perhaps the talk of "stronger reasons" is compatible with claiming that all things considered there is nonetheless most reason for the nasty bomber to proceed in the case where there are no other available pilots, and that it is therefore permissible (even obligatory) for him to do what is described in D2 (assuming he cannot rid himself of the problematic intentions and feelings), as I have claimed. Or perhaps it will be claimed that as long as the nasty munitions plant bomber adopts only the permissible plan of *bombing with the intention of destroying the munitions plant*, it is permissible for him to proceed despite his nasty feelings about the civilian deaths, as Wedgwood seems to suggest. Of course, this will not do if *his reason for*

---

[17] In discussing this sort of case McMahan (2009: 356) sometimes speaks not about whether it is *permissible* for the agent to act but about whether the agent *acts permissibly* in so acting. This difference may matter, as argued by Hanser (2005). I discuss this issue in part D of this section.

destroying the plant is in turn to kill civilians, which would make for an impermissible overall plan; and it may be hard to avoid this if he does not believe there is any real point in destroying the munitions plant by itself, given his own assessment of its military significance. But perhaps his further end is simply to obey his orders. Then perhaps he could adopt the plan Wedgwood endorses and his proceeding would come out permissible on this way of understanding the actual intention version of the DDE. If that is so, then perhaps this construal and application of the actual intention version accounts equally well for this case. That would not be an unwelcome result: it would show that the DDE can successfully meet the challenges raised by Rachels, Thomson, and Scanlon on *either* (something like) the actual intention construal or my alternative understanding of it. It is enough for my purposes to have shown that my version does at least as well as the actual intention version in capturing these complexities, and it remains an advantage in any case that I am not forced to construe the DDE as focusing primarily on thick act-types in connection with permissibility, allowing me more naturally to capture, in terms of thin act-types, the sense in which certain things remain permissible even when a given agent would act badly in doing them.

B. All the same points I have been making in defense of the DDE apply equally to Thomson's (1999) discussion of the case of a patient who requires such a high dose of morphine to control pain that it will foreseeably hasten death. Many of us, of course, hold that in such circumstances it may not actually be wrong for the doctor to aim at the patient's death, if the patient requests euthanasia and it is in her best interests; this is a plausible exception to the usual prohibition against intending the death of an innocent person. But suppose for the sake of argument we grant the Catholic position that even here death may not be aimed at as a means or end, though it may be brought about as a side-effect of controlling pain (where the drug controls the pain independently of causing death, rather than *by* causing death, though it also hastens death). Thomson imagines a case where the injection is approved but the only doctor available is one who would administer the drug with the wrong intentions, welcoming the hastened death as a means to permanent pain control, rather than aiming only at temporary pain control and regretting the death, though she does nothing medically different from any other doctor. Surely, Thomson says, it would be absurd to suppose that it would now be impermissible to administer the drug, so that the patient *must just be left to suffer* (1999: 514–15). Of course. But as should now be clear, the DDE is not committed to the absurd claim.

On my account, administering the drug is *permissible*, in abstraction from any facts about the actual intentions of particular agents, because there exists an otherwise adequate justification for it (even by Catholic standards) that *could* be acted upon by an otherwise good agent *without* engaging in any morally problematic intentions and acting badly. Of course, it's also true that this particular doctor would be acting badly, given her mental state, so that she has an agent-relative, *pro tanto* reason not to perform this sort of procedure. But it doesn't automatically follow that it is *impermissible* for her to proceed. It may be, if she could easily find another doctor to perform the same act, making it impermissible for her instead to go ahead with it and needlessly act badly. But if there is no other doctor available, then it is surely far more important that this patient be spared terrible suffering than it is for this doctor to keep her moral record clean by avoiding acting badly. So not only is it permissible for her to administer the drug, even though she will not act well in doing so, but she is plausibly obligated to do so.[18]

C. It is important also to consider how third parties figure into all of this. When a particular agent's bad intentions do make it *impermissible for her* to perform the action (because there are other agents available and she should avoid needlessly acting badly), the consideration in question—avoiding acting badly—is an *agent-relative* reason, and so at most implies that it is impermissible *for her* to perform the action rather than stepping aside. Nothing follows about obligations *third parties* such as commanding officers or medical supervisors might

---

[18] What if instead the patient's greedy nephew sneaks into the room and administers the injection with the intention of hastening death in order to get his inheritance sooner? One might be tempted to think that we must appeal to *his actual intentions* to understand the impermissibility, but that is not so. The primary reason why the nephew's act is impermissible is simply that there is *no sufficient justification of the act as performed by someone other than the doctor*, in terms of a sufficiently good end and otherwise unobjectionable means. The nephew's greedy desire for his inheritance doesn't constitute a good reason for hastening his aunt's death, and his means are ruled out in any case by the fact that his aunt has not waived *his* negative duty not to hasten her death, as she has done with respect to the doctor; he is thus violating her rights, making this case quite different from that of the nasty munitions plant bomber. Thanks to Matthew Liao for raising this objection.

have, e.g., to abort a bombing mission or to refuse to allow a certain physician to administer an injection. Suppose the doctor could easily find a replacement but insists on giving the injection herself. I have allowed that this may be an impermissible course of action for her. Nonetheless, her medical supervisor may have no obligation to stop what she is doing. If its impermissibility stems simply from the fact that the doctor is needlessly acting badly by doing something otherwise permissible but with bad intentions, and if the bad intentions do not adversely affect the patient, then the supervisor may plausibly say that this is the doctor's own business and allow it. And in the other case, where no other doctor is available and it thus remains permissible and even obligatory for this doctor to give the injection, there is obviously no problem with the supervisor requiring her to do so, despite the fact that the doctor will be acting badly in giving the injection. The absurd implications cited by critics are therefore once again avoided.[19]

D. Finally, before leaving this section, it is worth noting one further complication. Like Thomson and Scanlon, I have focused my discussion of permissibility on what Matthew Hanser (2005) helpfully calls "adjectival permissibility judgments": judgments that ø-ing is permissible, or that it is permissible to ø, or permissible for A to ø, where ø-ing stands for an act-type (such as bombing the munitions plant). There are also, however, what Hanser calls "adverbial permissibility judgments," where we're concerned with whether or not A *acted permissibly*, or *acted permissibly in ø-ing*, where ø-ing stands for an agent's concrete action. I have generally avoided the adverbial construction because I believe it is derivative and tends to be unhelpful or even misleading: we can say everything we need to say, and with maximal clarity, using a combination of adjectival permissibility judgments (in connection with act-types) and judgments about acting well or badly (in connection with concrete actions). Talk of agents "acting permissibly" or not tends to blend together issues that I think Rachels, Thomson, and Scanlon are right to insist be kept distinct, as it uses the language of permissibility or

---

[19] The above position on third parties—e.g., that they might reasonably command, advise or allow an agent to do something that will constitute acting badly, or even something impermissible for them to do—is similar in spirit to both Hanser's (2005: 465–6) and McMahan's (2009: 356–8) positions on this issue.

impermissibility to refer to what is in fact just a close approximation to what I have meant by talk of acting well or badly.[20]

Hanser, for example, agrees with the adjectival judgment that the nasty munitions plant bomber does what is *permissible* in bombing the plant, despite his bad intentions, but says that he nonetheless *acts impermissibly* in doing so, meaning that *he acts for reasons that are insufficient* on moral grounds to justify him in doing what he does (an illustration of what Hanser calls the "inferential account of permissibility," focused on adverbial permissibility judgments). I think the latter point—the negative adverbial evaluation of the concrete action—is more accurately expressed by saying that the agent *acts badly* in doing what he does (though Hanser is right to point out that this cannot simply be identified with the agent's being *at fault*, which is a different issue). I have argued, for example, that while the nasty pilot *acts badly* in *every* case where he flies the mission, in one case (where there is no other pilot available) it is permissible (even required) for him to do it while in another (where there are other pilots available) it is impermissible for him to do it. It muddies the waters to describe this by saying that he *acts impermissibly* in every case (since he's acting on the wrong reasons), though in one case *it is permissible for him to do what he does* while in another it is impermissible for him to do what he does. Better to keep permissibility—both in general and connection with a particular agent, as in these cases—distinct from the issue of acting well or badly in how a concrete action is carried out.

A final case nicely illustrates the problems with the adverbial construction. Suppose a certain bomber assigned to destroy a munitions plant isn't even aware of the tactical justification and thinks he is being sent on a terror bombing mission using the destruction of the munitions plant as the most efficient way to kill nearby civilians with the fallout from the explosions; he accepts the mission happily. Does he *act permissibly?* It does indeed sound odd to say this, of course, since it is only *accidental* that his act overlaps with the justified tactical bombing,

---

[20] Hanser's subtle discussion deserves greater attention than I can give it here, though I will say a little more about it in the text. There is in fact a great deal of substantive agreement between our overall positions (see esp. 450–7). The main disagreement is over which form of permissibility judgment is fundamental. Hanser takes adverbial judgments to be fundamental, whereas I see them as dispensable—not because the relevant evaluations of concrete actions aren't important, but because I think it's better to handle them in the way I've suggested.

and of course he acts badly by intending to kill civilians, all of which makes talk of "acting permissibly" problematic, since again the latter is closely bound up with the idea of acting well. But saying instead that he *acts impermissibly* is also misleading, as it at least suggests the claim that what he is doing is impermissible: bombing the munitions plant is permissible for others to do, but not for him to do. That's not right either. It's better to say simply that *he does something that, narrowly described ("bombing the munitions plant"), it is permissible to do, but for the wrong reasons, thus acting badly.*[21]

4. THE INDISPENSABILITY OF THE DDE

Suppose Scanlon accepts that my version of the DDE gives proponents everything they want while escaping his objection. He may nonetheless remain unconvinced of its truth, maintaining that we simply don't *need* the DDE in order to explain anything. We can, he thinks, fully explain all the relevant cases without appeal to the idea that intending harm to innocents is specially morally problematic. If he were right, while this wouldn't be decisive, it would at least take some of the wind out of the DDE's sails. I want to conclude, then, by showing that the alternative principle he proposes for the central cases we've been considering turns out merely to hide an implicit appeal to intention in its underlying justification: it may be plausible, but if we ultimately need to fall back on an appeal to intention to explain its plausibility, then he has not really supplied an alternative after all. The other principles he mentions likewise fail to undermine the importance of the DDE.

---

[21] I said above that Hanser's talk of "acting permissibly/impermissibly" is a close approximation to my talk of "acting well/badly." They are not, however, entirely equivalent. Suppose an akratic villain lets his victim go free and does so for the right reasons but thinking that they are bad reasons: he does what is permissible (even required), and for the right reasons, but only through weakness of will, failing to do what he (wrongly) thinks is right. On Hanser's view, he not only does what is permissible but also *acts permissibly*, since the reasons on which he acts are the right ones (2005: 454). Inasmuch as akrasia is a form of practical irrationality, however, he surely *fails* to *act well* despite doing the right thing for the right reasons. "Acting permissibly" and acting well thus come apart. Again, I'm not convinced we need a notion of acting permissibly in the first place: we can handle cases like this one just by saying that the agent (i) does what is permissible, (ii) for the right reasons, but (iii) still acts badly by acting akratically.

Scanlon's alternative proposal is that it is permissible to use deadly force in war "only when its use can be expected to bring some military advantage such as destroying enemy combatants or war-making materials" (Scanlon 2008: 28). This is a constraint on the justification of the use of deadly force in war, and is supposed to show that bombing the munitions plant may be acceptable as an exception to the general rule against doing something that will harm innocents, since it may be justified by a military objective, while terror bombing is not acceptable, since killing non-combatants is not a military objective. So he thinks he has explained the relevant intuitions without any appeal to intention. This will not do, however. Although there is no *proximate* military objective for destroying a village, such an act does serve more *remote* military objectives such as weakening military recruitment and turning public sentiment against the war. And the ultimate military objective of *defeating the opposing military force* is clearly served by destroying the village, spreading terror, and undermining support. So terror bombing does after all destroy something of significant strategic or military value to the enemy, bringing a military advantage, which means that the proposed constraint does not yet succeed in ruling it out.

Scanlon's principle would have to be strengthened to say that the use of deadly force in war is permissible only when justified by a *proximate* military objective or advantage, such as destroying a munitions plant; and since there is no proximate military objective or advantage in destroying a village, terror bombing is impermissible. This is better and I agree with it. But now the question is: how are we to *justify* this intuitively plausible principle? It does not make explicit reference to intentions, but can this principle itself be justified without falling back precisely on such an appeal? Scanlon will seek to motivate this principle by distinguishing between combatants and non-combatants: non-combatants are non-threats, and so have a different status from combatants: because they are non-threats, non-combatants are simply not appropriate targets of violence.[22] Again, this is all very plausible.

---

[22] In an earlier draft of the material in (2009: 29), Scanlon puts the point here by saying: "The civilians who would be killed in such a raid are not 'military targets' even if killing them would hasten the end of the war" (ms. p. 24). That they are not *military* entities, i.e., combatants, is already obvious and does not by itself settle the normative questions here. The important claim here is that *inasmuch as they are not combatants they are not appropriate targets of military violence.* That is entirely correct, but as discussed in the text that follows, *why*

But *targeting* is an intentional notion: it means *intentionally aiming at.* So what we're saying is that because non-combatants are non-threatening, and so relevantly innocent, it is not appropriate to intentionally aim our violence at them, which amounts to intending their harm as a means or as an end. And this brings us right back to the DDE and its constraint on justification: any proposed justification of a bombing mission by appeal to the fact that it will kill non-combatants is a bad one because it violates the adequacy condition at the heart of the DDE, and it does so because of the inappropriateness of intending harm toward innocents as a means.

To put the point another way, Scanlon agrees that a pilot acts badly if he takes the fact that civilians will be killed as a *reason to carry out the mission*, rather than as a reason *against* it that needs to be overcome. But why is that? Because non-combatants aren't appropriate targets of violence, not being of direct military significance. But why must they be of direct military significance to be appropriate targets? A consequentialist will point out that the non-combatants killed through tactical bombing are just as innocent as those killed through terror bombing (it's not fair that *any* of them should have to die), so if we've decided that the end nonetheless justifies the sacrifice of the former, why shouldn't it equally justify the sacrifice of the latter, by whatever means? Scanlon's principle offers no non-question-begging help here. To answer these questions we need to fall back on the principle about intending harm: non-combatants are not of direct military significance, and so are relevantly innocent, and it is inappropriate to *intend* harm against innocents *even* for good ends (and even where it might be appropriate to tolerate similar harm as a side-effect), for the reasons given earlier in defending the principle in (ii). That's why non-combatants aren't appropriate targets of violence.[23]

Scanlon's proposed constraint on justification therefore turns out to be just a disguised form of precisely the constraint on justification provided by the DDE as I have defended it: the difference is just that

this is so—i.e., why non-combatants do not fall under the class of exceptions to the prohibition against the use of *deliberate* deadly violence even while they *may* permissibly be killed as a matter of collateral damage—is precisely what needs to be explained. This is where the DDE comes in.

[23] Thanks to Matthew Liao again for pressing me to clarify my response to Scanlon on these issues.

the DDE brings out the deeper justification behind that constraint, telling us why candidate justifications of terror bombing are ruled out, even where they would serve remote military objectives, by telling us *why* the distinction between combatants and non-combatants matters when it comes to deciding how to target violence. Scanlon's alternative principle turns out not to be an alternative at all: he simply leaves out the deeper justification behind the intuitive principles to which he appeals, which involves the familiar thought about intention and harm. Oddly, he admits that he has "not offered any defense of these principles or an explanation of their moral status... [and] not offered any explanation or justification for the importance they attach to the distinction between combatants and non-combatants" (2008: 32). This makes it puzzling how he could claim to have showed that "these principles need not be understood as making permissibility depend upon intent" (32). For that, he would need to provide alternative principles *and* justifications for them that clearly involve no appeal to intention of the sort endorsed by the DDE.[24]

Finally, it is important to be clear about the dialectical situation here. Defenders of the DDE do not claim that it accounts for *all* non-consequentialist intuitions about cases. Philippa Foot (1967) showed long ago that many cases for which the DDE was once thought necessary can better be handled by other principles, such as one appealing to the distinction between doing and allowing, or negative and positive rights and duties. At best, the DDE should be understood as one principle among others, pointing to one factor among many that at least *sometimes* affect an act's permissibility, all depending on the *contextual interactions* among them.[25] The claim is just that the intend/

---

[24] Notice also that Scanlon's summary claim that the defender of the DDE has things backwards in the case of the terror bomber cannot be right. He says: "The intention is wrongful because the act intended is wrongful, and the act is wrongful because of its likely consequences, not (fundamentally) because of the intention" (29). Even apart from the justificatory problems just raised above, this claim is falsified by our nasty munitions plant bomber: all agree that his intention is wrongful, but this is clearly *not* "because the act intended is wrongful," at least on Scanlon's view (as well as my own): we're agreed that bombing the munitions plant is *permissible*, which means that the problem with the agent's intention cannot be a consequence of the impermissibility of the act. It should instead be explained just as the defender of the DDE claims.

[25] Kamm (1996, 2007) has stressed the importance of contextual interaction in thinking about normative ethical factors. While this point is now typically recognized in connection

foresee distinction sometimes does make a moral difference, so that if we ignore it we will lack a complete account of certain important judgments about permissibility as well as about degrees of badness of wrong actions. It is therefore no strike against the DDE if we can often come up with other factors that are sufficient to explain the impermissibility of certain acts without appeal to bad intentions. In some cases, we may simply have overdetermination: appeal to a person's rights to her own organs, for example, may sufficiently explain the impermissibility of forcibly taking her organs to use to save others, but the associated intention of harm may equally suffice or at least contribute to that impermissibility, as well as to the degree of badness of the action.[26] In other cases it may be that other factors alone account for impermissibility, as Scanlon suggests in reconsidering various cases he has discussed and proposing other wrong-making factors to explain them: even if he is right about many of these cases, this poses no problem for the DDE.

Scanlon also objects to the DDE on the grounds that in certain contexts intending harm as a means may not be impermissible after all, citing Thomson's (1985) "loop variant" of the trolley case (where turning the trolley onto a side track would do no good were it not for one large person on that track, since the track loops back around such that the trolley would just continue on to hit the five from behind were it not for being stopped by the one). This is problematic for two reasons. First, it's far from obvious that the moral claim here is true in the first place: Michael Otsuka (2008), for example, has given strong reasons to doubt that turning the trolley in loop cases is permissible.[27]

---

with the doing/allowing distinction, it seems often to be forgotten in connection with double effect, as illustrated below.

[26] With regard to the last point, it may be that given two impermissible acts one will be *worse* to the extent that performing it for the reasons given in the best available (though still insufficient) justification for it would necessarily involve intending harm toward innocents, while the other does not have this feature. For example, while it may be impermissible both to kill one for her organs (intending harm as a means) and to run over someone trapped on a narrow road on the way to save others (foreseeing harm as a side-effect), the former may be worse than the latter at least partly because of this difference. Even where double effect fails to justify an action it may mitigate its badness (though it needn't always, as in cases of extreme callousness).

[27] Kamm (2007) takes a different tack, arguing that while it *is* permissible to turn the trolley in loop cases, this is consistent with an improved version the DDE, i.e., the "doctrine of triple effect," since turning doesn't strictly involve intending the crushing of the one, but only a weaker stance that the DTE allows. I think Otsuka successfully shows that while Kamm's new

Second, even if it *is* permissible to turn the trolley in the loop case and remains so even if we grant that it involves intending harm, all that would show is that the negative significance of intending harm may be mitigated by other contextual factors, such as the fact that the act involves merely diversion rather than initiation of a threat. This is consistent with holding that the intentional factor still makes the loop variant more problematic than the simple trolley case, and that it still suffices for impermissibility in other contexts.

5. CONCLUSION

I have argued that when properly understood, the DDE shows how intention can plausibly play a fundamental or direct, and not merely derivative, role in affecting permissibility. Intention plays this role primarily by figuring directly into the rationale for a constraint on the justification of action, though this involves no appeal to the actual intentions of particular agents, and so has no absurd implications of the sort cited by critics. There is, however, also a secondary (though still direct) way intentions can sometimes affect permissibility, which does involve the actual intentions of particular agents: an agent's bad intentions can make it the case that she will act badly even in doing something otherwise permissible, and in circumstances where she could easily avoid so acting without violating other duties (e.g., by finding a substitute) it may be impermissible for her to perform the

---

distinction is legitimate, it does not apply to this case, which remains one of intending harm and is plausibly impermissible. In further support of that position, consider *Chase Down*: you're in a car, rather than a trolley, the brakes have failed, and you're heading toward a crowd. There are steep hills on both sides and you can turn up one of them, but this in itself will do no good because the car will then just roll back down onto the crowd. However, there is a large man on the hill, and if you were to run over him this would stop your car from rolling back down the hill. So you turn up the hill, toward this man. Naturally, he starts running. May you steer very carefully after him, as he runs and weaves in an attempt to get away, until you succeed in running him over? Like Thomson's loop case, this is a case of redirecting an existing threat, but it seems clearly impermissible, and the reason is that you are (literally) *aiming* at this person and his demise, using it for your purpose without his consent. The intention of harm here is admittedly more robust than in the loop case, given the ongoing adjustments you make, and in fact Kamm (2007: 97) would agree that Chase Down involves intending harm and is impermissible (cf. her *Extra Push* case). But the difference between the cases is only a matter of degree, for reasons Otsuka (2008) brings out, rather than the sort of difference in kind to which Kamm appeals. If the blatant nasty intention in Chase Down is problematic, then so is the similar type of intention in the loop case, even if less so.

act—though in other circumstances there are no such implications. This simply gives expression to the point that one always has some reason to avoid acting badly, which might sometimes (though often won't) make a choice of a certain action impermissible for one. Finally, I have tried to motivate the central principle driving the DDE and to show that Scanlon has not succeeded in providing a real alternative to explain familiar cases: his proposed principle for the war cases just involves a hidden appeal to intention in its underlying justification. It is therefore premature to dismiss the DDE as inessential, and it remains a plausible principle articulating the moral significance of the intend/foresee distinction.

REFERENCES

FitzPatrick, William (2003) "Acts, Intentions and Moral Permissibility: In Defense of the Doctrine of Double Effect," *Analysis* 63(4), 317–21.

——(2006) "The Intend/Foresee Distinction and the Problem of 'Closeness'," *Philosophical Studies* 128, 585–617.

Foot, Philippa (1967) "The Problem of Abortion and the Doctrine of the Double Effect," *Oxford Review* 5, 5–15.

Hanser, Matthew (2005) "Permissibility and Practical Inference," *Ethics* 115(3), 443–70.

Kamm, Frances (1996) *Morality, Mortality*, vol. II (Oxford University Press).

——(2007) *Intricate Ethics* (Oxford University Press).

McMahan, Jeff (2009) "Intention, Permissibility, Terrorism, and War," *Philosophical Perspectives* 23, 345–72.

Nagel, Thomas (1979) "War and Massacre," in his *Mortal Questions* (Cambridge University Press), 53–74.

——(1986) *The View From Nowhere* (Oxford University Press).

Otsuka, Michael (2008) "Double Effect, Triple Effect and the Trolley Problem: Squaring the Circle in Looping Cases," *Utilitas* 20(1), 92–110.

Quinn, Warren (1993) "Actions, Intentions, and Consequences: The Doctrine of Double Effect," in his *Morality and Action* (Cambridge University Press), 175–93.

Rachels, James (1981) "More Impertinent Distinctions and a Defense of Active Euthanasia," in Thomas Mappes and Jane Zembaty (eds.), *Biomedical Ethics* (New York: McGraw-Hill), 355–9.

Scanlon, T. M. (2008) *Moral Dimensions: Permissibility, Meaning, Blame* (Cambridge, MA: Belknap, Harvard University Press).

Thomson, Judith Jarvis (1985) "The Trolley Problem," *Yale Law Journal* 94, 1395–1415.

——(1991) "Self-Defense," *Philosophy and Public Affairs* 20, 283–310.

——(1999) "Physician-Assisted Suicide: Two Moral Arguments," *Ethics* 109, 497–518.

Walen, Alec (2006) "The Doctrine of Illicit Intentions," *Philosophy and Public Affairs* 34(1), 39–67.

Wedgwood, Ralph (2011) "Scanlon on Double Effect," *Philosophy and Phenomenological Research* 83(2), 464–72.

6

Kantian Intuitionism as a Framework for the Justification of Moral Judgments

ROBERT AUDI

Intuitionism in ethics has often been thought to lack a way to unify the plural standards it endorses. It has also been taken to have at best meager resources for explaining how we should resolve conflicts between prima facie obligations. On this resolution problem, W. D. Ross appealed to Aristotelian practical wisdom. He argued that neither Kantian nor utilitarian ethics (the two most promising rival views he considered) offers an adequate alternative.[1] There is, however, an interpretation of Kant's humanity formula of the categorical imperative for which this negative assessment is unduly pessimistic. This paper will show why. I am not implying, however, however, that dependence on Aristotelian practical wisdom in certain cases is a fatal defect in a Rossian intuitionism. There are, moreover, many cases of conflicting obligations for which, even if practical wisdom is required for their resolution, there is no reasonable doubt about what should be done. In any event, no plausible ethical theory makes dealing with conflicts of obligation easy or uncontroversial; and dependence on practical wisdom is a central element in any virtue ethics and, in some ways, indispensable for practical ethics even when it is guided by a plausible moral theory of some other kind. My aim, then, is not to eliminate dependence on

---

[1] See *The Right and the Good* (Oxford University Press, 1930), esp. 18–20. It is noteworthy that Ross evaluated Kantian resources on the assumption that they must accord with Kant's view that "there are certain duties of perfect obligation, such as those of fulfilling promises . . . which admit of no exception whatever in favour of duties of imperfect obligation, such as that of relieving distress" (p. 18). Whatever the status of Kant's apparent endorsement of this implausible position, no such view is required by every plausible interpretation of the categorical imperative framework, as will be indicated by this paper.

practical wisdom but to construct a broadly intuitionist ethical theory that helps us to enhance both the unity and the applicability of the intuitively acceptable moral principles it provides. Doing this will bring more resources to guide practical wisdom than Ross and later Rossian intuitionists have provided.

I. KANTIAN INTUITIONISM AS AN INTEGRATED VIEW

In early twentieth-century intuitionism, as in much earlier intuitionist writings, three ideas have been salient. First, basic moral principles have been held to be self-evident. Second, self-evident propositions have been claimed to be unprovable. Third, as suggested by the unprovability claim—which brings to mind the idea of propositions so basic as to be Aristotelian indemonstrables—the self-evident has been represented as a category of propositions whose truth a mature rational person can "just see" and can know only by such immediate insight. All three of these views have led to criticism of intuitionist ethics. But if, as I hold in contrast to Ross, Moore, and others, many self-evident propositions can be evidenced or even proved by other propositions, the way is open both to support Rossian moral principles by appeal to a more comprehensive principle or set of principles and to characterize the self-evident in a way that makes it easy to see why self-evident propositions may be not only far from obvious but also subject to rational disagreement.[2] Ross's list of apparently basic moral principles consists of eight: they posit prima facie obligations of (1) justice, (2) non-injury, (3) veracity, (4) fidelity to promises, (5) beneficence, (6) self-improvement, (7) reparation (e.g. for injuries to others), and (8) gratitude.[3] In earlier work (2004) I have represented a modified Rossian intuitionism, including two additional

---

[2] See chapters 1 and 2 of my (2004) for references to Prichard, Moore, and Ross's claims that the self-evident is unprovable and for a detailed account of self-evidence that indicates why this requirement is mistaken. Consider a simple case: If p entails q and q entails r but r is false, then p is false. This is self-evident but readily provable. The self-evident is justifiably believable without dependence on premises, but not (in general) incapable of receiving support from them.

[3] See Ross (1930), ch. 2. In ch. 5 of my (2004) I proposed adding two further Rossian principles that express prima facie obligations of two other kinds: those of respectfulness (understood in terms of the *manner* of action as opposed to its type) and of protection and enhancement of liberty. Both are elements in the Kantian intuitionism defended in this paper and their content will be clarified by examples and other aspects of the discussion below.

principles, as a good ethical theory, but have argued that a Kantian intuitionism that integrates it with a version of the categorical imperative is still better.

The version I have mainly appealed to is the formula of humanity. This might also be called the personhood formula or, alternatively, the intrinsic end formulation. I understand it along lines that, though they reflect some important elements in Kant's ethical texts, do not presuppose a specific interpretation of Kant. In particular, I have sought to show that its negative injunction—which prohibits treating persons merely as means—is explicable in terms of "descriptive" notions, and its positive injunction, which requires treating persons as ends, is explicable, if not descriptively, then at least without dependence on moral notions.[4] Showing this is important for defending Kantian ethics as well as for providing objective anchors for these notions. If the humanity formula is to serve as one of our *basic* guides in making moral judgments, we need a way to understand its requirements that does not depend on prior moral judgments.

A proponent of Kantian ethics might accept this constraint but still object that, first, if we adequately understand the categorical imperative, it will suffice by itself to lead us to correct moral judgments in any sufficiently well described case, and, second, that as a principle of final (overall) obligation, it cannot have prima facie principles (such as Rossian ones) as consequences.[5] Regarding the first, suppose the categorical imperative can lead us to correct (overall) moral judgments. This could be because it enables us to weight and take adequate account of the Rossian principles and thereby the considerations that ground prima facie obligation—something people with practical wisdom would do in any case. This point indicates why the second objection fails: the categorical imperative could be so interpreted as to imply the Rossian

---

[4] I developed Kantian intuitionism in (2001b) and further in (2004), esp. ch 3. Particularly in the latter I appealed to the notion of dignity as adding a dimension to the framework; but, contrary to the suggestion of Gert (2006), I did not depend on the notion for the clarity or defense of the overall view; and I sought to clarify the notion independently, e.g. on p. 99, pp. 157–8, and pp. 176–7. For a detailed discussion of Kant's conception of duty and of the proper treatment of persons see Stratton-Lake (2002), esp. chs. 2–4.

[5] One might take act-utilitarianism to provide such a principle; e.g., one ought to do what optimizes well-being (where overriders are ruled out). On some readings of Kant, the categorical imperative yields such final obligations. Ross was at least doubtful that any such principles are sound.

principles conceived as each indicating at least one moral element crucial for applying the imperative. In applying it to determine our final obligations, we must, for example, take into account promises, human needs, and potential harms. Indeed, I doubt that the categorical imperative can adequately guide moral decision *apart* from taking account of such factors, and, on the positive side, deeds that enhance non-moral goodness. Even if it could, it would surely do so better as integrated with principles according prima facie obligating force to those and other factors.

Given the detailed development of Kantian intuitionism that I have provided in earlier work, my aim here is to extend and clarify the framework in new ways. Addressing further objections will help in this. One objection is to the effect that the categorical imperative framework is no help in deciding what to do when, as is common, there is a conflict of prima facie obligations and we need to determine what obligation is final,[6] say an obligation to keep a promise to protect property and an obligation not to harm a person who is fleeing with stolen goods. A related objection is that Kantian intuitionism leaves unclear how *close* we may come to treating persons merely as means and that, without an account of this, the humanity formula cannot provide grounds for the Rossian obligations.[7] I take these objections in turn. The response to the first partly deals with the second.

Suppose I am correct in thinking that treating a person merely as a means is roughly treating the person not just *solely* as a means but (with some qualifications) also with a disposition *not* to be concerned with any *non*-instrumental aspects of the treatment. (This negative disposition is needed to account for the force of "merely.") An example of such merely instrumental treatment might be ordering a timid and willing employee to do a risky job, with an intention to let the person struggle alone even if the job becomes highly dangerous. If, as I think plausible, such treatment is prima facie wrong—wrong-making, in another

---

[6] This is suggested by Hurka (2007), and I have responded in detail in Audi (2007). Ross (1930) implies something similar in ch. 2.

[7] This objection was formulated by Peter Wicks in correspondence. The terminology to which he reacted had "negative ideal" where I now have "negative standard" and the objection indicated that the former could create the impression that there is a prima facie obligation to *maximize* distance from merely instrumental treatment of persons. This would be both misleadingly quantitative and too strong.

terminology—and prima facie wrong even if the act-type, ordering the job done, is not prima facie wrong in the context, then we have a morally relevant factor that supports fulfilling a Rossian obligation: roughly, a prima facie obligation of sufficient weight to yield overall obligation in the absence of conflicting considerations.

A different example may help: a conflict between the obligation of veracity in making a promise and an opportunity for beneficence. Suppose that, by making a promise I do not intend to keep, I would be getting the promisee, who expects to benefit from my keeping it, to do a very good thing for a third party. Making such a promise might also manifest the relevant disposition not to be concerned with non-instrumental aspects of the treatment of the promisee, say the person's suffering from the loss of an important opportunity when I break the promise. Let us assume this. The point that in making the insincere promise one would be using the promisee merely instrumentally weighs against making the promise or, if one does make it, favors reversing one's course and keeping it after all. It also supports the promissory obligation over the obligation of beneficence (though the support may not be overriding). The decision whether to keep the promise may still not be easy, though it might be. In any case, the point is that the added moral ground—that making the insincere, manipulative promise would be, or would at least approach, treating the promisee merely as a means—is helpful and potentially determinative; the point is not that it makes all the conflict cases easy to resolve. That is something no plausible moral view will achieve.

Consider now treating someone as an end, which is mainly a matter of doing—for its own sake—something that is (and is appropriately conceived by the agent as) for the good of the other person. Suppose I have to decide whether to punish a child for bad behavior by keeping the child at home and I know this punishment is reasonable but will make the child suffer. Suppose the retributive considerations, together with the good the punishment will do for the child in the long run, are just strong enough to make the choice between punishing and simply reprimanding difficult, given the desirability of avoiding the suffering. Now suppose that I consider, prospectively, as is appropriate to making a moral decision, not just the two act-types in question—which some other person could realize—but also how I would be *treating* the child in each case. *Treatment* is a matter of my *conduct*, in a sense in which that term expresses a three-dimensional concept encompassing these diverse elements: first, the act-type I would instantiate; second, the reasons(s) for which I would perform the act; and third, the manner in which I would perform it. There are two significantly different questions here. On the question of whether giving the punishment is justified by the disobedience, the answer might be positive. On the question whether I, as opposed to someone less emotionally involved, should give it, the answer might be negative. The explanation of this difference requires analysis.

II. THICK AND THIN MORAL QUESTIONS

I propose that we conceive the question of what my conduct should be as morally thicker than the question of what act-type I should perform. One difference is this. The thicker question partly concerns the fittingness of my expectable motivation in performing the prospective act of punishment to the context in which I envisage performing it, whereas the thin question concerns not that, but mainly the fittingness of the act-type to the factors that ground the basic prima facie obligations. The latter question is roughly a first-person application of "What should *be done?*" whereas the former is a conduct-specific version of "What should *I do?*" Suppose my concern is guided by a sense of the thick, conduct question. Here are two possibilities.

First, I might see that, in punishing, I would be acting mainly *from* intrinsic motivation to contribute to the overall good of the child, whereas in simply reprimanding I would be avoiding temporary suffering on the child's part and would be motivated mainly by avoidance of this painful consequence and to some extent by a desire to avoid having to hear the anticipated screams of protest. The realization that one action would be treating the child as an end and the other would not (which is not to say it would be treating the child merely as a means) might properly tip the balance in favor of punishing.

The second possibility also concerns treatment conceived as conduct but might be such as to favor either the reprimand or yielding the decision itself to someone else. Suppose I know that I am very angry with the child. I may still think the punishment is required but may believe that I would be administering it partly out of anger, perhaps mainly so. I think, then, that I would be doing the right thing but at least not mainly for the right reason. Here one might be reminded of what Socrates is believed to have said to a slave boy: I would beat you if I were not angry. In addition to thinking I would not be acting mainly for the right reason, I might also believe I would punish *angrily*, and this expectation about the manner of my act is a further significant consideration. My conduct, then, might well not be an instance of treating the child as an end. If it would not be, then on that count it would be morally deficient.

Prospective and retrospective conduct questions

The punishment case illustrates the important point that treating persons as ends goes beyond fulfilling the obligation of beneficence, which requires, chiefly, bringing about the relevant good with an appropriate connection to an awareness of the obligation to do so (this does not entail acting from the *virtue* of beneficence, which requires that the action be based on certain elements in one's character). The obligation of general beneficence is *already* taken into account in my weighing of the overall good that the act of punishment will do in comparison with the good of avoiding the suffering it would cause. The point here (which a plausible virtue ethics might also stress) is that there is additional moral reason to treat the person with a kind of good will *and* in a manner that manifests it. There is a good in the *doing* of the right, conceived as conduct; this conduct is not just something done that *is* right.

The case does not imply that in making moral decisions, even where treatment of persons is in question, we must *always* reflect on or even attend to how we would be treating whoever is in question. Often we see clearly what we ought to do, and even how we would do it, without any need for scrutiny or reflection. There is often no need to raise the thick question. Moreover, in many cases of conflicting obligations there would be no difference of the kind in question, on any of the competing options. Nonetheless, the kind of treatment of persons we would instantiate in doing one thing rather than another is morally important. Its importance is not an element in Rossian intuitionism but is compatible with the core of that position. Taking account of the difference, moreover—and of what might be called the kind of *aretaic good* that my view thereby accounts for (a kind of good in the doing of the right)— does not require either direct voluntary control over motivation or any greater knowledge of our own motivation than we may be plausibly thought to have.[8]

The conduct question, then, is three-dimensional. It takes account of the moral assessment not just of the act-type in prospect when we make a moral decision but also of the kind of treatment of persons that we would instantiate in doing one or another thing in question; that in turn is partly a matter of our motivation and our manner of action. The thin moral question concerns simply what act-type is morally appropriate for an agent in the relevant circumstances. I am of course assuming that the same act-type, such as requiring a child to stay home, can be tokened for different reasons. This should be uncontroversial but must be stressed; for there are also *conduct-types*. Conduct is not just instantiating an act-type; it is (roughly) instantiating it for a particular set of reasons and in a particular way. But, in part because we have indirect control over why we do things—if only through our power to abstain from or delay doing them—conduct is subject to moral evaluation as part of our record.

Conduct, then, is richer than action narrowly considered, but it is also an element in our manifest accomplishments in a way traits of character are not. This places it between elements of character on the dispositional side and overt performances on the behavioral side. It tends to reveal character, but is not an element in character. It requires action, but is not a matter simply of the type of act the treatment embodies. Granted, we can give a behavioral name to an act-type instantiated in a certain way, and many act-describing terms apparently reflect a sense of the importance of some of these double-barreled types. To yell, for instance, is to speak very loudly; to pace is to walk in a certain repetitive way. But yelling and pacing can be done in different ways. There are limits to the number of ways we can control the manner of our actions, but for a huge range of act-types we can consider realizing, *how* we should do the thing in question is morally significant.

The significance of thick questions can easily be missed. Ethics is easily taken to concern just what we ought to do. It certainly concerns that. But it also concerns the kinds of reasons for which we should do what we ought to do; and, as is less widely noted and sometimes ignored, it concerns *how*—in what manner—we should do what we

---

[8] The kind and degree of our voluntary control of our reasons for acting is explored in detail in my (2009a).

ought to do. The manner of an obligatory action is not fixed even by a specification of both the obligatory act-type it tokens *and* the reason(s) for which the agent realizes it. A person of moral virtue naturally tends to do the right thing for the right reason and in the right manner; but one need not be a virtue ethicist to acknowledge the value of singling out the three dimensions of conduct as I have.

The scope and comprehensiveness of prima facie obligation

These promissory and retributive examples might give the impression that the notions of merely instrumental and end-regarding treatment simply place two more prima facie obligations on a Rossian list and hence are no help either in its unification or in dealing with conflicts of obligations. I have indeed suggested that the non-moral grounds in question—the two kinds of treatment—generate prima facie obligations and seem to do so "in their own right." Suppose this were all we could say of these grounds: that there are prima facie obligations to treat persons as ends and to avoid treating them merely as means. This is significant in itself. The obligations would be morally important by virtue of their *instantial*, as opposed to systematizing, aspects. They would figure (as illustrated) in many cases that would otherwise be difficult or impossible to decide in an intuitively satisfactory way.[9] They are, however, both different in kind from Rossian obligations, since they concern conduct rather than act-types. They are also more comprehensive than Rossian obligations. One or the other of them can be seen as applicable in all (or virtually all) instances of Rossian obligation. For all of the Rossian obligations, many kinds of fulfillments can be cases of treating someone as an end; and violations of the "negative" obligations, for instance of non-injury, fidelity, and veracity, are the kinds of actions that tend to approach treatment merely as a means.

A further point is that the notions of avoiding merely instrumental treatment and aiming at end-regarding treatment express broad negative and positive aims proper to the *institution* of morality—a *telos* of morality, as it were. They characterize, in broad strokes, some of the kinds of evils morality opposes and some of the kinds of goods it

---

[9] I leave open whether it is self-evident that the two kinds of treatment ground prima facie obligations; they can play the indicated role even it this point is not self-evident.

supports. This purposive role that the two notions partly represent is a significant unifying element for the Rossian obligations.

Regarding the second line of objection, I begin with a clarification. In speaking of the categorical imperative as usable in systematizing the Rossian obligations, I have in mind at least this minimal kind of systematization: on my interpretation of it, the imperative provides three kinds of understanding: first, a way of conceiving the obligations as partially explained in terms of the wider obligations to avoid treating persons merely as means and to treat them as ends; second a way to view the Rossian obligations as in some way derivable from it (at least with some regimentation); and third, a way of interpreting and comparing those obligations in concrete cases (as will be illustrated (especially in Section IV). I have not implied (and do not hold) that the Rossian obligations are ontically *grounded* in the obligations to treat persons as ends and never merely as means, i.e., possessed in virtue of the fulfillment of those obligations being ways of meeting the deeper, treatment obligations. Rossian principles can be true "in their own right" even if they gain support from elsewhere. This brings us to a different kind of grounding, the epistemological. I have argued for the epistemological (and axiological) *groundability* of Rossian principles: roughly, for their being *justifiable* on the basis of the categorical imperative framework I have sketched or (consistently with this) of a certain theory of value, or by integrating the two (2004, pp. 149–50). Their justifiability (and knowability), however, does not depend on the imperative or on such a theory; and their epistemic groundability in these sources does not entail (and I do not assert) the ontic point that their *truth* depends on the categorical imperative or on axiological propositions (2004, pp. 141–2).

III. THE TREATMENT OF PERSONS AND THE ROSSIAN PRIMA FACIE OBLIGATIONS

As to the particular epistemic relations I take to exist between the humanity formula as I interpret it and the Rossian obligations, the weakest is that of providing a "justificatory rationale" (2004, esp. pp. 102–3). The idea is roughly that in the light of the former, the latter can be seen as reasonable. One might argue that wherever one set of propositions provides a justificatory rationale for another set, there is a regimentation of the former which *entails* the latter or a regimented version thereof. I have left this entailment possibility open and with it the possibility of a stronger epistemic relation than providing a justificatory rationale; but I do not think that such an entailment must be presupposed in order for the rationale to yield a significant degree of justification for what it rationalizes. It should be stressed that the possibility that self-evident Rossian propositions can receive justification from other propositions does not entail that they stand in need of it: justificatory overdetermination is a possibility even for the self-evident; and, for both self-evident and other kinds of propositions, it is realized in ethics as elsewhere.

It should also be emphasized that one can take each set of propositions to provide support for the other without holding (as a coherentist might but I do not) that each justifies (or explains) the other. I do hold the conceptual thesis that each may help to clarify the other, but the kind of mutual clarification in question does not imply mutual entailment and is consistent with various epistemic and explanatory connections.[10] My epistemological thesis here is that insofar as the humanity formula (correctly) explains, or is an essential explanatory element in what best explains, the Rossian principles, it receives support. This is because a proposition's having a certain kind of explanatory power in accounting for what is justifiably believable and true provides some degree of justification for it—a kind of abductive justification. The Rossian principles thus play a justificatory role regarding the humanity formula, even though they themselves are rationalizable by appeal to it. But this role is not that of *justifying* or directly supporting the formula; it is that of constituting truths whose explanation yields justificatory support for what explains them. Explaining what is true confirms the explainer.

A remaining question is what work the notion of treating merely as a means can do when it serves (as I intend) as a negative standard which we should avoid even approaching. The idea to be clarified is, in part,

---

[10] Olson (2006) raises (though he does not pursue) the question how all the relations I posit between the intrinsic end formulation and the Rossian obligations can obtain together. He is especially suspicious regarding the compatibility of the specification relation between the latter and the former and the explanation and (overdetermining) justification relations between the former and the latter (p. 542). This section should help to justify the overall integration between the two elements that my Kantian intuitionism maintains.

that we have reasons not only to avoid actually treating people merely as means but to avoid approaching this. There are at least four cases of such approach, for a given kind of instrumental act *A* whose perform-ance would constitute treatment of some person. 1. There is *approaching A*-ing, as in taking preparatory steps to send someone on a dangerous mission for a minimal payment, while aware that one is disposed not to be concerned with any non-instrumental aspects of sending the person, such as physical injuries. 2. A second case is *continuing to A*, say continuing to keep an employee working on an increasingly dangerous task, when one is approaching such an indisposition, as where the prospect of monetary gains fills consciousness and crowds out moral scruples. 3. A third case is less directly at odds with avoiding merely instrumental treatment. It is failing to avoid conduct that foreseeably strengthens one's motivation to exploit someone. This might occur with one's employees or in close personal relationships, as where a man employs a female assistant he knows he is likely to seduce and then abandon. 4. Similarly, a fourth case is failing to take opportunities to nurture or develop motivation that enhances the likelihood of treating as ends persons one interacts with. Refusing to hear about suffering friends one could easily help might be an instance of this.

Both 3. and 4. also bear on character development. One should resist conduct that makes one callous in such a way as to incline one to act with the disposition to treat people merely as means (such conduct might include doing something that tends to cause treating persons merely as means to cover up wrong-doing). One should, by contrast, enhance one's tendency to treat persons partly as ends, and we should do this even where they must be treated *partly* as means, as is common in much of normal life. (Treating someone merely as a means may be uncommon and presumably *is* quite uncommon among decent persons, and it is ruled out by treating someone even *partly* as an end, which we may hope is common.)

Taking account of cases 1. and 2. helps in deciding overall obligation, both by adding independent support to certain options and by clarify-ing the moral status of certain prospective conduct. This has been illustrated above in the punishment and promising examples 3. and 4. reflect the secondary obligation to support fulfillment of a primary one (the obligation to avoid treating persons merely as means). Moreover, since treating a person even *partly* as an end entails that one is not treating the person merely as a means, developing a tendency to treat persons even partly as ends, which 4. enjoins, reduces the likelihood of treating them merely as means.

These clarifications of Kantian intuitionism do not provide a formula for dealing with conflicts of obligation, but they do show that the notions of merely instrumental and end-regarding treatment of persons can play positive roles both in providing a comprehensive conceptual framework for understanding the Rossian obligations and for dealing with certain conflicts between those. I do not claim that every such conflict is better dealt with in the light of those notions, but many are. A main reason for this is that in dealing with these conflicts, we may often benefit from asking thick moral questions rather than just thin ones aimed at determining what is to be done (other reasons will emerge in Section IV. This enables us to do a fuller evaluation and, often, to conduct ourselves better.

IV. REASONS FOR ACTION AND FINAL OBLIGATION

I have been presupposing that a ground of obligation, such as making a promise, is also a reason for action, but not all normative reasons are moral. I have also taken no position on the (normative) strength of moral reasons relative to other kinds.[11] The possibility of conflict between moral and non-moral reasons, such as reasons of pure self-interest, can make more difficult the overall question of what one ought to do (what *to* do, if that question is understood normatively). Non-moral reasons may not only conflict with moral ones but may also support some moral reasons against other moral reasons. Here it is enough to indicate how, on my theory, we should conceive conflicting moral reasons. Some of what is said will apply to conflicts between moral and non-moral reasons.

To begin with, I take it that there is no a priori hierarchy among the moral reasons represented by the Rossian obligations. Thus, there are

---

[11] A theory of reasons and of the possible kinds of relations that hold between moral and non-moral reasons is provided in my (2001a), e.g. chs. 5 and 6. To be sure, the notion of a *moral* reason is not sharp. For extensive discussion of the relative weights of practical reasons and, in particular Sidgwick's problem of the dualism of practical reason, see Crisp (2006), esp. ch 5.

apparently no two categories of obligation, say justice and beneficence, such that *every* obligation in one will outweigh *any* (individual) obligation in the other. An implication of this view—a kind of particularism regarding normative ethical hierarchies—is that a moral reason corresponding to such an obligation is not a priori overridden in every case of conflict with a moral reason belonging to a different category of obligation. Note, too, that even on the assumption that a reason of one kind is always overridden in a pairwise conflict with a single reason of some other kind, certain coalitions of reasons on one side might still prevail over any single reason that would always override any one member of the coalition. If, for instance, in conflict cases, any reason of non-injury were to outweigh every reason of gratitude taken by itself, some of the former taken singly might not outweigh every set of the latter.

Weighting principles

Given the ethical theory so far outlined, we might formulate some rough generalizations which might be conceived as *weighting principles* that can guide one in dealing with conflicting prima facie obligations, whether between two or more of the ten I have posited or within a single category, as where two promises conflict. (I do not take the list of ten Rossian obligations I have formulated—Ross's and the two mentioned in note 3—as necessarily complete, but it is highly comprehensive and at present I see no clear need to extend it.) What follows are several candidates for weighting principles that might be plausibly thought to hold when other things are equal in terms of these Rossian obligations. The formulations are tentative, but seem defensible on some plausible reading. I do not claim, however, that any of these principles is self-evident or even broadly a priori; nor do I claim that all are implicit in my interpretation of the humanity formula. Not all are, but each is at least harmonious with that principle. They might be viewed as *adjunctive* relative to both that and the Rossian principles. I will illustrate these weighting principles in terms of choice among singular acts, but the formulations also apply where our options are certain principles of action. They are all forward-looking, formulated with making moral decisions in mind, but their application is not limited to prospective action. They can also be used in appraising deeds already done.

The first weighting principle indicates one way in which the categorical imperative bears on Rossian obligations:

1. *Treatment of persons.* If two options we have are equally well supported by conflicting Rossian obligations, then if one option is favored in terms of our (a) avoiding treating persons merely as a means or (b) treating persons as ends (or both), then that option is preferable, other things equal, with (a) having priority (other things equal) over (b) if (a) supports one option and (b) the other.[12]

The punishment case above illustrates this principle. The thick moral question concerning appropriate conduct is central for 1; and because the focus of the principle is on conduct-types rather than act-types, it differs from Rossian principles. It is also plausible, however, even as applied only to the relevant alternatives conceived as act-types *insofar as* identifying them is a reliable guide to the kind of treatment one will engage in. It should be added that although it is perhaps not obvious that Kant viewed the obligation to avoid merely instrumental treatment as, other things equal, weightier than the obligation to treat persons as ends, this view is independently plausible and provides greater determinacy for my interpretation of the overall moral force of the humanity formula.

For some of the same kinds of reasons why it is desirable to give more than one argument for a thesis, it may be desirable, in moral matters, to have (and act on) more than one reason. In this light one might give some weight to diversity of moral considerations, as follows:

2. *Moral diversity.* If two options we have are equally well supported by the conflicting Rossian obligations, but the number of distinct

---

[12] Two points should be noted here. First, although the obligations to treat persons as ends and never merely as means overlap the obligations of manner (a wide category of Rossian obligation introduced in ch. 5 of Audi 2004), the two sets are not equivalent, and an account of the latter is helpful in clarifying the former. The obligations of manner are *performative*; the others are largely *motivational*. This is why one could be treating someone nicely in manner, even nursing injuries, yet still treating the person merely as a means, say to preserve for later enslavement. Second, it may be true that whenever obligations of manner—*adverbial obligations*, as I called these in ch. 5 of Audi (2004)—are violated, so is some value represented among the obligations of matter (including the other nine Rossian obligations). Might obligations of manner, then, reduce to those of matter? Imagine that, e.g., being beneficent covers most of the former. Still, *being beneficent* is not an act-type, and I am construing the other nine Rossian principles as designating obligatory act-types, and have stressed (esp. in 2004, pp. 179–82) that any act-type can be performed in various *ways*, and that the manner of our performances is often morally important. (Treating merely as a means and treating as an end are not act-types, however—at least not behavioral act-types—a point that goes with their comprehensiveness.) The problem of specifying the connection between the adverbial obligations and the others was posed to me by Paul Audi.

obligations or of types of obligations favoring one option is greater, that option is preferable, other things equal.

The degree of preferability in question may be slight, but taking number of obligations or of types of obligations into account seems reasonable. In part, this is a matter of always giving some weight to the variety of *kinds* of considerations favoring an action; but it leaves open whether, other things being equal, number of types of obligations is more important than the number of individual obligations. One among other considerations here is that the number of obligations corresponds to the number of moral considerations that can be cited in support of an action. It seems reasonable to give the number of such reasons some weight, in part because error is less likely and because each kind of moral reason for an act is at once a pathway to understanding why it is obligatory, a potential motivational support for it and, if it is performed for that reason, at least a partial explanation of why it is performed.

The awarding of grants and fellowships might illustrate this principle. If A and B are approximately equally good candidates for the same award, then if the number of the criteria on which A merits the award is larger than the number on which B does, then—other things equal—choosing A tends to be slightly preferable. This is not to say one is required to prefer A. I take preferability to render the relevant choice rational and morally better, but not necessarily to render every competing alternative irrational or morally wrong.

It is uncontroversial that the number of people (even other sentient beings) affected by an act is relevant to its moral appraisal. This suggests the following principle:

3. *Distributive scope: number of affected people.* If one of two options equally well supported by the conflicting Rossian obligations negatively affects a smaller number of people than another, or positively affects a larger number of people than the other option, then the first is preferable, other things equal.

This has clear application to legislative and administrative decisions. A choice between healthcare plans might illustrate the principle regarding distribution of goods; a choice between plans for wartime military conscription might illustrate it for distribution of "bads." The principle might indicate one kind of respect for what Rawls has called the "separateness of persons." Everyone matters—we are all "ends." It is not just the collective human good that is morally important. 3. is also supported by some of the considerations cited in rationalizing 2. In positively affecting more people, for instance, we may in some cases tend to fulfill a larger number of types of obligations.

Still another weighting principle reflects the moral importance of equal treatment of persons:

4. *Equality.* If one of two options equally supported by the Rossian obligations treats the persons who would be affected more nearly equally, it is preferable, other things equal.

It must be granted that since promoting justice and eliminating injustice may be matters of equality, this adds nothing to the obligation of justice where that standard calls for pursuing equal treatment. But this rule would apply even where justice is not at stake, as where two needy groups of people compete for help not *owed* to either. If, moreover, we countenance *indirect* treatment, then where two sets of charities compete for one's donation (as a fulfillment of the obligation of beneficence), and one charity distributes its benefits in a more nearly equal fashion than the other, this principle would provide a basis for preference of the former.

A sound ethics should give some kind of priority to reducing suffering over enhancing positive well-being.[13] This suggests a principle like the following:

5. *Priority of the worse off.* If one of two options equally supported by the Rossian obligations benefits one or more persons who are worse off than the person(s) benefited by the other option, then, other things equal, it is preferable, and the more so the greater the disparity in well-being, or the worse off the latter set of persons is in absolute terms.

There are many prioritarian principles that reflect what might be called the stronger moral "claim" of the worse off, and the priorities may be specified more quantitatively. This principle may be less controversial than more quantitative versions. Once again, an illustration might come

---

[13] This priority of the worse off is related to the positive and negative aspects of beneficence discussed in my (2004), esp. pp. 175–77.

from choices between serving two groups of people or between choosing between two charities or grant applicants.[14] The principle reflects the plausible idea that the relief of pain or suffering is, other things equal, morally more important than the provision of positive benefits.

One could regard 5. as implicit in a proper understanding of beneficence, but that claim is probably controversial, and some theorists might give it a different interpretation that is incompatible with 5. It should also be noted that pain often impedes autonomy in our conduct, and the importance of that point is better, or at least differently, accounted for by the value of treating persons as ends than by considerations of beneficence. In any event, explicitness is best served by including this principle separately from that of beneficence.

It is natural to regard ethics as centrally concerned with how we should conduct ourselves as social beings. In this light, the following seems to be a natural weighting principle:

6. *Reducing alienation.* If one of two options equally supported by the Rossian obligations would be alienating to one or more persons affected, or would be more so than the other, or would reduce alienation less than the other, then the latter is preferable, other things equal.

This principle might apply to a choice between two government policies or two healthcare plans for a company. Alienation need not be a kind of injury, so this principle goes beyond emphasizing non-injury. Arguably, the principle exhibits an instance of according weight to giving people the sense of being treated as ends or at least of a disposition to avoid treating them merely as means. Providing this sense may be a kind of beneficence but it is not usually considered under that heading and is plausibly taken to go beyond beneficence. To be sure, if *A*-ing is morally positive, the sense of being treated as a target of the act tends to be positive; but that point does not imply that the treatment in question is a case of, or in any event nothing more than, beneficence.

---

[14] Insofar as equal treatment is considered in some way *proportionate*, for instance to need or effort, the intuitive importance of equality gives some support to the priority principle, which has results similar to those of the equality principle interpreted to require proportionate equality. But the moral importance of preference of the worse off is an independent consideration.

Here is a plausible counterpart of 6:

7. *Coordination values.* If one of two options equally supported by the
   Rossian obligations would be superior to the other in reinforcing or
   enhancing coordination among persons, it is preferable, other things
   equal.

No doubt enhancing coordination, for example by instituting car
pooling or a grievance policy to reduce conflicts, is by and large a way
of doing good for people; but whether it actually achieves this is a
contingent matter, and this rule is not simply reducible to according
additional weight to beneficence. Given both our social nature and our
interdependence as a condition of success in much that matters to us,
coordination is an indispensable element in human flourishing taken to
be essentially social. Abiding by this principle seems warranted even by
its instrumental value in contributing to flourishing. A certain kind of
coordination among persons also has inherent value, as where a team
wins a game by mutually supporting plays. Such inherent value would
provide further rationale for treating the principle as a distinctive
element in certain moral decisions.

Higher-order normative principles

The last two principles I want to suggest are different in being higher
order than 1.–7. Both can be rationalized by appeal to the humanity
formula, but they are better understood and can be better justified if
that principle is interpreted in relation to the determinate prima facie
requirements, such as equal treatment, liberty, and beneficence, that are
explicit in the Rossian principles. Both principles concern the sorts of
reasons appropriate for a kind of action or the apparent level of one's
justification for action relative to that of someone (possibly hypothetical) who disagrees. Both are particularly important in political contexts
in which, as with legislative decisions, interpersonal discussion is crucial
in the process of determination and justification of policy.

Legislative and public policy decisions often imply coercion and
should be justifiable in a way appropriate to both the idea that liberty
is important in its own right as a morally desirable good and the idea
that interpersonal conduct should be justifiable in broadly moral terms.
Particularly in the often difficult task of balancing religious considerations and "natural reasons"—which are such that any normal rational

person can accord them some degree of normative authority (which implies their secularity)—we need a principle that indicates what kind of reason is needed.[15] Here I suggest a principle that goes beyond those so far articulated in applying where reasons not singled out by them, mainly religious ones, might otherwise be thought to have sufficient weight to justify a coercive action:

8. *The principle of secular rationale* (roughly, of natural reason): Citizens in a free democracy have a *prima facie* obligation not to advocate or support any law or public policy that restricts human conduct, unless they have, and are willing to offer, adequate secular reason (roughly, natural reason) for this advocacy or support (e.g. for a vote).[16]

Here a secular reason for an action (or for a belief) is roughly one whose status as a justifier of action (or of belief) does not evidentially depend on (but also does not deny) the existence of God; nor does it depend on theological considerations, or on the pronouncements of a person or institution *as* a religious authority. This notion is epistemic, roughly a matter of evidential grounding, not a matter of the content of the reason. We can imagine a case in which a person's reasons for action include commitments based essentially on religious convictions. Consider a promissory obligation grounded in swearing on the Bible that one will keep a promise to one's priest to oppose same-sex unions. The secular rationale principle would call for abstaining from coercion (as opposed to persuasion) in this matter apart from having an adequate reason that does not depend in this way on religion or theology. If the material welfare of children could be shown to be adversely affected by such unions, there would be a secular reason. (The adequacy condition rules out the appropriateness of certain non-religious reasons, e.g. racist ones; but the prominence and special importance of religious reasons calls for a principle like 8.)

The principle of secular rationale can be supported by a very broad one that also applies to coercion even outside the political realm:

---

[15] The notion of natural reason needs explication, and I have outlined an analysis, and in doing so taken account of Aquinas's notion of natural reason, in (2009b).

[16] This formulation is drawn from Audi (2000), p. 86, though I published essentially the same version in (1989).

9. *The principle of tolerance*: If it not reasonable for proponents of coercion in a certain matter to consider themselves epistemically superior in that matter to proponents of the corresponding liberty, the former have a prima facie obligation to tolerate rather than coerce.[17]

The principle is meant to apply where there is an actual or hypothetical disputant who is, in the matter(s) at hand, an apparent *epistemic peer* of the person, i.e. (roughly) equally rational, possessed of the same relevant evidence, and equally conscientious in assessing that evidence. This principle reflects the value of liberty—respecting which is a partly constitutive element in treating persons as ends—but it is not entailed by simply taking some degree of protection of liberty to be, like promoting the well-being of persons, an object of prima facie moral obligation. Imagine someone's making a case that certain apparent harms justify coercion, whether institutional or in personal relations, to prevent them. The principle of tolerance would call for restraint if it is not reasonable for the would-be coercer to consider the proponent of liberty epistemically inferior in relation to the issue at hand. Thus, in what might otherwise be a case in which coercion is justifiable by the balance of conflicting obligations, this principle might determine that liberty should prevail.

Each of the weighting principles may conflict with at least one other, but they may still serve to reduce the difficulty of dealing with conflicts between Rossian obligations, and in any case conflicts at the level of weighting principles may be less common or (at least often) less serious, or both. As with the Rossian obligations, I see no a priori hierarchy. In any plausible ethic, judgment on the basis of practical wisdom of a kind that need not be a matter of applying *any* principle may at some point be needed. My aim is not to eliminate the need for practical wisdom but to assist it as much as possible by formulating principles congenial to it.

Might we also have a principle framed in terms of negative and positive obligations? Might we say that where a "negative" obligation—for example one of non-injury, fidelity, or veracity—conflicts

---

[17] I cannot explicate the notion of the reasonable here, but I take it to be stronger than the concept of the rational: what is reasonable is rational but not conversely. Detailed defense of this view is provided in my (2001a), esp. pp. 149–53.

with a positive one, say an obligation of beneficence or self-improve-ment, the former takes priority, other things equal? I suspect this is too broad to be helpful (I leave open whether some other formulation in this range might be sustained). Here the problem of deciding what has to be equal is even more difficult than in the case of the other rough generalizations.

The obligation of beneficence is particularly troublesome. In a world with as much suffering as this one has and with as good means as now exist for relieving some of it by charitable contributions, it looks as if the beneficence obligations of the prosperous are very weighty. Can they be weakened by making promises to one's children and friends to commit large proportions of one's resources to them? As these cases apparently show, a blanket preference for negative obligations, even when other things are equal, does not take account of the voluntary character of many of them. It is not plausible, for instance, to regard a prosperous person's obligations of beneficence as substantially reduced by promises of support which, with a view to rationalizing the reduction of charit-able contributions, are made (but not owed) to already flourishing children. This is not to say that promises made with such an evasive aim generate no prima facie obligations; but acting for that kind of reason is morally criticizable conduct, and (as in other cases) the resulting obligations may or may not be overridden. Nor should we deny that some promises, and certain other commitments, that it is morally reasonable to make to those close to us foreseeably limit our capacity for general beneficence. The problem here may not be soluble by any single principle of the kind just illustrated, and it remains a challenge to any ethical theory.[18]

* * *

The status of ethical intuitionism depends largely on our power to perceive truth by certain kinds of non-inferential discernment. This discernment may be intuitive and may or may not be accompanied by or even based on reflection. On rationalist versions of intuitionism, even general moral principles may be directly (non-inferentially) known—

---

[18] In (2004, pp. 94–101) I have dubbed this demandingness problem *the beneficence problem* and argued that the prohibition of treating persons merely as means indicates an important element in dealing with it.

though neither indefeasibly nor in a way that is wholly unmediated by reflection.[19] As I have developed intuitionism, the required power of reason to ground non-inferential knowledge of certain moral principles is essentially like the power needed for knowledge of the a priori in general; and the power of reason regarding singular judgments is highly analogous to the epistemic powers by virtue of which we acquire perceptual knowledge. These points hold for a modified Rossian intuitionism, which I consider a good theory even when not strengthened by integration with an interpretation of the humanity formula or some other comprehensive principle.

The integration achievable by Kantian intuitionism is supported in part by axiological considerations. The comprehensive theory that reflects this further unification of ethical considerations is developed in *The Good in the Right* (2004). Even apart from that theory, this paper enables us to see how the injunction to avoid treating persons merely as means and to treat them as ends figures both in systematizing Rossian obligations and in dealing with conflicts between them. The notions of merely instrumental and end-regarding treatment help us to take account not just of act-types appropriate to a situation of choice but also of conduct and of a related distinction between thick and thin moral questions. The notion of conduct is complex, and the question what our conduct should be has both behavioral and motivational dimensions. Answering it requires more than considering options conceived as act-types or even act-types and the consequences of instantiating them. The normative framework of the overall view is also enhanced by the formulation of certain weighting principles that can often help in resolving conflicts of prima facie obligations and connect these diverse obligations with such ethically important notions as scope of distribution, equality, and social coordination. Further clarification is needed, but it should now at least be clear how incommensurable moral

---

[19] It may be thought that noncognitivism avoids the problem of determining the scope of reason in ethical matters, as suggested by, e.g., Kappel (2002), p. 411. But any plausible noncognitivist view must provide an account of what constitutes a relevant (and indeed a good) reason for holding a noncognitive pro or con moral judgment. How we might know or justifiedly believe such an account seems to me a problem in moral epistemology much akin to the kind I have been dealing with here.

considerations can be rationally compared in a way that facilitates making justified singular moral judgments.[20]

REFERENCES

Audi, Robert (1989) "The Separation of Church and State and the Obligations of Citizenship," *Philosophy & Public Affairs* 18(3), 259–96.

——(2000) *Religious Commitment and Secular Reason* (Cambridge University Press).

——(2001a) *The Architecture of Reason* (Oxford University Press).

——(2001b) "A Kantian Intuitionism," *Mind* 110(439), 601–35.

——(2004) *The Good in the Right: A Theory of Intuition and Intrinsic Value* (Princeton University Press).

——(2007) "Kantian Intuitionism and Ethical Pluralism," in Timmons, Greco, and Mele, 213–18.

——(2009a) "Moral Virtue and Reasons for Action," *Philosophical Issues* 19, 1–20.

——(2009b) "Natural Reason, Secularity, and Neutrality Toward Religion," *Religion and Human Rights* 4, 1–20.

Crisp, Roger (2006) *Reasons and the Good* (Oxford University Press).

Gert, Joshua (2006) Review of Audi, *The Good in the Right, Mind* 497(15), 121–25.

Hurka, Thomas (2007) "Audi's Marriage of Ross and Kant," in Timmons, Greco, and Mele, 64–72.

Kappel, Klemens (2002) "Challenges to Audi's Intuitionism," *Ethical Theory and Moral Practice* 5, 391–413.

Olson, Jonas (2006) Review of Audi 2004, *Philosophical Review* 115(4), 540–42.

Ross, W. D. (1930) *The Right and the Good* (Oxford University Press).

Stratton-Lake, Philip (2002) *Ethical Intuitionism: Re-evaluations* (Oxford University Press).

Timmons, Mark, John Greco, and Alfred R. Mele (eds.) (2007) *Rationality and the Good: Critical Essays on the Ethics and Epistemology of Robert Audi* (Oxford University Press).

---

[20] Earlier, quite different versions of this paper have been presented to the Philosophical Society in Oxford, at the University of Muenster, at Wake Forest University, and at the Arizona Workshop on Normative Ethics. I have benefited from discussion on all those occasions and, for helpful comments, would particularly like to thank Mark Timmons and two anonymous readers for the Press.

7

An Uncompromising Connection Between Practical Reason and Morality

MICHAEL NELSON

J. David Velleman has argued for *compromised Kantianism* (Velleman 2004). The view is Kantian as it entails that only irrational agents act immorally. It is compromised as it allows that there are immoral but rational acts. On Velleman's view, the rationalist is right that only irrational agents act immorally and the arationalist is right that not all immoral action is irrational, as the weight of practical reason favors immorality in certain circumstances. I argue that this middle position is unmotivated, defending thoroughgoing moral rationalism, according to which every autonomous agent has most reason to do as morality requires and thus immoral action is always contrary to reason. I end by discussing Broome's widescopism about practical requirements, as it relates to Velleman's compromise, and defend the Kantian claim that the moral law is self-legislated against Velleman's objections.

While my overt aim is to respond to Velleman's arguments against moral rationalism, my discussion has broader significance. First, I defend moral rationalism by arguing that morality is grounded in a purely explanatory conception of practical reason. This is a novel approach, as standard defenses of moral rationalism take a normative conception of practical reason as basic. Second, I offer an account of how "should"-clauses detach from conditionals with merely factually true antecedents. This is of interest to the moral rationalist because it renders the claim that morality is authoritative for all autonomous agents consistent with the claim that some autonomous agents are also subject to anti-moral requirements. The view also allows us to solve a number of puzzles about practical requirements, which is of interest independently of moral rationalism.

Velleman's compromise is grounded in a skepticism concerning the scope of morality and morality's relation to reasons for action. Some agents, Velleman believes, lack reasons to be moral. These agents act immorally but not contrary to practical reason, as moral considerations fail to have overriding weight for them. So, in acting immorally, they do not act contrary to the weight of reasons that apply to them.

One alleged "hard case" is G. A. Cohen's Mafioso (Cohen 1996). Because of the kind of person he has become and the set of concerns, values, and commitments he has developed, what the Mafioso has most reason to do is break the fingers of the person late with his loan payments. Morality, we will suppose, requires that he not. Velleman thinks that the Mafioso lacks reason to do as morality requires. The weight of reason, for him, lies entirely in breaking the fingers; a lesson needs to be taught and a clear message sent. We are led, then, to compromise. The Mafioso lacks reason to be moral and so does not act irrationally, in the sense of acting contrary to the weight of reason, in doing what morality forbids. He is irrational for having become the sort of person he is, but does not act irrationally in breaking the borrower's fingers.

One claim that Velleman's case requires is that the Mafioso has most reason to break the borrower's fingers. A weaker claim is that, because of his contingent practical identity, the Mafioso has reason (although perhaps not *most* reason) to break the borrower's fingers. Cohen would not agree with either claim. Cohen introduced the Mafioso case to demonstrate that not all threats to one's practical identity generate obligation in any sense, even the weak *pro tanto* sense capsulated by the weaker claim. While letting the person off with a gentle warning may violate the Mafioso's conception of himself, still, that's what he should do, as that conception of who he is does not generate or support genuine reasons for action, those seeming reasons being silenced by morality.

I think that the strong claim is false and that the weak claim is true. So, I agree with Velleman and against Cohen that the Mafioso is subject to a practical requirement, stemming from his contingent concerns, cares, and values constitutive of his practical identity, to teach the person a lesson by breaking his fingers. This is because our practical identities provide us with reasons for action and at least some of these reasons give rise to practical requirements. But I also agree with Cohen and against Velleman that the Mafioso has *most* reason to not break the borrower's fingers. I argue that what even the Mafioso *really* should do is what morality requires. My view is that the Mafioso is subject to conflicting practical requirements and both moral requirements and the requirements stemming from his practical identity carry force, although moral requirements are overriding and so more weighty.

An agent can have both a reason to Φ and a competing reason to not-Φ in the same set of circumstances. Here I sit in front of a plate of cookies. They are delicious and I want to eat them. I have reason to eat the cookies. But I also know that they are for my daughter's party, so eating them would make her sad. So I also have reason to not eat the cookies. Almost everyone agrees that an agent can have competing and conflicting reasons for action. I am assuming a view where these reasons for action are transformed into practical requirements, associated with 'ought'-claims and so things the agent should do, when those reasons stem from things the agent cares about, values, or are based in aspects of her practical identity.[1] And the practical requirements an agent is subject to can conflict just as the reasons an agent has can conflict.

I argue for my position regarding the Mafioso in stages. I begin by arguing, very briefly, that the Mafioso is subject to a genuine practical requirement to break the borrower's fingers that stems from his contingent practical identity as a Mafioso (Section 2). I then argue, contrary to Velleman, that that requirement is overridden by moral considerations, which are authoritative even for the Mafioso (Sections 3–5). This argument constitutes the heart of the paper. In these sections I largely set the Mafioso to the side and argue for a general connection between autonomous practical reasoning and morality. All autonomous agents, I argue, are subject to the demands of morality. Insofar as our Mafioso is an autonomous practical reasoner, then, he too is subject to the demands of morality. Together with the claim that contingent practical identities generate practical requirements, this entails that the Mafioso is

---

[1] Thanks to an anonymous referee and Justin Coates for helping me sort through what I mean by a "practical requirement" and how it relates to reasons for action.

subject to conflicting requirements to both break and not break the borrower's fingers. I return to the topic of conflicting restrictions in Section 6, offering a solution to the threat of contradiction.

2. PRACTICAL IDENTITIES

One's self-conception is the set of properties that define one's practical identity and sense of what one is.[2] These changing conceptions enable one to both understand and govern one's decisions and behavior. Because I conceive of myself as my children's father, otherwise possible actions are unthinkable in deliberation and otherwise merely possible actions are nonoptional. My self-conception provides both important inputs and structure for my deliberation, framing the considerations that I bring to bear in my deliberations and helping determine their weights. Because of my self-conception, I do not need to start afresh every time I deliberate, choosing every factor dependent on my choice; I can simply take certain factors as given, which is necessary for finite beings like ourselves to navigate the complex world we live in. One's self-conception provides reasons for action and generates practical requirements precisely because, then, they play these structuring roles in practical deliberation. (I have helped myself to material from Velleman 2001, 2006a, 2006b.[3]) The considerations for acting connected to one's practical identity are not *mere* reasons for acting, considerations that *could* explain and justify one's behavior, like the pleasant aroma of food noticed when one does not feel like eating. The considerations connected to one's practical identity don't present themselves as mere invitations but as demands, precisely because of their

---

[2] I say *what* and not *who*. One's practical identity is not constitutive of one's personal identity. One's conception of what one is often changes quite drastically across time while one's identity as a person—who one is—remains the same. I might have conceived of myself first as a defiant teenager and then a parent. My conception of what I am varies yet my identity as a person remains the same. Even at a time I may have different, and perhaps conflicting, (at least dispositional) conceptions of what I am that become operative in different circumstances.

[3] Unlike Velleman (2006b), I do not think that one's self-conception provides one with an individuation of who among the world's population of persons one is and is not involved in one's self-thoughts. One does not individuate oneself in thought qualitatively. One's self-thoughts are directly about the person that one is, singling out a particular person merely in virtue of the metaphysical fact about the identity of the person doing the thinking and independently of one's conceptions.

connections to what we find important and valuable and our sense of what we are.

3. PRACTICAL REASON

So, I agree with Velleman that the Mafioso is subject to a practical requirement to break the person's fingers because of his self-conception as a Mafioso. But I disagree with Velleman that he is not also subject to a moral requirement to not break those fingers. Velleman's earlier view of practical reason (1996, 2000), I shall argue, provides the basis for an argument that all autonomous practical reasoners are subject to the demands of morality, although Velleman does not develop the view in this manner and has renounced these implications in later work (2009).

According to Velleman, practical reason is animated by an aim to act in accordance with reason. Velleman argues that to be motivated to act in accordance with reason is to be motivated to make sense of one's behavior, to have an explanation of what one is doing and why one is doing it. It is thus, as a starting point, an explanatory, not normative, aim. This is important as a thick, normative conception of agency is not presupposed but instead derived. Thus, the normative commitments that are squeezed from this starting point are less susceptible to skeptical doubt, insofar as even a skeptic grants a constitutive connection between practical reason and explanation.

Let's first see how this aim to make sense of oneself works and then turn to the argument, in the next two sections, that a commitment to morality follows from it. When I plan to raise my hand, I have in mind a goal the arm raising is thought to achieve. I explain the arm raising in terms of the end it is aiming at or constitutive of. The behavior is nonarbitrary, in at least the minimal sense that I, however implicitly, have available as I act some explanation of why I am so behaving. Without considerations that would explain why I am so behaving involved in the production of my behavior, I am a mystery to myself and my behavior cannot be seen as stemming from me. But things don't stop there. Unlike my cats, I don't have my ends simply given by instinct and bodily needs. I can reflect on and choose my ends; for better and sometimes worse, reason is involved in the adoption of ends.

Complete self-governance requires a complete explanation of what one is doing and why.

Granting that there is a connection between self-governance and explanation, the next question is what constitutes a complete explanation of what one is doing and why that is necessary for self-governance. In the following two sections I argue that the aim of making sense of oneself puts rational pressure on an autonomous agent to act only on considerations that can at the same time be consistently willed as universal law. Assuming without argument that morality requires that we only act on considerations that are universalizable, this result entails that any autonomous agent is under the authority of morality, providing her with a reason to act in accordance with its dictates. This constitutes my defense of the claim that all autonomous agents have reason to act morally, which undermines Velleman's compromise, as Velleman's case assumes, as we saw above, that some agents like the Mafioso are not subject to the demands of morality.

4. UNIVERSALIZATION

A reason for acting is a consideration in light of which an agent can make sense of what she is doing. (I shall argue that a consideration *justifies* action only if it, in the first instance, sheds explanatory light on what is happening. Its normative force, then, derives from its explanatory force.) Insofar as the agent acts autonomously in acting on a consideration, the consideration's effectiveness in producing behavior must be compatible with the agent being the nonarbitrary source of that behavior. In that case, the consideration must be seen as speaking for the agent. So, an agent's acting autonomously constrains what considerations she acts on: The considerations must shed explanatory light on what she is doing and why and be consistent with her viewing her behavior as flowing from herself. I now argue that considerations that fail to be universalizable fail to meet these conditions. I support this first by considering cases of nonautonomous action, trying to isolate what they lack.

I begin with unconscious motives. (Velleman 1992, 2000 uses such cases to illustrate the distinction between "full-blooded" human action and mere intentional behavior, which is related to my distinction between autonomous action and different forms of nonautonomous action.) I find myself in front of the local ice cream store while out for a walk. Later reflection tells me that I have been, from the beginning, guided by the aim of securing a treat. I unconsciously decided to get a treat and set out to realize that intention unaware of its presence. Because its operation was unconscious, I cannot see my behavior as both directed by that intention and stemming from myself. My behavior is intentional but not autonomous. In order for an intention's functioning in deliberation and action to count as my controlling my deliberation and action, I must be, at some level and however implicitly, aware of its operation at the time of action.

Unconscious motives provide one class of intentional, nonautonomous action. But there are other cases where the motive is perfectly conscious but its role in the production of behavior does not amount to the agent's guidance of her behavior. Consider first Harry Frankfurt's unwilling addict (Frankfurt 1971). The unwilling addict chooses to perform complex intentional actions, guided by the aim of getting high. Her behavior is done for reasons and she is aware of the existence and operation of the motives that animate her drug-taking behavior. But, for all that, she is not really in control of herself. Because of her alienation from those motives, explaining her behavior in light of them excludes her from being the source of her behavior. Acting autonomously requires that the behavior in question flow from the agent's sense of what to do while the unwilling addict's behavior flows from alien, because rejected and disvalued at the time of action, motives. Such cases show that there is a wedge between minimal notions of acting for reasons, acting intentionally, and acting intelligibly, on the one hand, and a more robust notion of acting autonomously.[4]

---

[4] The cases of unconscious and alien motives, which I think never involve autonomous action, should be distinguished from cases of habituation, which are sometimes instances of acting autonomously. For example, a boxer works drills until certain counter combinations are "automatic." Throw a straight right and Billy immediately fires back a left hook, without thought and reflection. Because the habit was formed intentionally through work with an aim of having the behavioral sequence unfold in the given circumstances, it is plausible to view the resulting habituated behavior as fully chosen by the agent, even if the behavior is not the effect of deliberation at the time of action. Furthermore, habituated behavior can be overridden, suggesting that the agent in fact is still in deliberative control of her behavior. The deliberation acts as a chaperone, as it were, ready to step in when things don't work out as they should. To return to the boxing case, if one's habituated counter is effectively countered by one's

Consider next cases of perversity. Perversity comes in degrees. Milder forms are cases of clear-eyed weakness, where one acts of one's own free will on considerations that one judges, at the time of deliberation and action, to be outweighed, in the circumstance, by competing considerations. I grab another cookie of my own free will. I am not overrun by passion; I do not act compulsively. But I am not identified with the motives that move me. Even while I reach out and start chewing, I really wish I wouldn't and despise my weakness. These cases demonstrate two points. The first concerns Frankfurt's claim of the connection between identification and acting of one's own free will.[5] The second concerns my main claim that there is pressure for universalization constraining the forms of explanation compatible with acting autonomously. I discuss each in turn.

Frankfurt employed the notion of identification in an account of acting of one's own free will. While Frankfurt didn't fully spell out what he thinks is involved in addiction, it is plausible that addiction undermines freedom of the will. An addict's motives determine her behavior independently of her own determination of what to do. So, the unwilling addict does not act of her own free will. This contrasts with cases of ordinary weakness. The phenomenology is that I simply *allow* myself to be determined by my desire for sweets—I am not overrun by rebellious motives—and so I act of my own free will. In both cases, the agent acts independently of her evaluative determination, but only in cases of addiction does the agent fail to act of her own free will.

The distinction between the unwilling addict and the person who willingly acts contrary to her evaluative judgments is related to Watson's

---

opponent, one readjusts and suppresses the habituated response through deliberative control. Billy doesn't continue to fire his habituated hook when Sam uses his straight right to open Billy for an upper cut. Such actions then are not really automatic in the sense incompatible with being autonomous and under deliberative control.

[5] This connection is made in Frankfurt's early work: in particular, (Frankfurt 1971, 1977, 1987). In (1992), Frankfurt introduced the notion of satisfaction into his analysis of acting of one's own free will. An agent is satisfied with a motive or consideration just in case she is not concerned to oppose that motive or consideration. In (1994) and particularly (2004), Frankfurt's view of autonomy changed more drastically, turning from higher-order desires and satisfaction to the attitudes of concern and love. My description of Frankfurt in the text focuses on Frankfurt's earlier views.

distinction between compulsion and weakness (Watson 1977).[6] The distinction proves problematic for Frankfurt's claim that acting on a motive with which one is identified is necessary for acting of one's own free will, as the merely weak agent acts of her own free will but on a motive with which she is not identified. Furthermore, weakness is compatible with moral responsibility; the weak, but arguably not the compelled, agent is morally responsible for her behavior.

Identification is not necessary for acting of one's own free will and being morally responsible. But, I will argue, acting *autonomously* does require being identified with the motives that move one. Frankfurt did not distinguish between acting of one's own free will and acting autonomously, which hampered his ability to do justice to the distinction between the unwilling addict and the merely weak agent. That failure also kept him from seeing the real role identification plays in the proper functioning of human agency.

Because I judge it better to not eat the cookies, I judge myself to have not done what I should. I am normatively deficient. But I am also a bit of a mystery to myself. The problem I have isn't *just* a normative problem, but an explanatory problem; indeed, on my view, it is a normative problem because it is an explanatory problem. "Why am I doing this?" I ask, without being able to adequately answer. Sure, the behavior has *something* going for it; it isn't like sticking tacks under my fingernails, which really has nothing to say in its favor. The wonderful taste and fabulous sensations of eating the cookies in some sense render my behavior intelligible. The behavior isn't aimless; it is directed at some end that has something to be said for it. Furthermore, given my past similar action, it is hardly surprising that I broke down; I always seem to when faced with a plate of cookies and a little free time. But there is still a mystery. What remains unexplained is why I am allowing myself to be directed by those considerations. Citing the pleasant

---

[6] Watson doubts that this distinction concerns whether or not the agent is able to resist the contrary motive. Instead he argues that the distinction is irreducibly normative and concerns whether or not the agent gave in to a passion that the possession of the normal degree of self-control would enable one to resist. The appeal to normality renders the analysis relative to expectations and norms. While I cannot adequately defend the point here, I think that a modal account of the difference between the compulsive and weak actor is viable, as the assessment of what an agent is able to do is in part determined by the factors Watson draws our attention to. Watson's rejection of the modal account rests on an overly simplistic semantics of "ability"-claims.

sensations and good flavors fails to make sense of *my* guiding my behavior. They provide a mere psychological explanation that is not compatible, in light of my negative assessment of the weight of those considerations, with my being the source of my actions. They are not connected up with my other views to properly enable me to make sense of myself as in control of my behavior while acting on those consider-ations. It is only when I deem a consideration as authoritative that my choosing to guide my behavior by it makes complete sense and has an explanation consistent with my self-determination. Absent endorsement of a motive, then, I do not act autonomously in acting on it. While noting my weak nature and recalling all the past times I acted in similar ways may make my behavior predictable and reveals something about me, in the end it only makes my failure all the more mystifying, as I still have no account of why I ever allow myself to be ruled by something I deem unfit to lead. Being defeated by an alien force I could not resist, as the compulsive agent is, is one thing while willingly giving into a consideration I deem to be outweighed is another.

When one voluntarily acts contrary to one's evaluative outlook, we cannot simultaneously see that behavior as being based on the deemed lesser considerations—the considerations that the cookies taste good, in the example above—and as stemming from the agent herself. This is particularly clear when considered from the first-person—*Why am I eating these cookies? Sure, they taste good, but my view is that I still shouldn't eat them. I see that reason as being outweighed. Sure, I always eat cookies left in front of me, but why do I do that given that I think I shouldn't and have the capacity to resist?* But the mystery remains in the third-person perspective, as someone cannot both act autonomously and act contrary to her conception of what she should, in the sense of what the weight of reason favors, do. They may be morally responsible for their behavior, when they were not compelled to act as they did, but they are not self-governing. So, I claim, there is a constitutive connection between acting autonomously and acting from one's evaluative perspective.

I have argued that acting autonomously requires acting from one's evaluative perspective. But then there is rational pressure to act from one's evaluative perspective in virtue of one's being an autonomous agent. Autonomy is the default position of practical deliberation. While we can fall short of our autonomy by acting nonautonomously, whenever we are making choices, we are subject to the demand to act autonomously. I argued above that one of the conditions of acting autonomously is the demand to act from one's evaluative judgments, acting only on motives with which one is identified. So, in virtue of our autonomy, we are subject to the demand of acting from our evaluative judgments.[7]

To summarize: I act of my own free will in eating the cookies but I do not act autonomously. I don't act autonomously because I act on a motive with which I am not identified. I am not identified with the effective motive because I judge it to not be among the best things to do given the circumstances. There is a constitutive connection between acting autonomously and acting from one's evaluative perspective, as only then can one have a complete explanation of why one is acting as one does consistent with viewing that behavior as being self-governed. Evaluative endorsement and self-governance are related because evaluative judgments constitute the agent's principled stand on what to do.

What does this have to do with my main claims about practical reason and universalization? Evaluative judgments are subject to demands of explanatory coherence. One cannot reasonably think, "Well, it's what I should do today as it is me and today" or "It is good for me and bad for you simply because it's me." Those grounds do not enter into an explanatory web with one's other beliefs and attitudes and hence are unreasonable. Reason seeks generalities in support of the particular. Reasonable evaluative judgments, then, must have supporting general grounds. One's evaluative perspective must be grounded in generalizations about what it is good for people of a certain kind—with certain aims, wants, in certain conditions, etc.— to do. Those grounds, then, apply to anyone with those characteristics. The grounds must support, then, others acting on those considerations as well. So, considering the way in which clear-eyed weak-willed action is defective supports my claim that there is a rational pressure for an autonomous agent to choose to act only on considerations that are universalizable in the sense that their grounds must be general. The considerations employed in explaining my behavior must have grounds

[7] While I am sure she would not be satisfied with my efforts, I thank Jennifer Morton for getting me to more carefully think through the connection I am positing between autonomy and acting from one's evaluative judgments.

that would equally render intelligible anyone else so acting in circumstances similar to my own.[8]

There is a second, complementary route to the same conclusion that does not require evaluativism about identification. Insofar as I am acting on an intention, then I believe that, all other things being equal, I will do as I intend. Intending to Φ requires having a belief that one will Φ.[9] That belief is not held in isolation. It must enter a web of other beliefs and be explanatorily related to those other beliefs. And there is pressure, as reason always seeks generalities, to explain why one will Φ (as well as the contents of other beliefs used in the immediate explanation) in more general terms, screening out considerations that are irreducibly particular as explanatorily unfit.

---

[8] Thanks to Benjamin Mitchell-Yellin for helpful discussions of this argument.

[9] The thesis that intention involves belief is controversial, perhaps even more controversial than the evaluativism of the previous argument. Proponents of the view, sometimes labeled *cognitivism*, include (Harman 1976, 1986), (Setiya 2007), (Velleman 1989, 2000, 2007), and (Wallace 2001). Michael Bratman is the most forceful opponent of the position (Bratman 1987, 2009a, 2009b). While there are multiple and complex issues, including the relationship between theoretical and practical rationality and the source of normative principles governing intention like the coherence principle and the means-end principle, one problem in particular facing the view is the problem of uncertainty. It seems that I can form an intention in the face of uncertainty as to whether or not I will carry it out. One such example is Bratman's case of intending to stop at the grocery store on the way home from work when one knows that one is likely to forget. While I cannot do justice to the case here, I want to raise two points in defense of cognitivism. In Bratman's case, I may have general grounds for doubting whether or not I will remember to stop; most of the time I start going home, I am on autopilot and make the trip without thought. But I lack specific grounds that on this particular case I will forget. If I did, and I didn't take steps to correct, then it is hard to see that I really intend, or at least rationally intend, to stop at the store. But general grounds for doubt are perfectly consistent with specific belief. So, belief that I will stop at the store is perfectly consistent with general grounds for doubting that I will. My second line of defense develops Harman's points about belief in the face of uncertainty. I believe that the sun will rise tomorrow, even though I am not certain that there will not be a cosmic catastrophe later tonight, in which case the sun will not rise tomorrow. While I am not certain, I am certain enough, and the stakes are sufficiently low, that I simply assume there won't be a catastrophe. The content of my belief is not the conditional *If there is no catastrophe, then the sun will rise*. Instead, the content is the unconditional *The sun will rise* which I believe conditional on background assumptions including that there will not be a cosmic catastrophe. Bratman's case turns on considerations of uncertainty. But I can be uncertain that I will do as I intend while still believing (in a conditional way) that I will do it. I intend to stop at the store in the face of uncertainty. A background assumption informing that intention is the assumption that I won't forget this time. Those same assumptions then condition my belief that I will stop at the store. The material in Section 6 about conditions receding into the background and conditioning an attitude can be applied to make this suggestion more precise. I hope to take these issues up in more detail in future work.

In the previous several paragraphs I have argued that only considerations that rest on general grounds—that is, considerations whose
grounds would equally well explain another person in my position
acting as I propose to act—can be used to render fully intelligible
autonomous action, either to the agent herself or to another.[10] But it
is a further step to say that those considerations must be universalizable, in the sense that, in acting on them, One must, however
implicitly, *will* that anyone else in similar circumstances act on
those considerations.[11] The rational egoist promises to provide an
example of the difference. This consideration is general. The egoist
does not act arbitrarily as the person who thinks that his behavior is
rendered intelligible by the fact that it is his doing it on Tuesday,
there being no general features about him or Tuesday in virtue of
which that behavior is intelligible. The egoist's basic principle of
choice is to satisfy his own interests, whatever the cost to others,
which he thinks is supported by the general principle that everyone
should act so as to satisfy his or her own interests whatever the cost to
others. He does not universalize that principle, in the sense that he
does not will that others satisfy their own interests, especially when
those interests conflict with his own. He views others and their
interests as potential obstacles for him to overcome, not themselves
acting on the same kind of considerations that he then needs to
incorporate as reasons for action in his own deliberations. So, he
acts only on considerations that are grounded in general principles,
but he does not will those principles as universal law. Yet he seems
perfectly rational and autonomous.

---

[10] I say that the grounds of the consideration, as opposed to the consideration itself, should
be general in order to attempt to allow special relations and some forms of "agent-relative"
considerations to play explanatory roles in autonomous action. For example, that I love this
particular person seems to be a consideration that explains a range of my behaviors. That
consideration is not general but essentially particular. However, for the consideration to
explain my behavior in the right way, it must be held in the background of thinking that
anyone who loves someone and bears the relations I bear to my beloved can be rendered
intelligible in acting as I did on the basis of a consideration of the same form of consideration
I act on. The consideration thus has a general ground.
[11] Thanks to William FitzPatrick, Elizabeth Harman, Elinor Mason, and Jennifer Morton,
among others, for pressing this on me and getting me to distinguish my claims about
generalization from my claims about universalization, which I had collapsed together in earlier
versions of this argument.

Appearances deceive. Insofar as the egoist wills that he do something in a given circumstance that he does not will others do were they in that circumstance, I think that he is arbitrary. He needs an explanation not only of what he is doing—say, making a false promise in order to get what he wants when he thinks he will get away with it—where this explanation may have general grounds. He also needs an explanation of his willing that he do what he does. If he wills only that he act on the principle that one do whatever is required to satisfy one's interest, then, given that that depends upon his choices, he needs to have some explanation of why he is willing that only he act on that principle and not others. And, as was observed before, it is not acceptable to simply say, "Well, it's because it is me." There must be some general characteristics in terms of which he explains the difference between himself and others, otherwise there is an air of arbitrariness that reason abhors. And because this is choice of a basic principle of choice, I do not see how those characteristics can be anything besides general features of one's autonomous agency as such. So, the egoist violates the rational demand of full explicability if he acts on principles that have general grounds but he does not will that others in similar circumstances act on principles with those grounds as well.

Acting on considerations that are not universalizable is defective because one does not have a complete and rationally acceptable explanation of one's behavior. Self-intelligibility is the constitutive aim of autonomous activity. So, our autonomy requires us to not act on considerations that are not universalizable. And, assuming the Kantian idea that the Categorical Imperative is the fundamental source of moral demands, this makes us subject, merely in virtue of our autonomy, to the demands of morality.

5. PERVERSITY AND UNIVERSALIZATION

Sometimes we act contrary to our evaluative judgments but not by giving in to the force of contrary passions, whether those passions be irresistible, as they are in the case of the unwilling addict, or resistible but unresisted, as they are in the case of weak-willed cookie eater. Rather, we act from a sort of rebellion. This may seem problematic for my view, as such behavior seems both autonomous but against the agent's evaluative outlook, thus calling into question the constitutive connection I have pressed between acting autonomously and acting from one's evaluative outlook. One alleged example of this type of action is St. Augustine and his youthful theft of pears (Augustine 397, bk 2). Augustine claims that he was attracted by a "love of mischief" and "enjoyed doing wrong for no other reason than that it was wrong." He seems to have been acting both intentionally and of his own free will. He was not driven by any ordinary passion like hunger or attraction to the taste of the pear. And he acted knowing that what he was doing was, by his own lights, wrong and delighted precisely in its wrongness. Milton's Satan is, on some readings, another example of this phenomenon. It is a deep and important fact that we are sometimes attracted to the bad because it is bad. These evaluative judgments do not appear to be mere lip service or from some external perspective not accepted by the agent. Yet, some will insist, the acts are autonomous precisely because they are not caused by "alien" motives.

Gary Watson (Watson 1987) argues against identification theories of acting of one's own free will along similar lines. He writes:

> When it comes right down to it, I might fully "embrace" a course of action I do not judge best; it may not be thought best, but is fun, or thrilling; one loves doing it, and it's too bad it's not also the best thing to do, but one goes for it without compunction. Perhaps in such a case one must see this thrilling thing as good, must value it; but, again, one needn't see it as expressing or even conforming to a general standpoint one would be prepared to defend. One may think it is after all rather mindless, vulgar, or demeaning, but when it comes down to it, one is not (as) interested in that. (168–9)

Watson claims that "there is no estrangement here. One's will is fully behind what one does." While I agree that one can act perversely of one's own free will, there being "no estrangement here" in the sense of there being no alien determination, I disagree with Watson that the agent is "fully behind what" she does. His mistake can be traced to a failure to distinguish acting of one's own free will from acting autonomously. Acting of one's own free will only requires an absence of alien determining forces. As estrangement involves alien determining forces, we can agree with Watson that the cases under consideration lack estrangement and so are instances of acting of one's own free will. But, being "fully behind" a piece of behavior is more robust, requiring a principled stance and not just an arbitrary plopping for a course of action. Thorough perversity seems to me unprincipled in a way that excludes being "fully behind" one's behavior, as opposed to merely not estranged from the motives that move one. Acting autonomously, being "fully behind" and directing one's behavior, requires that that behavior stem from a principled position in favor of so acting and not merely the absence of alien determination. So, we should be careful to distinguish a lack of alien determination, which cases of thorough perversity can possess, from a positive, principled determination, which I claim they cannot.

Perhaps Watson is imagining a case in which the agent determines what is best and then chooses the opposite, out of spite, say, as a rebellious teen. Then Watson faces a dilemma. Either the decision to act out of spite was itself unprincipled or it was principled. If the former, then we again have the ultimate determination of the behavior being unprincipled in a way incompatible with full self-governance; acting out of spite was either arbitrarily determined or perhaps imposed on the agent in a way that suggests estrangement. If, on the other hand, the decision to act out of spite was principled, say to exercise one's power by simply saying, "No," then the case is drained of its perversity. (And, as I have been arguing, that principle is taken up into an explanatory web that puts pressure to universalize. One quickly sees the self-defeating character of such rebelliousness taken as a positive principle that one will universally, which is why acting on it is irrational for autonomous agents.) Either way, the case of genuine perversity is not a case of fully autonomous action. So, I think that Watson is wrong to claim that the perverse actor is "fully behind" her choices in the sense that she acts autonomously. More generally, I think that it is wrong that there are cases in which one autonomously acts perversely.

There is a constitutive connection between self-governance, which involves both a negative freedom of not being determined by forces outside oneself and a positive freedom of not being random but being principled, and universalization. The argument mirrors Kant's argument, in the opening paragraphs of section 3 of the *Groundwork*, for the claim that the perfectly free will is bound by the Categorical Imperative. The autonomous agent needs principles to govern her choices, lest her behavior be random, lacking positive freedom. And those principles must be such that they make sense of the agent's choice, including the choice to have her choices governed by those very principles. Only the principle to act in accordance with reason fits the bill, as only that principle can be seen as arising from the nature of acting autonomously. But then principles that cannot be universalized are ruled out as unfit for determining the behavior of autonomous agents.

My response to Watson involves distinguishing acting autonomously from acting of one's own free will, which I have now connected to Kant's distinction between negative and positive freedom. Cases of compulsion and thorough manipulation fail the first, negative condition, involving behaviors that are wholly determined by alien, unauthorized forces. The compulsive agent does not act of her own free will and typically is not morally responsible for her actions. Cases of uncompelled weakness fail the second condition. While the agent may act of her own free will and may be morally responsible, she does not act autonomously. The explanation for an autonomous action must not appeal to considerations that the agent herself does not authorize or see the force of. This is because an adequate explanation of autonomous behavior can only appeal to considerations that the agent herself endorses, as she must be viewed as authorizing their effects. By viewing those considerations in a negative light, an agent separates herself from them and thereby renders them unfit to direct her behavior in her voice. Similarly, more extreme perversity fails the second condition, as such cases involve a lack of a principled stance necessary for positive freedom.

I have argued that we can derive a practical requirement to act only on considerations that are universalizable from the concept of acting autonomously, relying on Velleman's conception of practical reason as being animated by an aim to make sense of oneself. The aim of self-understanding combined with our autonomy requires that the considerations in light of which one can make sense of one's behaviors must ultimately stem from the nature of reason itself and in particular the aim of self-understanding. A consideration makes our behavior intelligible in the right sort of way only if we can see it as making intelligible *any* person's similar behavior, were that person in the general circumstances we are in.

This defense of the categorical status of the basic principles of morality is distinctive in that it starts with a non-normative, explanatory conception of acting for a reason. It does not assume as a starting point a concern to justify oneself to others. Rather, such a concern is derived as a consequence of the concern for self-understanding compatible with acting autonomously. Standard defenses treat the concern to justify oneself to others as basic, not being constitutive of bare autonomous agency as such. (See, for example, Scanlon 1998.) Such a position allows that it is possible to act autonomously without a concern to justify one's behavior to others. For if this concern is constitutive of autonomous agency, then the view collapses into one like the view I have articulated above. Insofar as the force of morality depends upon an extra-rational concern, a concern that is rationally optional, there can be autonomous rational agents who lack that concern. Such agents are immune to the demands of morality. But then the question, "Why should I concern myself with morality?" asked by such an agent does not have a satisfying answer. I don't claim that this is decisive. Proponents of the standard account can, for example, claim that such agents nonetheless have reason to do as morality requires that are not dependent on the concerns these agents have. I take it to be a virtue of my view that I do not need to countenance such external reasons. Because the concern to justify oneself is not a basic starting point in the derivation of the moral law, my account of the foundations of morality does not leave this skeptical question open. An agent who is completely immune to demands to justify herself to others is at odds with the constitutive aim of her own agency, the aim to make sense of her behavior in a way consistent with her acting autonomously, as that aim requires that she act only on considerations that are universalizable and hence carry justificatory force. We should act only on principles that others cannot reasonably reject. But that is because unreasonable principles do not render our behavior intelligible consistent with our acting on them autonomously.

Grant me the Kantian claim that moral requirements stem from the Categorical Imperative to not act on considerations that cannot be consistently willed as universal law. Then the arguments from above support the claim that every autonomous agent has reason to do as morality requires, as acting autonomously requires acting only on considerations that can be universalized. Armed with this claim, we can return to the Mafioso. Insofar as the Mafioso is autonomous, he is subject to the demands of morality. Velleman is wrong, then, that he is immune to the demands of morality. Velleman's case for compromise rests on the claim that there are autonomous agents who lack reasons to do as morality requires, which I have now argued is mistaken.

6. CONFLICTING PRACTICAL REQUIREMENTS

Given the Mafioso's contingent commitments, he should break the borrower's fingers. I have argued that he is also subject to morality's demand to not break the borrower's finger. The uncompromising Kantian claims that he has most reason to do as morality requires. So he should not break the person's fingers. It is a common assumption that moral requirements are overriding. My defense of the rational basis of morality suggests why: Moral requirements are based in the most general and widely applicable explanatory grounds of behavior and so acting against them is rationally unintelligible, while acting contrary to one's contingent practical identity need not be, as there are explanatory principles laying behind that contingent practical identity. So, what the Mafioso should do, all things considered, is not break the borrower's fingers. But the Mafioso is still subject to conflicting practical requirements, which is problematic. I won't compromise, but I also want practical identities to generate genuine practical requirements; I want it to be true that one *should* in some sense do the things required by one's practical identity. I need a solution, then, that allows for an agent to be subject to genuinely conflicting requirements without contradiction.

This puzzle is similar to puzzles John Broome discusses (Broome 1999). Sally smokes. She really shouldn't. But, because she does, she should smoke filtered cigarettes. The second seems to entail that she should smoke (after all, one can't smoke filtered cigarettes without smoking), which conflicts with the original claim that Sally should not smoke. So Sally, like the Mafioso on my view, seems subject to competing and conflicting practical requirements. She both should not smoke and she should smoke filtered. Let's start with the simpler case of Sally to see what light it can shed on the more complex case of the Mafioso.

According to one famous solution, "should" takes wide scope over the conditional and does not detach unless the antecedent of the conditional is something that should be. Because Sally should not smoke, we cannot infer that Sally should smoke filtered just from the fact that she smokes. Such an inference is akin to inferring that George is necessarily unmarried from the truths that he is a bachelor and that necessarily anything that is a bachelor is unmarried. I reject this as an adequate solution for claims about what an agent should do. Denying that Sally should smoke filtered cigarettes makes it mysterious how "should" conditionals govern the behavior of imperfectly rational agents. While Sally is not doing as she should in smoking at all, it would be rationally worse for her to smoke unfiltered cigarettes.

On my view, "should" functions as a modal, ranging over a class of situations (or states of affairs or events), true when applied to a sentence *s* just in case *s* designates a situation from that range that should be the case.[12] I intend that to be uncontroversial. The novel component is that the set of situations the modal ranges over is shifty. The antecedent in a "should" conditional limits the range of the modal attached to the consequent. (i) Sally should not smoke and (ii) if Sally smokes, then she should smoke filtered. Because Sally smokes, (iii) Sally should smoke filtered. But (iii) is true only when the range of the modal only includes situations in which Sally smokes (as is required by the truth of the antecedent in (ii)). Although "should" detaches from the conditional given the factual truth of its antecedent, a trace of its conditional truth remains. (iii) is true, but only when "should" has a restricted range of situations in which the antecedent of (ii) is true. This restriction is enforced by the truth of the antecedent and the fact that (iii) is inferred from a conditional. The conditions recede to the background against which the consequent is true.[13] Under such restrictions—restrictions in which the range of the modal only includes situations in which the antecedent of (ii) is true—(i) is false, as there is no situation in the

---

[12] For simplicity, we can take what should be the case as a primitive mode of truth. Of course, *p* does not follow from the fact that it should be that *p*. So, the characteristic T-axiom of alethic modal logic (namely, $\Box\phi| = \phi$) is invalid for the logic of the should-of-practical-reason modal.

[13] So (iii) is not a conditional, but it is, in some sense, conditionally true. A true conditional is explicit about the conditions under which the consequent is true. When those conditions recede into the background, as I am claiming happens when "should" is detached from a conditional whose antecedent is merely factually true, the claim in question has an unconditional form but the conditions of its truth are not explicit in the claim itself, even though its truth is affected by and dependent on those conditions being satisfied.

limited range in which Sally does not smoke. (i) is true only when the modal has a wider range, including situations in which Sally does not smoke. But then (iii) is false. This is because what Sally *really* should do is not smoke. Hence, if situations in which Sally does not smoke are included in the set of situations over which "should" ranges, then (iii) is false. The conflict between the truth of (i) and (iii) is only apparent. It is akin to the seeming "conflict" in my truly saying, "I wrote this here paper," and your truly saying, "I did not write this here paper." While the word forms seem to contradict each other, their joint truth is consistent as they are true in different contexts and what the one says (in its relevant context) does not contradict what the other says (in its relevant context). Similarly, on the view I am suggesting, (i) and (iii) do not really express related propositions, as the word "should" has a different content as it occurs in the two sentences.

There is a hierarchy of what an agent should do at a given time, dependent upon which states are taken for granted as background. The less that is taken for granted—the less "givens" there are functioning as background conditions limiting the range of situations the modal ranges over—the more revealing of what the agent *really* should do, all things considered or all things up for grabs, the truth of a "should"-claim is.[14] Sure, Sally should smoke filtered cigarettes; but that's only when we hold fixed that she is going to smoke. But that is holding fixed something that should be up for grabs (and is within her control, we are to suppose). So what she *really* should do, we want to say, is not smoke at all. That "should"-claim is more inclusive, in the sense that it is true in a broader class of situations serving as the range of "should," than the first "should"-claim, which is false when there are situations in which Sally does not smoke in the range of the modal. So, appealing to this hierarchy allows us to give content to the thought that what Sally *really* should do is not smoke.

This account of "should" conditionals is attractive in part because it allows us to make evaluative distinctions between less than practically ideal choices and it allows practical requirements to continue to guide imperfectly rational agents. Sally is not doing as she should by smoking.

---

[14] Typically we take as settled matters independent of the agent's choice, i.e., beyond the agent's control, at the time of deliberation. These aspects of the situation, then, are not "up for grabs," even when they are metaphysically contingent.

But there are better and worse ways to not do as one should. If she smokes unfiltered, that's worse than smoking filtered. The truth of (ii) can guide Sally's choices, even when she is not fully doing as she should. For agents like us, we typically don't want everything dependent on our will to be up for grabs in making our decisions. We want to rely on previous decisions we've made, previous plans and policies we have put in place. We want to take them as settled and decide what to do from there. That's why it is perfectly rational to background certain conditions; they are taken as given and condition the choice now being made because we are finite beings that cannot decide afresh with each decision.

Let's return to the case of the Mafioso and the conflicting requirements my view entails he is subject to. Call the Mafioso *Sal.* (i) Sal should not break the borrower's fingers, because morality forbids it and Sal is subject to the demands of morality. But (ii) if Sal is a good Mafioso, then he should break the borrower's fingers. Because Sal is a good Mafioso, (iii) Sal should break the borrower's fingers. We learned from the case of Sally that the mere existence of conflicting "should"-claims is not necessarily a sign of contradiction. (iii) is true only when the range of 'should' includes only immoral situations in which Sal is a good Mafioso. Under such a restriction, (i) is false. (i) is true only when 'should' has a broader range. But then (iii) is false, as situations in which Sal is not a Mafioso are in the range of the modal. So, there is no contradiction in the joint truth of (i) and (iii), in the sense of entailing that both a proposition and its negation are true.

There are important disanalogies between the cases of Sally and Sal that complicate extending my solution of the conflict in the former to the latter. It is reasonably clear what is involved in purging all situations in which Sally does not smoke from the range of the modal in rendering "Sally should smoke filtered cigarettes" true. But it is less clear what situations are excluded in the case of Sal. The antecedent of the Sally conditional is *Sally smokes*, which picks out a relatively clear class of situations in which Sally performs a certain action. The range of 'should' in (iii) is then the intersection of the original set of situations and the set of situations in which Sally performs this activity. But the antecedent of the Sal conditional is *Sal is a good Mafioso.* There are not overt activities picked out by the truth of this claim; instead, its truth more concerns what set of values and commitments govern Sal's deliberation and action.[15] Furthermore, with Sally I formed a hierarchy of things Sally should do—first, she should not smoke, but, short of that, she should smoke filtered instead of unfiltered cigarettes—by considering the practical dictates over successively narrower classes of situations all guided by a unified principle of evaluation or value—namely, concern for health. But there seems to be no such unity in the case of Sal. In other words, in Sally's case we ranked better or worse ways of caring for one's health, whereas in Sal's case we seem to be comparing the dictates of two radically different evaluative systems or sets of values and commitments—Mafioso values and morality values. These differences may lead one to accept my account of the consistency in the Sally case but question whether that helps with the Mafioso case of primary interest.

I think that these differences are important and make the account of Sally more certain than the account of Sal. But I still think the account extends. The truth of the antecedent of the conditional in the case of Sal selects by situations that conform to the Mafioso commitments and values Sal has adopted. That is, when (iii) is detached from the conditional (ii), situations that would not be chosen by someone operating with Mafioso commitments and values are excluded from the range of situations 'should' in (iii) ranges over. In that case, situations in which Sal lets the borrower off with a gentle reminder, or perhaps forgives the loan altogether, are excluded. And the key idea articulated with the case of Sally that the set of situations "should" ranges over is restricted by the truth of the antecedent when detached from a conditional applies to the case of Sal.

In Sally's case, a common commitment—concern for her health—is operative both in the "ideal" case of not smoking and in the less than ideal but not worse case of smoking filtered cigarettes. (If Sally were completely indifferent to her health, it is hard to see why it would be better for her to smoke filtered rather than unfiltered cigarettes.) There is similarly a common commitment operative in Sal's case: Namely, the commitment to make sense of oneself. That is the common aim that he achieves better if he does as morality requires, and which practical reason dictates as the best if all options are on the table, and

---

[15] Thanks to an anonymous referee for suggesting this way of bringing out the disanology.

next best, given his self-conception as a Mafioso (which, like smoking, practical reason advises against), by breaking the borrower's fingers. In Sally's case, a commitment to her health guides her nonideal choices to smoke filtered instead of unfiltered cigarettes given her decision to smoke. The seeds of Sally's rational demise are present, then, in the nonideal case. She is guided by a concern that would lead her, were she to fully follow where it leads and deliberate about matters she takes as settled—namely, that she is going to smoke—to revise her decision to smoke. The same is true for Sal. Even as a Mafioso, his reasoning is animated by an aim to make sense of his behavior. If the arguments from the earlier sections of this paper are sound, this commits him to morality in virtue of his autonomy. He does not follow that aim all the way to where it leads—namely, giving up his Mafioso values, commitments, and deliberative outlook. Like Sally, he takes things as settled in his reasoning that his own commitments pressure him to revise. So, I claim that, while there are important differences between the cases of Sally and Sal, they are nonetheless sufficiently similar for it to at least be promising that the account of conditional "should" claims I offered applies to both.[16]

I claim that Sal is subject to a practical requirement to break the borrower's fingers. This is correlated with a practical justification for so doing. That may seem problematic for the fan of morality, as he is hardly justified in doing what morality forbids. But remember, the requirement to break the borrower's fingers, while unconditional in form, obtains only in the background of a set of conditions, some of which shouldn't themselves obtain: Namely, the requirement presupposes that Sal is a good Mafioso, which he shouldn't be. The justification for breaking the borrower's fingers similarly obtains only when those same conditions, some of which are not justified, are taken as given. So, I think that the fan of morality can grant that Sal has both a practical requirement and practical justification for breaking the borrower's fingers. Both the requirement and the associated justification are overridden, all things considered, by moral requirements and obtain only in the background of conditions that should not be and are not justified.

---

[16] Thanks to Justin White for very helpful discussion of the differences between the two cases.

They have the same status, then, as Sally's justification for smoking filtered cigarettes.

7. WILLING THE LAW

I end by briefly considering Velleman's argument against the Kantian claim that the moral law is self-imposed. My account of the connection between autonomous practical reasoning and morality provides a way of understanding the thesis that is immune to Velleman's objection.

Velleman argues that the self-legislation thesis gives an inadequate account of the authority of morality, as anything that depends upon the will of an agent can be undone by that same will, thus undermining morality's inescapability and necessity. Morality is inescapable, in the sense that it does not depend upon a rationally contingent aim that can be disavowed. I should stretch if I want to be flexible. I evade the demand to stretch by abandoning the end(s) to which it is a necessary means. Morality is not like this. But, if morality's force derived from an act of self-legislation where one chooses to be under the Categorical Imperative (CI), then the same will that legislated the CI can undo it by an opposing legislative act, draining morality of its inescapability.

Velleman assumes that the legislative act through which an autonomous agent self-imposes morality is an arbitrary act of the will. It is arbitrary in the sense that there are no antecedent forces tipping the balance in favor of morality. Velleman assumes this because otherwise morality would depend upon those factors and not the act of self-legislation. And if there are no antecedent considerations favoring morality, then it is equally possible for the agent to have imposed a different principle—say, the principle of self-love—and to undo its commitment once made.[17]

---

[17] A substantial portion of Velleman's discussion targets Korsgaard's defense of the self-legislation thesis. I think that his criticisms of Korsgaard are largely successful, but that there are better ways of defending the self-legistlation thesis. Whereas Korsgaard seems to concede the conception of morality being imposed by an arbitrary act of will, I argue below that we should deny that conception. I think that this is to give up on constructivism as the correct metaethical account of the source of morality in favor of some form of realism, but the issues are complex and beyond the scope of this paper. I take them up in my "The Practical Irrationality of Immorality."

My account of the connection between autonomous practical reasoning and morality outlined above suggests an alternative. The CI is self-imposed in the sense that it is constitutive of autonomous willing as such. When one wills autonomously, one is implicitly willing one's intention as universal law, whatever the content of one's willing. This is because, as I argued above, there is a constitutive connection between acting autonomously and universalization. One is thereby, in virtue of the commitments of autonomous willing as such, subject to the requirements of universalization and hence subject to the CI. Morality is self-imposed, but not by an arbitrary act of will in the sense described in the previous paragraph. This commitment does not arise from the agent's reflecting on the CI itself and choosing it over some other principle. Rather, it arises from the constitutive connection between autonomous willing and the CI and the fact, which we cannot help, that we are autonomous agents. We can, of course, freely adopt an alternative principle of choice, such as the principle of self-love. But we are still, even in that choice, subject to the demands of morality and the CI simply in virtue of our autonomy. That is the sense, I believe, in which the moral law is self-imposed.[18] And that kind of self-imposition cannot be unimposed by a competing act of self-legistlation.

REFERENCES

St. Augustine (397) *Confessions*, trans. H. Chadwick (Oxford University Press, 1991).
Bratman, M. (1987) *Intention, Plans, and Practical Reason* (Cambridge, MA: Harvard University Press).
——(2009a) "Intention, Belief, and Instrumental Rationality." In D. Sobel and S. Wall (eds.), *Reasons for Action* (Cambridge University Press), 13–36.
——(2009b) "Intention, Belief, Practical, Theoretical." In S. Robertson (ed.), *Spheres of Reason: New Essays in the Philosophy of Normativity* (Oxford University Press), 29–61.
Broome, J. (1999) "Normative Requirements," *Ratio* 12, 398–419.
Cohen, G. A. (1996) "Reason, Humanity, and the Moral Law." In C. Korsgaard, *The Sources of Normativity* (Cambridge University Press), 167–88.
Frankfurt, H. (1971) "Freedom of the Will and the Concept of a Person," *Journal of Philosophy* 68, 5–20. Reprinted in Frankfurt 1988, 11–25.

[18] See (Reath 1994) for a sophisticated interpretation of the self-legislation thesis in Kant.

—— (1977) "Identification and Externality." In A. Rorty (ed.), *The Identities of Persons* (Berkeley: University of California Press), 239–51. Reprinted in Frankfurt 1988, 58–68.

—— (1987) "Identification and Wholeheartedness." In F. Schoeman (ed.), *Responsibility, Character, and the Emotions* (Cambridge University Press), 27–45. Reprinted in Frankfurt 1988, 159–76.

—— (1988) *The Importance of What We Care About* (Cambridge University Press).

—— (1992) "The Faintest Passion," *Proceedings and Addresses of the American Philosophical Association* 66, 5–16. Reprinted in Frankfurt, *Necessity, Volition, and Love* (New York: Cambridge University Press, 1998), 95–107.

—— (1994) "Necessity, Volition, and Love." In H. F. Fulda and R. Horstmann (eds.), *Vernenftbegriffe in der Moderne: Stuttgarter Hegel-Congress 1993* (Stuttgart: Klett-Cotta). Reprinted in Frankfurt, *Necessity, Volition, and Love* (New York: Cambridge University Press, 1998), 129–41.

—— (2004) *The Reasons of Love* (Princeton University Press).

Harman, G. (1976) "Practical Reasoning," *Review of Metaphysics* 29, 431–63.

—— (1986) *Change in View* (Cambridge, MA: MIT Press).

Milton, J. (1667) *Paradise Lost.* In A. Fowler (ed.), *Paradise Lost* (London: Longman, 1998).

Reath, A. (1994) "Legislating the Moral Law," *Noûs* 28, 435–64.

Scanlon, T. (1998) *What We Owe to Each Other* (Cambridge, MA: Harvard University Press).

Setiya, K. (2007) "Cognitivism about Instrumental Reason," *Ethics* 117, 649–73.

Velleman, J. D. (1989) *Practical Reflection* (Princeton University Press).

—— (1992) "What Happens When Someone Acts?," *Mind* 101, 461–81. Reprinted in Velleman 2000, 123–143.

—— (1996) "The Possibility of Practical Reason," *Ethics* 106, 694–726. Reprinted in Velleman 2000, 170–99.

—— (2000) *The Possibility of Practical Reason* (Oxford University Press).

—— (2001) "Identification and Identity." Reprinted in Velleman, *Self to Self: Selected Essays* (Cambridge University Press, 2006), 330–60.

—— (2004) "Willing the Law." Reprinted in Velleman, *Self to Self: Selected Essays* (Cambridge University Press, 2006), 284–311.

—— (2006a) "Introduction." In *Self to Self: Selected Essays* (Cambridge University Press), 1–16.

—— (2006b) "The Centered Self." In *Self to Self: Selected Essays* (Cambridge University Press), 253–83.

—— (2007) "What Good is a Will?" In A. Leist and H. Baumann (eds.), *Action in Context* (Berlin: de Gruyter/Mouton), 193–215.

—— (2009) *How We Get Along* (Cambridge University Press).

Wallace, R. J. (2001) "Normativity, Commitment, and Instrumental Reason," *Philosophers' Imprint* 1, 1–26.

Watson, G. (1977) "Skepticism about Weakness of Will," *Philosophical Review* 86, 316–39. Reprinted in Watson 2004, 33–58.

——(1987) "Free Action and Free Will," *Mind* 96, 145–72. Reprinted in Watson 2004, 161–96.

——(2004) *Agency and Answerability* (Oxford: Clarendon Press).

8

Coercion and Integrity*

ELINOR MASON

In his discussion of 'negative responsibility', Bernard Williams is trying to show us that utilitarianism is an impoverished account of morality. In particular, the examples are supposed to show that utilitarianism, being a consequentialist theory, rules out a certain sort of consideration: 'a consideration involving the idea, as we might first and very simply put it, that each of us is specially responsible for what he does, rather than for what other people do' (Williams 1973, p. 99). In one of Williams' cases, an innocent botanist, Jim, comes across a situation in the middle of the jungle: the Captain has captured twenty Indians, and is about to kill them. He proposes to Jim that if Jim takes the gun and kills one person, the Captain will let the other nineteen go free. Williams' point is not primarily that Jim should *not* kill one of the Indians (though Williams does think that maybe Jim should not). His point is rather that because utilitarianism is concerned only with outcomes, the utilitarian must take other people's projects, including evil ones such as the Captain's, as shaping his own options irrevocably, and this, Williams claims, is an attack on the agent's integrity.

In this paper I am going to argue that utilitarianism does not rule out the idea that each of us is specially responsible for what he does in Williams' sense. Of course utilitarianism, like any moral theory, should say that we are *only* responsible for what we do—distant avalanches are not and cannot be the sort of thing we are responsible for. On the other hand it is true that the world shapes our options and sometimes we will

* Thanks to audiences at The Uehiro Centre for Practical Ethics (Oxford) symposium on Kamm's *Intricate Ethics*, The University of Copenhagen, Glasgow University, York University, and the Workshop in Normative Ethics, Tucson, January 2011. Thanks also to Ben Colburn, Mike Ridge, Vinit Haksar, and two anonymous referees for OUP for comments on earlier drafts.

be faced with unpleasant choices. But there is something special about cases like Jim's. I will argue that the real issue in the Jim example is *coercion*, and because Jim is coerced he is not responsible for the bad effects of his action. This is something that a utilitarian can say as much as anyone can.

Consequentialism makes no distinction between doing and allowing. The classic cases are trolley problems—should I divert an out of control trolley and thereby kill one but save five, or should I do nothing, allowing five to be killed? The debate over this might be seen as central to the debate between consequentialism and other moral theories—it seems essential to consequentialism that the right answer is to divert the trolley. I take it for granted that consequentialism cannot and should not accept a doing/allowing distinction. But that does not imply that the agent is to be held responsible for everything that happens—that would be absurd. Rather, consequentialists take agents to be responsible for (roughly) things that they could have prevented as well as things they brought about—and some suitable account of what that means, compatibilist or otherwise, is in the background. For consequentialism, allowings are just a subset of doings.

However, there is something else going on in Williams' discussion of negative responsibility. There are two sorts of case: general cases of allowing, and cases of allowing where another agent is involved.[1] The second sort of case, cases where there is an intervening agent, are a subset of cases of allowing. Jim is the classic example—Jim is innocently botanizing, and along comes the villainous Captain and makes his actions dependent on Jim's. So one of the things that Jim will be 'allowing to happen' if he refuses the Captain's offer will be the Captain killing twenty innocent people.

Williams approaches the example by arguing that Jim would not necessarily be responsible for the deaths of nineteen Indians if he refuses

---

[1] The case of George the chemist is an example of the first sort of case, though it is a little more complex than trolley problems. Williams' worry is that George should not have to take into account that if he doesn't take the job making chemical weapons someone more zealous than him will. Williams obviously thinks that George should think only of his own possible actions and not worry about what other people will do. For a consequentialist, the predictable actions of other people in cases like George's are just like other predictable events, and must be taken into account as part of the consequences. I argue below that Jim's case is not like this. There are various things consequentialists can say about the George example, but I will not go into them here.

to shoot. Frances Kamm approaches from the other direction, arguing that Jim is not necessarily responsible for the death of the one Indian if he *does* shoot (Kamm 1999, 2007).[2] Kamm and Williams are both very persuaded by the thought that the responsibility is the Captain's whatever happens. However, Kamm's approach raises more interesting issues. Williams' complaint, that Jim might not be responsible for the deaths of twenty Indians when he refuses the Captain's offer, focuses our attention on the doing/allowing distinction in general. Kamm, by contrast, in concentrating on the possibility that Jim is not responsible even if he does accept the Captain's offer, immediately focuses on the intervening agent.

KAMM'S ACCOUNT

Kamm thinks that a non-consequentialist can say that it is permissible for Jim to kill one Indian (2007, pp. 306–8). She comes up with variations on the Captain case to show that in order for responsibility to stay with the Captain, it is crucial that the instigator of the deal is the Captain. Kamm argues that when Jim does kill, it is the Captain, not Jim, who is responsible. On Kamm's view, it is much less clear that Jim is permitted to kill in a variation of the case, where the Captain makes no offer but Jim has the results of a brain scan that show that the Captain will refrain from killing any of the Indians if Jim offers to kill one.[3]

Part of what Kamm is doing here is giving an account of the normative intricacies in the various differing cases. Just as in trolley cases, tiny differences to the cases make differences to our intuitions, and Kamm's view is that these intuitive reactions reflect real normative differences. Kamm also claims that the Captain 'keeps responsibility' when he is the instigator of the offer. If there is no offer, and Jim acts off his own bat so as to maximize the good (as in the brain scan case), Jim is fully responsible for the bad as well as the good consequences of his actions.

---

[2] Alan Gewirth (1981) makes the same point in a slightly different context. Like Kamm, Gewirth hints at an explanation for the shift in responsibility from the immediate agent to the intervening agent, but his discussion does not go very far (see especially p. 12)—he is chiefly concerned with the normative facts.

[3] There are other variations, but I shall leave them aside here.

There are various different issues here: Kamm's main concern is with *when* responsibility shifts, but we should also ask *why* responsibility would shift, and most importantly, what responsibility in this context *is*. Kamm makes some suggestions as to why responsibility shifts, but I will leave them aside as they raise issues that are not relevant to my project here. Kamm's account of what responsibility is not always completely clear, though she makes various interesting remarks. Kamm says that when the Captain makes the offer, Jim becomes 'the Captain's agent', and thus the Captain and not Jim bears responsibility for what happens. She talks mostly about 'positive responsibility'—by which she means responsibility for an act that has been done (as opposed to negative responsibility, which is being responsible for what you allow to happen[4]). She first explains what this means as follows:

the Captain has positive moral responsibility for the consequences of Jim's act. I take this to mean that he is to be held completely morally responsible in the sense of being to blame for, being at fault for, the negative consequences of Jim's act. He is also completely responsible in the sense of being accountable, for the negative consequences (i.e. liable for criticism, punishment, or compensation for the death). This is true even though ... Jim is causally responsible ... his choice to shoot was what I shall call a responsible one, because it was voluntary and he was in a sound state of mind. (2007, p. 311)

There are three ideas here—voluntariness, accountability, and a third slightly mysterious one—'morally responsible in the sense of being to blame for, being at fault for, the negative consequences of Jim's act'. Later on, Kamm explicitly makes a distinction between three aspects to positive responsibility: *voluntariness, accountability,* and *moral responsibility.* I assume that Kamm is using these terms in the following more or less standard way: voluntariness is the primary condition of responsibility—libertarians claim that we are responsible in that sense only when we have genuine alternate possibilities and we freely choose between them. Compatibilists claim that we are free in that sense when we have the right relationship to our actions, and that alternative

---

[4] As I say above, the idea that we have 'negative responsibility' is just the denial of the doing/allowing distinction. But there is something else of interest here, hence the shift to talking about positive responsibility in Captain cases.

possibilities are not required.⁵ In what follows I tend towards a reasons responsiveness account of moral responsibility, such as that favoured by Susan Wolf (1990) or Fischer and Ravizza (1998). I do not offer a full account of compatibilist voluntariness; rather my aim is to elucidate one particular way in which voluntariness can be undermined.

Accountability is a quite different notion—it is about when an agent should be *held* responsible (or accountable)—when it is appropriate to punish or reward the agent.⁶ Voluntariness is a precondition for accountability, but beyond that, variations in accountability might not be explained by variations in voluntariness. We might not be accountable for merely self-regarding acts, for example, or for certain sorts of harm to others—not because our acts are not voluntary, but because of the moral rules surrounding those sorts of acts.

This leaves the third element, 'moral responsibility'. Kamm is not at all clear what she means by that. In fact, in Kamm's descriptions of the various cases, moral responsibility and accountability never come apart, so in Kamm's discussion the notion of moral responsibility is redundant. As a consequence, Kamm's story is all about accountability, which we could understand as depending purely on the moral rules that are in play in the situation. We could treat her account of the Captain cases as having nothing to do with *responsibility*—in the sense that Jim acts voluntarily in all the cases, and so is responsible in all cases. Kamm is providing an account of how instigation has an effect on the moral situation, in just the way that promises have an effect on the moral situation. If I make you a promise I am bound to you in a new way—I have new duties. Similarly, one might think, the Captain's instigation of the offer excuses Jim from duties of reparation that he would otherwise have had when he kills someone.

But this does not seem enough in Jim's case. The sense in which Jim is not responsible is not simply that he is not accountable—though I agree that Jim is not accountable. The reason that Jim is not

---

⁵ This is a very rough characterization of compatibilism—there are many different accounts of the conditions which make our actions 'free' in the compatibilist sense.

⁶ The term 'accountability' has, so far as I can see, come into popular use in the moral responsibility literature since Gary Watson (1996) made a distinction between what he claims are two faces of our concept of responsibility, 'attributability' and 'accountability'. Watson's is a rather more complex distinction than I intend to use here—by 'accountability' I mean simply liability for sanctions.

accountable, however, goes deeper than Kamm's account suggests. It is not merely a consequence of the moral rules surrounding the instigation of offers.[7] Jim is not accountable because he lacks responsibility in something more like the voluntariness sense—the act is not really Jim's act. On the other hand, in one sense Jim's act is voluntary— he is not hypnotized or blown by the wind. So to make sense of Jim's case we need to say something a bit more subtle about voluntariness.

COERCION

I agree with Kamm that there is a big difference between Williams' original case and the case where Jim sees the results of a brain scan and decides on his own to kill one person. In the original case, Jim is coerced, in the brain scan case he is not. Coercion is what undermines the agent's responsibility. Coercion is a form of manipulation—one agent gets another agent to do something through a coercive proposal. In what follows I shall say more about the conditions of coercion with a view to making sense of the way in which coercion undermines voluntariness.

1. Choice

I am going to argue that the mark of coercion is that the agent's act is not fully voluntary. However, it is not involuntary either—being coerced is not like being blown by the wind—coercion essentially involves a choice. As Aristotle puts it, actions done out of fear of greater evils, such as when a villain will kill your family unless you do something shameful, do not seem to be involuntary. One chooses to do them—and yet they are not completely voluntary either—they are mixed.[8]

---

[7] To be fair to Kamm, some of what she says suggests that she does think there is more to Jim's lack of responsibility than lack of accountability. What I say below could be seen as expanding on some of Kamm's remarks about Jim being the Captain's agent.

[8] See Aristotle (1999), p. 30. It is common to argue that a choice made when the alternatives is unacceptable is not a properly voluntary choice. See e.g. Dworkin (1970), Cohen (1988), Olsaretti (1998, 2004). Note that the terminology can be confusing here—being free, acting freely, being forced, and so on, are used in different ways by different writers. Note also that coercion is only one sort of non-voluntary choice—one where another agent is involved.

2. *The other agent*

It is crucial to coercion that another agent's will is dominating the situation.[9] Only agents can coerce—we cannot be coerced by the blind forces of nature. Furthermore, accidental coercion is not conceivable—the coercer must have a *mens rea*.[10] I'll come back to details of this; for now it is sufficient to note that coercion, as opposed to other sorts of non-voluntary choice, must be defined with reference to both the coercer and the coercee.

3. *Reasons and motivation*

There are different ways that agents can be manipulated. Coercion obviously involves creating a powerful motivation for an agent to do the coercer's desired action. However, there are different sorts of motivation. A coercer might threaten a coercee by playing on non-rational motivations: by threatening to do something the agent is terrified by, or offering something that a very greedy agent is unable to resist. In these cases, the agent may be made to do something very bad, something that the agent should not have done. But we understand that the agent is under huge psychological pressure, and we excuse them to some extent. On the other hand, a coercer might manipulate an agent by manipulating his *reasons*. This is what happens in Jim's case. Jim does not have any irrational motivational quirks that the Captain is playing on. Jim's moral view, by hypothesis, tells him that it is better to kill one person than allow twenty to die. Jim does what he ought when he accepts the Captain's proposal. These are very different sorts of manipulation.

Threats involving phobias are often used as examples of coercion in the literature, thus apparently coming down on the side of formulating coercion in terms of non-rational motivations.[11] Phobias are an extreme

[9] Nozick makes the point in his account of coercion (1969). This idea is also in Kamm (2007), who talks about how Jim has become the Captain's agent, and in Yaffe (2003), who talks about the coercee being the 'toady' of the coercer.

[10] Again, I am in agreement with Nozick here (1969), p. 443.

[11] E.g. Gideon Yaffe (2003), though Yaffe's official definition is of reasons coercion. Yaffe allows both rational and irrational responses to a coercer to count as coercion—on Yaffe's account, either the coercer provides reasons that it is rational to respond to, or, as Yaffe puts it, 'The coercer may be aware of the victim's imperfect tendencies to respond to reasons and may manipulate the victim only by bringing it about that she *takes herself* to have reason to do what he wants her to do, even when she does not, in fact, have any reason to do it' (2003, p. 351). However, Yaffe's example is of a hydrophobe being threatened with water, which does not fit

case of non-rational motivation, but there are many more common cases—the standard cases of weakness of will, where we are driven to act by laziness, greed, jealousy, and so on.[12] In these more common cases, it is hard to distinguish between motivation by reasons the agent (wrongly) takes herself to have, and her non-rational motivations. Imagine that my colleague is very lazy and very averse to grading, but is not a bad person. On the one hand he may over emphasize the weight of his reasons to avoid grading (he places too much weight on the pain it causes him and not enough on the benefit to the students or the burden to his colleagues when he shirks). On the other hand there may be situations where he really does know that he ought to do his grading, all things considered, and yet he doesn't do it. So it may not always be clear from the outside, and even from the agent's own point of view, whether an apparent case of coercion is a case where the agent is acting on reasons she takes herself to have or whether it is a case where she is acting on her non-rational motivations.

But there is a big difference between reasons coercion and non-rational coercion. When an agent is coerced by reasons coercion, there is an important sense in which he does what he ought—he does what he has reason to do. Whereas when an agent is coerced by manipulation of his non-rational motivations, it is quite possible that he does something he ought not to do, and even if the coercer gets him to do what he ought by this method, the agent lacks some virtue—he is not acting for the right reasons. In so far as coercion is an excuse then—something that excuses an agent from responsibility—it will work differently for reasons coercion than for non-rational coercion.

Of course, there is disagreement about what the conditions for excuses are. As Austin points out, we do not use the supposedly contrasting terms 'justification' and 'excuse' clearly. As Austin puts it, 'In the one defence [justification], briefly, we accept responsibility but deny that it was bad: in the other [excuse], we admit that it was bad but don't accept full, or even any, responsibility' (1956, p. 176). It is

---

into either of Yaffe's categories. Yaffe does not consider the possibility that the agent is acting in a way that she knows herself to have no reason to act.

[12] One important sort of case that I do not discuss here is manipulative sexual relations. See Conly (2004) for a good discussion of the ways in which weakness of will and coercion relate to manipulative sexual encounters.

presumably not accidental that Austin uses the word 'bad', rather than its close relatives, 'wrong' and 'ought not'. What Jim does is not wrong in the circumstances, and it is not the case that he ought not to have done it. Jim is, in that sense, justified in killing one person. So Jim has both an excuse and a justification. Whereas someone who acts out of fear or greed in response to a coercive proposal has an excuse (at least a partial one) but no justification.

It is fairly easy to see how non-rational coercion can undermine agency. Agency is usually thought of as being closely connected to our capacity to reason, so in activating a non-rational motivational force, the manipulator is pretty clearly doing something that undermines agency. But it is a rather different sort of oppression when an agent manipulates another agent's reasons. It is tempting to think that if you are acting for reasons, you must be responsible.[13] But that is too quick. In this paper I argue that reasons coercion undermines agency in an important way.

There is one last clarification to be made about my account of reasons coercion. There is a distinction between the reasons that there are (even in some modest sense) and the reasons that agents take themselves to have. In cases like Jim's, the coercer provides reasons, and the coercee understands those reasons and does what is there is overall reason to do. In the other sort of case, the coercer appeals to reasons that the coercee takes herself to have, but does not actually have. For example, the Captain seems to take himself to have reason to seize power in his region. I could coerce him by threatening to arm his most powerful enemies if he does not do what I want. There is a sense in which the Captain's only rational course of action is to give in to my demands— although in fact the Captain does not have a 'true' reason to take over the region. I think in this situation it is fair to say that I have coerced the Captain.

I am thus giving a 'subjective' account of reasons coercion. An agent counts as being coerced when the reasons *she takes herself to have* are manipulated by another agent. There are two reasons that an account of coercion needs to appeal to subjective reasons. First, in order for a coercive proposal to be effective, the coercer must use the actual beliefs

---

[13] This is what Frankfurt seems to think, which is why he characterizes coercion in terms of overpowering desires. Frankfurt focuses on non-rational motivation, but otherwise his position is like mine, in that he defines coercion in terms of the agent's subjective reaction.

that an agent has. It is crucial that an account of coercion focuses on the actual pressure that is applied, and that relies on the actual beliefs about reasons that the coercee has. On the other hand, we want to rule out accidental coercion—it shouldn't count as coercion if someone makes an idle threat and is unpredictably taken seriously. So we need to take into account both the beliefs of the coercer and the beliefs of the coercee, and we should take the actual beliefs in both cases, even if they are unjustified. If the coercer believes that the coercee takes something to be a reason and attempts to use it to coerce her, it is attempted coercion (if he has a false belief of course it will not be successful coercion). And if the coercer does not believe that he is providing reasons to the coercee, then even if, by her lights, he is, it will not count as coercion.

The second justification for a subjective account is that the deeper issue here is about responsibility. I argue that when agents' reasons are manipulated by someone else, the agent is thereby rendered less responsible. Reasons that are not accessible to the agent are not something that can affect the agent's responsibility: we cannot hold agents responsible for getting things right, we must hold them responsible for something that is (again, in some suitably compatibilist sense) under their control. So when an agent has false beliefs about reasons or anything else, we can hold them responsible for that mistake if they have not tried hard enough to reach a true belief, or if they have been deliberately self deceptive. However, we cannot hold them responsible for a mistake just because they have made a mistake.[14]

In sum, there is a belief condition on coercion—both the coercer and the coercee believe that the coercee takes herself to have been given reason to do what the coercer wants her to do. There is no requirement that these beliefs are justified, they must only be sincere. Of course, some agents have crazy ideas about what their reasons are—someone who believes every living creature, no matter how small, has an absolute right to life can be coerced into causing serious pain to a human (which by her lights is preferable to the death of any creature) by the threat to kill some protozoa. Such a belief system is absurd of course, but this does not mean that it is any less coercive to use it to manipulate someone.

---

[14] I come back to this issue below. I defend subjectivism about obligation at length in my manuscript, 'Subjective Consequentialism'.

4. Substantial reasons

It is not enough to say that someone is coerced into A when the coercer gives them a reason to do A—the reason has to be powerful—in the sense that the reason (by the coercee's lights) easily overrides or outweighs all other reasons in play. If the proposer renders the action only slightly more eligible, then even though it is true that the agent has more reason to do that act, it is not true that she is coerced into it. Take Kamm's own description of a situation that she takes to be parallel to Jim and the Indians:

> Suppose that Albert is about to tell a story that will embarrass twenty people. However, he makes Jim an offer: If Jim tells a story that embarrasses only one of the people, Albert will desist. (2007, p. 338, footnote 18)

Kamm's point about this example is that it is parallel to the Jim and the Indians case in that if the offer is instigated by the Captain/Albert, then the responsibility for the bad effects of Jim's accepting the offer stays with the Captain/Albert. However, it seems intuitively right that in the case of Jim and the Indians, Jim is coerced, but in the case of Albert and the embarrassing story, Jim is not coerced. First, the reason that Albert gives Jim to tell the embarrassing story is not a comparatively powerful enough reason. Even a consequentialist, who is most likely to think that Albert has given Jim sufficient reason to tell the embarrassing story, should admit that the balance of reasons is not overwhelming. For a start, it must be difficult to judge that the bad effects of giving in to Albert on this occasion wouldn't swamp the bad effects of letting him go ahead. Second, even if the final judgement is that letting Albert go ahead is worse than accepting the offer, there is not an enormous amount at stake here. The embarrassment of twenty people is not a huge deal. For a case to be coercion, the stakes must be high.

Of course, it is not always clear when a reason is powerful enough for a case to count as coercion. In real life cases we do not find it easy to say whether people were coerced—by the Nazis, the Stasi, the camp commander, the kidnapper, and so on. Sometimes cases of collaboration with evil are just that—cases where someone has voluntarily collaborated with evil. This difficulty is an inevitable part of a theory of coercion.[15]

---

[15] Here I am in agreement with Zimmerman (1981, p. 125).

5. Threats and offers

Nozick formulates his account of coercion in terms of threats, and much of the literature on coercion since Nozick's influential paper on the topic is concerned with the distinction between threats and offers.[16] One of Nozick's worries is that if we allow that offers could be coercive, any time someone renders one option substantially more desirable than another they would count as having coerced you. If someone offers you a huge salary to come and work for them, it would count as coercion. If someone puts their merchandise on sale at a great price it would count as coercion. This is ridiculous. The point here is that threats seem damaging in a way that offers do not—it seems plausible to say that threats, unlike offers, undermine the voluntariness of the recipient's choice.

Nozick's approach is to define threats and offers in terms of a baseline (1969). A threat would make you worse off than a baseline, where that baseline can be understood morally (how well off you ought to be) or non-morally (how well off you would have been in the normal course of events).[17] However, a non-moralized baseline does not seem to be able to do the work required of it here—what is expected in the normal course of events does not seem relevant if that is itself immoral. Nozick imagines a slave owner, who habitually, for no good reason, beats his slave. One day he says to his slave, 'Tomorrow I will not beat you if and only if you now do A' (1969, p. 450). This is an offer when compared to the expected course of events, but it is a threat if we consider the morally expected course of events, where the slave owner does not beat his slave, and indeed, does not own another person. Nozick suggests that we should use the moralized baseline, at least when the recipient of the proposal would do better off if we did. As Nozick himself recognizes, this introduces a crucial indeterminacy into his definition—whether something counts as a threat or an offer depends on what we think is morally expected. Imagine someone who proposes to a drowning man that she will rescue him for a sum of money. This is a threat if we think

---

[16] See Anderson's *Stanford Encyclopedia of Philosophy* entry for a summary.

[17] A baseline approach could be put in agent neutral terms, so that the issue would become whether or not a threatened state of affairs would be better or worse than the alternative state of affairs.

there is a standing obligation to rescue in such circumstances, and an offer if not.

The issues become even thornier if we think about what is 'morally expected' more broadly. Nobody should own slaves, so *every* proposal that the slave owner makes takes place against a background where what is happening is not what is morally expected. Is every proposal a threat? Take a classic case: Ann has no other employment prospects and is offered a hazardous job at low pay. Is Ann coerced by the employer? On the one hand we might say that the normal and morally expected course of events is that the employer does not hand over a salary to Ann, and so this is an offer—Ann is better off in the offer situation than in the pre-offer situation. But on the other hand, we might think that the circumstances in which Ann finds herself are unjust, and so it is not fair to talk about pre-offer situation without taking this into account.[18]

Nozick's answer to what we should say about the more general situation in which a choice is made comes in his later work (1974). Nozick's definitions of freedom and voluntariness are *moralized*: a person is free if the restrictions on their choices have not infringed their claim rights, and a person's choice is voluntary so long as others have acted within their liberty rights: 'Other people's actions place limits on one's available opportunities. Whether this makes one's resulting action non-voluntary depends upon whether those others had the right to act as they did' (1974, p. 262).[19] Thus, according to Nozick, job offers are not coercive, and the worker's acceptance is voluntary, so long as the offerer has not done anything she did not have a right to do.

As critics of Nozick have pointed out, moralizing voluntariness is extremely problematic: first, it does not relate to our usual notion of voluntariness—for example, it is clear that one can be involuntarily though justly incarcerated. Yet on a moralized definition of voluntariness, just incarceration comes out as voluntary. Second, if the definition of voluntariness is moralized, then Nozick's defence of free market transactions is circular—voluntariness cannot be used to show that a

---

[18] Zimmerman (1981) argues that offers can be coercive when the proposer's actions keep the recipient in a weak position. I do not think that this condition is necessary.

[19] Wertheimer also defends a moralized account (1987), p. 250. For criticisms of Nozick see e.g. Zimmerman (1981, 2002), Cohen (1988), and Olsaretti (1998, 2004). Olsaretti points out that Nozick's accounts of voluntariness and freedom are actually different, though Nozick himself, and most of critics, do not notice that (2004, pp. 123–124).

transaction is just. We cannot argue, as Nozick does, that voluntary exchanges are permissible *because they are voluntary.*

Yet it is obvious that there are 'offers we cannot refuse'—in other words, that offers can undermine voluntariness in the usual sense. It is very plausible to say that the worker's acceptance of a hazardous and low paid job is not fully voluntary. It is a different question whether or not the employer in this situation is acting within his rights, and another different question whether the employer is coercing the worker. The point of this discussion is that we cannot characterize voluntariness in terms of an agent being made better or worse off by a proposal where that is a moralized notion. A proposal could make you better off while still rendering your choice non-voluntary.

Relatedly, it is not enough to say that if a proposal would make you worse off it must be coercive. Some non-trivial proposals that make us worse off are not coercive, because they do not impact on the voluntariness of our choice. The government effectively threatens me into paying my taxes, and I am worse off as a result (worse off compared to free riding, anyway). Yet I pay my taxes voluntarily.[20] The focus on better off and worse off does not capture what is crucial to coercion—the impact on voluntariness. Of course, there may be a correlation between what makes us worse off and what renders choice non-voluntary, but the two ideas are not identical.[21] Thus we need to move away from better off and worse off, and hence from the distinction between threats and offers, and talk directly about voluntariness.

6. Voluntariness, domination and alienation

The limiting of options is not, by itself, what makes a choice non-voluntary. This is essentially Frankfurt's point about the irrelevance of alternative possibilities—what really matters for moral responsibility is the agent's own attitude to her choice—whether *she* feels it to be her choice (Frankfurt 1969). Compare two cases. In both cases the Captain makes Jim a proposal: kill one or I will kill all twenty. In one case Jim ('Sadistic Jim') has always wanted to kill someone, but has worried

---

[20] A consequence of my view is that the state's coercive proposals are only full blown coercion for those who obey the law only because of the threat of punishment. Law-abiding citizens obey the law voluntarily, and so are not coerced into it.
[21] For some related points, see Olsaretti's dicussion (2004, pp. 146–8).

about the consequences. He is delighted by the Captain's proposal; it gives him an opportunity to do what he has always wanted to do without having to worry that he will be held responsible. He knows that killing one is better than killing twenty—he is not an amoralist, and he would not kill someone without having a reason such as the one provided by the Captain. Nonetheless, he does not feel that the Captain has taken over his choices; rather the Captain has done him a favour. The other case is the standard case—Jim is a botanist, and is reluctant even to kill flowers. Jim takes himself to have very good *pro tanto* reason not to kill anyone, but the Captain has taken over the situation and set up the reasons so that that reason is overridden. Jim is now made to do something that horrifies him, and because the reasons are very powerful, he feels that he has no other options. He is completely dominated by the Captain.

In the example above, Sadistic Jim welcomes the threat—he was looking for an excuse to kill someone, and this certainly seems close to the reason that Sadistic Jim is not coerced. In his early work on coercion (1969), Nozick suggests that what is crucial about coercion is that the agent is dominated by another; the agent's choice is not his own. Nozick cashes this out by saying that part of what characterizes a coercive proposal is that it is unwelcome.[22] However, in Nozick's own account unwelcomeness is not really in the driving seat—Nozick's real account of a coercive proposal is that it is one that would make the recipient worse off, and it is only secondary to this that it would be unwelcome by a rational agent. So Nozick's account rests on his unsatisfactory account of threats and offers.

Coercive proposals do seem to be essentially unwelcome, but coercive proposals are not the only ones that might be unwelcome—there are all sorts of esoteric reasons that a proposal might be unwelcome. The bare psychological fact of unwelcomeness is not very explanatory—we need to know why a proposal is unwelcome. One tempting thought is that it is coercion when you are made to do something that you would not otherwise do, or that you think prima facie wrong, or that you regret. However, this does not capture what is crucial about coercion. It is

---

[22] Part of Nozick's justification for restricting coercion to threats is that he thinks that a threat dominates in a way that an offer cannot. Nozick expresses this by saying that whereas a threat would not be welcomed by a rational man, an offer would be.

possible to be coerced into doing something that is harmonious with one's ends.[23] Perhaps I could be coerced into choosing tea rather than coffee by a man with a gun to my back; perhaps I can coerce my students into handing in their assignment on time by threatening very harsh penalties; perhaps I can even coerce *myself* in some circumstances—for example by arranging for a friend to fine me if I do not do my work.[24]

I suggest then, that we go back to domination. An agent is coerced when she is dominated. But what is it to be dominated? The crucial point is whether the agent feels herself to be the author of her own actions—when she is dominated by another she becomes alienated from her own actions. Alienation is the *feeling* that one is not in control of one's actions—it may or may not be related to a fact of the matter about whether one is. From the perspective of theoretical considerations about determinism, we are never in control, but notoriously that is not how things feel. I usually feel as if I am making my own decisions. This may be an illusion, but it is an indispensable one. It is an uncomfortable thing to start to doubt one's ownership of one's actions.[25] Usually, being reasons responsive is not alienating, although of course being led by reason is a way of being determined. It is an interesting fact about us that we do not feel out of control when we are led by reason—that in fact, the freedom we want is the freedom to do what reason dictates.[26] However, if we feel that some other agent is in control of setting up

[23] Thanks to audiences at Glasgow (especially Ben Colburn), York, and Tucson (especially David Shoemaker and Elijah Millgram) for good examples of this. For the same sort of reason I reject Dworkin's suggestion that "A does X freely if and only if A does X for reasons he doesn't mind acting from" (1970, p. 381)—we may be acting from reasons that, in general, we wouldn't mind acting from, but on a particular occasion nonetheless be coerced into acting from those reasons.

[24] Deci and Ryan's research into self-determination (1987) that shows that self-pressure has much the same effects as pressure from other people. This is promising for an account of self-coercion, but there are difficulties. In standard cases of coercion, the other agent is crucial, as I argue below. I am not sure how an account of self-coercion can accommodate the sense of lack of control that comes from the intervention of another agent.

[25] Coercion is not the only thing that can cause alienation. Usually, knowledge of determinism is not enough to cause this sort of alienation, though dwelling on the issue can cause it.

[26] As Wolf argues, autonomy cannot be the freedom to act against both our desires and our reasons (Wolf, 1990). The idea that reasons responsiveness is crucial in one way or another is found in much (too much to list here) contemporary work on moral responsibility, autonomy, and agency.

reasons, being reasons responsive does begin to feel like a way of being controlled.

In cases of coercion, the fact that another agent set our reasons up (rather than blind forces) is crucial. There is a crucial difference in the *way* that our freedom is undermined—akin to the difference in Frankfurt's cases between determined by the casual history of the universe, and being determined by the interventions of a crazed neuroscientist (1969). Compatibilists agree on the crucial point illustrated by Frankfurt's examples, that whereas determination by the causal history of the universe does not interfere with moral responsibility, being determined by another agent *does*. My point about the difference between reasons set up by agents and reasons set up by blind forces is just a version of this more general point. Just as we would appropriately resent a crazed neuroscientist if we found out that our brains had been interfered with, and yet would not resent (in fact, do not resent) the causal history of the universe for interfering with our brains, we should resent a coercer in a way that we should not resent blind forces. What agents do to us is different to what non-agents do to us. Compare being kicked deliberately with being kicked accidentally. It is a different experience— a different event has taken place, even if the only physical difference is in whatever neurological process corresponds to the intentions of the kicker.

It is thus part of our concept of moral responsibility that responsibility is undermined by the interventions of other agents. The point is that when there is another agent, that agent takes the place of 'self' in self-determination. Other agents are qualified to do that because they themselves have wills and are self-determining—the blind forces of nature cannot take over in the same way. This is what creates the feeling of alienation in the coerced agent—the sense that another agent is dominating the situation, and that the original self has become a mere object. The coercer is treating the coercee like an object, in that she has treated the coercee's reasons responsiveness as a feature to be manipulated, not to be met head on. In Strawson's terminology, she has approached the coercee's reasons responsiveness in the objective mode, not the reactive mode. When agents interact with each other as agents they listen to each other's reasons—they respond to other agents as agents. But this is not happening in a coercive exchange. It is pointless for the coercee to express herself—her point of view, her own reasons, her interests have all been ignored.[27]

This is both a conceptual matter (our concept of moral responsibility is such that what other agents do to us is different to what just happens), and an empirical one. Richard Holton, in his brief discussion of coercion and autonomy cites empirical research that shows that our sense of self-determination is undermined by threats, rewards, and even deadlines (Holton 2007, quoting Deci and Ryan 1987).[28] According to Deci and Ryan's findings, our motivation to continue the activity we have been induced to engage in is seriously weakened by these external inducements. Further, these external inducements make us miserable in general—the effects are surprisingly wide ranging. When we feel that someone else is setting up our reasons, being reasons responsive takes on a new character: it is no longer the source of freedom, but the source of oppression.

7. Subjectivism

An agent is dominated when she feels alienated from her action as a result of another agent's actions. But of course different agents will be differently susceptible to alienation. One agent might be very robust— she feels that she is in the driving seat no matter what life throws at her, and even when other agents interfere with her reasons, she feels that she is fully self-determining in doing what the reasons dictate. On the other hand there could be someone who is extremely fragile—who feels that she is at the mercy of every change in the direction of the wind, and is easily disrupted by even minor threats and offers.[29]

---

[27] Korsgaard talks briefly about coercion in her discussion of what is wrong with lying—as she puts it, 'According to the Formula of Humanity, coercion and deception are the most fundamental forms of wrongdoing to others—the roots of all evil. Coercion and deception violate the conditions of possible assent, and all actions which depend for their nature and efficacy on their coercive or deceptive character are ones that others cannot assent to' (1986. p. 333). The point that coercion cannot be assented to is essentially the point that I am making here. Similar points are made by Mark Fowler (1982) and David Zimmerman (1981).

[28] See also Deci and Ryan (2002). According to Deci and Ryan, having our self-determination undermined also undermines our enjoyment, our creativity, our trustingness, makes us more aggressive, and is bad for our health.

[29] Of course the condition that the reasons must be very powerful for a threat or offer to count as coercive will rule out many of the cases where the super fragile agent feels alienated.

On my account, 'coercion' is a term for a sort of psychological harm that one agent inflicts on another. It is like the concepts, 'to bully', or 'to intimidate'. One agent may act in a bullying or intimidating way to another, but if the target is not cowed or intimidated, then she has not been bullied or intimidated. Some people are more easily bullied or intimidated than others. Likewise, identical coercive proposals may constitute coercion in some cases, but not in others. Robust agents will be hard to coerce, and fragile agents, easy to coerce. If a proposal meets the other necessary conditions for coercion (it is credible; provides strong reasons, and the coercer has a *mens rea*), what determines whether the proposal is coercion in a particular case is the actual reaction of the agent.

As support for this point, take one of the difficult cases. One might wonder if it is possible to coerce people under general conditions of consent. For example, take the threats that I might make in order to motivate my students to get work done. What actually happens when a student does her work because of a threat? It may be that the threat just gives her the incentive to sit down at her desk, and that once she is in the flow of her work she does it entirely for its own sake. Or, it may be that the threat never leaves her consciousness—that she sits at her desk and churns out an essay only to avoid the penalty—the work itself never animates her motivational states. In the former case, it seems right to say that this is not really coercion. And I would hope that most cases where people consent to inducements are like this—the inducement serves only to overcome some sort of initial weakness: it is not the whole story about the agent's motivation to do the act in question. If it is the whole story, however, we have a genuine case of coercion. In reality, it will not always be easy to tell when a proposal is coercive, because it is not easy to tell, even introspectively, whether one is truly alienated from an action. There is nothing odd about the question to oneself, 'was I coerced into that, or did I do it of my own free will?'[30]

---

[30] In the case of fragile agents the substantial reasons condition and the *mens rea* requirement mean that many of the cases of alienation will not be cases of coercion. In the case of robustness, remember that attempted coercion is also something bad. Also, agents' robustness might change over time—robustness can have different causes, including false consciousness. The very complex sort of non-voluntariness that is involved in false consciousness is a topic for another paper.

All this is by way of showing that a subjective account of coercion does not take us too far from our pre-theoretical notion. But the real justification for a subjective account is that non-voluntariness is the sort of thing that has to be made sense of in terms of what is going on inside the agent, not what is going on outside her. Compare Olsaretti's account of non-voluntariness. Olsaretti says that an account of voluntariness should meet two conditions: it should be explanatory (i.e. it must explain how the nature of the options affects the agent's will), and it must not be subjective (2004, p. 153). On Olsaretti's account, a choice is non-voluntary when it is chosen only because all of the alternatives are unacceptable, and she adds a necessary condition in order to meet her anti-subjectivism desideratum: that the alternatives are in fact *objectively* unacceptable. Olsaretti gives no justification for anti-subjectivism except that she wants to rule out examples of people being overly demanding about their alternatives—you don't get to count as having been forced into a choice unless the alternatives really were unacceptable.

I agree that Picky, who is very demanding about what he finds 'acceptable' should not count as being coerced, but not for the reason that Olsaretti focuses on. Olsaretti focuses on the fact that Picky *should not* find options unacceptable unless they really are. Effectively, Olsaretti makes voluntariness a moral notion—you earn the status of non-voluntariness by having reasonable preferences. But, as Olsaretti herself argues, voluntariness is not a moral notion. Voluntariness is just about an agent's control over her action. As compatibilists have argued both explicitly and implicitly, if we want to avoid talk of metaphysical freedom, we have to characterize an agent's control over her action in terms of her attitude to it. Picky appears as a possible counterexample to Olsaretti's account because Olsaretti's characterization of what voluntariness consists in is misleading. On her view, if the agent finds the alternatives unacceptable, her action is not voluntary. But it is too easy to interpret 'finding unacceptable' in terms of mere desires and preferences. Of course it is still possible to be acting voluntarily when one does not particularly like one's alternatives. The solution to this is not to go for an objective notion of acceptability; rather it is to find a more fundamental subjective state.

The subjective state that I focus on is a much deeper one—alienation. The character of Picky does not arise in the same way when we consider an account in terms of alienation. On my account, if an agent is alienated from her action by a proposal, then her act is not voluntary. The criterion is subjective in that it is about whether or not the agent actually suffers alienation, not about whether she is justified in suffering alienation. But we are not tempted to say that fragile agents—those more prone to alienation—are 'picky'—it does not seem to be something that they are somehow culpable for. When a coercer (someone with a suitable *mens rea*) rides roughshod over them, we should accept that in this case, for this person, the choice was not properly voluntary, even if for other people it would have been. Being alienated from one's action by another person is a way of having one's identity damaged. It is a serious issue, no matter how it came about. Not getting what you want, by comparison, is trivial.

Thus my account of coercion is subjective in this sense: non-voluntariness is a necessary condition for coercion, and whether a choice is non-voluntary depends on what happens inside the agent. It is also subjective in various other ways: coercion depends on what the coercer and the coercee actually believe about each other's reasons and reasoning capacities, whether or not those beliefs are justified, and it depends on the coercer having a certain sort of bad intention. Coercion is not about whether people are made better or worse off, it is about how people make each other feel.

8. *The coercer's* mens rea

Clearly the coercer does not have to intend that the coercee is alienated from her action. The alienation that results from coercion is not essential from the coercer's point of view. Rather, the *mens rea* of the coercer consists in his disregard of the coercee as an agent. The coercer is trying to dominate the coercee. As I said, this is helpfully put in Strawson's terms: the coercer approaches the coercee in the objective mode. The coercer sees the coercee as an object to be controlled, even if it is through reason responsiveness.

Of course this guilty mindset will be hard to determine in many cases. But there are some clear external signs. If the proposer is in a position where he is clearly in a superior power relation to the recipient—whether that is by threat of violence or something institutional (a president has power over an intern), and particularly if the proposer has deliberately created the power imbalance, then a *mens rea* is more

likely.[31] If the alternatives to accepting the proposal a
unacceptable, then a *mens rea* is more likely. If the propos
something he does not have a right to do, a *mens rea* is more
none of these guarantee a *mens rea*, and where there is n
there is no coercion. There may be other wrongs: expl
example. And where exploitation shades into coercion mig

Take again, a classically difficult case. An employer,
directly responsible for the unjust situation whereby Ann
prospects, offers Ann a hazardous job at a low wage. Ann's
not voluntary, but it is not clear that she is being coerced
course, other ways that we can criticize the employer with
he is coercing Ann—we could say, for example, that he is
What would it take for him to be coercing her? Jus
employer does not care at all about Ann's point of
two different lines of thought in these circumstances:
employer thinks, 'Ann needs a job, I'll offer her one
subsistence wage—that's as much as I can afford whil
profits my shareholders demand, and it should seem r
Alternatively, the employer might think, 'Ann is in
I can pay her subsistence and still get her to work, so
The first line of thought does not disregard Ann's p
misrepresents it. This is not properly coercion. Self-c
worker's point of view, rather than disregard, is
common attitude in exploitative exchanges. Only
thought constitutes the *mens rea* necessary for coer

In sum, my account of coercion is this:

The coercer makes a proposal to the coercee, an
reasons for the coercee to do what the coercer (
attempting to dominate the coercee: the coerc
coercee as an agent, but as an object to be ma
finds the proposal credible, and accepts the reasc
tial. As a result of the proposal, the coercee is do
from her action.

---

[31] See Anderson (2008) for a discussion of the import
coercion.

CONCLUSION

My purpose in giving an account of coercion is to show that we can give a deep explanation for the normative situation that results from certain sorts of interaction. I agree with Kamm that when Jim accepts the Captain's proposal, the Captain remains accountable for the negative consequences of Jim's act. As I argued in section 1, I do not think this is best characterized as a bare normative fact. We need to say something about the way in which Jim's agency is undermined. We need an explanation of why the coercer keeps accountability for the negative consequences of the act done, and why the coercee does not have that accountability. The first part of that is not difficult—the coercer has brought about a certain situation (albeit via another agent) and so is accountable. But accountability is not a zero sum game—why is the coercee accountable in some ways but not in others?

I have argued that coercion renders an agent's choices non-voluntary. This is not the same as *involuntary*—an agent who makes a choice is still functioning as an agent, and her act is an act rather than event, even if her choice is not fully voluntary. This complexity gives us the resources to say the complicated things we want to say about accountability. Jim accepts the Captain's offer, Jim does not seem accountable for the death of the one person he kills—the Captain is fully accountable for that. Yet Jim does seem praiseworthy for having saved the lives of nineteen others. He is praiseworthy because, although he was coerced, he was reasons responsive—he did not collapse under the pressure and do something that he did *not* have good reason to do. Of course this is not a full account of the relationship between non-voluntariness and accountability—it is just a start.

Let me close by making some brief remarks about integrity and utilitarianism. Williams' complaint was that utilitarianism undermines the integrity of the agent in so far as it allows the projects of others to determine what we should do.[32] Williams diagnoses the problem as

---

As has been pointed out by many critics of Williams, the complaint had better not beg the question—Jim's integrity is not undermined just because he has to choose the option that maximizes the good—a utilitarian agent is not undermined by doing what utilitarianism requires. So it is not entirely clear what Williams' complaint is, and most likely, there are several things he meant to say.

resting on the fact that consequentialism assigns value impartially to states of affairs. Williams thinks that this entails that it makes no difference to consequentialism how a state of affairs comes about—in particular, it makes no difference if another agent intervened. As he puts it in his discussion of Jim, '. . . for consequentialism, all causal connexions are on the same level, and it makes no difference, so far as that goes, whether the causation of a given state of affairs lies through another agent, or not' (1973, p.94).

In one sense this is true, but in another it is clearly not. In *ranking* states of affairs consequentialism takes no account of how they came about. But consequentialism is not just a theory about goodness, it is also a theory about rightness—about what agents should do, and about how we should praise and blame agents. So far as rightness is concerned, *of course* it matters how a state of affairs did or could come about. Consequentialism understood merely as a theory of the good includes in its rankings physically impossible states of affairs (it might be best for me to sprout wings and fly to the rescue of a drowning child right now), but such states of affairs are irrelevant to consequentialism as a theory of rightness. A theory of what agents ought to do it is limited by an account of responsibility.

In developing a theory about what agents ought to do, and what counts as right and wrong, we have various options about which account of responsibility we tie consequentialist rankings to. One bad option would be to embrace a 'consequentialist' account of responsibility. There is no reason why consequentialists should be forced to say that we are responsible for an action when it would have good consequences to say that we are responsible for an action. The goodness of consequences is relevant to actions, but it is not relevant to attributions of responsibility. Instead, we can tie consequentialist rankings to a reasons responsiveness account of responsibility: agents are responsible for an act when the agent has reasoned to that act. This gives us the resources to say that agents are not responsible for distant avalanches, and they are not responsible for what other people do, and sometimes, for example when there is an intervening agent, they are less than fully responsible for what they themselves do. That has been the argument of this paper.

So consequentialists as much as anyone can say that agents are not fully responsible when they have been coerced. And consequentialists as much as anyone can say that coercion is an attack on an agent's integrity. As I have defined coercion, this is a plausible claim: coercion is the undermining of the agent's feeling that her act is her own. This seems like as good a characterization of integrity as we are likely to find.

REFERENCES

Anderson, Scott 'Coercion', *The Stanford Encyclopedia of Philosophy* (Fall 2008 Edition), ed. Edward N. Zalta. <http://plato.stanford.edu/archives/fall2008/entries/coercion/>

——(2008) 'Of Theories of Coercion, Two Axes, and the Importance of the Coercer', *Journal of Moral Philosophy* 5(3), 394–422.

Aristotle (1999) Nicomachean Ethics, ed. Terence Irwin (Indianapolis, IN: Hackett).

Austin, J. L. (1956) 'A Plea for Excuses', *Proceedings of the Aristotelian Society* 57, 1–30. Reprinted in J. L. Austin, J. O. Urmson, and G. J. Warnock, G. J., *Philosophical Papers* (Oxford University Press, 1979).

Bayles, Michael D. (1974) 'Coercive Offers and Public Benefits', *The Personalist* 55, 139–44.

Cohen, G. A. (1988) *History, Labour, and Freedom* (Oxford University Press).

Conly, Sarah (2004) 'Seduction, Rape, and Coercion', *Ethics* 115(1), 96–121.

Deci, Edward L. and Ryan, Richard M. (1987) 'The Support of Autonomy and the Control of Behavior', *Journal of Personality and Social Psychology* 55, 1024–37.

——(2002) *Handbook of Self-Determination Research* (Rochester, NY: University of Rochester Press).

Dworkin, Gerald (1970) 'Acting Freely', *Noûs* 4, 367–83.

Feinberg, Joel (1986) *Harm to Self* (New York: Oxford University Press).

Fischer, John Martin and Ravizza, Mark (1998) *Responsibility and Control: A Theory of Moral Responsibility* (New York: Cambridge University Press).

Fowler, Mark (1982) 'Coercion and Practical Reason', *Social Theory and Practice* 8, 329–55.

Frankfurt, Harry (1969) 'Alternate Possibilities and Moral Responsibility', *Journal of Philosophy* 66, 828–39.

——(1988) 'Coercion and Moral Responsibility'. In *The Importance of What We Care About* (Cambridge University Press), 26–46.

Gewirth, Alan (1981) 'Are There Any Absolute Rights?', *Philosophical Quarterly* 31, 1–16.

Haksar, Vinit (1976) 'Coercive Proposals', *Political Theory* 4, 65–79.

Holton, Richard (2007) 'Freedom, Coercion and Discursive Control'. In Geoffrey Brennan, Robert Goodin, Frank Jackson, and Michael Smith (eds.), *Common Minds* (Oxford: Clarendon Press), 104–17.

Kamm, F. M. (1999) 'Responsibility and Collaboration', *Philosophy & Public Affairs* 28, 169–204.

——(2007) *Intricate Ethics: Rights, Responsibilities, and Permissible Harms* (Oxford University Press).

Kant, Immanuel (1998) *Groundwork of the Metaphysics of Morals*, ed. Mary Gregor (Cambridge University Press).

Korsgaard, Christine (1986) 'The Right to Lie: Kant on Dealing with Evil', *Philosophy and Public Affairs* 15(4), 325–49.

Nozick, Robert (1969) 'Coercion'. In Sidney Morgenbesser, Patrick Suppes, and Morton White (eds.), *Philosophy, Science, and Method: Essays in Honor of Ernest Nagel* (New York: St. Martin's Press), 440–72.

——(1974) *Anarchy State and Utopia* (Oxford: Blackwell).

Olsaretti, Serena (1998) 'Freedom, Force and Choice: Against the Rights-Based Definition of Voluntariness', *Journal of Political Philosophy* 6(1), 53–78.

——(2004) *Liberty, Desert and the Market: A Philosophical Study* (Cambridge University Press).

Strawson, P. F. (1993) 'Freedom and Resentment'. In *Freedom and Resentment and Other Essays* (Abingdon: Routledge), 1–28.

Watson, Gary (1996) 'Two Faces of Responsibility', *Philosophical Topics* 24, 227–48.

Wertheimer, Alan (1987) *Coercion* (Princeton University Press).

Williams, Bernard (1973) 'A Critique of Utilitarianism'. In J. J. C. Smart and Bernard Williams, *Utilitarianism: For and Against* (Cambridge University Press), 77–150.

Wolf, Susan (1990) *Freedom Within Reason* (New York: Oxford University Press).

Yaffe, Gideon (2003) 'Indoctrination, Coercion and Freedom of Will', *Philosophy and Phenomenological Research* 67(2), 335–56.

Zimmerman, David (1981) 'Coercive Wage Offers', *Philosophy and Public Affairs* 10, 121–45.

——(2002) 'Taking Liberties: The Perils of "Moralizing" Freedom and Coercion in Social Theory and Practice', *Social Theory and Practice* 28, 577–609.

9

The Best Expression of Welfarism[1]

CHRISTIAN COONS

The term "welfarism" is used in a variety of ways in moral philosophy, political theory, and economics. In this paper, following L. W. Sumner, it refers to a view about the foundations of morality—the view that "nothing but welfare matters, basically or ultimately, for ethics" (Sumner 1996: 184).[2] Again following Sumner, welfarists believe:

Axiological Monism: The list of foundational goods contains a single item: well-being. Only states of individual well-being are intrinsically good.

The Priority of the Good: Facts about which states are intrinsically good explain which duties and moral reasons we have. The point of ethics is to bring about good (or better) states of affairs.

Agent-Neutrality: The foundational ethical values are agent-neutral—there is a reason for each agent to promote it, or aim to bring it about. (Sumner 1996: 184–5)

I do not defend welfarism, though I briefly rehearse some of its attractions. Instead, my concern is which specific normative theory welfarists should adopt. Of course, if one begins simply with the three theses above it's hard to avoid arriving at anything other than a form of maximizing act utilitarianism. I argue, however, that the best expression of welfarism—i.e. the most compelling normative theory consistent with the three theses above—isn't utilitarian at all. Instead, it is a kind of *ideal carer* theory. My inspiration is not a nostalgic yearning for the benevolent spectators of early proto-utilitarian history; rather it is Elizabeth

---

[1] My thanks to the anonymous reviewers, Connie Rosati, Pekka Väyrynen, Kelly Sorensen, Simon Keller, David Faraci, Mark Timmons, David Schmitz, Ellie Mason, Doug Portmore, David Sobel, David Shoemaker, Chris Heathwood, Guy Fletcher, Elizabeth Guthrie, and Tom Dougherty for comments on this paper.

[2] Keller (2009) characterizes welfarism slightly more broadly.

Anderson, Steven Darwall, and David Velleman's more recent insight that there is a difference between *valuing welfare* and *valuing welfare for the sake of those to whom it accrues*.[3] Recognizing this difference allows us to develop a normative theory (as well as a "theory of beneficence"— a theory which ranks states of affairs according to welfare value) that better captures the spirit of welfarism, while avoiding some seemingly intractable problems that beset the traditional utilitarian approach. What's more, my theory can be applied without knowing what exactly welfare consists in, or how to quantify it *intra-* or *inter*-personally.

WHY WELFARISM?

A full discussion of welfarism's strengths and weaknesses would fill a long book; I won't attempt that here. Nevertheless, allow me to briefly outline some of the view's charms, especially because I'll argue the view that I propose best captures these charms.

Why accept Sumner's welfarist thesis that "ethics has ultimately to do with ensuring that lives go well"? To begin with, this view is already deeply embedded in our moral thinking. Stereotypically wrong acts (e.g. killing, theft, rape, deception, disloyalty, etc.) seem to share one and only one obvious and unique characteristic: they each tend to be bad for their victims. Moreover, the relative seriousness of these sins tends be proportional to how bad these acts are for others. Indeed, if someone tells you you something is your duty, one might challenge the speaker by asking—"Is it? Whom would it benefit? For whom is it worth doing?" Similarly, if you are told something is forbidden, one might ask—"Really? What's the harm in it?"[4] But these questions function as intelligible *challenges* to the original speakers only to the extent that harms and benefits are the *only* factors relevant to moral assessment. Thus, our tendency to think these questions as challenges indicates our welfarist leanings.

---

[3] Perhaps the most important difference between the type of theory endorsed by Hume and Smith and the one I will defend here lies in the relevant emotional response. For Hume and Smith a kind of empathy is the relevant sentiment. But "care" is a different, but related, state that Darwall (2002) also calls "sympathetic concern." This particular state, as distinguished from types of empathy, has become an object of psychological study: see Hoffman (1981, 1991), Batson (1991, 2009).

[4] Some rhetoric here is cribbed from Sumner (1996: 191).

Of course, one might deny welfarism and hold that harm and benefit are central to moral assessment. For example, consider a deontological position consisting of a single prohibition: *Intend no harm.* One can hold such a view without being a welfarist by denying that *one's being harmed* is bad, or by denying that the wrongness of intending harm is in any way explained by its actual or hypothetical tendency to make things worse. Either denial is obscure. What then would justify the prohibition? Surely harming is wrong in virtue of the *bad* that typically results from it?

Thus, welfarism not only provides a plausible understanding of what our moral practice is about—it is also able to *justify* it. After all, why shouldn't we view moral norms as mere evolutionary or cultural artifacts that bear no real relevance to what I should do all things considered? Welfarists have a powerful answer: rather than insisting that moral rules have no or are not in need of justification, they insist that the point of these requirements is to make the world better in the only way it can be: by improving our lives—for our sake. In short, moral acts do what is best for everyone.

Even when welfarism profoundly conflicts with our "intuitive" judgments, its appeal is resilient. For example, welfarism's most straightforward manifestation—act utilitarianism—may sometimes horrifically recommend hanging an innocent, torturing a child, or pushing a fat man off a footbridge. Even here, we must concede that the utilitarian has one heck of a point. If performing these acts really would be what's best for everyone—what's most worth doing for our "collective sake"— why shouldn't we? Despite the objections the utilitarian welfarist faces, answering that question remains difficult. For if morality really advised us to do something other than what's best for everyone then, as Simon Keller asks, "would we not be *better off* with something other than morality?" (2009: 91). On one reading, the answer to Keller's question is a trivial "yes." But surely, if there is a correct moral theory, it is not something we'd be better off without. If that's right, welfarist theories emerge as our most natural candidates for moral truth.

WELFARISM AND MAXIMIZATION

Welfarism tells us that moral norms are a function of the good; but it does not precisely identify how to "derive" these norms (Sumner 1996: 198). Welfarists hold that moral norms are (roughly) norms to "promote" well-being; but promote it when, for whom, how, and to what extent? The position, by itself, offers us no direct advice. Nevertheless, initially only one approach seems available—to *maximize* the well-being of *all* welfare subjects. Welfarism's priority of the good tells us that facts about which states are intrinsically good explain which duties and moral reasons we have. It is difficult to see how any moral considerations that might be raised to defend, for example, a *satisficing* or *rule* utilitarianism, or a restriction to only *human* well-being could be justified by or founded in an appeal merely to the value of well-being itself. By taking the priority of the good seriously, the welfarist seems committed to no less than *maximizing* welfare.

MAXIMIZING WELFARE AND POPULATION ETHICS

The idea that welfare is to be maximized needs specification. It is most naturally interpreted as an injunction to maximize *total* well-being—the sum of individuals' well-being in a state of affairs. But this view generates a repugnant conclusion that Derek Parfit famously called "the Repugnant Conclusion":

RC: There is always some number n such that a world containing n creatures whose lives are barely worth living is better than any world with a smaller number of creatures who are very well-off. (1984: 381–90)

To illustrate this conclusion's repugnance, consider the famous situations below:

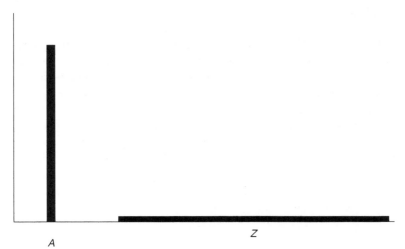

A

Z

Figure 9

Here, height represents levels of individual well-being and width the size of the population. Thus, in *A* suppose that 10 billion individuals fare 20 times better than the individuals in *Z*, but *Z* contains a population of 210 billion people. We may face a choice between situations like *A* and *Z* when we can spur or curb population growth in contexts of limited resources.

Maximization, therefore, can sometimes be an affront to the very ideas that make welfarism attractive. Choosing to move from a world like *A* to a world like *Z* certainly does not seem to be doing what's "best for everyone"—what's most worth doing for our sake.[5] Rather, moving to *Z* from *A* seems to make things go much worse for people. Here, unlike pushing the fat man or hanging the innocent, the characteristic pull of the utilitarian position is lost; indeed one is hard-pressed to see *any reason at all* to choose *Z*.

But our reactions to the Repugnant Conclusion do not reveal our implicit rejection of welfarism. Our view that *A* is better than *Z* is not explained by implicit deontological intuitions that challenge welfarism's priority of the good. For were the move from *A* to *Z* to occur via some natural disaster—a procreative explosion—things still have become worse. RC also does not indict welfarism's axiological monism. We don't object to a move from *A* to *Z* because doing so sacrifices important values such as freedom, preference-satisfaction, or autonomy; were the beings in *A* and *Z* squirrels, and thereby incapable of manifesting these other values, the move would make things worse, and worse *for* squirrels. Increasing the number of squirrels, at great expense to their average well-being, isn't worth doing *for their sake*. RC does not indict welfarism, it indicts expressing it in terms of maximizing *total* well-being.

Expressing welfarism in terms of maximizing *average* well-being fares no better. Simply "removing" people who are less well-off than average raises average well-being, but it does not make the world better, or better for us. To sharpen the point, imagine a world occupied by three children suffering in the 6th circle of hell. If we give birth to another occupant of this hellish world, one who suffers the mere tortures of the 5th circle, this improves average well-being, but the world is worse. Giving birth to this less tortured child wouldn't be what's

[5] Some, for lack of better options, now embrace the RC; see: Huemer (2008), Broome (2004), and Tännsjö (2002).

worth doing for our or anyone's sake—it's not what's "best for us." So, characterizing welfarism as an injunction to maximize average well-being also betrays what makes the view compelling.[6]

This is puzzling. Even non-welfarists tend to believe we have a moral reason to promote well-being; and welfarists believe that this is simply what morality is "all about." But sometimes there is no reason to maximize well-being, and welfarist reasons *to avoid* doing so. And a "hybrid" theory that somehow tries to appropriately weigh both average and total well-being cannot solve the puzzle.[7] Such views predict that we should produce "burdensome children"—children who are so happy that they promote *both* total and average welfare but reduce the well-being of everyone who existed before their birth. Arguably, the very poor are often able to produce such children, but their doing so would not be what's best for us, or anyone at all. Similarly, such views entail that "replacing" the current population with an ever so slightly (but currently non-existent) happier population would be an improvement. Surely this is not at all what the welfarist has in mind. As Jan Narveson once put it: we care about well-being because we value making *people happy*, not making *happy people* (1976).

PERSON-AFFECTING CONSTRAINTS

Narveson's rhetoric points to a feature shared by each of these problematic cases. In each case we have an improvement in average or aggregate well-being, but no one *for whom* the outcome was better. For example, Z (relative to A) has greater total well-being, but it's not better for anyone in particular. And when we improve average well-being by merely removing, adding, or replacing someone, there is no person for whom it is an improvement.

To avoid these problems, we might adopt a "person-affecting" welfarism.[8] There are various ways to characterize the person-affecting approach, but the basic view may be stated as:

---

[6] This sort of example, I believe, first appears in Parfit (1984: 422).

[7] Sidgwick (1907) may be the first to suggest such a view—see Driver (2009).

[8] See Narveson (1976). For a more sophisticated contemporary approach, see Roberts (1998) and (2004).

Person-Affecting Constraint: Actions or states of affairs are better or worse only insofar as they are better or worse for particular person(s).

This constraint is *too* constraining when our actions affect the identities of future individuals—Parfit calls these "Non-Identity" cases (1984: 351–79). Parfit illustrates with an example: imagine a woman who could have a child at age 14 or at 30. Suppose that the child she would have at 30 cannot be identical to the child she would have at 14, and that if she has the child at 14 it will fare worse than the child she would have had at 30. All else being equal, we tend to think it would be better if the woman had the child at 30. However, no one would be benefited by her doing so, and no one would be harmed or made worse-off were she to have a child at 14. Thus, person-affecting views are saddled with the result that it is no better if she has the child at 30.[9] Similarly, suppose that our decision to prevent global warming also affects *who* lives in 150 years—the future population contains completely different sets of individuals depending on our decision. The person-affecting approach would seem to entail that it is no better to prevent global warming: those come to exist cannot claim to have been harmed, for they would not exist were we to have done otherwise; and if we *do* prevent global warming, those who come to exist cannot claim to have been benefited or "spared" because there's no alternative in which they fared worse.

AN IRRESOLVABLE SET OF PROBLEMS?

These puzzles, first noticed by Sidgwick, came into sharp focus in Derek Parfit's *Reasons and Persons*.[10] The problem, of course, is not whether we can find a theory of how to rank states of affairs with respect to welfare value that allows us to avoid the Repugnant Conclusion; the problem is to find a theory that can avoid the Repugnant Conclusion, the Non-Identity Problem, and any other deeply unsavory commitment. Parfit suspected that no such theory—a "Theory X"—exists, and some claim to have formally proven that such a theory is impossible.[11] Accordingly how to deal with the Repugnant Conclusion has turned into "one of the cardinal challenges of modern ethics" (Ryberg et al. 2008).

[9] A more developed critique of person-affecting views appears in McMahan (1998).
[10] Sidgwick (1907) and Parfit (1984).
[11] See, for example, Arrhenius (2011) and Rachels (2004).

In the years since Parfit posed these problems, various solutions have been advanced, but the consensus is that none of these proposals has been satisfying. Though I cannot give proper hearing to all of the extant theories of beneficence here, most believe that each putative solution either falls victim to a variation on one of the standard problems above, or has an unacceptable implication of its own. Many approaches have been employed and some evoke other values in addition to welfare or deontic constraints. These approaches actually give up on welfarism—the first violates axiological monism and the second violates the priority of the good. In any case, these approaches are phenomenologically inaccurate: if our verdicts in these cases were explained by goods or requirements distinct from well-being, we should at least feel *some* conflict where well-being provides us with reasons that are "dominated" or outweighed by competing evaluative or deontic concerns. Yet I can see no reason to have burdensome children, add the person to the 5th circle of hell, or prefer *Z*. Consequently, the trouble appears not to lie with other values or deontic constraints, but with something peculiar about the value of well-being itself.

If well-being was always good, we would always have some defeasible reason to promote it—either in total, average, or perhaps via some more complex process of aggregation—but we don't. So while we may retain the welfarist idea that well-being is intrinsically good and the *only* intrinsic good, we also seem forced to deny well-being's unconditional value—we sometimes lack agent-neutral reasons to promote it. We need a principled account of *when* it matters, and hopefully one that still does justice to the spirit of welfarism. Furthermore, we don't just want a theory that is consistent with our intuitions about cases, we want one that can explain and vindicate our intuitions. "Theory X"—if it exists—should not merely faithfully "match" our intuitions, it should capture what grounds them.

TOWARD A SOLUTION

I submit that if we want to know *when* welfare matters, we should step back and ask ourselves *why* it matters. Some theorists cannot adopt such a strategy; for them we cannot explain *why* well-being is good; *it just is.* This view has no hope of addressing the axiological problems above; luckily however, welfarists are not condemned to it. Even if welfare is the only non-instrumental and intrinsic good, it does not follow that we can say nothing about why it has value—why it, rather than pain and suffering, is good. Welfarism only limits the *sort* of explanation we can give: *axiological monism* entails that we cannot explain welfare's value in terms of any other *good*, and *the priority of the good* prohibits the use of deontic claims in our explanation. So is there a plausible explanation of why welfare is good? Sumner offers a suggestion:

> In the case of human beings the idea that we should promote their good surely owes at least some of its appeal to the fact that we can do so for their sake . . . this notion of furthering someone's good for her own sake can be generalized beyond the boundaries of our species; I have a perfectly good sense of what it means to take my cat to the veterinarian for her sake. (1996: 211)

On the one hand, Sumner notes something seemingly obvious and important: we value well-being because it is worth promoting *for the sake* of individuals. And indeed this may be a plausible constraint on any putative good—i.e. nothing could be good or worth promoting unless it was worth promoting for the sake of some individual(s). On Sumner's view, welfare matters because it matters for the individuals to whom it accrues (1996: 214). If this is right, we now know we shouldn't express welfarism in terms of simple maximization—because, as we have seen, increasing average and total welfare is sometimes not worth doing for anyone's sake. On the other hand, we might worry that Sumner's explanation is empty. After all, isn't promoting an individual's well-being just *what it is* to act for that individual's sake? If so, Sumner's proposed "explanation" is no explanation at all—he has expressed a tautology.

I believe Sumner is on to something: we've already identified a number of cases where maximizing well-being does not appear to be what is worth doing for anyone's sake; so apparently there *is* an extensional difference between what *maximizes our well-being* and *what's best for us*—what is most worth realizing for our sake. But this appearance cannot be vindicated, nor help us find a better theory, without identifying a corresponding conceptual difference. To appreciate the import of Sumner's insight, and how it may lead us to an improved version of welfarism, it will help to first consider the difference between *acting for someone's sake* and *promoting her welfare*.

ACTING FOR AN INDIVIDUAL'S SAKE VS. PROMOTING HER WELFARE

What is it to act for someone's sake?[12] The natural answer is that acting for *x*'s sake is acting to promote *x*'s well-being. But this isn't quite right. After all, a young child may share with or console a playmate *for that playmate's sake* without having yet acquired a conception or theory of well-being. Indeed, care apparently precedes our particular theories of well-being and not vice versa.[13] Furthermore, some—namely G. E. Moore, Thomas Hurka, and Don Regan—question the very intelligibility of a "good for a person," yet we have every reason to suspect that they sometimes act(ed) for the sake of others (Moore 1903; Hurka 1987; Regan 2004).

One can also act so as to promote an individual's well-being, but not act for her sake. Selfish foster parents who aim to promote the well-being of their foster child only so as to continue receiving government checks surely do not act for the child's sake. Acting for one's sake also is not acting with the *non-instrumental* aim to promote one's well-being. Imagine a civil servant at the Department of Human Welfare who is so consumed by his work that he becomes single-mindedly concerned with, and non-instrumentally aims to promote, human well-being. Further imagine that he does not care for anybody (not even himself). Our civil servant's obsession with welfare seems fetishistic; it is just this sort of person who might promote well-being by adding happy people or "subtracting" those with less than average well-being. And, again, these policies do not appear to be worth adopting for anybody's sake. The difference seems to be that when we promote an individual's welfare for that individual's *sake*, an attitude towards that individual underlies our aim. Typically, this attitude is care. Caring for someone is incompatible with denying that her welfare matters. But our civil servant illustrates that caring for someone isn't *merely* valuing her welfare. As appearances suggest, *care for* an individuals is an attitude we bear towards individuals, not outcomes. We don't literally care *for*

---

[12] The contribution of "sake" to expressions of this form isn't clear: "I did it for John" and "I did it for John's sake" seem to be equivalent except in the rare case where the former expresses that one did something in John's stead.

[13] See Jaworska (2007) and Darwall (2002: 50–72); for evidence from experimental psychology see Thompson (1987) and Zahn-Waxler et al. (1992).

outcomes, though we can care *about* them. Nevertheless, care indirectly involves wanting certain outcomes. As Steven Darwall puts it:

> Any desire for another's good that springs from concern for that person is also for *his sake*, the object of care is the individual . . . Mill claims that people come to desire wealth even when it lacks instrumental value because of its psychological associations with other things they intrinsically desire. Were a desire for someone's good to arise similarly, it might involve no concern whatsoever for the person himself. One might simply desire intrinsically *that* another's good be realized without desiring it for his *sake*. (2002: 1–2)

We're now in position to see that Sumner's explanation, though obvious, is not vacuous. It *does* make sense to claim that we value an individual's well-being for that person's sake. This is just to say that we value it out of care for that individual—which is not simply caring *about* their well-being.[14] And this explanation seems correct. We all know that people who hate themselves tend to be imprudent, and that those who hate others have little regard for anyone else's well-being.[15] But these cannot be conceptual truths; they're psychological corollaries of how and why we value well-being.

This psychological explanation tells us only something about why we value well-being, not what makes it valuable. Having certain attitudes towards a person—in this case *care*—does not explain why that person's well-being has value. If we ceased to care, their well-being would still matter. Furthermore, the explanation has a problem: we often value the well-being of distant individuals whom we may never meet—but it's a stretch to claim we care about those *particular* people. I submit that we value the well-being of people that are unknown to us not because we care about them in particular, but because we think they are of a *type of being* that warrants or merits our care. We can care for types of individuals without caring for particular individuals of that type. And we will not view their welfare as *worth promoting* unless we view such individuals as *worth caring for*. Thus, we arrive at a corresponding metaphysical explanation for welfare's value: *Our welfare matters only when and to the extent that we merit care.* This seems correct. Even if we

---

[14] For concerns about Darwall's claim that we can characterize care independently of well-being, see Heathwood (2003: 616–17).
[15] For similar arguments, see Darwall (2002: 6) and Velleman (1999: 611).

hate someone, but reluctantly acknowledge that they too merit care, we're committed to seeing their well-being as worth promoting. And we would be utterly perplexed by a utilitarian who denied that welfare subjects are worth caring for.

Elizabeth Anderson defends this view, and it later appears in the works of Stephen Darwall and David Velleman. On their shared view, personal well-being does not matter, and is not an appropriate object of moral concern, unless persons merit concern. As Anderson puts it in *Value in Ethics and Economics*:

if it does not make sense to value the person (in a particular way) then it does not make sense to care about promoting her welfare [...] enemies, who hate each other have no reason to promote each other's welfare [...] what gives the pursuit of or desire for welfare its only point is that we ought to care about the people who enjoy it. (1993: 22)

The same position appears in David Velleman's "A Right of Self-Termination?"

things that were good for you would not actually merit concern unless you merited concern; and if you didn't, then despite their being good for you, they wouldn't ultimately be worth wanting, after all. [...] A person's good only has hypothetical or conditional value, which depends on the value of the person himself. (1999: 611)[16]

And in Darwall's *Welfare and Rational Care*:

What gives considerations of someone's welfare or personal good the status of [agent-neutral] normative reasons is having a value that makes him worthy of care, as one accepts when ones cares for him. (2002: 8)

Given these authors' employment history, let us call their shared position "The Michigan Condition" and characterize it as follows:

Michigan Condition (MC): Being good for some individual, *x*, is not itself a good-making feature of any state of affairs unless *x* merits care.

---

[16] Velleman's view has changed slightly. In "Beyond Price" (2008), he departs from Anderson and Darwall by claiming that the particular emotional response that's relevant to well-being is *love*. For more concerns about sympathetic concern as the attitude that's appropriately relevant to a person's good, see Rosati (2006).

Of course, this principle cannot help us develop an improved welfarist theory if it is itself inconsistent with welfarism. And there may be grounds for concern. For example: can well-being have *intrinsic value* if its value depends on the value of something else—the "value" of the individuals to whom it accrues—i.e. their *meriting care*? The answer rests on two issues: what we mean by "intrinsic value" and whether facts of the form *x merits A* are evaluative facts—do they attribute value to an object? Only one combination of these views makes *MC* inconsistent with welfarism. Specifically, if (1) "intrinsic value" simply refers to value that an object has that is independent of the value of anything else, and (2) claims of the form *x merits A* are claims about *x*'s value, then *MC is* inconsistent with welfarism. But, as I will explain, very few accept this pair, and given the way welfarists tend to use "intrinsic value," *MC* and welfarism are not in conflict.[17]

A predominant and traditional use of "intrinsic value" refers to value an object has in virtue of its intrinsic properties.[18] On this view, well-being can be intrinsically valuable even when its value depends on the value of individuals. To illustrate, if *Christian's being well-off* is good, and *MC* is true, then it follows that my being well-off is intrinsically valuable. For were it not for my "value"—my meriting care—this state would not be good, but the state is nevertheless good in virtue of an intrinsic constituent—me. In more rough, but vivid, terms: if my well-being *matters* because *I matter*, my faring well would still be good, as Moore would say, "in isolation." So, given this traditional and common understanding of "intrinsic value," *MC* and welfarism are consistent even if the value of well-being depends on the value of individuals.

But let's sidestep tedious debates about how to best characterize a term of art, and suppose the worst-case scenario: suppose that, for whatever reason, *any* plausible view of intrinsic value must reject the

---

[17] Only Anderson, to my knowledge, accepts this pair. Although I don't think this puts her in *substantive* dispute with others. Her commitment to (2) is apparent in her well-known contention that the value of states of affairs depends on the value of individuals (Anderson 1993: 17–43). Her commitment to (1) is revealed when she describes extrinsic values as items it makes sense to value only because it makes sense to value something else (Anderson 1993: 19).

[18] See Moore (1951: 260) and Feldman (1997: 136–39). For a defense, see Bradley (2002).

possibility that an item's intrinsic value could depend on the value of something else. Even this supposition won't impugn the compatibility of *MC* and welfarism unless our *meriting care* entails that we *have value*. But only fitting-attitude theories of value license this entailment. Extant welfarists, as broadly consequentialist, would not accept such an account. The consequentialist injunction to *promote value*, which runs through welfarism's various forms, becomes silly on a fitting-attitudes account. It becomes an injunction to promote items that merit particular attitudes. So if people were valuable in virtue of meriting care, we'd have some reason to produce more people even if we knew that they'd fare poorly! Clearly, a consequentialist would not believe any such thing even if they became convinced that some individuals merited care.

Thus, consequentialists apparently use "value" to refer to a different concept than those who accept fitting-attitude accounts.[19] This result is not surprising. When the welfarist says "only well-being has intrinsic value" we may paraphrase him as saying "only states of well-being are non-instrumentally *good* or *desirable*" or that "such states are worth wanting or preferring, even if nothing else is." Sumner, for example, characterizes intrinsic value as being "worth having or pursuing for its own sake, not merely by virtue of some further good with which it is connected or associated" (1996: 190). This is another common account of intrinsic value. And we know that it is incompatible with the view that *animals merit care* entails that *animals have value*—meriting care does not make one a suitable object of possession pursuit! Ultimately then, *MC* and the idea that well-being is the only intrinsic value are not in conflict. More importantly, given the way welfarists tend to use "intrinsic value," such a conflict is impossible.

Nevertheless, these observations suggest a different conflict: perhaps *MC* conflicts with welfarism's *priority of the good*. After all, if some individual(s) *merit* an attitude, isn't it true that we *have reason* or *ought to* bear this attitude towards them? And if this is so, then shouldn't we conclude that facts about the good are not the basis of all of our moral duties and moral reasons? This concern rests on a dubious, yet common,

---

[19] For a compelling argument along these lines, see Bradley (2006).

substantive assumption about the normative import of the *merits* relation—I call it "the deontic assumption" (or "*DA*").[20]

DA: If some attitude is "merited" or "fitting" (etc.), then we have a reason (or
ought to) have this attitude.

I reject *DA*, and I think others should too. For one thing, we can all
acknowledge—even consequentialists can acknowledge—that some
animals are *fearsome*—that they merit or are fitting objects of fear; but
then insisting that one really has a reason or ought feel fear towards such
animals seems silly. After all, "what's the point" in feeling a negative
emotion provided that we can keep ourselves out of danger without it?
So just as it is an open question whether you should wear a shoe simply
because it fits, one can sensibly ask whether one has any reason at all to
feel as is fit. Accordingly, *DA* is substantive normative thesis that is both
in need of defense and something a defender of *MC* can reject.

More importantly, we have strong grounds for rejecting *DA*—for it
may entail that the *priority of the good* is impossible! To see this, consider
two widely shared, putative conceptual truths: *being good just is being
desirable*, and *being desirable just is being a merited/worthy object of desire*.
If *DA* were true, then these apparent truths would entail that we have
reasons, or ought, to desire the good regardless of whether doing so
would promote the good. This is precisely what the priority of the good
denies. So *DA* allows us to dismiss traditional consequentialism and its
priority of the good out of hand. Surely these positions cannot be so
easily dispatched by a dubious assumption about the deontic import of
the *fits* or *merits* relation. Therefore, we should doubt *DA*, and this is
especially true of those who, like welfarists, accept the priority of the
good. Without *DA*, the most formidable objection to pairing the
Michigan Condition and welfarism goes away.[21,22]

---

[20] I've used the expression "merits care" but, to my mind, the expressions "worth caring
for," "fitting object of care," or "appropriate object of care" serve just as well, and often refer to
the same concept. Although 'merit' sometimes connotes that the relevant individual deserves
(in the sense that they have *earned*) the relevant attitude. I do not intend that sort of reading;
I use "merits" because it is the shortest.

[21] One might worry that my conclusion is too weak: perhaps *MC* is consistent with
welfarism, but that does not show that it is a welfarist view! Indeed, neither Velleman,
Anderson, nor Darwall happen to be welfarists. But hold your horses, I don't claim that *MC*
is welfarist, I use it to develop a welfarist view (below).

[22] Not only is it dubious whether these relations entail deontic relations to do/feel as is fit,
entailments also do not go in the other direction. To illustrate, imagine a world populated by
infants. Surely these infants merit care. But it is false that they *ought* to be cared about—no one

TOWARD AN IMPROVED WELFARIST THEORY OF THE GOOD

Our observations so far seem to be pointing in a common direction: If we accept . . .

- Welfarism is appealing because it directs us to do what would be best for everyone—to do what is most worth realizing for our sake.
- Sumner's claim that promoting welfare is good because it is worth promoting for the sake of individuals.
- Anderson, Darwall and Velleman's point(s) that promoting welfare for the sake of some particular person is to promote it out of care for them. And that one's well-being would not be worth promoting unless one merited care.

. . . then it seems the welfarist theory of what states are best—what is worth wanting or realizing for the sake of welfare subjects—should be somehow based on "what it makes sense" to want out of care for welfare subjects. Unfortunately, how to do this is not immediately clear.

First, we might take a cue from Darwall. On his view, what is good for an individual, *I*, is what it is *rational* to desire for *I* insofar as one cares about *I* (2002: 4). Thus, our corresponding theory about what states are impersonally best—which states are most worth realizing for the sake of welfare subjects in general—would look like this:

D: States are good (better) to the extent that it is rational to want (prefer) them out of care for welfare subjects.

My worry about *D* is that *care*, as a kind of feeling, cannot yield commitments. Having this feeling can certainly explain why a person does something, just as feeling dizzy might, but it is at least contentious whether, like a belief, such a feeling can *rationally commit* one to

---

in the world is cognitively equipped to care about them—so no one *can* care about them. Meriting care is also not being such that one ought to care, *if one can*. If I promise a plant-loving friend that I will really care for (and not merely tend to) his plants while he is away, then I ought to care for his plants. But that fact does not entail that the plants merit care. My own view about how fitting attitudes are normative, without being deontic or evaluative in the ordinary sense, will become clearer below. In short, on my view, the special normative role of the merited attitudes are as the conative elements that supplement *formal* ideal practical deliberation—they are what to attribute to any ideal observer used as standard or heuristic for resolving practical questions.

anything. And insofar as it can, its commitments seem problematically agent-relative because what it is rational to do in light of an attitude is characteristically dependent on an agent's other attitudes. For example, suppose that care for x commits one to valuing what one takes to be good for x; and suppose that I believe that a drug will improve John's health, and you believe that the drug is bad for John's health. Provided we both care for John, it is rational for me to want John to take the drug, while rational for you to want him to not take it. Consequently, on its face, Darwall's view entails that what's best for everyone would become implausibly indeterminate and "carer-relative." Though Darwall does not intend this result, it not easy to see how to avoid it.

Darwall sometimes alternatively states his view as the view that what's good for a person is what one *ought to want* out of care for her. Accordingly, we might characterize the welfarist impersonal good in terms of what we ought to want out of care for persons generally. But this alternative now conflicts with welfarism's priority of the good because it makes facts about the good dependent on facts about what one *ought* to do out of care. Furthermore, this view may now be conflict with the Michigan Condition itself. Remember, Darwall claims that well-being provides no agent-neutral grounds for acting unless the relevant welfare subject(s) *merits care*. But if this is right, the natural conclusion is that there is nothing we (agent-neutrally) ought to do *merely* out of care for an individual, because the relevant individual(s) must also merit care. Thus, this alternative characterization conjoined with *MC* yields an "error-theory" about well-being. Of course, Darwall surely does not intend this entailment. Darwall may be able to explain why these concerns are misguided; my aim is not to challenge the coherence of his view. I'm only suggesting that no clear and obvious interpretation of the view can be taken "off the shelf" to assist in our search for an improved theory of beneficence.

A second suggestion is inspired by Elizabeth Anderson who writes that, "the mediating function of concern for people can never be made transparent: the appropriateness of desires for states of affairs must be subject to the constraint that they adequately express their correlative attitudes toward people" (1993: 29). Anderson, thus, appears to endorse the following principle:

A: States of individual good are valuable to the extent that realizing them would adequately express care for those individuals that merit care.

This formulation also faces problems. First, it is obscure how to determine whether an act *adequately expresses* care for B. Furthermore, because *expresses* appears to be a communicative concept, and "what communicates what" seems relative to both speakers and listeners, this view appears subject to the same sort of relativity that moved us away from the first suggestion inspired by Darwall.

Anderson's proposal also seems to be in conflict with welfarism. It is an instance of a more general view that Anderson often invokes in *Value in Ethics and Economics*. If it makes sense to value a state, S, only because an individual, x, merits an attitude, A, then one should not pursue S through means that do not express A for x (1993: 17–43). This "expressive principle" lies behind Anderson's ultimate view that there are deontic constraints on our promotion of our good. On her view, though it is possible to manipulatively or ruthlessly promote someone's well-being for her sake (i.e. out of care for her), these acts don't *express* care—indeed these types of acts communicate just the opposite. Her expressive principle does not merely tell us that we sometimes have no reason to promote well-being, it positively entails substantive norms not to promote well-being in particular ways. The resulting view denies the priority of the good, a conclusion Anderson embraces.

So Anderson's expressive principle is questionable, and it looks like it's in tension with welfarism. In any case, it's certainly not obvious, and it is apparently false. I may value the state *Christian's being on the opposite side of the street from Fido*, because Fido is fearsome (i.e. Fido merits fear), but I clearly have no reason whatsoever to only take measures to cross the street that express my fear! On the contrary, that may be what will set him off![23]

---

[23] One might object that I'm equivocating on the meaning of "express." Perhaps one might say that, A can express I in the sense that (i) is *motivated*, or is *guided by*, I, or in the alternative sense where A (ii) can *display*, or *communicate* the relevant attitude. But Anderson clearly seems to have the latter in mind (see Anderson, 1993: Chapters 1–2, especially pp. 3, 11, 18). Anderson believes that if we a looked just at what one would *want* insofar as one were impartially caring, we would again arrive at the *repugnant conclusion* because impartial care would lead one to prefer Z for the sake of the people who do not exist in A: these people would be "better off" in Z, because non-existent in A (1993: 28). I think Anderson is wrong about this. First, she seems to dubiously assume that bringing into existence (with a life "worth living") is a benefit.

Perhaps we'll be more successful if we turn our attention to what care moves us to want or do, and forget about what it *makes rational, commits us to*, or what *adequately expresses* it. But here again, indeterminacy creeps in: What *I* might prefer in light of caring for someone may be different than what *you* might, especially if you and I have different theories of well-being. Furthermore, it's not clear the resulting theory will be suitably normative—what we *actually* prefer will be influenced by false background beliefs, poor inferences, or other idiosyncratic elements of our psychologies. These should play no part in determining what's actually best for us. Our best option here is to idealize. Building our theory on our actual dispositions only tells us how care manifests itself in the ignorant and irrational. To avoid these distorting influences, we may invoke an Ideal Carer ("IC")—a fully-informed, formally, instrumentally, and theoretically rational being—and ask what it would do and want insofar as it cares for welfare subjects.[24,25] Of course, this option famously has indeterminacy problems of its own. Couldn't more than one hypothetical being qualify as an IC, and yet each wants and does different things? For example, full information and formal rationality will not guarantee a convergence in views about

---

Second, her conjecture is phenomenologically inaccurate: as a carer I do not feel pangs of conflict in thinking about how we might create even more people. The carer just is, all else being equal, indifferent to "mere addition." Her view, instead, appears to be the odd suggestion that care for people *moves* one to add more people, but doing so is somehow in conflict with how one meaningfully *expresses* one's care.

[24] More precise characterizations of the relevant idealization will need to be made. Here, I'm merely sketching, not mucking through the details. However, an "insofar as" clause is needed because the IC will have some dispositions merely in virtue of being formally rational and fully-informed. We will not want these dispositions to deliver moral verdicts—e.g. the formally rational person draws valid inferences, but it's not plausible to thereby claim that doing so is morally optimal. The "insofar as" clause ensures the relevant response would not have occurred *but for* the IC's care.

[25] Darwall considers a position like this but opts instead for the "normative" view that well-being is what one *ought* or what it *makes sense* to want insofar as one cares (2002: 31). He appears to move away from a view like mine because it would fail to capture well-being's normative character—a caring person could recognize that certain states would be preferred by an IC, but ask "So what? How does that bear on what I should prefer?" I'm not moved by this worry for two reasons. First, caring agents presumably will be committed to approximating the preferences of the IC, because they are committed, as agents, to not acting on faulty or incomplete information and to meet the formal constraints of practical and theoretical reasoning. So they really cannot coherently ask, "What's it to me?" Second, my aim is not to provide an account of the *concepts* of well-being or even what's best for us, but to give a substantive characterization of which states fall under the extension of these concepts across worlds.

what's good for people—e.g. couldn't one IC be a hedonist about well-being while the other is not?

My response is simple—the IC should have no view about what's good for people. Indeed, our IC should have *no attribute* that is not necessitated by our description of it. Any addition would either be (a) superfluous, if it makes no dispositional difference, or, (b) yield "junk" outputs if it does make a dispositional difference. If we want to identify the purest, least-arbitrary, and immaculate manifestations of care, then we should not add anything that might make a dispositional difference that is not directly attributable to its care or the idealizing conditions themselves. So unlike Firth's "Ideal Observer" (1952), who does not have the relevant care, and is "otherwise normal," the IC has no desire to sing while listening to the radio—normal though it may be. So, the proper view of the IC is not as *any* or *a* being that cares for all welfare subjects and is fully-informed (etc.). Instead, the IC is the *least complex* being who meets these conditions. With that clarification, the problem of "many" ICs with different dispositions goes away.

In short, using the IC gives us the most plausible way to model what care "recommends." Care, obviously, does not *literally* recommend anything, and similarly it's a stretch (and perhaps even a category error) to say it renders some actions intelligible or reasonable—that there are acts that *make sense* or that *one ought to perform* in light of caring. And few acts beyond hugs, facial expressions, and speech-acts actually express care, if this means anything beyond providing evidence for its presence. But we can, and should, turn our attention to the *non-arbitrary* and *error-free* outputs or manifestations of care. The IC's idealization aims to ensure these outputs are not infected by error or ignorance. Its minimal complexity ensures the outputs are not arbitrary.

Of course, now one might worry that the IC cannot translate its care into action—a caring person tries to do what's best for those for whom they care, but with no theory of well-being, the IC's care cannot recommend any response. This objection is empirically implausible. We care for people, but almost none of us have a clear or robust theory of what is best for the people for whom we act. Again, children and G. E. Moore can act from care, even if they haven't the faintest sense of what the good for us is supposed to be. Yes, caring people want what is best for those for whom they care. But if that is so, I cannot see how the caring person, when formally rational, fully and vividly informed about the non-normative, and devoid of all normative views (for example a theory of well-being!) will fail to hit its mark—what they desire actually *will* be what's good for the person. What further information could the IC require? The IC's dispositions would at least appear to be a perfectly reliable *indicator* of what is best for us; this is does not commit us to Darwall's stronger claim that welfare *just is* what it makes sense to want insofar as you care for someone.[26]

The alternative—that the IC's responses *would not* track what is best for us—seems mistaken. It is not merely that children, some non-human mammals, and G. E. Moore are capable of acting from care without a theory of well-being, it is also true that when they act from care they can do a reasonably good job of wanting what actually is good for those for whom they care. In fact, we are inclined to attribute care *because of* successful sensitivity to those states that promote an individual's well-being. For example, we are tempted to infer that mother bears have feelings of care for their cubs because they tend to do things that promote their cubs' well-being. But the bear, we assume, lacks judgments about what well-being is, and how to measure it. Consequently, we assume that care (plus adequate non-normative information) is sufficient to allow you to be sensitive to what is actually good for an individual.

Think of it this way, imagine that you have a difficult choice to make, and you wonder which would be *best for* you. You consult two people. First, you consult a good friend. She is intelligent and cares deeply for you. She knows you and your circumstances rather well. However, your friend has not thought much about well-being before. Indeed, were she to study the matter she might, like many of us, find herself unable to settle on a view—shifting from varieties of hedonism, to informed-

---

[26] A concern about this view is that care for individuals may involve dispositions which clearly cannot be used to characterize what is good for them. For example, caring for others may often dispose us to tell others that we care, but telling someone that you care may not be part of what's good for them. In short, caring persons have other dispositions that go beyond wanting or preferring what is in fact good for the person. If so, an IC's wants or preferences would not reliably indicate the caree's good. But I submit that desires to communicate one's care, etc. are often founded on values, desires, and aims other than pure care itself. Indeed, it may not be possible for an attitude to be partly constituted by disposition to communicate itself; for a regress looms. Consequently, while what actual caring people tend to want for others may not be a reliable indicator of person's good, a minimally complex IC's desires for others would remain so.

desire views, to various objective-list views and back again. Alternatively, you can consult your colleague—a leading scholar with a considered substantive view about well-being. Your colleague knows you and your circumstances quite well, but does not care for you. He is willing and able to faithfully apply his theory to your decision. Who would you consult? Whose advice is likely to be more reliable? The IC, like your friend, does not need a theory of well-being, or views about how to measure it.

This points to an important advantage in using the IC to characterize what is best for us—it requires no substantive assumptions about what is good for us, how to measure it, or how to do interpersonal utility comparisons. Indeed, I submit that determining the IC's dispositions would finally allow us to settle those issues; they would reveal what well-being is, and what is best for welfare subjects in general. But our welfarist axiology must do more than identify "good" states—it also needs to *rank* them. Accordingly, we should look to the IC's *preferences*:

C: State, S, is better than a state, S', iff S would be preferred to S' by a minimally complex IC insofar as he cares for welfare subjects.

WILL THIS HELP WITH THE PROBLEMS IN POPULATION ETHICS?

I've offered an abstract case for using the IC's preferences to refine our welfarist axiology. But the proof is in the pudding—will this theory really avoid the cases that cast doubt on the maximizing approaches?

First, notice that caring persons will not prefer policies that improve total or average well-being merely by adding people. Caring for a type of creature does not involve preferring more of them. For example, most of us care, and think it is appropriate to care, for children. Obviously, if you care for children you'll want the children who come to exist to be as happy as can be, and you will disvalue outcomes where children suffer. But care for children does not involve preferring *more* of them, even if we're certain that the additional children will be happy. Or consider our care for fictional characters: caring for Huckleberry does not incline me to want a happy version of him, or someone like him, to actually exist. Therefore, this view, like the otherwise problematic "person-affecting" views, can capture and explain why we ought to make people happy, not happy people. The proposal can also similarly explain why we have no standing reason to reproduce, or to create burdensome children even if the addition of such children would raise total or average well-being.

The view also avoids the problems that beset the "person affecting" approach. But to see why we need to first discuss *how* our IC cares for welfare subjects. Notice that we can either (1) care only for the particular individuals that happen to meet a description, or, (2) we can care for individuals (whatever their particular identities, if any) under a description. Anderson holds that properly expressed care for people is directed only towards *each particular* person, for otherwise it simply amounts to a perverse concern for well-being itself, and the Repugnant Conclusion looms (Anderson 1993: 27–29, 35). But these are not our only options. To illustrate, an amnesiac woman—upon discovering scars from an apparent C-section—might be struck by an apparent and profound feeling of care for *her children*, even if it turns out that she does not have any. So does she care for her children or not? In the first sense she does not, and in the second sense she does. We might say that the woman has a *de dicto* care for her children rather than a *de re* attitude directed at particular individuals that meet that description. But this attitude towards *her children* gives her no reason to *have* a child, even if she knows it will fare well.

Notice also that individuals do not merit care because of their particular identities—e.g. because one is Bob, Suzy, or Gary. *Because Bob is Bob* is not a reason to care for him. Rather, we think that persons merit care not because of *who* they are, but *what* they are. Thinking otherwise violates the putative conceptual truth that evaluative facts cannot vary without a relevant qualitative difference. For the pure welfarist, the relevant feature will not be *being a particular person at t,* or even *being human,* but rather *being a welfare subject*—being an individual for whom things can go better or worse. Our characterization of the IC should reflect this fact; doing so allows us to handle the non-identity cases. The IC does not simply care for all the particular individuals who happen to be welfare subjects (e.g. Bob, Suzy, and Gary); rather the IC has *de dicto* care for *welfare subjects,* just as the amnesiac cares for the children she may or may not have.[27]

---

[27] My description of care here is, in one respect, a radical departure from the way it is discussed by both Anderson and Darwall. Specifically, they often characterize it as directed at particular individuals, and obviously I deny that. Kelly Sorensen brought this to my attention.

Now consider the older/younger mother case that introduced the non-identity problem. On its face, we now have every reason to suspect that the IC will prefer the outcome where the mother has the child at 30 to the outcome where she has it at 14. As argued above, caring agents don't prefer the addition of happy individuals, but they do want whoever comes to exist to be as well-off as possible. Apparently, an agent who cares for welfare subjects and not merely for the particular individuals that happen to be welfare subjects, would prefer Child at 30 to Child at 14. Were someone indifferent between these options, it would be reasonable to ask "don't you care about your children?" Thus, we need not appeal to the otherwise unacceptable claim that welfare is independently good to explain the non-identity cases. And though it initially sounds odd, we can now see how a state may be worth realizing for welfare subjects without being worth realizing for the sake of any *particular* welfare subjects.[28] Importantly, though this move "gets us out of a jam" it's not *ad hoc*; rather it is the most sensible move when we consider *why* individuals possess moral standing, and why we value well-being. Earlier approaches tried to avoid deeply counter-intuitive implications with specific suggestions as to *whose* welfare matters (actual individuals, future individuals, possible individuals... etc.) and *how much*—each answer beset with its own set of problems. Appealing to care allows us to avoid this. Like the amnesiac mother, it is possible to qualify as caring for individuals under a description without caring for any particular entities—actual or merely possible. Caring does not require *there being* particular individuals that are the object of care. Some children care for unicorns or imaginary friends, though such beings may be metaphysically impossible.

So the theory looks promising: thus far, the dispositional profile for care corresponds perfectly to our verdicts about when welfare is worth

---

However, this does not mean we're talking about different affective states under the same name. Rather, I think the cases above (caring for types of beings and impossible beings) illustrate that the very same affective state can have no particular beings as its object. The IC *does* care for Gary, Suzy and Bob, but it does so in virtue of its more general attitude toward beings of their type.

[28] See Hare (2007) for a related move. Hare also appeals to the distinction between particular individuals that happen to meet a description and individuals under a description. My argument appeared prior to the publication of his article in my 2006 dissertation. In conversation, I learned that he also developed his argument in *unpublished* form before I did.

promoting. Nevertheless, these observations only point to a research program; and some may worry that any such program is doomed. After all, Parfit suggests that, and others claim to have formally *proven*, that a satisfactory axiology for welfare is impossible (Parfit 1984: 419; Arrhenius 2001, 2011). The proofs begin by listing extremely plausible constraints on any defensible theory. In Parfit's informal proof, one constraint is that the theory must not entail the Repugnant Conclusion—e.g. it must not entail that *Z* is better than *A*. The proofs then purport to show that when we compare states of future generations with different sized populations, the constraints cannot be jointly satisfied. The upshot is that our reasoning about value appears to be incoherent, and that perhaps we should conclude that there are no *facts* about what makes the world go better or worse for us (Arrhenius 2011: 19–23).

If these proofs succeed, my theory must violate one of the adequacy conditions, thereby "proving" it is intuitively unacceptable, incoherent, or both. In fact, it's actually *very* easy to show that my view violates some of these putative constraints. To see this, consider *A* and *Z* again. In an abstract sense, if we were like a caring deity, and had to choose between *A* or *Z*, it certainly seems that all else being equal, we would prefer *A*. This seems like good news, because it suggests the theory will avoid the Repugnant Conclusion. But not so fast. The IC's preference will change when it is not (like a deity) choosing between *A* and *Z ex nihilo*. For example, suppose that the prevailing state of affairs were *Z*. Would things *go better* if we stayed in *Z* or immediately changed our world into *A*? Would a caring person prefer that almost everyone be annihilated, so that a (relatively) small number could be much happier? No. If the prevailing state of affairs were *Z*, then surely the carer *would* prefer *Z* to *A*. But if *A* were the prevailing state of affairs, then a carer would prefer *A*—caring people don't prefer the addition of many poorly-off people, especially when adding them would make everyone else much worse off. Thus, my theory yields the following results:

A is *better than* Z, if the current world is A.
Z is *better than* A, if the current world is Z.

The lesson we are *supposed* to draw from these results is that the theory is repugnant and incoherent. After all, the theory predicts both the repugnant verdict that *Z* is better than *A*, and *even worse*, it then later predicts that *A* is better than *Z*! The proofs typically assume no theory could have such "unacceptable" outputs. But, I hope you'll agree that there's nothing wrong with these results; these are the right results, something is wrong with the constraints.

The primary concern about this view would be that it makes the *better than* relation intransitive. But that is not so. Yes, a carer's preference for A or Z is sensitive to facts about the current world, and this makes it possible for the relative value of A and Z to change. Nevertheless, the variation in the carer's particular preference orderings makes perfect sense. The orderings depend on stable and transitive preferences regarding *types of changes*. For example, when the view predicts that:

A is better than Z, when the current world is A—because the IC prefers no change (A *to* A) to a change from A *to* Z.

Z is better than A, when the current world is Z—because the IC prefers no change (Z *to* Z) to a change from Z *to* A.

A is better than Z, when no one currently exists—because the IC prefers the change from an empty world to A to the change from an empty world to Z.

It is *these* preferences—preferences for types of changes—that order the IC's further preferences for worlds *at a time*. The lesson *is not* that the "better than" relation is intransitive; it is that states of the world *at a time* have value only in virtue of the value of changes that they instantiate. The more fundamental evaluative relation holds among changes, and here, the *better than* relation remains transitive. This type of view, one excluded by the terms of the current debate, offers the most faithful rendering of how we value well-being. I believe that only this type of view will properly explain why, for example, the world goes better *when our lives are improved,* rather than *replaced with improved lives*—for these are claims about the value of different changes, not states at a time.[29]

USING THE IC IN A WELFARIST NORMATIVE THEORY

So far, we've used the Ideal Carer to rank and evaluate outcomes—to deliver a refined welfarist axiology. Effectively, the theory tells us which outcomes are best (and better) for us—which outcomes are most worth realizing for our sakes. But to get a refined welfarist *normative theory*, we

---

[29] Obviously, more needs to be said about this approach, but space limits us here. For an extended defense and articulation of this approach, see Coons and Weber (2011).

still need to decide how to characterize our moral obligations in light of the good—for example, whether we should adopt an act or rule consequentialist theory. But I think we can sidestep, and potentially resolve, debates about how welfarists should characterize our obligations by again appealing to the IC. The IC's various types of disposition will offer us a natural way to distinguish the various types of moral assessment, including the *right*, the *merely permissible*, the *morally optimal*, and the *supererogatory*. Traditional (consequentialist) approaches famously have trouble finding a principled account of these different categories. Using the IC helps us carve out the appropriate conceptual distinctions while allowing for the substantive possibility that there are no supererogatory acts. For example, the *wrong* designates a set of acts that, morally speaking, the will mustn't perform—here unlike the *supererogatory*, one does not have the moral option to sacrifice one's virtue. Thus, if the IC embodies the moral perspective, we may characterize the *wrong* in terms of what it would *will* that you *not do* (i.e. cases where it would override your freedom to choose for yourself), the *right* in terms of what it would *will* that you *do*, and the *supererogatory* as perhaps just the class of actions that it would prefer that you do, but would not *will* that you do. The issue of whether there are any supererogatory actions is open and depends on whether the IC *always wills* that you do what it *wants* you to do; an affirmative answer would vindicate a view akin to traditional act consequentialism.

So, as a first approximation, the best expression of welfarism may look something like this:

One might suspect that these standards run afoul of welfarism's priority of the good—notice that none of them make reference to the good or to welfare! But this is misleading. On closer inspection, these standards positively entail the priority of the good. After all, the IC's dispositions will be some function of his *desires* and *preferences*—the dispositions that correspond to our axiological theory. Less abstractly, it seems that a caring person has no basis for willing that anyone do anything unless there are beings whose lives could be made better or worse—so it is well-being that provides the ground for his dispositions.

The Morally Optimal:	An action, *x*, is **morally optimal** in a circumstance *C*, for an agent *A*, iff a minimally complex, formally rational, fully-informed being would most want *A* to *perform x* in *C* insofar as it cares ("de dicto") for welfare subjects.
The Morally Required:	*A* has a **moral duty** to do *x* in *C* iff a minimally complex, formally rational, fully-informed being would *will* (not merely want, hope, or wish) that *A* do *x* in *C* insofar as it cares for welfare subjects.
The Supererogatory:	X is **supererogatory** for *A* in C iff a minimally complex, formally rational, fully-informed being would most *want* but not *will* that *A* do *x* in C insofar as it cares for welfare subjects.
The Permissible:	X is **permissible** for *A* in C iff a minimally complex, formally rational, fully-informed being would not *will* that *A* not do *x* in C insofar as it cares for welfare subjects.

BUT IS THIS THEORY OF ANY PRACTICAL USE?

Whether this is "best expression of welfarism" or not, it's interesting because we've arrived at a pure and uncompromising welfarism that is not necessarily utilitarian. However, one might worry that the theory suffers from unique and intractable epistemic hurdles. Specifically, we might worry that it is useless as a guide for discerning what is right, wrong, optimal, or best for us, because we cannot access the IC's dispositions. This concern is less serious than it seems. My proposal, I submit, substitutes a tractable and empirically investigable research question—*what is the dispositional profile of sympathetic concern?*—for the more difficult and perhaps intractable questions of *what is well-being?* And *how can it be quantified and measured within and among individuals?* Care is familiar to us; we've each felt it for others. And though the term 'care' is ambiguous, the affective state that I (and Darwall) appeal to is also an object of psychological study.[30] Presumably, we can identify those who have care for others and those that do not. Identifying both will be useful—for we can compare the dispositional profile of those who care for others versus the profile for those who do not. Obviously, none of our subjects will be "minimally complex." But I presume that with careful experimental design and a large and diverse sample size, we can begin to identify

[30] See Hoffman (1981, 1991), Batson (1991, 2009), and Batson and Shaw (1991).

which responses among the caring are attributable to their care. Advances in neurology may even allow us to identify which brain-states or processes are associated with care, and which response-types it prompts.

Finally, given that none of us are fully informed, we might worry that knowing what care disposes us to do tells us little about the IC's dispositions. But actually it tells us an awful lot. It tells us what the IC would do if the circumstances were as we take them to be. And we can control for differences among subjects' non-normative background beliefs by asking them to respond to detailed thought experiments, or scenarios where the circumstances are stipulated. Control for the influence of different normative background beliefs could be achieved with a large and diverse set of subjects. Generalizations should emerge, and these may function as moral or axiological principles depending on the relevant response-type. Of course, we should be careful about pronouncing from the armchair which conclusions we might reach. I'll leave open a deep meta-ethical question about these principles: whether or not the IC *tracks* these truths or its responses *make* them true. For practical purposes, that question is irrelevant. But the view is not an ideal-observer or response-dependent theory "all the way down" because it is built on the independent moral assumption that those whose lives can go better or worse merit care.

Of course, even if this research project is viable, there is only so much we can know about the IC's dispositions. Nevertheless, if welfarism is true, the theory gives us a moral ideal that we can approximate by: (1) cultivating impartial concern for sentient creatures; (2) isolating and acting only upon that affective response; and (3) cultivating the epistemic virtues. The extent to which you can accomplish 1–3 is the extent to which you and your actions approximate the moral ideal. Perhaps that's all we need: perfection is for the idealized; improvement is all we can hope for here on Earth.

REFERENCES

Anderson, E. (1993) *Value in Ethics and Economics* (Cambridge, MA: Harvard University Press).
Arrhenius, G. (2000) "Future Generations: A Challenge for Moral Theory." FD Diss., Uppsala University, Dept. of Philosophy (Uppsala: University Printers).
——(2011) "The Impossibility of a Satisfactory Population Ethics." Unpublished manuscript.

Batson, D. (1991) *The Altruism Question: Toward a Social-Psychological Answer* (Hillsdale, NJ: Lawrence Erlbaum Associates).

——(2009) "Two Forms of Perspective Taking: Imagining How Another Feels and Imagining How You Would Feel." In K. D. Markman, W. M. P. Klein, and J. A. Suhr (eds.), *Handbook of Imagination and Mental Simulation* (New York: Psychology Press), 267–79.

——and Shaw, L. (1991) "Evidence for Altruism: Towards a Pluralism of Pro-Social Motives," *Psychological Inquiry* 2, 107–22.

Bradley, B. (2002) "Is Intrinsic Value Conditional?" *Philosophical Studies* 107, 23–44.

——(2006) "Two Concepts of Intrinsic Value," *Ethical Theory and Moral Practice* 9, 111–30.

Broome, J. (1999) *Ethics Out of Economics* (Cambridge University Press).

——(2004) *Weighing Lives* (Oxford University Press).

Coons, C. and Weber, M. (2011) "Transitional Consequentialism and the Mere Addition Paradox." Unpublished manuscript.

Darwall, S. (2002) *Welfare and Rational Care* (Princeton University Press).

Driver, J. (2009) "The History of Utilitarianism." The Stanford Encyclopedia of Philosophy (Summer 2009 Edition), ed. Edward N. Zalta <http://plato. stanford.edu/archives/sum2009/entries/utilitarianism-history/>

Feldman, F. (1997) *Utilitarianism, Hedonism, and Desert: Essays in Moral Philosophy* (Cambridge University Press).

Firth, R. (1952) "Ethical Absolutism and the Ideal Observer," *Philosophy and Phenomenological Research* 12, 317–45.

Hare, C. (2007) "Voices From Another World: Must We Respect the Interests of People Who Do Not, and Will Never, Exist?" *Ethics* 117, 498–523.

Heathwood, C. (2003) "Welfare and Rational Care (Review)," *Australasian Journal of Philosophy* 81, 615–17.

Heyd, D. (1988) "Procreation and Value: Can Ethics Deal With Futurity Problems?" *Philosophia* 18, 151–70.

Hoffman, M. (1981) "Is Altruism Part of Human Nature?" *Journal of Personality and Social Psychology* 40, 121–37.

——(1991) "Is Empathy Altruistic?" *Psychological Inquiry* 2, 131–3.

Huemer, M. (2008) "In Defence of Repugnance," *Mind* 117, 899–933.

Hurka, T. (1987) "'Good' and 'Good For'," *Mind* 96, 71–3.

Jaworska, A. (2007) "Caring and Internality," *Philosophy and Phenomenological Research*, 74(3), 529–68.

Keller, S. (2009) "Welfarism," *Philosophy Compass* 4(1), 82–95.

McMahan, J. (1998) "Wrongful Life: Paradoxes in the Morality of Causing People to Exist." In Jules Coleman and Christopher Morris (eds.), *Rational Commitment and Social Justice: Essays for Gregory Kavka* (Cambridge University Press), 208–47.

Moore, G. E. (1903) *Principia Ethica* (Cambridge University Press).

——(1951) *Philosophical Studies* (Atlantic Highlands, NJ: Humanities Press).

Narveson, J. (1976) "Moral Problems of Population." In M. D. Bayles (ed.), *Ethics and Population* (Cambridge, MA: Schenkman), 59–80.

Parfit, D. (1976) "On Doing the Best for Our Children." In M. D. Bayles (ed.), *Ethics and Population* (Cambridge, MA: Schenkman), 100–15.

——(1982) "Future Generations: Further Problems," *Philosophy and Public Affairs* 11, 113–72.

——(1984) Reasons and Persons (Oxford: Clarendon Press).

Parsons, J. (2002) "Axiological Actualism," *Australasian Journal of Philosophy* 80(2), 137–47.

Rachels, S. (2004) "Repugnance or Intransitivity: A Repugnant but Forced Choice." In J. Ryberg and T. Tännsjö (eds.), *The Repugnant Conclusion: Essays on Population Ethics* (Dordrecht: Kluwer), 163–86.

Rawls, J. (1971) *A Theory of Justice* (Cambridge, MA: Belknap).

Regan, D. (2004) "Why Am I My Brother's Keeper?" In R. J. Wallace, P. Pettit, S. Scheffler, and M. Smith (eds.), *Reason and Value: Themes from the Moral Philosophy of Joseph Raz* (Oxford University Press), 202–30.

Roberts, M. (1998) *Child versus Childmaker: Future Persons and Present Duties in Ethics and the Law* (Lanham, MD: Rowman & Littlefield).

——(2004) "Person-Based Consequentialism and the Procreation Obligation." In J. Ryberg and T. Tännsjö (eds.), *The Repugnant Conclusion: Essays on Population Ethics* (Dordrecht: Kluwer), 99–128.

Rosati, C. (2006) "Darwall on Welfare and Rational Care," *Philosophical Studies* 30, 619–35.

Ryberg, J., Tännsjö, T., and Arrhenius, G. (2008) "The Repugnant Conclusion." The Stanford Encyclopedia of Philosophy (Fall Edition), ed. Edward N. Zalta <http://plato.stanford.edu/archives/fall2008/entries/repugnant-conclusion/>.

Sider, T. (1991) "Might Theory X be a Theory of Diminishing Marginal Value?" *Analysis* 51, 265–71.

Sidgwick, H. (1907) *The Methods of Ethics*, 7th edition (University of Chicago Press).

Sikora, R. I. (1975) "Utilitarianism: The Classical Principle and the Average Principle," *Canadian Journal of Philosophy* 5, 409–19.

Sumner, L. M. (1996) *Welfare, Happiness and Ethics* (New York: Oxford University Press).

Tännsjö, T. (2002) "Why We Ought to Accept the Repugnant Conclusion," *Utilitas* 14, 339–59. Reprinted in J. Ryberg and T. Tännsjö (eds.), *The Repugnant Conclusion: Essays on Population Ethics* (Dordrecht: Kluwer), 219–38.

Temkin, L. (1987) "Intransitivity and the Mere Addition Paradox," *Philosophy and Public Affairs* 16, 138–87.

—— (1993) "Harmful Goods, Harmless Bads." In R. G. Frey and C. W. Morris (eds.), *Value, Welfare, and Morality* (Cambridge University Press), 291–324.

Thompson, R. A. (1987) "Empathy and Emotional Understanding: The Early Development of Empathy." In N. Eisenberg and J. Strayer (eds.), *Empathy and its Development* (Cambridge University Press), 119–45.

Velleman, J. D. (1999) "A Right of Self-Termination?" *Ethics* 109, 606–28.

—— (2008) "Beyond Price," *Ethics* 118, 119–212.

Warren, M. A. (1978) "Do Potential People Have Moral Rights?" In R. Sikora and B. Barry (eds.), *Obligations to Future Generations* (Philadelphia: Temple University Press), 14–30.

Zahn-Waxler, C., Radke-Yarrow, M., Wagner, E., and Chapman, M. (1992) "Development of Concern for Others," *Developmental Psychology* 28(1), 126–36.

10

Rawlsian Self-Respect[1]

CYNTHIA A. STARK

Self-respect is a good whose value seems undeniable. As a consequence, it presents itself as a notion capable of justifying the value of other goods. Indeed it has been employed in this way by a number of philosophers (Boxill 1976; Held 1973; Postow 1979; Miller 1982; Mohr 1988). The most prominent of these is John Rawls. Rawls appeals to the good of self-respect to justify many features of "justice as fairness"—the highly influential account of distributive justice presented in *A Theory of Justice*.

Most who have considered the role of self-respect in Rawls's theory, throughout the four decades since the publication of *A Theory of Justice*, have agreed that Rawls's argument rests upon an irreparable equivocation between two different ideals of self-respect (Doppelt 2009; Eyal 2009; Moriarty 2009; Thomas 1978a, 1978b).[2] In the face of this critical consensus, I attempt to resurrect Rawls's approach. I show first that Rawls relies upon an unambiguous notion of self-respect, though he sometimes is unclear as to whether this notion has merely instrumental or also intrinsic value. I show second that Rawls's main objective in arguing that justice as fairness supports citizens' self-respect is not, as many have thought, to show that his principles support citizens' self-respect generally, but to show that his principles counter the effects of the market on lower class citizens' sense of worth. This discussion

[1] I owe thanks to Jeffrey Moriarty and the participants in the Second Annual Arizona Workshop in Normative Ethics, especially Ernesto Garcia, Thomas Hurka, and Elijah Millgram, for their feedback on this paper. I am also grateful to two anonymous referees for their helpful comments.
[2] See also, Deigh 1983; Labukt 2009; Lane 1982; McKinnon 2003; and Yanal 1987. Distinctions among different types of self-respect that have bearing upon the supposed equivocation contained in Rawls's account are discussed in Darwall 1977; Dillon 1992; Hudson 1980; Massey 1983; Middleton 2006; and Sachs 1981.

establishes that Rawls, in the end, sees self-respect primarily as an intrinsic good.

I proceed as follows. First I outline the equivocation objection. Second I argue that that Rawls's view of self-respect should be interpreted as the belief that the activities that make up one's contribution to a scheme of social cooperation matter. Third I establish that this interpretation is consistent with all of Rawls's arguments justifying justice as fairness by appeal to self-respect. Finally, I show that these arguments are primarily designed to demonstrate that justice as fairness upholds the self-respect of lower class citizens in spite of their diminished class position.

THE ARGUMENT AND THE STANDARD CRITIQUE

Rawls's argument that his principles of justice preserve citizens' self-respect has the following structure. First, Rawls claims that self-respect—the secure conviction that one's plan of life is worth carrying out—is what he calls a "primary social good." It is, along with wealth, liberties, and opportunities, a necessary all-purpose means for citizens (as moral persons) to achieve their ends. He maintains, second, that because self-respect has this special role, the provision of self-respect is a matter of justice. Indeed, political arrangements can be judged just or unjust in part on the basis of whether those arrangements sustain self-respect. Third, he argues that the arrangements proposed by justice as fairness indeed secure citizens' self-respect.[3] He concludes that those arrangements are, to that extent, just.

Rawls's critics claim that this argument breaks down because the attitude Rawls identifies as a primary social good, and hence as necessary for agents to achieve their ends, is not the same attitude as the one he shows his principles to promote.[4] The former attitude consists in believing one's conception of the good to have value; the latter consists in recognizing one's equal standing as a citizen. So, Rawls has not shown

---

[3] For a discussion of the ways in which Rawls's two principles of distributive justice support citizens' self-respect see Cohen 1989.

[4] Though there are subtle differences in meaning between such terms as "support," "promote," "secure," "advance," and the like, for stylistic reasons, I use these interchangeably when discussing Rawls's idea that social arrangements and principles of justice can contribute to or detract from citizens' self-respect.

that his principles ensure that citizens have the sense of worth they need to pursue their ends.

Furthermore, the argument goes, this problem cannot be fixed because the attitude said to be supported by justice as fairness is not plausibly counted a primary social good: one need not recognize one's equal civil status in order to pursue one's ends. And, the attitude Rawls identifies as a primary social good is not plausibly supported by his principles of justice. While the equal distribution of liberty, for example, might help citizens recognize their equal civil status, it will not likely cause them to believe their conceptions of the good to be valuable.

RAWLS'S ACCOUNT OF OUR SENSE OF WORTH

In *A Theory of Justice*, Rawls defines self-respect (or self-esteem—he uses the terms interchangeably) as follows: "First," he says, "... [I]t includes a person's sense of his own value, his secure conviction that his conception of the good, his plan of life, is worth carrying out. And second, self-respect implies a confidence in one's ability, so far as it is within one's power, to fulfill one's intentions" (1971: 440). Later, in *Political Liberalism*, Rawls characterizes self-respect[5] thusly: "Self-respect is rooted in our self-confidence as a fully cooperating member of society capable of pursuing a worthwhile conception of the good over a complete life ... The importance of self-respect is that it provides a secure sense of our own value, a firm conviction that our determinate conception of the good is worth carrying out" (1993: 318). So, there are two separate aspects to Rawls's account of self-respect. One involves confidence in one's capacity to pursue a conception of the good. Call this the "self-confidence aspect." The other involves a secure belief that one's conception of the good is worth pursuing. Call this the "sense of one's value aspect." Now, as it turns out, the self-confidence aspect of Rawls's account does very little justificatory work in his theory. His arguments that various features of justice as fairness support citizens' self-respect rarely invoke the self-confidence aspect. So, I will set aside, for the purposes of this paper, this aspect of Rawls's view and focus on the sense of worth aspect.

---

[5] By now Rawls maintains that self-respect and self-esteem are not the same attitude and refers to the notion of self-worth that concerns him as "self-respect." See Freeman 1999: 260.

ATTITUDES TOWARDS OUR ACTIVITIES

Let us assume, then, that Rawls is primarily concerned that citizens see their conceptions of the good as worth carrying out. That is to say, for Rawls, self-respecting citizens attach value of some sort to their conceptions of the good. And those who lack self-respect fail to attach such value to their ends. As mundane as this idea might seem, it is actually puzzling as an account of self-respect, for it seems to render self-respect an empty concept. To see this, consider someone—call him Marty—who has a career as a chef. Suppose Marty has adopted gourmet cooking as a substantial aspect of his conception of the good. Suppose, in other words, that Marty has adopted gourmet cooking as an end. Cooking for him is not merely an interest, an inclination, or a pastime. It is something to which he is committed.

Surely it follows directly from the fact that Marty has taken gourmet cooking as an end, that he values (in some sense) gourmet cooking. Given that gourmet cooking is at the center of Marty's conception of the good, to state that he values it is not to make an additional claim about his relation to gourmet cooking, for the claim that one values the components of one's conception of the good is plausibly counted a conceptual truth. It is hard to see how one could not value something that is by definition part of his set of values.

Taking a cue from Rawls's later characterization of self-respect, in which he invokes the idea of the citizen as a "fully cooperating member of society," I propose that we see Rawlsian self-respect not as a valuing stance toward one's ends or conception of the good, but as a valuing stance toward the activities that make up one's contribution to a scheme of social cooperation. There is no conceptual barrier to a person failing to value these activities—to one's failing to see these activities as worth pursuing. And one's failing to see these as worth pursuing would indeed be likely to hinder one's pursuit of one's ends. It follows that viewing as worth doing the activities that make up one's contribution to a scheme of social cooperation fits Rawls's characterization of a primary social good—a good that is necessary for one to pursue one's ends, whatever they are.

There are three cases where we can see how a failure to value the activities that make up one's contribution to a scheme of social cooperation would impede one's pursuit of one's ends. If I am right that it is a conceptual truth that persons value their ends, it follows that if a person fails to value her contribution to a scheme of social cooperation that contribution is not an end for her. If she has no other ends, then she is, at it were, "at loose ends" and is hindered in the pursuit of her ends simply by not having any. In the more likely case that she does have other ends—other activities that she values to which her contribution to a scheme of cooperation is a means—then not valuing her contribution will make it difficult for her to pursue her ends simply by making it difficult to undertake the activities she must in order to pursue her ends.[6] Another way that not valuing one's contribution to a scheme of social cooperation can hinder one's pursuit of one's ends is that, in making one's (unvalued) contribution, one is not pursuing one's ends. One's ends and one's contribution pull apart and so one is deprived of the experience of fulfilling one's ends through the activities that one spends much of one's life doing. Indeed, I suspect that in claiming that social arrangements should encourage citizens to value their conceptions of the good what Rawls has in mind is that those arrangements should encourage, or at least allow, citizens to regard the activities that make up their contributions to society as among their ends.

So, let us suppose that Rawls's concern about citizens' self-respect is the concern that citizens believe that the activities that make up their contribution to a scheme of social cooperation are in some sense valuable. There are three ways that we might understand the attitude of valuing that one might have toward one's contribution.[7] A person might see his contribution as valuable

---

[6] I realize that this interpretation represents a significant departure from Rawls's stated view and that this interpretation—or perhaps, more accurately, modification—ultimately requires more argument than I have provided. I think this modification can be supported by the link, suggested in Rawls's work, between self-respect and the ideal of reciprocity that Rawls claims is expressed by his principles of justice. He says, for instance, that while the least advantaged in society "control fewer resources, they are doing their full share on terms recognized by all as mutually advantageous and consistent with everyone's self-respect" (2001: 139). Thanks to Jeffrey Moriarty for pointing out to me this passage.

[7] Larry Thomas has interpreted this valuing stance as seeing oneself as having worth for her success in the pursuit of her conception of the good. I do not think that interpretation is supported very well by Rawls's writings, though there are some grounds for thinking that this notion is what Rawls has in mind in his description of the self-confidence aspect of self-respect. See Thomas 1978a and 1978b.

(1) in the sense of being "meritorious,"[8] or
(2) in the sense of thinking it is good *for him* to undertake it, or
(3) in the sense of judging that it matters.

We can get a grasp on these different attitudes of valuing by appealing again to our example of Marty. Let us suppose now, for the sake of simplicity, that Marty does not value cooking as an end; it is not part of his conception of the good. (Let us say that his conception of the good revolves around coaching soccer, which is what he does much of the time when he's not cooking in a restaurant.) Cooking is simply the career Marty has chosen and he values it as a means to his ends. One way in which we might understand the valuing stance that Marty takes toward cooking is that he thinks that the activity of gourmet cooking has merit. He believes that gourmet cooking has high value in comparison with other activities as measured on an objective scale. Marty thinks, for example, that cooking endeavors, in comparison to, say, real estate sales endeavors have considerably more worth. Indeed, he has chosen cooking over real estate sales, let us say, for this reason.

A different attitude of valuing that Marty might have toward his cooking activities is that he might see cooking as good *for him*. In this case, he does not think that cooking is objectively better than, e.g., real estate sales. He simply thinks that cooking is a better activity for him than, real estate sales, given his attributes, dispositions, etc. Perhaps he founds this judgment on the fact that he is good at cooking, or enjoys it, and that cooking does not require him, as real estate sales would, to talk to strangers, which he dislikes. This type of valuing is subjective in the following sense: one judges the value of an activity strictly in terms of its suitability for oneself without making a judgment about the value of the activity *per se*. The judgment is not "one ought to cook (rather than sell real estate)" but rather "given the sort of person I am, I ought to cook (rather than sell real estate)."

Consider now the last attitude of valuing listed above. This is the belief that one's contribution matters. If Marty, our cook, has this attitude then he thinks that gourmet cooking is important—that it is not pointless or trivial or dispensable. He thinks that gourmet cooking is worthwhile; that it counts. He thinks that gourmet cooking meets a

---

[8] Labukt 2009 and Yanal 1987 interpret Rawls along these lines.

threshold of being worth doing. He believes, in other words, that there is a place for it in society. In thinking this, he ascribes to gourmet cooking a kind of standing.

Moreover, to be self-respecting, Marty need not think that he is making an especially significant contribution to society. If he later decided to join a monastery and take up the contemplative life, Marty would have to admit that the nature of his contribution is not significant compared, to, say, policing or manufacturing. Indeed if the mattering view required one to believe that one's contribution was significant, the view would begin to collapse into the merit view, for one would be judging one's contribution on a scale of merit that attaches merit to contributions in reference to how significant those contributions are for a given society.[9] The value associated with mattering, as I am understanding it, is independent of various judgments about the relative virtues of various contributions. It is a type of valuing that is orthogonal to the type of valuing one engages in when assessing contributions on the basis of their merits. Whatever citizens believe about the merits of their contribution to a system of social cooperation, to be self-respecting, citizens believe that their contribution is legitimate—that it has weight.

Now, if the source of the value of one's contribution on the mattering view is not its significance (or its other merits) but it nonetheless matters objectively, on what basis, one might ask, does it matter? Here, what I think Rawls has in mind is simply that one's contribution matters because it is what one has to offer. To deny that the contribution that one is suited or able to make to one's system of social cooperation matters is to say that one has nothing to offer to that system. So when Rawls claims that a just society preserves the self-respect of its citizens, he is saying that it is a matter of justice that citizens believe that they have something to offer—that they are never led to believe that,

---

[9] An anonymous referee suggested to me that the mattering view might be understood along the following lines: one respects oneself when one judges oneself a good cooperator. One sees one's chosen activities as helping to form an overall better scheme of cooperation. My worry about such a view is that the notion that one ought to be a good cooperator seems as though it belongs to a comprehensive doctrine. It expresses a moral ideal of what sort of person one should strive to be. So, an ideal of self-respect founded upon this notion would be incompatible with Rawls's commitment to political liberalism.

though they are participating, they have no contribution to make.[10] Self-respecting citizens, on my reading of Rawls, believe that whatever they are equipped to do to take part in their system of social cooperation is worth doing.

GROUNDS FOR THE MATTERING INTERPRETATION

We can reject the merit interpretation of Rawlsian self-respect fairly swiftly. There is plenty of textual evidence, which I consider below, that implies that the merit view is not what Rawls has in mind. More importantly, though, if this *were* what Rawls has in mind, his view of self-respect would conflict with his view of conceptions of the good. Because Rawls thinks that every citizen should have self-respect, he would be committed, on the merit interpretation, to the idea that every citizen should have as part of his conception of the good the idea that persons' contributions can be assessed on an objective scale of merit. He would not be committed to a particular view of *which* contributions have merit—he would not be, that is, committed to a particular standard of merit. But he would be committed to the notion that all persons should have an objectivist view about the merit of various types of human activities. In the language of the later Rawls, we can say that Rawls would be committed to the idea that a reasonable comprehensive doctrine as such must contain the view that the various sorts of contributions people make to a scheme of social cooperation can be ranked on a scale of merit. But Rawls clearly does not restrict reasonable comprehensive doctrines in this way (1993: 58–66). He counts among the reasonable comprehensive doctrines those that deny the existence of an objective standard for assessing the merit of various human activities. So, we have a fairly strong reason to conclude that Rawls does not see self-respect as a secure conviction in the merit of our contributions to a scheme of social cooperation.

That leaves us with the good-for-oneself and the mattering interpretations of Rawlsian self-respect. Before outlining my argument for the

---

[10] There may be, in rare cases, adult members of society who have virtually nothing to offer to a scheme of social cooperation. To encourage them to have self-respect, then, would be to encourage them to have a false belief. This problem is set aside by Rawls's conception of the citizen as a fully cooperating member of society.

246 Cynthia A. Stark

mattering interpretation, I must make a distinction between two types of circumstances that Rawls thinks sustain citizens' self-respect. When he explains that self-respect is a primary social good, Rawls gives us what I will call the "personal circumstances" that support individuals' self-respect. These include, first, the conformity of one's activities to the Aristotelian Principle and, second, the appreciation of one's activities by one's associates. When he explains why the tenets of justice as fairness secure citizens' self-respect, Rawls is identifying what I will call the "political circumstances" that support self-respect. There are three of these. The first is the duty of mutual respect, which Rawls thinks would be adopted by the parties in the original position along with his two principles of distributive justice. The two principles of distributive justice include, first, the equal liberty principle, which prescribes the equal distribution of the maximal degree of liberty compatible with its being distributed equally. The second allows inequalities of wealth provided that there is substantive equality of opportunity and that the inequalities maximally benefit the person with the least wealth. The second of these constraints on inequality is termed the "difference principle."

The second political circumstance that supports citizens' self-respect, according to Rawls, is the difference principle and the third is the "lexical ordering" of his two principles, also known as the doctrine of the priority of liberty. This doctrine prohibits constraining liberty for the sake of increased wealth.

In what follows, I examine Rawls's explanation of both the personal and political circumstances that sustain self-respect. I show that citizens' self-respect is supported by all of these circumstances when self-respect is understood as the mattering notion. However, citizens' self-respect is supported only by the personal circumstances, and perhaps by one of political circumstances, when self-respect is understood as the good-for-oneself notion. It follows that if Rawls were offering the good-for-oneself view in his account of self-respect as a primary social good, then he would indeed by offering an equivocal account of self-respect, as critics have maintained.

Moreover, Rawls, to a certain degree, invites this objection because the passages explaining the political circumstances that secure self-respect are often cryptic. Rawls is attempting in these passages to show that certain aspects of his view are justified by the fact that they promote self-respect. Yet, in each case, he briefly describes the aspect that he wishes to justify and then simply asserts that this aspect advances citizens' self-respect. He does not make explicit the connection between the aspect and self-respect and he rarely speaks in terms of the definition of self-respect that he has proposed—the conviction that one's endeavors are worth carrying out. The reader, then, is left wondering how the feature of Rawls's view that is said to secure citizens' self-respect in fact advances the ideal of self-respect he has identified as primary social good.

As I see it, critics have, first, taken Rawls to be defending the good-for-oneself or the merit view when he describes the personal circumstances that support self-respect. Second, they have argued (not implausibly) that the political circumstances cannot be understood to promote self-respect when it is interpreted in this way. The political circumstances, they claim, suggest a different notion of self-respect, namely a belief in one's equal worth as a citizen.[11] My contention is simply that all the circumstances that Rawls identifies as sustaining self-respect are consistent with the mattering interpretation of self-respect. So the generous reading of Rawls attributes to him that interpretation.

THE PERSONAL CIRCUMSTANCES SUPPORTING SELF-RESPECT

Rawls says, "[T]he circumstances that support the first aspect of self-esteem, the sense of our own worth, are essentially two: (1) having a rational plan of life, and in particular one that satisfies the Aristotelian principle; and (2) finding our person and deeds appreciated and confirmed by others who are likewise esteemed and their association enjoyed" (1971: 440). The Aristotelian Principle is a principle of human psychology that says "other things equal, human beings enjoy the exercise of their realized capacities (their innate and trained

---

[11] Doppelt sees Rawls as characterizing self-respect as an appraisal of the value of the life one pursues and an appraisal of the standards that are most appropriate for judging that life. He claims that this ideal is "an empirical notion devoid of normative content" and that it is "subjective" (2009: 128, 134). Eyal characterizes Rawlsian self-respect as "confidence in the value of one's plans" but does not state what sort of value he thinks Rawls has in mind (2009: 202). He claims that, in any case, this confidence is distinct from the Kantian ideal of self-respect as "confidence that one has the dignity of persons" (2009: 203). This is the ideal he thinks Rawls invokes throughout most of *A Theory of Justice*. Doppelt makes a similar claim (2009: 133).

abilities), and this enjoyment increases the more the capacity is realized, or the greater its complexity" (1971: 426).[12] One's activities satisfy the Aristotelian Principle when they make sufficient use of and adequately contribute to the cultivation of one's capabilities.

The Aristotelian Principle is related to self-respect in the following straightforward way: one is more likely to respect oneself to the extent that one undertakes activities that fulfill the Aristotelian Principle. Rawls says,

> I assume then that someone's plan of life will lack a certain attraction for him if it fails to call upon his natural capacities in an interesting fashion. When activities fail to satisfy the Aristotelian Principle, they are likely to seem dull and flat, and to give us no feeling of competence or a sense that they are worth doing. A person tends to be more confident in his value when his abilities are both fully realized and organized in ways of suitable complexity and refinement. (1971: 440)

In other words, the more one's activities incorporate the exercise and development of one's talents, the more likely one is to value them and, in this sense, be sure of one's own worth.

The second personal circumstance that supports individuals' self-respect—others' appreciation of our life plans—is influenced by the Aristotelian Principle. Rawls asserts,

> For while it is true that unless our endeavors are appreciated by our associates it is impossible for us to maintain the conviction that they are worthwhile, it is also true that others tend to value them only if what we do elicits their admiration or gives them pleasure. Thus the activities that display intricate and subtle talents, and manifest discrimination and refinement, are valued both by the person himself and those around him. (1971: 441)

So, the degree of complexity in the activities that make up one's life plan influences one's self-respect both directly and indirectly. One's sense of worth is bolstered by one's engaging in complex activities and by one's associates' appreciation of one's endeavors. But one's associates' appreciation of one's endeavors depends upon one's endeavors incorporating complex activities.

---

[12] For a critical discussion of the Aristotelian Principle, see Shue 1975.

Now, Rawls is aware that it might seem that only very talented people who are surrounded by other very talented people are likely to have self-respect on this view of what encourages self-respect. He denies that this is the case, however, because the Aristotelian Principle, he says, "is always relative to the individual" (1971: 441). A person's activities fulfill the Aristotelian Principle if they are suitably complex *given his capabilities*.[13] Moreover, societies are diverse in their associations so a person can find a group of people with similar tastes and capability levels who will affirm his undertakings (1971: 441–2). As long as this is the case, then, each person, no matter the extent of his capabilities, will have the opportunity to come to value his endeavors.

Rawls's account of the relation between self-respect and both the Aristotelian Principle and the appreciation of others is consistent with both the good-for-oneself and the mattering interpretations of self-respect. If one finds one's activities challenging and engaging one will be lead to think that those activities are both suitable for oneself and that they matter. Insofar as Marty, for example, finds gourmet cooking challenging, he is inclined to think that gourmet cooking is an activity that *he* should pursue. He is inclined to think that gourmet cooking is good for him to do. But it is also likely that Marty would conclude from the fact that he finds cooking interesting and engaging that cooking *itself* matters—that cooking is good to do *simpliciter*. If our endeavors bring us satisfaction, we tend to think, as Rawls says, that they are worth doing.

Likewise, if others appreciate our undertakings, we are likely to make a number of inferences about the worth of those undertakings. Suppose Marty's friends and neighbors appreciate his cooking skills. They commend him for his cooking, let us say, and seek out opportunities to sample his food. This fact might encourage Marty to believe that cooking is a good activity for him to engage in. He might interpret the appreciation of his associates as confirming his judgment that *he* ought to pursue cooking. It is certainly likely, though, that Marty will infer from the appreciation of his associates that cooking is worth pursuing in other senses. In particular, this appreciation is likely to cause him to think that cooking itself matters—that cooking is a worthwhile and

---

[13] This notion strongly suggests that Rawls does not see self-respect as a belief in the objective merit of one's conception of the good.

important activity. Surely he is likely to think not just that gourmet cooking is good for *him* to do, nor merely that *his* gourmet cooking matters *to his friends*, but that gourmet cooking is a worthwhile activity. So, Rawls's appeal to the Aristotelian Principle and the appreciation of others as personal supports for self-respect is consistent with both the good-for-oneself and the mattering interpretations of self-respect.

THE POLITICAL CIRCUMSTANCES SUPPORTING SELF-RESPECT

The duty of mutual respect

After describing the two personal circumstances that support citizens' self-respect, Rawls intimates that they are not sufficient to ensure citizens' self-respect. He suggests that they are sufficient only "... whenever in public life citizens respect one another's ends and adjudicate their political claims in ways that also support their self-esteem. It is precisely this background condition," he continues, "that is maintained by the principles of justice" (1971: 442). So, the public norm requiring citizens to *respect* one another's contributions referred to in this passage is to be distinguished from the *appreciation* of one another's contributions that takes place within associations.

We can get an idea of what is involved in respecting one another's contributions by looking at Rawls's account of the duty of mutual respect, for Rawls claims that the parties in the original position would adopt the duty of mutual respect *precisely because* the self-respect of those whom they represent would be at risk in a society in which this duty is absent (1971: 178–9). So, it is reasonable to conclude that the attitude expressed through the observance of the duty of mutual respect is part of what is involved in the respecting of others' contributions that is necessary for citizens to have full self-respect.

The duty of mutual respect, Rawls says,

[I]s the duty to show a person the respect that is due to him as a moral being, that is, as a being with a sense of justice and a conception of the good.... Mutual respect is shown in several ways: in our willingness to see the situation of others from their point of view, from the perspective of their conception of their good; and in being prepared to give reasons for our actions whenever the interests of others are materially affected. (1971: 337)

If this duty is plausibly seen as encouraging citizens to believe, among other things, that their contributions to a scheme of cooperation matter, then we have grounds for thinking that the view of self-respect he describes as a primary social good consists in that belief. I submit that the passage above implies that showing respect includes recognizing that others' contributions matter. Moreover, if we assume that the kind of respect one is shown determines the kind of *self*-respect one acquires, then we can conclude that when one's contribution is judged by others to matter, one tends oneself to judge that one's contribution matters. It follows that Rawls's account of the duty of mutual respect gives us grounds for attributing to him a view of self-respect as the belief that the activities making up one's contribution to a scheme of cooperation matter.

Consider the two actions or attitudes that Rawls identifies as paradigmatic of respecting others: being willing to see things from their point of view and being willing to give them reasons for our actions. A willingness to see things from another's perspective conveys one's belief in the legitimacy of that perspective. It conveys a sense that one regards the other's point of view as having standing. One may not fully understand the other's point of view or agree with it. One may in fact feel alienated from it. But in being willing to take it up, as it were, one shows that one regards it as significant or important, not trivial or silly. A willingness to provide reasons for one's actions expresses one's realization that we may act in ways that might interfere with or limit others' projects only if there are good reasons for doing so. It expresses, in other words, the idea that one sees another's projects, again, as having standing, and acknowledges that others are entitled, all things equal, to undertake their projects.

Both of these attitudes would likely encourage individual citizens to think that their contributions to the cooperative scheme in which they are participating with other citizens matters. When one's fellow citizens acknowledge the standing of one's perspective and projects, they acknowledge that one's perspective and projects matter. Given that our perspectives and our projects are intimately bound up with our contributions to a cooperative scheme, acknowledging the standing of our perspectives and projects includes acknowledging the standing of our contributions, and hence recognizing that our contributions matter. For example, to see, in the public forum, Marty's situation from his point of view, the fellow citizens of Marty would have to see things from the point of view of someone who has a career as a chef. And in being prepared to give reasons for their actions that affect others' interests, Marty's fellow citizens would have to be willing to justify their support for policies that might negatively affect restaurant workers. By acting in these ways, Marty's fellow citizens would fulfill the duty of mutual respect and in so doing convey their belief that Marty's contribution to the scheme of cooperation they share with him matters. So, by acting in these ways, Marty's fellow citizens encourage Marty to believe that his contribution matters. It follows that the duty of mutual respect can be seen to support citizens' self-respect where their self-respect is understood as the belief that their contribution to a scheme of social cooperation matters.

Notice that a failure to be respected by one's fellow citizens would not typically cause one to cease to think that the activities making up one's contribution are good for oneself. That others disrespect those activities would not likely make one change one's mind about the suitability of those activities for oneself. One's judgment that an activity is good for oneself is founded primarily upon features of oneself, not upon factors such as the respect of other citizens who are not, in Rawls's words, one's associates. One might be dismayed that the activities one judges good for oneself to undertake are not respected by one's fellow citizens, but this is different from doubting whether one's activities are well suited to the kind of person one is. Being disrespected in the public forum, then, is not likely to diminish one's self-respect if self-respect is understood as a belief that one's contribution to a scheme of social cooperation is valuable for oneself. It follows that Rawls's discussion of the duty of mutual respect does not support the good-for-oneself interpretation of self-respect.

The difference principle

The difference principle, which is a principle governing the distribution of wealth, allows inequalities, but only those that maximally benefit the least well off. Part of Rawls's argument that the difference principle supports citizens' self-respect is contained in his remarks about envy. Envy, Rawls says, "is the propensity to view with hostility the greater good of others . . . . We envy those persons whose situation is superior to ours . . . and we are willing to deprive them of their greater benefits even if it is necessary to give up something ourselves" (1971: 532).

Rawls is concerned about envy because he thinks that the unequal distribution of wealth in a society can damage citizens' self-respect to an extent that gives rise to envy and in turn to instability. Indeed, he claims that the primary cause of envy is the absence of self-respect. "[T]he main psychological root of the liability to envy," Rawls says, "is a lack of self-confidence in our own worth combined with a sense of impotence" (1971: 535). Moreover, according to Rawls, when people's self-respect is damaged by their having considerably less wealth than others, the envy that they feel toward the better off is excusable. That is to say, we cannot expect the less fortunate to overcome their envy in that case; rather we are obliged to change the political arrangements that reduce their self-respect and foment envy. Because Rawls's theory allows for inequality of wealth, he must consider whether his theory recommends arrangements that are likely to induce excusable envy.

In the end Rawls thinks that the difference principle will *not* generate excusable envy because, first, it does not encourage large disparities of wealth, and second it allows only those disparities that are to greatest advantage of those who have the least wealth. Citizens are not inclined toward envy when "the greater advantages of some are in return for compensating benefits for the less favored" (1971, 536). We can set aside the issue of whether or not this is a strong argument. I simply want to pinpoint the notion of self-respect that is at work in Rawls's claim that distributive inequality can seriously injure citizens' self-respect and that this injured self-respect tends to generate envy.

A plausible reconstruction of the reasoning behind Rawls's contention that distributive inequality may damage the self-respect of the less well off is as follows. If one's contribution is remunerated far less than the contributions of others, then one will come to see one's endeavors as unimportant or insignificant. The relatively small reward one receives for making one's contribution inclines one to judge that others see one's contribution as mattering little and this leads one to doubt oneself that one's contribution matters. If "what we do in everyday life" brings us a scanty wage or salary, which in turn gives us access to few of the advantages our scheme of social cooperation creates, then we are inclined to conclude that what we do does not matter (1971: 441). This feeling that what we do does not matter can induce hostility toward those who engage in activities that we see as mattering on account of the high compensation garnered by those activities. And this hostility can generate a desire to impose a loss, even at a cost to ourselves, on those who engage in those activities.

Notice that if one's activities are poorly remunerated one does not typically cease to see those activities as good for oneself. If one thinks that e.g., gourmet cooking is good for oneself, the fact that one gets remunerated little for it is not likely to change that assessment. Again, this is because one's judgment that an activity is good for oneself is founded upon features of oneself, not upon factors such as prestige or compensation. One might, of course, choose to make a contribution that involves activities for which one is not well suited because one prefers wealth and prestige. But this phenomenon is compatible with the idea that one's judgment about what is good for oneself is generally unaffected by how well remunerated one is for one's activities. Having considerably less wealth than others, then, is not likely to diminish one's self-respect if self-respect is understood as a belief that one's contribution to a scheme of social cooperation is valuable for oneself. It follows that Rawls's discussion of envy does not support the good-for-oneself interpretation of self-respect.

The priority of liberty

The doctrine of the priority of liberty is justified by Rawls largely in terms of its support for citizens' self-respect. This doctrine states that, when a society has reached a level of wealth that allows all citizens a decent standard of living, constraints on liberty that would increase citizens' wealth should not be permitted. The merits of Rawls's argument for the priority of liberty have been much discussed (Doppelt 1981; Shue 1974/75; Hart 1979; Neilson 1979; Taylor 2003). I do not hope here to add anything to that discussion; I confine myself to showing that Rawls's argument for the doctrine supports the idea of self-respect as a conviction that one's contribution to a scheme of social cooperation matters.

There are two types of restrictions on liberty, according to Rawls, that might be imposed for the sake of increasing wealth (1971: 244). First, liberty might be less extensive but still distributed equally. Second, liberty might be distributed unequally—it might be limited for only some citizens. The first type of restriction might seem justified if it resulted in an increase in wealth, consistent with the difference principle, for all citizens. The second type of restriction might seem justified if it resulted in an increase in wealth, consistent with the difference principle, for those with less liberty. Both types of restriction, Rawls thinks, are in fact unjustified because they would damage citizens' self-respect. He argues that the parties in the original position, as they are concerned to promote the good of self-respect, would therefore adopt the doctrine of the priority of liberty.

There is no doubt that Rawls's argument that an *unequal* distribution of liberty would damage citizens' self-respect invokes the importance of civil equality. Unequal liberty, he tells us, would damage the self-respect of those with fewer liberties by

publicly establishing their inferiority as defined by the basic structure of society. This subordinate ranking in the public forum experienced in the attempt to take part in political and economic life, and felt in dealing with those who have a greater liberty, would indeed be humiliating and destructive of self-esteem. (1971: 545)

The idea seems to be that people would lack self-respect if they were forced to see themselves as civilly inferior to their compatriots. This idea is compatible with a notion of self-respect as a secure conviction in one's civil equality. But it is also compatible with a notion of self-respect as a secure conviction that one's contribution to a scheme of social cooperation matters. The reason for this mutual compatibility is that the fact that civil inferiority can *cause* diminished self-respect, as the quoted passage suggests, does not entail that the content of self-respect is (or is only) a belief in one's civil equality. Indeed Rawls implies that it is not merely the civil inequality itself that undermines the self-respect of the civilly inferior but also "the hardships arising from political and civic inequality and from cultural and ethnic discrimination" (1971: 545). Surely having an inferior civil status has a host of effects on one's sense of oneself. And it seems reasonable to think that being marginalized and discriminated against can lead one to believe that one's more politically advantaged compatriots care little about one's contribution to society, and this can lead one to doubt oneself that one's contribution matters.

Rawls's account of the injuries to self-respect that arise from civil inferiority strongly suggests that injuries to self-respect would arise also from economic inferiority. Surely having a low rank in an economic hierarchy would impose hardships on citizens similar to those imposed by having a low rank in a political hierarchy. Though not literally second-class citizens, the poor are often politically powerless and disenfranchised. The poor no doubt feel their inferiority in attempting to take part in political and economic life alongside the wealthy and are prone to experience humiliation and diminished self-respect. So, it appears that inequality of wealth would also damage citizens' self-respect. Yet Rawls's theory permits this kind of inequality.

Rawls gets around this problem in the following way. His argument for the priority of liberty assumes that citizens have what he calls "a need for status." This is the need to be valued by others, which valuing, Rawls claims, is a prerequisite for self-respect. This need can be met in the political domain either by one's economic status or one's civil status. Rawls thinks political institutions should be arranged so that the need for status is met by something that gives people equal status, because this will support the self-respect of all citizens. Because there are independent reasons, according to Rawls, for allowing inequality of wealth, then if wealth is positioned as the ground for status, the need for status will be satisfied by something that gives people unequal status, and so will put the self-respect of those with less status at risk. It follows that the need for status should be satisfied by an equal distribution of liberty. Rawls concludes,

In a well-ordered society then self-respect is secured by the public affirmation of the status of equal citizenship for all; the distribution of material means is left to take care of itself in accordance with pure procedural justice. Of course doing this assumes the requisite background conditions which narrow the range of inequalities so excusable envy does not arise. (1971: 545)

Rawls's argument that an equal but less expansive liberty undermines self-respect also supports the mattering interpretation of self-respect. His argument is as follows. As the economic conditions of a society improve, so that everyone enjoys a comfortable standard of living, citizens' interests in pursuing their life plans as they see fit increases. They are no longer preoccupied with subsistence and so can focus on, e.g. their spiritual needs. Human beings, as such, develop and pursue their plans, Rawls says, within "communities of interest." They undertake their endeavors, that is, by means of attachments to others who share their interests and ideals. The associations that are necessary for people to pursue their life plans flourish only when citizens are afforded extensive liberties (1971: 542–43).[14] Liberty, in short, gives rise to pluralism.

One of the reasons pluralism is required for citizens to undertake their projects is because it is within various associations that citizens come to attach value to their activities—to regard their activities as worth doing. One can pursue one's ends adequately only when one values the activities that make up one's contribution to a cooperative scheme, and the primary way one comes to value those activities is by being surrounded by similar others who confirm their value. Because liberty is required for the emergence and survival of communities of interest, liberty is required for citizens to experience their associates appreciating their endeavors, and it is therefore required for citizens believing in the worth of their endeavors. Liberty sustains citizens' self-respect, then, by securing one of the personal circumstances that upholds self-respect. Because the mattering notion of self-respect is supported by Rawls's claim that self-respect depends upon the appreciation of others, the mattering notion is supported by Rawls's claim that self-respect depends upon a more expansive liberty since the role of liberty is to afford citizens the opportunity to feel that their activities are appreciated by others.

(Notice that the good-for-oneself view of self-respect is also supported by Rawls's claim that liberty secures citizens' self-respect by creating one of the personal circumstances upholding self-respect. This follows from the fact that Rawls's account of the personal circumstances is compatible with both the good-for-oneself and the mattering interpretations of self-respect.)

SELF-RESPECT, PRIMARY GOODS, AND SOCIAL HIERARCHY

I have argued that Rawls's theory of justice employs a univocal notion of self-respect as the belief that the activities that make up one's contribution to a scheme of social cooperation matter. In what follows, I maintain that Rawls nonetheless equivocates on the value

[14] For the importance of social groups for the development of self-respect see McKinnon 2000.

of self-respect, sometimes regarding it as merely instrumental and other times as intrinsic. I argue further that his main interest in stressing the importance of self-respect is to explain how justice as fairness avoids what he sees as an objectionable outcome of markets—the specific sense of inferiority that might burden those at the bottom of class hierarchies. Rawls thinks, on my reading, that unless institutions within market societies are carefully designed, citizens who lose out in market competition will fail to see the worth of their contribution to a system of cooperation that nonetheless relies on their contribution. The centrality of this preoccupation reveals that Rawls sees self-respect, in the end, as having intrinsic worth.

In identifying self-respect as a primary social good, Rawls claims that self-respect is good chiefly as a means—like wealth and opportunities, its value lies in its enabling us to carry out our ends, or at any rate to do with ease or with pleasure. Moreover, his account of the personal circumstances supporting self-respect suggests that Rawls sees the risk of diminished self-respect as equally distributed throughout the population. Each of us, to be fully self-respecting, he says, needs to undertake activities that are sufficiently complex and needs for our associates to affirm these activities. It seems that any of us might fail in these regards.

But it is clear that the political circumstances are what really matter on Rawls's view, for he tells us that these personal circumstances are sufficient only in an environment of mutual respect, equal liberty, and limited inequality of wealth.[15] His account of the political circumstances, moreover, suggests that Rawls is largely concerned with the self-respect of citizens who have less wealth and prestige than others. This is especially obvious in his treatment of envy where he assures us that under the difference principle *the less fortunate* will lack grounds to doubt their worth. This concern, however, is also implied by his discussions of the duty of mutual respect and the priority of liberty. In those passages Rawls strongly suggests that so long as the economically less well off are treated with respect by other citizens in the public forum and afforded equal liberty, they will have secure self-respect.

---

[15] I leave out expansive liberty here because Rawls's argument for the importance of expansive liberty for sustaining self-respect is that such liberty is a precondition for one of the personal circumstances sustaining self-respect.

Now, if the value of self-respect resides merely in its enabling us to fulfill our ends, then we should expect that Rawls's concern for the security of the self-respect of the less fortunate would be a concern that the less fortunate will be hindered in fulfilling their ends. It appears from his discussion of the political circumstances, though, that Rawls is not worried that the less fortunate will be hindered in this way. Rather he seems concerned with the bare fact of the potentially diminished self-respect of the less fortunate.

Consider again his accounts of the connection between self-respect and the difference principle, the duty of mutual respect and the priority of liberty. In these accounts at no point does Rawls say or imply that self-respect is important so that citizens can adequately fulfill their ends. It seems quite clear that in these discussions Rawls takes a diminished or insecure sense of worth to be bad in itself. To be encouraged to think less of oneself by having one's projects publicly demoted or one's perspective ignored or by being given fewer rights is to be wronged, Rawls thinks, regardless of the effects of this damaged sense of worth upon one's ability to pursue one's ends. On my interpretation of Rawlsian self-respect, then, Rawls thinks that when citizens are encouraged by political institutions to believe that their contributions to society do not matter, they have been wronged. And this is regardless of the debilitating effects this belief may have on their carrying out their life plans.

I have maintained that Rawls's account of self-respect does not have the major flaw that has been attributed to it. Rawls offers us one notion of self-respect. It is the conviction that the activities making up one's contribution to a scheme of social cooperation matter. Rawls suggests that this conviction is instrumentally good insofar as it helps us to pursue our ends, or at least to pursue them with pleasure. But that is not its chief importance. He thinks that this conviction is also intrinsically good, for he clearly regards its absence as bad in itself. It is the hallmark of just society, Rawls believes, that it secure this belief for everyone, especially lower class individuals who are at risk of thinking that their contributions are not worthwhile.

260   *Cynthia A. Stark*

REFERENCES

Boxill, Bernard (1976) "Self-Respect and Protest," *Philosophy and Public Affairs* 6, 58–69.

Cohen, Joshua (1989) "Democratic Equality," *Ethics* 99, 727–51.

Darwall, Stephen (1977) "Two Kinds of Respect," *Ethics* 88, 36–49. Reprinted in Dillon 1995, 181–97.

Deigh, John (1983) "Shame and Self-Esteem," *Ethics* 93, 225–45. Reprinted in Dillon 1995, 133–56.

Dillon, Robin (1992) "How to Lose Your Self-Respect," *American Philosophical Quarterly* 29, 125–39.

——— (ed.) (1995) *Dignity, Character and Self-Respect* (New York: Routledge).

Doppelt, Gerald (1981) "Rawls' System of Justice: A Critique From the Left," *Noûs* 15, 259–307.

——— (2009) "The Place of Self-Respect in *A Theory of Justice*," *Inquiry* 52, 127–54.

Eyal, Nir (2009) " 'Perhaps the Most Important Primary Social Good': Self-Respect and Rawls's Principles of Justice," *Politics, Philosophy and Economics* 4, 195–219.

Freeman, Samuel (ed.) (1999) *John Rawls: Collected Papers* (Cambridge, MA: Harvard University Press).

Hart, H. L. A. (1979) "Rawls on Liberty and Its Priority." In Norman Daniels (ed.), *Reading Rawls* (Stanford University Press), 230–52.

Held, Virginia (1973) "Reasonable Progress and Self-Respect," *The Monist* 57, 12–27.

Hudson, Stephen (1980) "The Nature of Respect," *Social Theory and Practice* 6, 69–90.

Labukt, Ivar (2009) "Rawls on the Practicability of Utilitarianism," *Politics, Economics and Philosophy* 8, 201–21.

Lane, Robert E. (1982) "Government and Self-Esteem," *Political Theory* 10, 5–31.

McKinnon, Catriona (2000) "Exclusion Rules and Self-Respect," *Journal of Value Inquiry* 34, 491–505.

——— (2003) "Basic Income, Self-Respect and Reciprocity," *Journal of Applied Philosophy* 20, 143–58.

Massey, Stephen (1983) "Is Self-Respect a Moral or a Psychological Concept?" *Ethics* 93, 246–61.

Middleton, David (2006) "Three Types of Self-Respect," *Res Publica* 12, 59–76.

Miller, David (1982) "Arguments for Equality," *Midwest Studies in Philosophy* 7, 73–87.

Mohr, Richard (1988) "Dignity vs. Politics: Strategy When Justice Fails." In Mohr, *Gays/Justice: A Study of Ethics, Society and Law* (New York: Columbia University Press), 315–27.

Moriarty, Jeffrey (2009) "Rawls, Self-Respect and the Opportunity for Meaningful Work," *Social Theory and Practice* 35, 441–59.

Neilson, Kai (1979) "Radical Egalitarian Justice: Justice as Equality," *Social Theory and Practice* 5, 209–26.

Postow, B. C. (1979) "Economic Dependence and Self-Respect," *Philosophical Forum* 10, 181–205.

Rawls, John (1971) *A Theory of Justice* (Cambridge, MA: Harvard University Press).

——(1993) *Political Liberalism* (New York: Columbia University Press).

——(2001) *Justice as Fairness: A Restatement*, ed. Erin Kelly (Cambridge, MA: Harvard University Press).

Sachs, David (1981) "How to Distinguish Self-Respect from Self-Esteem," *Philosophy and Public Affairs* 10, 346–60.

Shue, Henry (1974/75) "Liberty and Self-Respect," *Ethics* 85, 195–203.

——(1975) "Justice, Rationality and Desire: On the Logical Structure of Justice as Fairness," *Southern Journal of Philosophy* 13, 89–97.

Taylor, Robert (2003) "Rawls' Defense of the Priority of Liberty: A Kantian Reconstruction," *Philosophy and Public Affairs* 31, 246–71.

Thomas, Larry (1978a) "Morality and Our Self-Concept," *Journal of Value Inquiry* 12, 258–68.

——(1978b) "Rawlsian Self-Respect and the Black Consciousness Movement," *Philosophical Forum* 9, 303–14.

Yanal, Robert (1987) "Self-Esteem," *Noûs* 21, 363–79.

II

Exploring Alternatives to the Simple Model: Is there an Atomistic Option?[*]

LUKE ROBINSON

I. INTRODUCTION

How do morally relevant factors combine and interact to make right acts right and wrong acts wrong? It's easy to assume that such factors combine in a simple, additive way, like weights on a scale. The right-making factors (e.g., LIFE-SAVING or PROMOTING-THE-OVERALL-GOOD) go on one side of the scale, so to speak, while the wrong-making factors (e.g., PROMISE-BREAKING or DOING-HARM) go on the other side. And the "balance" of these factors determines the moral statuses of the various options (their permissibility, impermissibility, etc.). Call this, the *simple model*.

The simple model is an intuitive and familiar model (or theory) of how morally relevant factors combine and interact. Moreover, it coheres with an equally intuitive and familiar—albeit controversial—model (or theory) of moral deliberation, that figuring out what one ought morally to do is a matter of weighing the moral reasons for and against relevant alternatives with the aim of ascertaining which of those alternatives is favored by the balance of those reasons.

But the simple model is arguably too simple. For it's not consistent with certain plausible (albeit controversial) views about particular cases and how morally relevant factors combine and interact therein. To

* A draft of this paper was presented as "Can an Atomist Explain Why the Governing Function is Not Additive?" at the Second Annual Arizona Workshop in Normative Ethics. I am grateful to Mark Timmons and members of that audience for helpful discussions thereof. I owe special thanks to two anonymous referees and to my colleagues at Southern Methodist University, especially Philippe Chuard, for their criticisms of subsequent drafts.

sketch but one example, one might think, not only that it's permissible to harm a wrongful aggressor in self-defense, but also that SELF-DEFENSE prevents DOING-HARM from having the wrong-making effect it normally has *even though* it doesn't outweigh or counterbalance DOING-HARM (as, say, LIFE-SAVING arguably does in certain cases). But the simple model entails that this view is false (see §2).

How could we accommodate the aforementioned views and, in particular, the sorts of complex combinations and interactions they take to occur? In short, how could we accommodate *the relevant views and interactions?*

Shelly Kagan suggests that we could accommodate them by rejecting *either* of two (logically independent) assumptions made by the simple model,[1] which he refers to as "the assumption that the governing function is additive" (or "the additive assumption") and "the assumption of independent contributions" (or the "independence condition") (1988: 16–17, 20–1 n. 8). To a first approximation, the object of my inquiry is whether we could, in fact, accommodate the relevant views and interactions by rejecting the first of these assumptions *rather than* the second.

As I will understand it, the first of these assumptions is that the moral status of an act is determined by the sum (or net balance) of the contributions made by each of the factors relevant thereto.[2] (Compare how the weights of each of the objects in the pans of a balance scale combine to determine whether and to which side that scale tips.) Hereinafter, I will refer to this first assumption as *additivity*. [A caveat: Kagan often refers to the *conjunction* of this first assumption and the next as "the assumption that the governing function is additive" (or "the additive assumption"). But all I mean by "additivity" is this first assumption. Moreover, unlike Kagan, I won't regard it as an assumption about a supposed "governing function."]

As I will understand it, the second of these two assumptions is that neither the size nor the direction of a factor's contribution can be

---

[1] He calls it "the additive model."

[2] "Each factor makes its own individual contribution to the status of the act, and the overall status is [determined by] the sum of these contributions"; "[T]he overall status of the act is [determined by] the sum of the separate contributions of the individual factors" (Kagan 1988: 15, 16).

affected by other factors (or by variations in other factors).[3] (Compare how neither the weight nor the placement of an object on a balance scale is affected by the other objects thereon.) So understood, it's the negation of two forms of *moral holism*. The first of these is *valence holism*, the view that the moral "valence" of a factor (or the *direction* of its contribution) may be affected by other factors (or by variations in other factors) such that (e.g.) what is a right-making factor (a factor that makes a positive contribution) in one case may not be one in another, or may even be a wrong-making factor (a factor that makes a negative contribution) given suitable circumstances. This first holism is a version of what Jonathan Dancy calls "the holism of the right-making relation" (2004: 79).[4] The second is *weight holism*, the view that the moral "weight" of a factor (or the *size* of its contribution) may be affected by other factors (or by variations in other factors) such that (e.g.) what is a right-making factor with a particular weight in one case may have more or less weight in another.[5] Hereinafter, I will refer to this second assumption as *atomism*.[6]

Both additivity and atomism require further elucidation (see §2). But I can now state the object of my inquiry with greater precision. We could accommodate the relevant views and interactions by rejecting atomism—provided, that is, that weight and valence holism are tenable. Indeed, the relevant views are among the very sorts of views that are used to motivate holism: ones that appear to entail that one factor (e.g., SELF-DEFENSE or GUILT) can and does affect the valence or weight of another factor (e.g., DOING-HARM or SUFFERING). But could we (also) accommodate them by rejecting additivity *rather than* atomism, as Kagan suggests? In other words, is there an *atomistic option*, a way of

---

[3] "[V]ariations in the *other* factors will *not* affect the contribution made by the factor in question" (16–17; see also 16 n. 7).

[4] I take it to be the most plausible version of the holism of the right-making relation, which Dancy (implicitly) defines as the view that a feature that is a right-making reason in one case may be no reason at all, or an opposite reason, in another (2004: 74, 79). The holism of the right-making relation should be distinguished from what Dancy calls "the holism of the favoring relation," which is a parallel view about normative reasons for action and belief, including distinctly moral reasons for action (2004: 79). Unfortunately, these two holisms are frequently not distinguished, and it's not always possible to tell whether a particular author intends both or only one of them. I intend only the one.

[5] Cf. Kamm's "Principle of Contextual Interaction," which states that "a property's role and, most important, its effect may differ with context" (1996: 51).

[6] For contemporary expressions and defenses of atomism see, e.g., Crisp 2000; Hooker 2008; Raz 2000.

accommodating the relevant views and interactions without rejecting atomism? If there is, then the relevant views don't entail holism. In which case, holists can't use them to motivate holism, at least not without further argument. And atomists could accept them as true, rather than reject them as false, as they currently do. Moreover, these views could be true even if weight and valence holism prove untenable.

The remainder of the paper is structured as follows. Section 2 considers the simple model, its assumptions (additivity and atomism), and its limitations. Section 3 considers how we could accommodate the relevant views and interactions by rejecting atomism in favor of weight and valence holism. Section 4 considers the suggestion that developing an atomistic option would involve replacing the simple model with an alternative one that assumes atomism but not additivity (see Kagan 1988: 20–1 and n. 8). And section 5 argues that developing an atomistic option requires offering a *conception of contribution*—an account of just what it is that contributory right-making factors contribute—that renders coherent the particular claims that must be true if there is, indeed, such an option. Finally, section 6 considers whether Rossian pluralism—the *locus classicus* for the idea of a contributory right-making factor—offers the conceptual and metaphysical resources necessary to offer such a conception. In the process, it considers whether Rossian pluralism could accommodate the relevant views and interactions other than by rejecting atomism.

Before I proceed, a few points of clarification may be in order. First, by exploring ways of accommodating certain (admittedly controversial) views that the simple model entails are false, I don't mean to dismiss the possibility that the simple model is actually correct. And I certainly don't mean to suggest that either weight or valence holism is untenable, as I'm elsewhere engaged in their defense. But, here as elsewhere, exploring alternatives is simply good methodology. Moreover, exploring alternatives to the simple model is consistent with defending that model *and its assumptions*. For having first explored those alternatives, one might then defend the simple model by arguing that none of them is tenable. And though my arguments here do not show that there is no atomistic option, they do raise doubts about the tenability of such an option. Hence, they might ultimately contribute to just such a defense of the simple model. On the other hand, they might also contribute to the defense of weight and valence holism by helping to rule out an alternative way of accommodating the relevant views and interactions.

Second, I use the terms "holism" and "atomism" as they are generally used in the literature on moral particularism and moral generalism. In that literature, "holism" usually refers to either or both of (1) the holism of the right-making relation—of which valence holism is a version—or (2) a parallel view about normative reasons for action and belief (see n. 4).[7] Likewise, "atomism" usually refers to the negation of one or both of these views, although here I use it to refer to the negation of both valence and weight holism. I choose this terminology both because my arguments here bear directly on issues in that literature, and to retain terminological continuity with my other work.[8]

2. THE SIMPLE MODEL, ITS ASSUMPTIONS AND LIMITATIONS

To begin, let's consider a familiar (albeit controversial) view of the sort that all *relevant* parties will agree the simple model gets right. Suppose that I can't keep my promise to meet Able for a pint without failing to save Baker's life and, second, that Able will be disappointed if I don't meet him. And, to keep things simple, suppose that there are only three morally relevant factors here: PROMISE-KEEPING, LIFE-SAVING, and DIS-APPOINTMENT.[9] These are contributory right- and wrong-making factors. Each makes a (positive or negative) contribution to the moral status of each of these (possible) acts, meeting Able and saving Baker. And the "balance" of these factors (or these contributions) determines the moral status of each of these acts, the rightness of saving Baker and the wrongness of meeting Able.

All of this is consistent with the simple model and, in particular, with both additivity and atomism. First, the moral status of each of these acts

---

[7] See, e.g., Dancy 2004: ch. 5; McKeever and Ridge 2006: ch. 2; McNaughton 1988: 192–3; Robinson 2006; Väyrynen 2006: 717–18.

[8] These same terms are used with different and variable meanings in the literature on intrinsic value and organic unities. See, e.g., Brown 2007; Hurka 1998. Note also that what Brown calls "Additivism" (roughly, the view that the value of a whole is equal to the sum of the values of its parts) isn't analogous to additivity, in part because the value of a whole isn't analogous to the moral status of an act. (For instance, being morally required is *at best* analogous, not to being good "on the whole," but rather to being better than available alternatives.)

[9] For present purposes, it doesn't matter whether we think of these factors as features of acts (e.g., being the keeping of a promise) or as circumstances, or features of situations (e.g., my having promised to meet Able).

is determined by the sum (or net balance) of the contributions made by each of the factors relevant thereto, which is just to say that the moral status of each of these acts is determined by how these contributions "add up" or "balance out," just as whether and to which side a balance scale tips is determined by how the weights of the objects in each of its pans "add up" or "balance out." Indeed, one could use a balance scale and three coins of appropriate weights to model how these three contributions determine the moral status of each of these acts: place a relatively heavy coin in one pan to represent the contributions made by LIFE-SAVING and place sufficiently lighter coins in the other pan to represent the contributions made by PROMISE-KEEPING and DISAP-POINTMENT, and the scale will tip toward the first pan, indicating that saving Baker is right and that meeting Able is wrong. And what additivity claims is that the same holds true in all (possible) cases— that the moral status of an act is determined by the sum of the contributions made by each of the factors relevant thereto.

Second, neither the size nor the direction of any of the contributions made by these factors is affected by other factors (or by variations in other factors). For instance, LIFE-SAVING doesn't reduce the weight of PROMISE-KEEPING, or the size of the contribution it makes to the moral status of my meeting Able. Nor does it affect its valance, or the direction of that contribution. It just "outweighs" PROMISE-KEEPING, just as a heavier coin in one pan of a balance scale outweighs a lighter coin in the other. And what atomism claims is that the same holds true of all factors in all (possible) cases—that, *contra* weight and valence holism, neither the weight nor the valence of a factor can be affected by other factors (or by variations in other factors).

Note two things. First, atomism, weight holism, and valence holism are all views about factors that are of fundamental (or non-derivative) moral relevance. Suppose, for example, that LIFE-SAVING is only of derivative relevance, and that the relevant fundamental factor is PRE-VENTING-HARM. In that case, atomism doesn't entail that other factors can't affect the weight or valence of LIFE-SAVING. Moreover, whenever I speak of factors, I am speaking of factors that are of fundamental moral relevance. (Which factors are of fundamental moral relevance is, of course, a matter of considerable dispute.)

Second, atomism doesn't entail that a factor's weight and valence are invariable *simpliciter*. And I take it that the most plausible version of atomism will insist only that a factor's weight and valence can't be affected by other factors (or by variations in other factors), and will reject the further claim that they can't be affected by variations *in that factor*. For example, it won't deny that the weight of DISAPPOINTMENT or DOING-HARM varies as the amount of resulting disappointment or harm varies (see Hooker 2008: 21). And if, say, guilt and innocence are two possible values of a single factor, CULPABILITY, it won't deny that CULPABILITY can contribute either positively or negatively to the moral status of punishing a person, depending on whether that person is guilty or innocent (see Kagan 1988: 6 n. 3).[10] Conversely, holism doesn't entail that there are no factors whose weights or valences cannot be affected by other factors (or by variations in other factors).[11] Moreover, I take it that the most plausible versions of holism will allow that whether the weight or valance of a particular factor can be affected by other factors can be a contingent matter, because it can (in the case of at least some factors) depend on whether there are, in fact, any factors that are capable of affecting that particular factor's weight or valence. (Compare, for example, how whether a particular disposition can be masked[12] is contingent on the existence of something with the power to mask it.)

Now, as the example above illustrates, the simple model assumes that we can distinguish the *contribution* a factor makes to the moral status of an act from the *effect* it has thereon. This distinction will be important in what follows. So it bears some attention.

The effect a factor has on the moral status of an act is just the difference it makes to that status. Suppose, for example, that I could both meet Able and save Baker. In that case, PROMISE-KEEPING would have a right-making effect on the moral status of my meeting Able: it would make the difference between what the moral status of this act is (required) and what that status would be in its absence (permissible). In this sense, PROMISE-KEEPING would make this act right. But in the case as described, PROMISE-KEEPING doesn't have this right-making effect: it doesn't make this act right. Or consider LIFE-SAVING. This factor has a

---

[10] I take the most plausible versions of atomism and holism to insist that any variation in the weight or valence of a factor must be either the effect of variations in that factor or the effect of other factors (or variations in other factors).

[11] See, e.g., Dancy 2004: 77; Robinson 2006: 337; Väyrynen 2006: 712.

[12] See note 30 below.

right-making effect on the moral status of my saving Baker. But it also has a wrong-making effect on the moral status of my meeting Able: it makes the difference between what the moral status of this act is (impermissible) and what that status would be in its absence (required). In this sense, LIFE-SAVING makes this act wrong. (Although in another sense, it's the overall "balance" of PROMISE-KEEPING, LIFE-SAVING, and DISAPPOINTMENT, or of the contributions they make, that makes this act wrong.) Now one might, of course, think that there's more to an act's moral status than merely its deontic status.[13] But my discussion will be confined to right- and wrong-making effects.

It's considerably harder to say just what the *contribution* a factor makes to the moral status of an act is. (Moreover, the view that right- and wrong-making factors are contributory factors is not uncontroversial.) Currently, many—including many atomists and holists— understand contributory factors in terms of moral reasons, as factors that provide moral reasons of various weights and valences.[14] On this view, the contribution a factor makes to the moral status of an act is the (*pro tanto*) moral reason that factor provides to perform or not to perform that act. This isn't how I prefer to think of these contributions,[15] but it will do as a first approximation. I will, however, continue to speak of contributions rather than moral reasons. (The reason for this will become apparent in the final sections of the paper.)

Now let's consider two views that the simple model entails are false, both of which are offered by Kagan to show that it's controversial.[16] It should be said that these views are themselves controversial (as Kagan acknowledges). But the point here isn't that the simple model is false. Rather, the point is simply that it's not consistent with certain views, because these views imply that morally relevant factors can and do combine and interact in certain complex ways that the simple model entails they can't.

---

[13] For example, one might think that it would be morally worse to kill the victims of a famine than it would be to let them die, even though neither is permissible (cf. Kagan 1988: 6–7).

[14] This seems to be how Kagan understands such factors (1988: 14–15).

[15] See Robinson, forthcoming-b.

[16] More precisely, Kagan offers them to show that the conjunction of additivity and atomism is not only controversial, but also "likely to be false on most moral theories" (1988: 18).

The first view makes three claims. First, there's no moral difference whatsoever between defending one's own life by pushing a wrongful aggressor into a pit, expecting the fall to kill him, and defending one's own life by not warning an aggressor that he is about to fall into a pit, expecting the fall to kill him. In particular, both of these acts—pushing the aggressor and not warning the aggressor—are permissible, and there's no other moral difference between them. Second, there's no moral difference between these acts *because* one factor, SELF-DEFENSE, prevents another factor, DOING-HARM, from having the moral effect(s)—i.e., making the moral difference(s)—it otherwise would. In particular, SELF-DEFENSE prevents DOING-HARM from making pushing the aggressor wrong, rather than permissible. Third, SELF-DEFENSE does *not* do this by making a contribution that combines additively with the negative contribution made by DOING-HARM—e.g., a positive contribution that counterbalances the latter's negative contribution.[17]

The second view makes three claims about a case in which we can aid either Trixie or Fritz, both of whom are suffering because Trixie's scheme to harm Fritz went awry and harmed her more than it harmed Fritz. First, Trixie's greater suffering notwithstanding, we ought to aid Fritz rather than Trixie: aiding Trixie is wrong, rather than right. Second, this is so *because* GUILT prevents GREATER-SUFFERING from having the moral effect it otherwise would. In particular, her guilt prevents Trixie's greater suffering from making aiding her right, rather than wrong. Third, Trixie's guilt does *not* do this by making a contribution that combines additively with the positive contribution made by her greater suffering—e.g., a negative contribution that outweighs the latter's positive contribution.[18]

The simple model entails that each of these views is false. It assumes that the moral status of an act is determined by the sum of the contributions made by each of the factors relevant thereto. (This is additivity.) But that's true only if *each* of the factors relevant to the moral status of an act makes a contribution thereto, which contribution

[17] "It seems a mistake to treat the factor of self defense as though it made . . . a contribution to be added to that made by other factors . . . . A more natural interpretation . . . would be to view [it] more like a zero multiplier" (1988: 19).

[18] "It will seem more appropriate to view the factor guilt/innocence not as making an independent contribution, but rather as a multiplier—this one able to range from one to zero" (Kagan 1988: 20).

combines additively with those of every other such factor to determine that act's moral status. And, on these views, that's not what SELF-DEFENSE and GUILT do: *ex hypothesi,* neither of these factors makes such a contribution. Rather, what they do is prevent other factors—DOING-HARM and GREATER-SUFFERING—from having the moral effects they otherwise would. And they don't do this in the way that, say, LIFE-SAVING prevents PROMISE-KEEPING from having the right-making effect it otherwise would on the moral status of my meeting Able. That is, they don't do this by making contributions that outweigh or counterbalance the contributions made by other factors. And that is the only way that the simple model allows that they could do this. Hence, the simple model entails that each of these views is false.

Now, the claim that SELF-DEFENSE and GUILT don't make contributions that combine additively with the contributions made by other factors is ambiguous. Do they (*a*) make no contributions, or (*b*) make contributions that don't combine additively with the contributions made by other factors? This is a matter for stipulation. I would prefer to say *b*. But contributory factors are generally characterized as having weights and valences. And if we did say *b*, we would then need to distinguish between the kinds of contributions that the simple model contemplates (additive contributions?) and other kinds of contributions that it doesn't (non-additive contributions?). Thus, I'm going to say *a*, they make no contributions. But we should keep in mind that on some accounts of what's going on in these cases it might be more natural to say *b*, rather than *a*. Moreover, when I say that a factor "makes no contribution," I'm not denying that it makes a contribution that doesn't combine additively with the contributions made by other factors. On the contrary, I'm asserting it.

Finally, these views are (as I said) controversial. And proponents of the simple model would say what atomists typically say about these and similar views.[19] Some would say that such views are mistaken about how SELF-DEFENSE and GUILT prevent DOING-HARM and GREATER-SUFFERING from having the effects they otherwise would. They do this, they would say, by making contributions—e.g., contributions that counterbalance or outweigh the contributions made

---

[19] See, e.g., Crisp 2000; Hooker 2008.

by DOING-HARM and GREATER-SUFFERING. Others would say that these views misidentify the relevant factors. For example, they might say that the relevant factors aren't DOING-HARM and GREATER-SUFFERING, but rather DOING-UNDESERVED-HARM and GREATER-UNDESERVED-SUFFERING. But, as I said, the point here isn't that the simple model is false. Rather, the point is that it's not consistent with these views. Moreover, this isn't because these views imply that contributory factors can be complex factors that require fine-grained descriptions (e.g., DOING-UNDESERVED-HARM). For these views imply nothing one way or the other about how complex contributory factors can be. Rather, it's because these and similar views imply that morally relevant factors can and do combine and interact in certain complex ways that the simple model entails they can't.[20]

3. THE HOLISTIC OPTION

Now one might assume that atomism is *by definition* committed to rejecting the foregoing views as false. It's certainly true that atomists do reject them as false. And it might be that some think of atomism in such a way that it is, by definition, committed to doing so. For example, some might think of atomism as the view that a factor can't have an effect, or make a moral difference, in one case unless it has that same effect, or makes that same difference, in any case. But we can't think of atomism in that way without (e.g.) thinking that Ross, who is supposed to be *the* paradigmatic valence atomist, is a holist simply because he allows that some factors can outweigh others. And if by "atomism" we understand the view that neither the size nor the direction of a factor's contribution can be affected by other factors (or by variations in other factors), then it's simply false that atomism is *by definition* committed to rejecting either the foregoing views or others that take morally relevant factors to combine and interact in similarly complex ways. Moreover, Kagan suggests that we could accommodate such views and the sorts of complex combinations and interactions they

---

[20] For that same reason, one couldn't defend the simple model by successfully codifying the complex ways in which such views imply that morally relevant factors combine and interact. (Thanks to Holly Smith, Daniel Star, and Christian Coons here.)

take to occur—i.e., the relevant views and interactions—by rejecting additivity *rather than* atomism.

But before we consider Kagan's suggestion, it will help to first consider the option he mentions in a footnote but doesn't explore: accommodating the relevant views and interactions by rejecting atomism (1988: 20 n. 8). For understanding this *holistic option* will make understanding and assessing Kagan's suggestion easier.

First, consider the view that SELF-DEFENSE prevents DOING-HARM from making pushing the aggressor wrong, rather than permissible. If we reject atomism in favor of valence holism, we can attribute this (posited) variation in the moral *effect* of DOING-HARM to a variation in its moral *valence* that is due to SELF-DEFENSE. On this holistic view (call it H1), DOING-HARM doesn't have the wrong-making effect it otherwise would *because* it doesn't have the negative valance it otherwise would: it doesn't make pushing the aggressor wrong *because* it doesn't make the negative contribution to the moral status of pushing the aggressor that it otherwise would. (Or, if you prefer, it doesn't provide the moral reason not to push the aggressor that it otherwise would.) Moreover, this variation in valance is due to SELF-DEFENSE: SELF-DEFENSE prevents DOING-HARM from having the negative valence it otherwise would (i.e., it's a *disabler*). On this view, SELF-DEFENSE prevents DOING-HARM from having the wrong-making effect it would otherwise have *by* preventing it from having the negative valence it would otherwise have, or making the negative contribution it would otherwise make.

Next, consider the view that her guilt prevents Trixie's greater suffering from making aiding her right, rather than wrong. If we reject atomism in favor of weight holism, we can attribute this (posited) variation in the moral *effect* of GREATER-SUFFERING to a variation in its moral *weight* that is due to GUILT. On this holistic view (call it H2), Trixie's greater suffering doesn't have the right-making effect it otherwise would *because* it has less weight than it otherwise would: it doesn't make aiding Trixie right *because* it makes a smaller positive contribution to the moral status of aiding her than it otherwise would. (Or, if you prefer, it provides less moral reason to aid her than it otherwise would.) Moreover, this variation in weight is due to Trixie's guilt: her guilt reduces the weight of her suffering (i.e., it's an *attenuator*). On this view, Trixie's guilt prevents her greater suffering from having the right-making effect it would otherwise have *by* reducing its weight, or the size of the positive contribution it makes.

Finally, consider the following view, which is an alternative to the previous one. Because it's due to her wickedness, rather than merely her own wrongdoing, Trixie's greater suffering has a *wrong-making* effect on the moral status of aiding her: rather than (merely) failing to make aiding her right, Trixie's greater suffering makes aiding her wrong (and would do so even if we could aid her after first aiding Fritz). If we reject atomism in favor of valence holism, we could attribute this (posited) variation in the moral *effect* of GREATER-SUFFERING to a variation in its moral *valence* that is due to WICKEDNESS. On this holistic view (call it H3), Trixie's greater suffering has a wrong-making effect on the moral status of aiding her *because* it has a negative valence: it makes aiding Trixie wrong *because* it makes a negative contribution to the moral status of aiding her. (Or, if you prefer, it provides a moral reason not to aid her.) Moreover, this variation in valence is due to Trixie's wickedness: her wickedness reverses the valence of her suffering (i.e., it's a *reverser*). On this view, Trixie's wickedness reverses the effect that Trixie's greater suffering has *by* reversing its valence, or the direction of the contribution it makes.

Notice that these holistic views are not *additive* views. For they entail that additivity is false. Now, holism itself doesn't entail that additivity is false. Suppose that some factor *both* makes a contribution *and* affects either the weight or the valence of another factor (the size or the direction of its contribution). In that case, atomism would be false, but it could still be true that the moral status of an act *is* determined by the sum of the contributions made by *each* of the factors relevant thereto.

But these holistic views do entail that additivity is false, because each supposes that some factor that is relevant to the moral status of an act doesn't make a contribution thereto, but rather (only) affects the weight or valence of another factor (and thereby the effect it has). For instance, if—as H2 claims—Trixie's guilt makes no contribution, but rather reduces the weight of her greater suffering, then the moral status of aiding Trixie is *not* determined by the sum of the contributions made by *each* of the factors relevant thereto.[21] For at least one of those factors makes no contribution. Likewise, if—as H1 claims—

---

[21] Given my earlier stipulation, to say this *is* to say that it's not determined by the *sum* of the contributions made by each of the factors relevant thereto (i.e., these statements are notational variants).

SELF-DEFENSE makes no contribution, but rather prevents DOING-HARM from making the (negative) contribution it otherwise would, then the moral status of pushing the aggressor is *not* determined by the sum of the contributions made by *each* of the factors relevant thereto.

It bears noting that these holistic views *are* consistent with the following assumption, which is considerably weaker than additivity: the moral status of an act is determined by the sum of the contributions made by those factors that make contributions thereto. (Which isn't to say that this weaker assumption is warranted.) For this weaker assumption allows that some factors don't make contributions, but rather (only) affect the weights and valences of other factors. Thus, none of our holistic views entails either that what Selim Berker (2007) calls "the combinatorial function" isn't additive or that there's no such function.[22] Berker defines the combinatorial function as "the function that takes as inputs the [possibly holistically-determined] valence and weight of all the reasons present in a given possible situation and gives as output the rightness and wrongness of each action available in that situation" (120). Since what Berker means by a "reason" here is what I mean by a contributory factor (115–18), the claim that there is an additive combinatorial function entails only that the moral status of an act is determined by the sum of the contributions made by those factors that make contributions thereto. And none of our holistic views entails that there isn't an additive combinatorial function, much less that there's no combinatorial function.[23] However, I mention this only to lay it aside. In what follows, I won't be concerned with whether there's a combinatorial function or whether, if there is one, it's additive.

4. NON-ADDITIVE MODELS

As the foregoing illustrates, we could accommodate the relevant views and interactions by rejecting atomism. But the object of my

[22] For similar reasons, none of them entails that what Brink calls the "additive assumption" is false (see 1994: 217 n. 5).
[23] It follows that the "combinatorial function" could be additive even if additivity is false. Thus, the question Berker considers (which is whether there is a coherent conception of a reason for action that is consistent with both valence holism and the view that "the combinatorial function . . . is not finitely expressible (and so . . . not additive)" [122, 124–34]) is orthogonal to the questions I consider here.

inquiry is Kagan's suggestion that we could also do this by rejecting additivity *rather than* atomism: the possibility of an atomistic option. Unfortunately, Kagan doesn't develop such an option (presumably because doing so isn't necessary to his project, which is to criticize arguments that presuppose both additivity and atomism). Nor is he particularly clear about how it would differ from the holistic option. So we must do some work before we can assess its prospects.

I begin with the suggestion that developing an atomistic option would involve not only rejecting additivity and the simple model along with it, but also replacing the simple model with an alternative one that assumes atomism but not additivity (Kagan 1988: 20–1 and n. 8). Now Kagan doesn't develop such a model himself. But we can get a rough, but good-enough idea of how one might work by considering some simple (and rather crude) *non-additive models*, which adapt his suggestion that SELF-DEFENSE and GUILT act more like "multipliers"— i.e., like the variable x in the equation $S = x \times y + z$—than factors that make contributions that combine additively with those made by DOING-HARM and GREATER-SUFFERING (19).[24]

First, consider the view that SELF-DEFENSE prevents DOING-HARM from making pushing the aggressor wrong, rather than permissible. And consider the following model, which treats SELF-DEFENSE as a "zero multiplier."[25]

$$\text{M1} \quad E = d \times s$$

To capture the view in question, we must make some stipulations. First, E represents the effect, if any, that DOING-HARM has on the moral status of an act A that involves doing harm. Negative values indicate a wrong-making effect: $E < 0$ if DOING-HARM makes A wrong. And zero indicates no effect: $E = 0$ if DOING-HARM makes no difference to A's moral status. Second, d represents DOING-HARM and, in particular, the effect it has on acts that involve doing harm in the absence of perturbing factors (e.g., SELF-DEFENSE). Since this effect is a wrong-making one, d is a negative number. Third, s represents SELF-DEFENSE. It equals zero (is a "zero multiplier") if A is an act of self-defense; otherwise, it equals one.

---

[24] Berker (2007) describes some non-additive models, but they model "combinatorial functions" and, thus, aren't applicable (see above).

[25] See note 17 above.

Given these stipulations, M1 represents SELF-DEFENSE as a factor that (when present) prevents DOING-HARM from making acts that involve doing harm wrong. If A is not an act of self-defense, s equals one; so the value of E is the same as the value of d, which is negative.

$$E = (d \times 1) = d < 0$$

In other words, if A is not an act of self-defense, DOING-HARM makes A wrong. But if A is an act of self-defense, s equals zero; so the value of E is zero.

$$E = (d \times 0) = 0$$

In other words, SELF-DEFENSE prevents DOING-HARM from making A wrong. Hence, M1 captures the view that SELF-DEFENSE prevents DOING-HARM from making pushing the aggressor wrong, rather than permissible. Moreover, M1 is not additive (in the relevant sense): it doesn't assume that the moral status of an act is determined by the sum of the contributions made by each of the factors relevant thereto.

Next, consider the view that her guilt prevents Trixie's greater suffering from making aiding her right, rather than wrong. And consider the following model, which treats GUILT as "a multiplier . . . [that can] range from one to zero."[26]

$$\text{M2} \quad E = s \times g$$

Here, too, we must make some stipulations. First, E represents the effect, if any, that a person P_1's greater suffering has on the moral status of aiding her rather than another person P_2, who is suffering less. Values greater than some threshold value t, a positive number, indicate a right-making effect: $E > t$ if GREATER-SUFFERING makes aiding P_1 right. And values equal to or less than t indicate no effect: $E \leq t$ if GREATER-SUFFERING makes no difference to the moral status of aiding P_1. Second, s represents GREATER-SUFFERING and, in particular, the effect it has on aiding one who is suffering more rather than another who is suffering less in the absence of perturbing factors (e.g., GUILT). Since this effect is a right-making one, s is greater than t. Third, g represents GUILT and, in particular, P_1's degree of guilt, or culpability. It is less than one but

---

[26] See note 18 above.

greater than or equal to zero if Pr is guilty to some degree; otherwise, it equals one.

Given these stipulations, M2 represents GUILT as a factor that can (when present) prevent GREATER-SUFFERING from making aiding one who is suffering more rather than another who is suffering less right. If Pr is not guilty, g equals one; so the value of E is the same as the value of s, which is greater than t.

$$E = (s \times 1) = s > t$$

In other words, if Pr is not guilty, GREATER-SUFFERING makes aiding Pr right. But if Pr is guilty, g is less than one; so the value of E is less than the value of s.

$$E = (s \times g) < s$$

Moreover, for some values of g (including zero), E will be less than t. In other words, if Pr is *sufficiently* guilty, GUILT prevents GREATER-SUFFERING from making aiding Pr right. Hence, M2 can capture the view that her guilt prevents Trixie's greater suffering from making aiding her right, rather than wrong. Moreover, M2 is not additive (in the relevant sense).

Finally, M2 can be modified to capture the alternative view that, because it's due to her own wickedness, Trixie's greater suffering makes aiding her wrong. We need only stipulate (1) that g is less than zero if and only if Pr's greater suffering is due to her own wickedness, rather than merely her own wrongdoing,[27] and (2) that negative values of E indicate that Pr's greater suffering has a wrong-making effect on the moral status of aiding her: $E < 0$ if GREATER-SUFFERING makes aiding Pr wrong.

On this revised model (call it M3), if Pr's greater suffering is due to her own wickedness, g is less than zero; so the value of E is negative. (Note that $s > 0$.)

$$E = (s \times g) < 0$$

---

[27] Cf. "A more pronounced version of this view might allow the multiplier to range between positive one and negative one ... [to allow that] the wicked deserve to be unhappy" (Kagan 1988: 20).

In other words, WICKEDNESS reverses the effect that GREATER-SUFFERING has on the moral status of aiding P1. Hence, M3 can capture the (alternative) view that, because it's due to her own wickedness, Trixie's greater suffering makes aiding her wrong. Moreover, like M1 and M2, M3 is not additive (in the relevant sense).

Now (as I said) these models are crude. For instance, they represent the effect that a particular factor has on the moral status of an act as being determined by itself and a second factor, which is not generally the case. Moreover, unlike the simple model, none is a general model of how morally relevant factors combine and interact. Nevertheless, they do give us a rough idea of how an alternative to the simple model might work and, in particular, of how the specifically non-additive aspects of such a model might work. And for present purposes, that's all we need. For it allows us to see that alternative models are of no help in developing an atomistic option.

First, consider that non-additive models as such don't assume atomism and, in particular, that these models don't. Take M1, for instance. M1 represents SELF-DEFENSE as a factor that (when present) prevents DOING-HARM from making acts that involve doing harm wrong. But M1 makes no assumptions about the means by which SELF-DEFENSE does this. True, it doesn't represent SELF-DEFENSE as doing this *by* preventing it from making the (negative) contribution it otherwise would. But neither does it represent SELF-DEFENSE as doing this by some other means. If an act A that involves doing harm is an act of self-defense, s equals zero and the value of E is 0, indicating that SELF-DEFENSE prevents DOING-HARM from making A wrong. And this is so even if, as H1 claims, SELF-DEFENSE does this by preventing that other factor from making the (negative) contribution it otherwise would. Moreover, the same is true, *mutatis mutandis*, of M2 and M3, which make no assumptions about the means by which GUILT and WICKEDNESS alter the effect of Trixie's greater suffering.

Next, consider the objection that all this shows is that these are the wrong models. What we want aren't non-additive models. Rather, what we want are non-additive models *that assume atomism*. M1–M3 treat SELF-DEFENSE and GUILT as multipliers of the *effects* that DOING-HARM and GREATER-SUFFERING have in the absence of perturbing factors, like SELF-DEFENSE and GUILT. But what we need are models that treat them as multipliers of the *contributions* that DOING-HARM and

GREATER-SUFFERING make in the absence of perturbing factors, which—
if atomism is true—are the same contributions they make in the
presence of such factors. Unlike these (merely) non-additive models,
such models would be of help in developing an atomistic option. Or so
goes the objection.

But such models would be of no such help. What's a multiplier of the
contribution that a factor makes in the absence of perturbing factors?
One thing it could be is (1) a factor that affects the size or direction of
another factor's contribution. But if atomism is true, it can't be that.
The only other thing it could be is (2) a factor that alters the *effect* that
another factor has *other than by* altering the contribution that second
factor makes (its size or direction). But that tells us precisely nothing we
didn't already know. For we already knew that accommodating the
relevant views and interactions by denying additivity *rather than* atomism requires saying that SELF-DEFENSE and GUILT alter the effects that
DOING-HARM and GREATER-SUFFERING have other than by altering the
contributions they make. Moreover, the proposed models would
assume atomism only if we stipulated that the multipliers are of the
second type, rather than the first.

And there's the rub. For—as I will now argue—we don't know
whether we can make that stipulation. More specifically, we don't
know whether what it says is coherent.

5. THE RUB AND THE CHALLENGE

First, let's review what developing an atomistic option requires us to *say*.
What it requires us to say is that one factor (e.g., SELF-DEFENSE) *can* alter
the effect that another factor (e.g., DOING-HARM) has *other than by* doing
one of the following:

(i) making a contribution of its own—e.g., one that outweighs the
    contribution made by that second factor; or
(ii) altering the contribution that second factor makes (its size or
    direction).

Second, what the aforementioned stipulation says is that a multiplier of
the contribution that a factor makes in the absence of perturbing factors
is a factor that alters the effect that another factor has other than by

doing (ii). But the rub is that we don't know whether we can *coherently* say either of these things. For whether we can coherently say them depends on whether there's a conception of contribution, an account of just what the contribution a factor makes to the moral status of an act *is*, that renders these assertions coherent.

Now, to see that this is the rub, we need only suppose (*contra* the simple model and all relevant parties) that the contribution/effect distinction is merely terminological—i.e., that the *contribution* a factor makes to the moral status of an act is nothing other than the *effect* it has thereon under a different description. In that case, the key claim—that one factor can (or does) alter the effect that another factor has *other than by* doing (ii), altering the contribution that second factor makes—is incoherent. For given this *effect conception* of contribution, to alter the effect that another factor has *just is* to alter the contribution that it makes.

Now it might be said that holism—and even the simple model—are in much the same boat, that absent a suitable conception of contribution, we don't know whether the claims they make about how one factor can alter the effect that another factor has are coherent. But while that's true, it's irrelevant. For the object of inquiry is the possibility of an atomistic option. And what we would need to develop such an option is a conception of contribution that renders coherent the claims *it* makes.

Call the challenge of offering such a conception the "Challenge." And note that it has two parts, because a suitable conception of contribution must both (*a*) identify what a factor's contribution is such that it's something other than the effect it has, and (*b*) render coherent the claim that one factor can alter the effect that another factor has *other than by* doing either (i) or (ii).

Obviously, atomists *as such* bear no obligation to meet this challenge. They may choose, instead, to defend the simple model. (Although even that requires meeting the first part of the Challenge.) But developing an atomistic option would require meeting it. Moreover, we can't, *ex ante*, rule out the possibility that it can be met. We can only consider possible conceptions of contribution to determine whether they are suitable ones. And that some aren't doesn't show that none is. Thus, we should inquire whether atomists *could* meet the Challenge.

6. COULD ROSSIAN ATOMISTS MEET THE CHALLENGE?

In this final section, I consider whether Rossian pluralism offers the conceptual and metaphysical resources that atomists would need to meet the Challenge. I focus on Rossian pluralism for a number of reasons, of which I'll mention two. First, Ross's *The Right and the Good* (1930) is the *locus classicus* for the idea of a contributory right-making factor. He maintains that various factors can contribute to the *prima facie* rightness or wrongness of an act, and that the right act in any given situation is the one "whose *prima face* rightness ... most out-weighs its *prima facie* wrongness ..." (46). Second, discussions of valence holism originated in particularist critiques of Rossian pluralism, critiques that objected to its (supposed) valence atomism.[28] Thus, Rossian pluralism is a natural place to begin an inquiry into whether atomists could meet the Challenge.

Contrary to what the term "*prima facie*" suggests, it's clear that *prima facie* rightness is not apparent rightness (1930: 19–20; 1939: 84–5). But there are different ways of understanding just what it is, or different conceptions of *prima facie* rightness. So I'll consider whether atomists could appeal to *some* conception of *prima facie* rightness to meet the Challenge. And in the process, I'll consider whether Rossian pluralism could accommodate the relevant views and interactions other than by rejecting atomism.[29]

On one conception, *prima facie* rightness is "conditional rightness,"

the property, not necessarily of being right but of being something that is right if the act has no other morally relevant characteristic. ... (1930: 138)

On this *conditional conception, prima facie* rightness is the property of being right "where other considerations do not enter the case" (135).

At first blush, conditional rightness and conditional wrongness might seem like what atomists would need to meet the Challenge. Consider an act that DOING-HARM makes wrong—e.g., whatever Trixie did that harmed Fritz. Such an act is conditionally wrong: it has the characteristic of being wrong *if* its only morally relevant characteristic is

---

[28] See, e.g., Dancy 1983; McNaughton 1988.
[29] Perhaps I should add that I think Rossian pluralism (broadly construed) can accept both weight and valence holism.

that it involves doing harm. Moreover, its conditional wrongness is something different from the effect that DOING-HARM has on its moral status. Now consider pushing the aggressor, which DOING-HARM doesn't make wrong because SELF-DEFENSE prevents it from doing so. The same is true of it. It's conditionally wrong, and its conditional wrongness is something different from the effect, if any, that DOING-HARM has on its moral status (which we are supposing is none). And, as this shows, its conditional wrongness is unaffected by SELF-DEFENSE. Moreover, we may suppose that SELF-DEFENSE doesn't counterbalance or outweigh DOING-HARM, but merely prevents it from making pushing the aggressor wrong.

But atomists would need more than conditional rightness and wrongness to meet the Challenge. For an act's conditional rightness or wrongness isn't itself a contribution to its moral status. And an act's being conditionally right or wrong doesn't guarantee that the ground of its conditional rightness or wrongness makes a contribution to its moral status. Suppose, as H1 claims, that SELF-DEFENSE prevents DOING-HARM from making pushing the aggressor wrong by preventing it from making the negative contribution it otherwise would to its moral status. In that case, pushing the aggressor is conditionally wrong, but the characteristic that grounds its conditional wrongness (DOING-HARM) makes no contribution to its moral status.

On a second conception, *prima facie* rightness is a dispositional property, the "tendency to be right" (1939: 79). This fits Ross's characterization of "*prima facie* duties" both as acts that tend to be duties and as acts that tend to be right, as well as the analogy he draws between the moral tendencies of such acts and the physical tendencies of bodies subject to gravitation and other physical forces (1930: 18 n. 1, 28–9, 46; 1939: 86, 89). On this *dispositional conception, prima facie* rightness is the tendency or disposition to be right. And an act can tend to be right without being right, just as a body can tend to move in line with a given force without so moving (1939: 86).

Here, too, this dispositional conception of *prima facie* rightness and a correlative conception of *prima facie* wrongness might seem like what atomists would need to meet the Challenge. But again, atomists would need more than a tendency to be right or wrong to meet the Challenge. For such a tendency isn't itself a contribution to an act's moral status. And an act's having such a tendency doesn't guarantee that the ground of that tendency makes a contribution to its moral status. Suppose, for example, that the following is correct. Pushing the aggressor involves doing harm. This characteristic (DOING-HARM) grounds a tendency in this act to be wrong—a tendency that would, in the absence of perturbing factors, manifest, thereby making it wrong. But pushing the aggressor is an act of self-defense. And this second characteristic (SELF-DEFENSE) is a perturbing factor: it masks that tendency, thereby preventing it from manifesting.[30] If this view is correct, then pushing the aggressor has a tendency to be wrong. But there's no guarantee that DOING-HARM does anything beyond grounding this (masked) tendency, such as making a (negative) contribution to its moral status.

Now one might well argue that this is the wrong way to think about the tendency to be right and the tendency to be wrong. One might argue that we should understand these tendencies in the way that Ross suggests, as analogous to the tendencies of bodies subject to physical forces. On this view, these tendencies are consequent upon moral forces. Or one might argue that we should understand these tendencies *as* moral forces (Brink 1994: 19–20).[31] In either case, atomists might then attempt to meet the Challenge by identifying a factor's contribution with a moral force contributed by that factor. In which case, their atomism would amount to the view that right- and wrong-making factors contribute moral forces whose magnitudes and directions can't be affected by other factors (or by variations in other factors).

If tenable, this third, *force conception* of *prima facie* rightness would provide atomists with what they need to meet the first part of the Challenge: something to identify with a factor's contribution that isn't the effect it has, a moral force. But there would seem to be nothing in this conception that would allow atomists to meet the second part of the Challenge, which—in this iteration—is to render coherent the claim that one factor can alter the effect that another factor has other than by (i′) contributing a force of its own or (ii′) altering the force contributed by that second factor (its magnitude or direction). Consider that Trixie's suffering is greater than Fritz's. Atomists must, therefore, say that her suffering contributes a greater positive moral force than Fritz's

---

[30] A masking disposition (or masking power) is one whose manifestation prevents another disposition from manifesting without making its bearer lose that disposition.

[31] Cf. Robinson, forthcoming-a; forthcoming-b.

suffering does. But then how could they allow that we ought to aid Fritz instead—that the balance of moral forces favors aiding *him*? It would be false to the (stipulated) facts of the case to say that Trixie's guilt contributes a third force that combines with the force generated by Fritz's suffering to defeat the force generated by Trixie's suffering (or that we've misidentified the relevant factors). For one of those facts is that Trixie's guilt makes no contribution (contributes no force). And it seems incoherent to say that Trixie's guilt (somehow) alters the balance of forces without either contributing a force or (à la weight holism) altering the magnitude of the force contributed by her suffering.

Moreover, this form of atomism is itself false to the (stipulated) facts of our examples. Suppose (as per this form of atomism) that neither the magnitude nor the direction of the moral force contributed by Trixie's suffering is affected by her guilt. In that case, we ought to aid Trixie rather than Fritz, because that's what the balance of moral forces favors. Moreover, if we aid Fritz instead, we have *as much* cause to (e.g.) regret or apologize for not aiding Trixie as we would if she were innocent and we failed to aid her.[32] But all of this is false to the (stipulated) facts of the example: we ought to aid Fritz rather than Trixie; and if that's what we ought to do, then we either have *no* cause to regret or apologize for not aiding Trixie or else we have *less* cause to do so than we would if she were innocent and we failed to aid her. Or take the view that there's no moral difference whatsoever between (*a*) pushing the aggressor and (*b*) not warning the aggressor. If neither the magnitude nor the direction of the moral force contributed by DOING-HARM were affected by SELF-DEFENSE, then there *would* be a moral difference between *a* and *b*, and one *would* have more cause to (e.g.) regret *a* than *b*.

Given the foregoing, I conclude that atomists couldn't appeal to either the dispositional conception or the force conception of *prima facie* rightness to meet the Challenge.

On a fourth conception, *prima facie* rightness is moral suitability or fitness, not to a particular situation, but rather to some aspect thereof (1939: 51–5, 84–5). More specifically, it's the (relational) property of being "morally suitable to a certain degree, and in a certain respect"

---

[32] I'm assuming here and below that one reason for positing a defeated moral force or reason in conflict cases is to explain why one has cause for (e.g.) regret or apology in such cases, even if one acts rightly (see, e.g., Brink 1994: 220–3; Dancy 2004: 3–4).

(52–3). This fits Ross's partial definition of rightness, which identifies rightness with "the greatest amount of [moral] suitability possible in the circumstances" (53). On this *suitability conception*, *prima facie* rightness is the moral suitability or "fitness . . . of an . . . act *in certain respects*" (84). And a particular act is *prima facie* right in a particular situation just to the degree that it fits aspects of that situation.

Here, too, we might grant that this conception provides atomists with what they need to meet the first part of the Challenge: a degree of suitability or unsuitability. But here, too, there would seem to be nothing in it that would allow them to meet the second part, which—in this iteration—is to render coherent the claim that one factor can alter the effect that another factor has other than by (i″) contributing a degree of suitability or unsuitability itself or (ii) altering the contribution that second factor makes (its size or direction). Given that Trixie's suffering is greater than Fritz's, atomists must say that aiding her is more suitable than aiding Fritz in that respect. But then how could they allow that we ought to aid Fritz instead—that aiding Fritz is more suitable than aiding Trixie? It would be false to the (stipulated) facts to say that Trixie's guilt makes aiding her unsuitable in another respect (or that we've misidentified the relevant factors). And it seems incoherent to say that her guilt (somehow) makes aiding Trixie less suitable than aiding Fritz without either contributing a degree of unsuitability to aiding Trixie or (à la weight holism) reducing the degree to which her suffering makes it suitable.

On a fifth conception, *prima facie* rightness is *pro tanto* moral reasonableness. Although Ross himself never characterizes either *prima facie* rightness or the correlative notion of a "*prima facie* duty" in terms of reasons, many others do.[33] Philip Stratton-Lake's account is representative.

For an act to be *prima facie* right is . . . for [it] to have some feature that gives us a moral reason to do it. (2002: xxxiii–xxxiv)

On this *reasons conception*, *prima facie* rightness is the property of being favored by a moral reason, which property an act may have even if it's not favored by the "balance" of such reasons.

---

[33] See, e.g., Brink 1994: 216; Dancy 2004: 5–7, 18–20; Stratton-Lake 2002, xxxiii–xxxviii.

Again, we might grant that this conception provides atomists with what they need to meet the first part of the Challenge: a degree of reasonableness. But again, there would seem to be nothing in it that would allow them to meet the second part. Indeed, for present purposes, the reasons conception seems not to be relevantly different from the suitability conception.

Finally, we might add that atomism about moral reasons is also false to the (stipulated) facts of our examples. Suppose (as per such atomism) that neither the weight nor the valence of the moral reason provided by Trixie's suffering is affected by her guilt. In that case, we ought to aid Trixie rather than Fritz, because that's what the balance of moral reasons favors. Moreover, if we aid Fritz instead, we have *as much* cause to (e.g.) regret or apologize for not aiding Trixie as we would if she were innocent and we failed to aid her.[34] But all of this is false to the (stipulated) facts of the example. Or take the view that there's no moral difference whatsoever between (*a*) pushing the aggressor and (*b*) not warning the aggressor. If neither the weight nor the valence of the moral reason provided by DOING-HARM were affected by SELF-DEFENSE, then there *would* be a moral difference between *a* and *b*, and one *would* have more cause to (e.g.) regret *a* than *b*.

Given the foregoing, I conclude that atomists couldn't appeal to either the suitability conception or the reasons conception of *prima facie* rightness to meet the Challenge. And I'm aware of no other conception of *prima facie* rightness that might do the trick. Therefore, I conclude both that Rossian pluralism lacks the conceptual and metaphysical resources that atomists would need to meet the Challenge, and that Rossian pluralism could accommodate the relevant views and interactions only by rejecting atomism. However, it bears repeating that my arguments here don't show that there is no atomistic option. For we can't, *ex ante*, rule out the possibility that the Challenge can be met. And that Rossian pluralism lacks the resources that atomists would need to meet it doesn't entail that it can't be met.[35]

---

[34] See note 32 above.

[35] Kagan likens the rejection of the simple model to Moore's principle of organic unities (1988: 23 n. 10). And one might ask whether Moore's principle might help atomists meet the Challenge. Space prevents me from doing justice to this question, but note that Moore's own account of why this principle is true is consistent with value-theoretic analogs of both additivity and atomism—which account is (roughly) that the factors that determine the value of a whole "on the whole" can include not only the values of its parts, but also its value "as a whole," which value results from the specific way in which its parts are combined (Hurka 1998). (Thanks to Tom Hurka and Guy Fletcher here.)

REFERENCES

Berker, Selim (2007) "Particular Reasons," *Ethics* 118, 109–39.
Brink, David O. (1994) "Moral Conflict and Its Structure," *Philosophical Review* 103, 215–47.
Brown, Campbell (2007) "Two Kinds of Holism About Values," *Philosophical Quarterly* 57, 457–63.
Crisp, Roger (2000) "Particularizing Particularism." In Brad Hooker and Margaret Little (eds.), *Moral Particularism* (Oxford University Press), 23–47.
Dancy, Jonathan (1983) "Ethical Particularism and Morally Relevant Properties," *Mind* 92, 530–47.
——(2004) *Ethics without Principles* (Oxford University Press).
Hooker, Brad (2008) "Moral Particularism and the Real World." In Mark Lance, Matjaž Potrč, and Vojko Strahovnik (eds.), *Challenging Moral Particularism* (New York: Routledge), 12–30.
Hurka, Thomas (1998) "Two Kinds of Organic Unity," *Journal of Ethics* 2, 299–320.
Kagan, Shelly (1988) "The Additive Fallacy," *Ethics* 99, 5–31.
Kamm, F. M. (1996) *Morality, Mortality* (New York: Oxford University Press).
McKeever, Sean and Michael Ridge (2006) *Principled Ethics: Generalism as a Regulative Ideal* (Oxford University Press).
McNaughton, David (1988) *Moral Vision* (Oxford: Blackwell).
Raz, Joseph (2000) "The Truth in Particularism." In Brad Hooker and Margaret Little (eds.), *Moral Particularism* (Oxford University Press), 48–78.
Robinson, Luke (2006) "Moral Holism, Moral Generalism, and Moral Dispositionalism," *Mind* 115, 331–60.
——(Forthcoming-a) "A Dispositional Account of Conflicts of Obligation," *Noûs*.
——(Forthcoming-b) "Obligating Reasons, Moral Laws, and Moral Dispositions," *Journal of Moral Philosophy*.
Ross, W. D. (1930) *The Right and the Good* (Oxford University Press).
——(1939) *Foundations of Ethics* (Oxford University Press).
Stratton-Lake, Philip (2002) "Introduction." In W. D. Ross, *The Right and the Good* (Oxford University Press).
Väyrynen, Pekka (2006) "Moral Generalism: Enjoy in Moderation," *Ethics* 116, 707–41.

Moral Dumbfounding and Moral Stupefaction

DANIEL JACOBSON

Several prominent moral psychologists and philosophers have recently made much of a phenomenon they term *moral dumbfounding*, defined as "the stubborn and puzzled maintenance of a moral judgment without supporting reasons" (Haidt et al. 2000: 1).[1] This phenomenon, most thoroughly discussed in Jonathan Haidt's (2001) influential paper, "The Emotional Dog and its Rational Tail," has been utilized in antithetical ways. Haidt and his collaborators hold it to support a descriptive and normative theory, social intuitionism, which is anthropocentric and sentimentalist, and claims to vindicate moral knowledge; whereas Peter Singer (2005) and Joshua Greene (2008) hold that dumbfounding supports a hyper-rationalist consequentialism, which they claim to be the only alternative to moral skepticism. Yet the proponents of dumbfounding agree that the phenomenon shows something important about ordinary moral judgment, even where people are not dumbfounded. Specifically, they claim that it supports their view that reasons and reasoning typically play little or no role in judgment. What passes for moral reasoning is, quite generally, better viewed as post hoc rationalization of decisions made on other, non-rational grounds. Let us call this the pessimistic view of moral reasons and reasoning.

In this paper I will dispute the evidence for such pessimism drawn from dumbfounding, despite accepting the existence of moral

---

[1] I would like to thank audiences at the Arizona Workshop in Normative Ethics, Franklin & Marshall College, the Murphy Center at Tulane University, Syracuse University, and the Ethics Discussion Group at the University of Michigan for their helpful comments on earlier drafts of this paper. I am especially grateful to Justin D'Arms, William FitzPatrick, Simon May, David Sobel, and two anonymous referees.

dumbfounding more or less as described. That is, I grant that sometimes people are unable to support their evaluative judgments with reasons. This much seems evident from everyday life and has been widely noted by philosophers. In their renowned but unpublished study, Haidt and his collaborators interviewed 30 undergraduates and discovered that they often could not articulate reasons in support of their condemnation of a couple of outlandish hypothetical scenarios titled Incest and Cannibal. Moreover, evidence drawn from morally neutral situations supports the idea that, in struggling to make sense of themselves and their behavior, people sometimes unwittingly make up stories that falsify the real causes of their action: they confabulate.[2] But no one doubts that in a host of mundane cases, we do act for reasons and know the reasons on which we act. Sometimes a person eats because he is hungry; that fact both *explains* why he ate and *justifies* it (at least by his own lights).

In the moral domain, however, Haidt and others press a very strong claim: they doubt whether we ever reason our way to moral judgment. "The central claim of the social intuitionist model," Haidt (2001: 817) writes, "is that moral judgment is caused by quick moral intuitions and is followed (when needed) by slow, ex post facto moral reasoning." In this view "the core of the model gives moral reasoning a causal role in moral judgment, but only when reasoning runs through other people" (Haidt and Bjorklund 2008: 181). Moreover, such social persuasion works mostly to secure the conformity of people's intuitions, not to make them more sensitive to reasons. Although this picture does not quite rule out the possibility of genuine moral reasoning, as opposed to mere post hoc rationalization, it claims to capture "the great majority of moral judgments made by the great majority of people" (Haidt and Bjorklund 2008: 193).

The term "dumbfounding" has a negative connotation, suggesting as it does that those who cannot give reasons for their moral judgment are confounded: struck dumb with confusion. Indeed, dumbfounding is put forward as the quintessential case for pessimism. Social intuitionists

---

[2] In a classic paper, Nisbett and Wilson (1977) review and summarize an already lengthy literature on such confabulation. Haidt (2008: 189) expressly recalls their analogous claim, writing that Nisbett and Wilson "demonstrated such post hoc reasoning for causal explanations. When people are tricked into doing a variety of things, they readily make up stories to explain their actions, stories that can often be shown to be false."

and hyper-rationalist consequentialists alike claim that because dumb-founded subjects are unable to articulate their reasons, their moral judgments about the scenarios can have no rational justification.[3] According to the descriptive model of moral judgment they share, reasons and reasoning play a scant role in our moral judgments. The phenomenon of moral dumbfounding seems to support this conclusion because dumbfounded subjects stick to their moral judgments dogmat-ically, despite being unable to support them. Or so it is expressly and repeatedly claimed. Yet the pessimistic view holds that the dumb-founded are not so different from the rest of us. Haidt (2001: 814) compares the role of reasoning in moral judgment to "a lawyer trying to build a case rather than a judge searching for the truth," or the spin of a presidential press secretary whose job is to tell credible lies that make the president look as good as possible (Haidt 2005). The difference between the ordinary case, where people support their moral judgments with reasons, and cases of dumbfounding amounts merely to the difference between a competent and an incompetent press secretary. Both lie by nature and job description—it's just that when we are dumbfounded, reason has failed at its task of constructing bogus rationalizations.

But I contend that the claim that the dumbfounding study supports this pessimistic conclusion rests on a shaky foundation. Several alterna-tive explanations of the phenomenon would arise were there good reasons for the dumbfounded subjects' moral judgments, even though they are unable to articulate them under the experimental conditions. I will argue that there are in fact good reasons for critical moral judgments in all of the cases Haidt considers—indeed, obviously good reasons—his claims to the contrary notwithstanding. The fact that these reasons have somehow been overlooked in this literature suggests that the subjects are not *dumbfounded* by these cases so much as certain (extremely intelligent) psychologists and philosophers are, rather,

---

[3] Haidt and Bjorklund (2008: 181) hold that the social aspect of their theory provides non-rational justification to moral judgment, but their account of justification and moral know-ledge is deeply problematic. I have argued that their theory amounts to a form of cultural relativism, despite their claims to the contrary, and does not succeed in justifying moral judgment (Jacobson 2008). However that may be, Haidt and Bjorklund hold that these judgments would be unjustified without the social element; while Singer and Greene hold that ordinary moral judgments, not founded on first principles like Sidgwick's axioms of ethics, are unjustified.

stupefied by their moral theories. To be morally stupefied in this fashion is to be rendered unable to see obviously good reasons, because you are in the grip of a theory too narrow-minded to accommodate them. In particular, philosophers committed to the claim that judgments of wrongness must be grounded in harm cannot presume that others have no moral reasons simply because they have no harm-based reasons. Perhaps they have no *good* reasons—though I will argue otherwise—but to be dumbfounded is not to have substantively bad reasons; it is to have no reason at all in support of one's judgment.

In fact, I think that specifically moral stupidity is an important and fascinating subject in its own right, in that very smart people can in various respects be stupefied by ideology, conformism, group polarization, and even by misguided theory, into making profound moral errors. These errors tend to be mistakes of proportionality and false moral equivalence, as when the (obviously true) fact that no country or culture is without blemish gets used to imply that all are equally worthy. Moreover, sometimes people promote their self-interest and display their partiality while dressing up their reasons in the trappings of morality and objectivity, without realizing what they are doing. Although these observations reveal an important truth at the core of Haidt's view, it is important to note that too strong a pessimistic claim obscures the point by assimilating all moral reasoning with its defective instances. Thus while I accept a modest form of the *primacy of affect* thesis, according to which factors we are unaware of play a significant role in driving evaluative judgment, the plausible versions of this thesis cannot be so strong as to imply the (near) causal impotence of reasons and reasoning, as the pessimistic view claims.

My first goal in this paper is to illustrate a flaw in Haidt's central example, Incest, which undermines the support it provides for the arguments given by proponents of dumbfounding. The trouble with this scenario is that there are perfectly good *harm-based* reasons for moral condemnation, despite the fact that Haidt repeatedly claims that the moral intuition scenarios were "carefully written to be harmless" and hence that it is "extremely difficult to find strong arguments" to justify judgments of wrongness (2000: 7). He concludes that subjects who stick to their moral judgments do so "in the absence of reasons" (2000: 6) and thus without justification. But critical moral judgments about such scenarios cannot be discounted simply because the actions considered are *in some sense* harmless, if they are needlessly dangerous or violate rules well designed to prevent harm (or promote good). In order to be plausible, the harm-based theories that the dumbfounding literature seems to presuppose must adopt a more complex conception of the connection between harm and wrongness.

Next I argue that Haidt's other primary example of a scenario that produces dumbfounded moral intuitions, Cannibal, fails for a similar reason. Here too there are perfectly good reasons to judge the act wrong. Although these reasons do not advert *directly* to harm, they are available to any moral theory sophisticated enough about the connection between harm and wrongness to be tenable. The important point for present purposes is that claims of dumbfounding cannot presuppose a specific moral theory, especially not one that has a peculiarly narrow view of what counts as a reason. Since I contend that *all* of the most plausible action-guiding moral theories yield the conclusion that the actions described in Incest and Cannibal are wrong, I need not adopt any particular theory in order to display the good reasons for moral condemnation.

Moreover, the Cannibal scenario illuminates a blind spot in Haidt's treatment of his secondary cases: putatively "harmless taboo-violation" tasks and scenarios. One need not be under the spell of magical thinking or irrational taboo in order to balk at the tasks that Haidt and his collaborators ask their subjects to perform. The implicit argument that people's aversion to these tasks and actions cannot be justified with reasons rests on an impoverished conception of action, which ignores its symbolic and expressive aspects and the reasons that arise from them. In the final section of the essay, I consider these aspects of action and argue that any psychologically adequate moral theory cannot ignore this aspect of who we are and what we do. I deploy such arguments, along with considerations about the vices manifested by the protagonists in these scenarios, against the rest of the dumbfounding cases, including both the taboo-violation tasks considered in the dumbfounding study and the judgments about "offensive yet harmless" actions given elsewhere (Haidt et al. 1993), where he anecdotally reports similar results.

The primary aim of this paper is to show that the prominent and influential dumbfounding study does not work on its own terms. Its examples ignore crucial distinctions concerning harm, wrongness, and reasons. Moreover, this is not just a problem of poorly chosen examples;

it illustrates a larger issue facing Haidt and the dumbfounders. Because they fail to differentiate between inarticulateness and insensitivity to reasons, they have not yet fixed on true dumbfounding—the sort that could support their pessimism. The fact that we are sometimes dumbfounded and sometimes confabulate does not imply that commonplace reasons offered for moral judgment are mere post hoc rationalizations.

We sometimes make up reasons in order to rationalize actions and decisions that would otherwise be inexplicable. These are rationalizations rather than reasons because they play no causal role in our judgment and action; the best explanation of what we think and do does not advert to such confabulations. Thus I grant that *sometimes* people are truly dumbfounded in a way that undermines the justification of both their moral claims and their aversion to acts that can aptly be called taboo, in that the only grounds for avoiding them is that they are anathema to accepted social norms. In other cases, however, people are simply unable to articulate the good reasons to which they are genuinely sensitive. Then their judgments and aversions are not unjustified simply because they cannot readily adduce their justification. In order to distinguish these two very different cases, we would need better examples and more careful argument. The modest claim that we sometimes confabulate moral reasons, sometimes cannot articulate reasons to which we are nonetheless sensitive, and sometimes can articulate genuine reasons that both cause and justify moral judgment (at least by our own lights), is significantly less exciting than the strong pessimistic claims made by the champions of dumbfounding. Yet it has the virtue of giving a more plausible account of our moral psychology.

I. HARM AND WRONGNESS

The connection between harm and wrongness, even according to those theories committed to somehow grounding wrongness in bad outcomes, is considerably more complex than the dumbfounding literature acknowledges. In this section, I argue that *none* of the three most prominent action-guiding moral theories is committed to denying the wrongness of such speciously harmless action as described in Incest— the case where Haidt's study finds dumbfounding most prevalent by far.[4] Although the good reason for moral condemnation of Cannibal does not advert directly to harm, it too can be accepted even by consequentialist moral theories, which pose the most challenging case. (I will give rough-and-ready glosses of these technical terms as we go.)

After making these arguments, I proceed in §2 to suggest that a powerful but perhaps not action-guiding approach, virtue ethics, suggests an undermining explanation for the dumbfounded response to scenarios like Incest and Cannibal which can be accommodated by other theories as well. In short, the explanation is that the scenarios are both grossly under-described and psychologically unrealistic. The most realistic ways of filling in the details of these toy cases renders them morally dubious. In §3, I consider the secondary examples of dumbfounding given by Haidt, concerning ostensibly harmless taboo violations and offensive actions, in ways foreshadowed by the discussion of his primary cases. All these examples were expressly designed to elicit strong intuitions of wrongness based on negative emotional responses to actions where, *because no one is harmed*, these responses are claimed to be extremely difficult to justify with supporting reasons. The discussion seems to presuppose that there are no defensible grounds for condemning harmless action. But this is an extremely controversial view, to say the least, and the primary dumbfounding scenarios hang on just the sort of case where even those theories most tolerant of harmless action must make exceptions.

We need to begin by briefly considering how various action-guiding moral theories view the connection between harm and wrongness. By an *action-guiding* moral theory, I simply mean one that aspires to advise agents prospectively about what to do, not merely to offer a criterion for evaluating action after the fact. The three most promising action-guiding theories are subjective act consequentialism, rule consequentialism, and deontology. It is more problematic whether virtue ethics is best construed as an action-guiding theory—but, as we will see, virtue ethics only raises further problems for the dumbfounders.

---

[4] Haidt considers *statements of dumbfounding*—such as "I know it's wrong, but I just can't come up with a reason why"—to be the clearest evidence of the phenomenon. He reports that such statements "were made 38 times in response to the Incest story and 24 times in response to the cannibalism story" (2000: 12).

According to deontological theories, certain types of action are inherently wrong, either in all cases or at least when there aren't compelling reasons to the contrary, such as those given in a catastrophe clause. These countermanding reasons may but need not advert to harm, since such theories draw no principled connection between harmlessness and permissibility. According to rule consequentialism, actions are permissible if they do not violate the best set of rules, where what counts as the best set of rules is somehow determined by their consequences (the details do not matter for present purposes). The crucial point here is that harmless token actions of a typically harmful type will often be prohibited by the best moral rules. Because the connection between harm and wrongness is indirect, the theory has no problem prohibiting dangerous actions that turn out fortunately—and are, in that superficial sense, harmless—such as drunk but lucky driving. Both deontology and rule consequentialism make the violation of rules their criterion of wrongness, but they have different foundations. Whereas rule consequentialism grounds right and wrong in the outcomes of actions, albeit indirectly, deontology holds certain types of actions to be inherently, though perhaps not invariably, wrong. Thus although both theories can hold that it is (generally) wrong to break one's promises, for rule consequentialism this fact issues from the utility of a rule prohibiting it, while for deontology it issues from the nature of the action itself.

Matters get more complex when we consider act consequentialism, although we need not pursue many of the complications. According to this theory, the right action is the one that brings about, or is likely to bring about, the best consequences. It is a separate matter what is valuable and, hence, what count as good or bad consequences. The crucial distinction for our purposes is between *subjective* and *objective* versions of act consequentialism. Objective theories take the actual results of an action as their criterion of wrongness, whereas subjective theories use the expected results given the agent's evidence at the time of decision (again there are various complications irrelevant for present purposes). The difference between the two can be illustrated with seatbelts, which usually protect passengers in car accidents but occasionally harm them—for instance, when being thrown through the windshield prevents an even worse fate. Consider just such a statistically unlikely but not bizarre case. The subjectively prudent act is to wear your seatbelt; that has the better expected result, since one cannot predict freak accidents. The objectively prudent act, however, is the one that actually has the best consequences—which on this occasion, we are stipulating, is not wearing the seatbelt. Thus it is not actual harm that matters for subjective theories, or even the balance of harm and benefit, but *expected* costs and benefits.

Objective act consequentialists do not put their view forward as action guiding, because one cannot try to bring about the best consequences except by putting oneself in a good epistemic position and then doing what has the best expected results. Thus in its advisory role the theory reverts to a subjective form. We can note afterwards that, in the event, not wearing the seat belt would have produced a better outcome (and hence is right according to the objective criterion). But this judgment can only be offered after the fact, when it is too late to guide the original action; moreover, because the outcome was unlikely, it offers no guidance for future actions either. It's great to get lucky but "Get lucky" is useless advice, whereas "Don't wear your seatbelt, you might be better off being thrown through the windshield" is terrible advice. By contrast, subjective act consequentialism takes expected value as its criterion precisely because this can be action guiding. It gets the correct result here, since it is always subjectively prudent to wear your seatbelt. This is not an argument against objective versions of the theory, but a demonstration of why—even according to their proponents—such theories do not purport to give prospective advice to agents.

With these distinctions in hand, we can now turn to the specific cases adduced by the literature. The central dumbfounding example, Incest, concerns a scenario in which two adult siblings, Julie and Mark, engage in consensual incest without any harmful consequences. Here is the prompt Haidt and his collaborators (2000: 20) gave their subjects:

Julie and Mark, who are brother and sister, are traveling together in France. They are both on summer vacation from college. One night they are staying alone in a cabin near the beach. They decide that it would be interesting and fun if they tried making love. At [the] very least it would be a new experience for them. Julie was already taking birth control pills, but Mark uses a condom too, just to be safe. They both enjoy it, but they decide not to do it again. They keep that night as a special secret between them, which makes them feel even closer to each other. So what do you think about this? Was it wrong for them to have sex?

Many of Haidt's subjects continued to hold that this action was wrong despite the fact that, under pressure from an experimenter playing devil's advocate, they cannot give any good reason for this verdict. (Or so it is claimed.[5]) As Haidt (2000: 8) describes the protocol, "following the Incest and Cannibal stories, if the participant responded that what the person or persons did was wrong, the main counter argument was that no harm was done, and that the fact that an act is disgusting does not make it wrong." The result was that the Incest scenario primarily, and Cannibal to a lesser extent, showed evidence of significant dumbfounding. Indeed, only Incest and Cannibal had a statistically significant result on more than one of four measures.[6]

The fundamental problem with Haidt's discussion of Incest is that he does not recognize that there is a perfectly good, if somewhat nuanced, harm-based argument for the supposedly dogmatic conclusion that Mark and Julie act wrongly. Nor does he consider the possibility that the 30 undergraduates surveyed, almost all of whom were between 18 and 20 years old, might have been browbeaten into giving up a good argument by an experimenter in a position of authority who insists that because no harm was done, no harm-based reason can apply. Or it just might not have been worth it to the subjects to fight for their conclusion in the face of crude resistance. The crudeness of the devil's advocate's argument is evident mainly in its notion of harmlessness.

The dumbfounding study seems to presuppose that because it is stipulated that no harm is done in the Mark and Julie scenario, no harm-based moral theory can criticize their act. Haidt (2000: 8) states repeatedly that the stories were "carefully written so as to be harmless," and Greene (2008: 57) overtly claims that "consequentialists do not

---

[5] As will be discussed, even this result is questionable because the experimenters do not seem to acknowledge the existence of any good reasons to judge the act wrong, which casts into doubt the claim that none were offered.

[6] Only the Incest story showed a statistically significant difference in *unsupported declarations*, such as "It's just wrong," as compared with a common moral dilemma case that was "expected to trigger dispassionate moral reasoning" (Haidt 2000: 7). Haidt considers *statements of dumbfounding*, where participants "directly state that they know or believe something, but cannot find reasons to support their belief" to be "the clearest evidence of dumbfounding" (ibid.: 8). Such statements occurred 38 times in Incest, as compared to 24 times in Cannibal. These were the only scenarios or tasks where anything like this degree of dumbfounding occurred.

condemn harmless actions" such as these.[7] These assumptions are built into the experiment, since the two counterarguments that the devil's advocate uses to undermine the subjects' critical judgments are that "no harm was done" and "the fact that an act is disgusting does not make it wrong." But there are perfectly good reasons to condemn Mark and Julie's consensual incest in various ways, including as morally wrong, even by consequentialist standards.

In order to illustrate this point, we must note some of the many problems with the claim that consequentialists do not condemn harmless actions. In the first place, this depends on the theory of value adopted: forms of consequentialism that do not adopt a utilitarian conception of value—on which pleasure or happiness is the only intrinsic good, and pain or unhappiness the only bad—may condemn many harmless actions. I will therefore focus on the utilitarian version of consequentialism in what follows. Second, indirect forms of utilitarianism often condemn acts harmless in their specific consequences that belong to a generally harmful type of action. Finally, even the simplest utilitarianism will condemn harmless action whenever it precludes more beneficial actions. It would be more accurate to say that utilitarianism (let alone consequentialism) does not concern harmlessness as such at all.[8]

Consider first what subjective act utilitarianism—which I will refer to hereafter simply as utilitarianism—holds about Incest. While Haidt can stipulate whatever he likes about the consequences of Mark and Julie's

---

[7] Greene (2008: 37–9) suggests that by "consequentialist" he does not mean the theory commonly referred to by that name, but a way of moral thinking he associates with that theory: the practice of thinking about actions solely in terms of their consequences. If so then the most sophisticated forms of consequentialism are not "consequentialist" in Greene's sense. It is still false that moral thinking that focuses solely on consequences cannot condemn harmless action, however, since Singer (1972) and other single-minded consequentialists would claim that it is wrong for Mark and Julie to travel to France rather than donating their vacation money to Oxfam, where it would do more good.

[8] Perhaps classical liberalism—which many of the first generation of philosophical utilitarians also held—does not *morally* condemn harmless action. But even that claim would be misleading in respects crucial to the dumbfounding cases, because classical liberalism can and must condemn various "harmless" actions, such as drunk but lucky driving, to take just one pertinent example (Jacobson 2000). Furthermore, there are other forms of criticism that the liberal can level at Mark and Julie. Since consent suffices to make any action permissible, in this view, their action is not morally wrong. Nevertheless, it can be criticized in other terms: as foolish, self-indulgent, and even perverse. In any case, consent rather than harmlessness is morally paramount.

behavior, these stipulations do not change the *expected* utility of their action, only its actual utility. Compare a scenario I'll call Gamble, in which Mike and Judy—who have no creditors or dependants, but have been diligently saving for their retirement—take their nest egg, head to Vegas, and put it all on one spin of the roulette wheel. And they win! Suddenly their retirement becomes about 40 times more comfortable. Having gotten lucky once, they decide that they will never do anything like that again. Was what Mike and Judy did prudent? Of course not, it was a foolish and reckless thing to do. Utilitarianism has no problem explaining why: they took a risky bet they couldn't afford with money needed for retirement. The fact that they got lucky, while doubtless crucial to them, is irrelevant to the criticism of their action. Reckless but lucky actions are just as foolish as reckless and unlucky ones. Although one might call a "winning" play of Russian roulette harmless, any notion of harm that ignores danger by focusing solely on actual outcomes cannot be action guiding in our sense. No matter how well things turned out, in relevantly similar circumstances one should act differently.

Now suppose that Mike and Judy made their gamble not with their own retirement but with their children's college savings. According to utilitarianism (and any other reasonable action-guiding moral theory) what they do is wrong—regardless of whether their lucky number comes up. Although one can stipulate that there are no bad remote effects, and hence that the act is in some sense harmless, this makes no relevant difference. Again it should be obvious why what Mike and Judy do in this version of Gamble is wrong: it recklessly endangers their children's welfare. Even if they happen to get lucky.

What relevance does Gamble have to Incest? This too should be obvious to philosophers, though perhaps not to a handful of undergraduates facing cross-examination by a devil's advocate who insists that if an action turns out to do no harm then it is harmless, and that if an act is harmless then it cannot be wrong. What Mark and Julie do is similarly *dangerous*. This point seems lost on the study's proponents, whether or not it was evident to their subjects. Haidt reports that several of the undergraduates in the study fix on the possibility of birth defects. He dismisses that unfounded worry by pointing out that its likelihood is minuscule, since Julie is on the pill and Mark uses a condom. This response is reasonable enough, as far as it goes. But the scenario's focus on birth control seems like a red herring: a salient but irrelevant point that distracts from the real issue. The great danger in Incest is of course that Mark and Julie do irreparable harm to their relationship as siblings. This is hardly an insignificant matter, and the point is rather obvious. After all, a lifetime of family get-togethers, funerals and weddings—perhaps even Mark and Julie's respective weddings—lie in the future. These events might be a touch awkward, even when there isn't an open bar. Moreover, as Twain observed: "Two people can keep a secret, as long as one of them is dead."

For most people, sex can have serious emotional repercussions, and although one might hope that a youthful experience could fade into the past, the potential benefits are negligible. (This point highlights the most serious problem with Greene's claim that consequentialism does not condemn harmless actions: the crucial issue isn't harm but relative *net* happiness; and the dumbfounding scenarios are, without exception, actions with little prospect of gain.) We are told in the Incest scenario that Mark and Julie think having sex might be "interesting and fun" or at least "a new experience." That isn't much to recommend risky behavior. It would be bizarre to think that there are no dangers present in Incest just because pregnancy is extremely unlikely, and it would be crazy to claim that an act wasn't dangerous just because it turned out well. I will not belabor this point any further. According to utilitarianism, the balance of expected utility determines an action's moral status, and in this case it surely condemns the Mark and Julie affair.

The case against Incest is even easier to make in rule utilitarian terms. Surely in any society roughly like ours, given obvious and widespread human psychological tendencies, some rule against incest would be justified by the likelihood of harmful emotional effects.[9] When we consider what a deontologist should say about Incest, though, an interesting point becomes apparent. Since deontology does not have to ground its judgments of inherent wrongness in harm, there is nothing to prevent it from holding that what Julie and Mark do is wrong simply *because it is incest.* Yet those who are putatively dumbfounded about the scenario cannot be confused about the type of action described (or else

---

[9] It is true but irrelevant that anthropologists can tell us about cultures where the definition, meaning, and consequences of incest differ from ours. Those are not Mark and Julie's circumstances.

their problem is deeper than moral dumbfounding). Rather, they are unable to come up with further reasons in a situation where, according to the theory, no further reasons must exist. That is just what it means to say that incest is inherently wrong. The devil's advocate's arguments are an irrelevant distraction.

The dumbfounding literature seems to beg the question against intuitionist forms of deontology, according to which moral judgment is non-derivative and immediate—like perception, to use a word without negative connotation.[10] Hence I will not consider quasi-perceptual forms of deontology any further with respect to moral judgment, where most philosophers find them inadequate (but cf. Stratton-Lake 2002). An analogous view of aesthetic judgment seems much more compelling, however. If you can't see what is beautiful about that sunset, or smell what is disgusting about raw sewage, then there is something wrong with your sensibility—not with my inability to provide you with a reason. This will become relevant when we consider Haidt's cases of offensive and disgusting but harmless action, in §3.

That should suffice to make the initial, relatively modest point that Incest is a bad example for Haidt and the dumbfounders. Moreover, it is crucial to remember why the scenarios were constructed as they were. As Haidt (2000: 6; emphasis added) explains:

> We interviewed people about situations that were likely to produce strong intuitions that an action was wrong, yet *we engineered the situations to make it extremely difficult to find strong arguments* to justify these intuitions.

In order for the inability to adduce a reason to be dumbfounding rather than mere inarticulateness, it is necessary to construct cases where there are no strong arguments—or simply good reasons—to be found. Thus Incest is poorly suited for making the dumbfounders' case. Not only

---

[10] H. A. Prichard (1912: 29) claimed, "We do not come to appreciate an obligation by an argument, i.e. by a process of non-moral thinking," and it is a mistake to think we should. Rather, such judgments are, as they should be, direct and immediate perceptions of our moral reasons. Prichard was thus skeptical of reasoning, but not of reasons. Reasoning, understood as a process of discrete inferential steps, often gets conflated with acting on reasons in this literature, although one might simply see what one has most reason to do without inferring it in some stepwise process. The significant claims about confabulation and ex post facto rationalization, which threaten to undermine the justification of moral judgment, follow not from the denial of reasoning but from the claim that moral judgment is not caused by reasons to which the agent is responsive.

is there a compelling harm-based reason to condemn the action as wrong, but the example obscures this reason in two ways: the scenario hangs crucially on a somewhat subtle point about the difference between risk and harm, and the experimental protocol uses a devil's advocate to blur just this distinction by insisting that Julie and Mark's behavior was harmless. Indeed, Haidt and his collaborators—along with their philosophical allies—seem oblivious to the decisive moral argument condemning Incest, as the quotation above attests.

The larger question then becomes whether the problem with Incest just amounts to faulty engineering, or if there is something more deeply problematic about the implications drawn from the dumbfounding study. I contend that a deeper worry infects all of Haidt's examples and cannot be solved simply by reengineering the cases. The deep problem lies in the danger of conflating two quite different circumstances: those where an agent has no reason, just some brute aversion that is rationalized after the fact; and those where an agent is responsive to a reason without being immediately able to articulate what it is.[11] To illustrate the latter possibility, imagine that one of the dumbfounded subjects continued to think about the case and soon realized that the morally relevant point in thinking prospectively about what to do is what was likely to happen, not what actually happened. This is such a compelling point that it should not be dismissed as post hoc rationalization too quickly. There is evidence from non-evaluative domains that people can be sensitive to reasons they cannot adequately articulate, for instance when experts prove reliable at discerning forgeries by such subjective criteria as their "feel." The presence of an affect-laden intuition does not undermine the possibility of reason-responsiveness either. Perhaps fear sometimes alerts us to environmental cues that we cannot identify, such as the body language of an approaching stranger. These are just a couple of examples of how we might be responsive to reasons without being able to articulate them.

Recall that Haidt (2000: 1) defines moral dumbfounding as "the stubborn and puzzled maintenance of a moral judgment without

---

[11] Indeed, there are other possibilities. The aversion might not simply be brute, but inculcated (deliberately or not) specifically because it is typically beneficial. Such inculcation might be first or second nature, the product of evolution or habituation. I am grateful to Eric Mack for noting this point and its implications.

supporting reasons." What is now at issue is whether being unable to state a reason is tantamount to not having one at all. Only the latter possibility is real dumbfounding, in the sense that supports the pessimistic view of moral reasoning as mere post hoc rationalization. The former merely shows that we cannot always articulate the reasons on which we act. But if we sometimes respond to reasons without being able to articulate them, then scenarios where there are good reasons to be found, though subjects can't seem to find them, cannot differentiate between dumbfounding and mere inarticulateness.

2. RULES AND REASONS

Thus far I take myself to have shown that the central example of the dumbfounding study, where the phenomenon was most robust, does not work as advertised. Contrary to Haidt's claims, it is quite easy to justify a critical moral judgment about Incest as long as one avoids the "good outcome, therefore good decision" fallacy. Two important questions remain: whether these problems extend to all of his examples of moral dumbfounding, and whether this is merely an engineering problem which could be solved by better scenario design. Consider the prompt for Haidt's other primary case, Cannibal:

Jennifer works in a medical school pathology lab as a research assistant. The lab prepares human cadavers that are used to teach medical students about anatomy. The cadavers come from people who had donated their body to science for research. One night Jennifer is leaving the lab when she sees a body that is going to be discarded the next day. Jennifer was a vegetarian, for moral reasons. She thought it was wrong to kill animals for food. But then, when she saw a body about to be cremated, she thought it was irrational to waste perfectly edible meat. So she cut off a piece of flesh, and took it home and cooked it. The person had died recently of a heart attack, and she cooked the meat thoroughly, so there was no risk of disease. Is there anything wrong with what she did?

Since what Jennifer does has no obviously harmful consequences, Haidt contends that it is extremely difficult to find a strong argument that she acts wrongly. As we've seen, this begs the question against those forms of intuitionist deontology on which there are no *further* reasons, just the inherent wrongness of cannibalism. I would not want to defend such a view myself. But is it really so hard to find a good utilitarian argument against Cannibal?

Recall that according to rule utilitarianism, what makes an action wrong is that it violates the best set of rules, which are themselves justified by the utility of their acceptance. This means that the theory counts any consideration suggesting that some action would violate warranted moral rules as a reason. Although Cannibal is a toy case presented with little context, one must presume that there are standard protocols in Jennifer's lab of the sort found in any medical laboratory. While such rules will vary in minor respects, we can be confident that the protocols of *every* lab will rule out the desecration of corpses—even those about to be cremated. Again this justification should be obvious to anyone who isn't stupefied by a theory on which such superficially harmless actions cannot be condemned. Surely there would be far fewer cadavers available for research if those who would otherwise donate their body to science knew that a perverse lab assistant might violate their corpse. Furthermore, better scenario design would not help matters. Although Haidt could have stipulated that Jennifer's act remains secret, so donations are not deterred, rule utilitarianism justifies moral rules not by the consequences of a toy case but by those of the whole class of realistic cases.

Now consider subjective act utilitarianism, which will be my focus in the rest of the paper for two reasons. In the first place, it is the hardest case for me, since this is the action-guiding moral theory on which it is most challenging to condemn action that seems to have no bad *specific consequences*—as opposed to consequences that arise from repetition of the same type of action. Second, utilitarianism illustrates the crucial point that once one distinguishes a theory's criterion of rightness from its recommendations for moral thinking, this opens up a broad sphere of what I'll call *non-criterial* reasons. Such reasons advert not to considerations that are part of the theory's criterion of right and wrong, but to features of situations that properly minded agents should take as reasons: considerations the theory itself recommends treating as reasons. This will show why hedonist utilitarianism need not advert only to considerations of pain and pleasure as reasons to act, for instance, although only those considerations are recognized by its criterion of rightness. The same point holds for forms of consequentialism that adopt a more complex theory of value.

It is now widely acknowledged that utilitarianism, like other forms of consequentialism, offers a criterion of rightness; it does not entail any particular view about how to engage in moral thinking. In particular, it *need* not advise the agent always to aim at maximizing the good, and there are compelling reasons to think that the theory *should* not do so (Hare 1981). This is important because once it is acknowledged that sophisticated versions of utilitarianism recommend other sorts of moral reasoning than single-minded promotion of net goodness, it becomes evident that consequentialism must recognize a broader class of reasons than those that appeal directly to its criterion of rightness—that is, to criterial reasons. Vulgar consequentialist reasoning, which is limited to criterial reasons, would likely make us biased and inefficient promoters of the good. This point leads most philosophers to conclude that utilitarianism would do better, by its own standard, to make us into decent people concerned primarily with our own actions and character, and committed to specific projects and particular relationships out of proportion to their place in the utility calculus. The theory should encourage us to be reasonably virtuous agents: averse to cheating, cruelty and the like, and disposed to take such properties of action as providing non-criterial reasons. Although cheating isn't inherently wrong (since nothing is), and the fact that an action constitutes cheating isn't literally a wrong-maker (as it isn't criterial), "That would be cheating" counts as a reason not to do it (though not always conclusive reason).

One particular type of non-criterial reason is especially important because so often neglected. These considerations focus on the consequences of action on the agent himself, which are seldom the effects of any specific act but are inculcated through repetition. Behavior that is rewarded tends to be repeated. Hence when cheating pays off, this leads the agent to become a cheater: someone disposed to cheat when he thinks he can get away with it. Whenever performing some type of action would make you vicious through habituation, as a non-specific consequence of repeated acts, then you do well to inculcate an aversion to so acting. An analogous point holds of virtuous action. Moreover, you should endorse these aversions and attractions by conceptualizing them in evaluative terms (such as *perversion* or *generosity*) and accepting these concepts as reason-giving. It is a good thing that we are averse to incest and cannibalism, and that we endorse that aversion by taking people to have reason not to engage in such acts *because they are perverse or disgusting*. Since this reason does not advert directly to happiness, it is non-criterial by utilitarian standards. Nevertheless, such reasoning, which focuses on the character of the agent, should be embraced by utilitarianism—especially given that people often mistakenly identify acts as harmless by ignoring their non-specific consequences. Which of course is precisely how the dumbfounding scenarios are engineered.

Whether or not virtue ethics should be considered an action-guiding moral theory, its focus on character and motivation helps explain putative dumbfounding. When one reads Incest and especially Cannibal, it is hard to construct a plausible picture of the motivations of the protagonists. We are told that Jennifer defiles the corpse because she thinks it "irrational to waste perfectly edible meat" (2000: 20). Seriously? Someone genuinely motivated all the way to action—action that violates basic lab protocols and, if discovered, would risk her job and subject her to widespread contempt—would surely have taken less drastic waste-reduction measures previously. She might have petitioned the lab to allow the cadavers to be widely distributed to soup kitchens rather than cremated, so that they can be served to the poor. Any such suggestion would have no chance of success, of course, assuming her supervisors are sane. But if Jennifer has thought this through and decided instead on direct action, wouldn't she already be living on a diet of road kill and dumpster diving? Are we supposed to imagine that Jennifer, despite being a moral vegetarian, lacks the normal abhorrence toward eating human flesh? The dumbfounding scenarios are incredible as stated, particularly regarding the motive explicitly ascribed to Jennifer (frugality) and the dispositions implicitly denied (aversion to cannibalism). What Jennifer does is so perverse as to suggest that she is motivated by something deeper and darker than frugality—and something much easier to condemn. If subjects simply can't make sense of Jennifer and her motives as described, then they aren't so much morally dumbfounded as bewildered about what they are being asked to imagine.

What then does utilitarianism say about Cannibal? If the theory has any problem criticizing Jennifer, it is the view's familiar difficulty condemning actions that have no bad specific consequences when considered in isolation. The point of reengineering Cannibal so as to rule out the most obvious reasons to condemn Jennifer's action is to illustrate that non-specific consequences can ground non-criterial reasons to judge cannibalism wrong—at least when it's done with such a flimsy rationale as thrift.[12] Even if her behavior remains secret, we cannot ignore the consequences of Jennifer's action on her own character and dispositions to act in the future. It is unrealistic to stipulate that there will be no such effects, because she will have just as much reason to do the same thing tomorrow—and having done so once, she will be more likely to do it again. If utilitarianism should endorse an aversion to cannibalism, as seems plausible, then there are several good non-criterial reasons to condemn her act: what she does is cannibalism, it breaks warranted moral rules, and it threatens to turn her frugality into perversity.

Now recall Incest. What traits of character do Mark and Julie display on their carefree French vacation? Consider that their only reasons for deciding to have sex are that it would be interesting, novel, and fun. I grant that these are fine reasons to do certain things, such as try an exotic cuisine or play a new game. But they are rather lightweight reasons to think that having sex with a live sibling or a dead chicken might be worth trying—even if you thought you might like it. Indeed (and this is part of the point), sometimes the thought that one might like it provides the strongest reason *not* to experiment. Whereas Jennifer's stipulated motivations are so bizarre as to queer the thought experiment, Mark and Julie exhibit the less exotic vices of recklessness and licentiousness.[13] The frivolity of their risky behavior provides a reason to condemn it that is available not only to virtue ethics but, as a non-criterial reason, to other normative theories as well. A perfectly good reason to condemn Mark and Julie's action is that it is reckless and licentious. And a perfectly good argument against Jennifer's action is that what she does is perverse—again, *without any serious prospect of benefit.*

---

[12] This judgment need not lead to an absolute prohibition. The good reason not to engage in cannibalism, reflected in our endorsed aversion to it, is outweighed by the even better reason not to starve to death in a Donner Pass scenario: a forced choice between cannibalism and starvation.

[13] I am of course well aware that licentiousness is no longer a popular term of disapprobation, and it's not one I frequently invoke myself. But you don't have to be a prude to deem *some* acts licentious; rather, you have to be morally stupefied to deny that anything is. One might consult Suetonius's *The Twelve Caesars* as a reminder of this point, or simply use the *reductio* example of necrophilia.

Admittedly, utilitarianism must treat non-criterial reasons as contingent and defeasible, and as actually defeated in exceptional cases. Nevertheless, no serious consideration is offered as a defeater of the prima facie reasons provided in these scenarios by non-criterial reasons. Given how lame "it might be fun" is as a reason for risky behavior, or "it would reduce waste" is as a reason to eat human flesh, every tenable action-guiding moral theory should condemn these actions. Thus the simplistic conception of the relation between harm and wrongness assumed by the dumbfounders spoils their primary cases, those best supported by the data. Their secondary cases are flawed in somewhat different ways.

3. THE SYMBOLIC AND EXPRESSIVE ASPECTS OF ACTION

Considerations to which virtue ethics has been most sensitive, but that can and should be incorporated into any moral theory, contribute significantly to our understanding of Incest and Cannibal intuitions. Similar reasons figure in both Haidt's "taboo-violation" tasks from the dumbfounding study, which he calls Roach and Soul, and in judgments about certain admittedly offensive actions he considers elsewhere (Haidt et al. 1993). Although the latter cases were not part of the dumbfounding study, Haidt (2001: 817) claims in subsequent work that many survey participants were dumbfounded about these cases as well, which is to say that they were unable to articulate good reasons for their condemnation of "offensive yet harmless [actions], such as eating one's dead pet dog, cleaning one's toilet with the national flag, or eating a chicken carcass one has just used for masturbation."

I have argued that Incest and Cannibal are only superficially harmless, and that any tenable moral theory can condemn them. The taboo-violation tasks and offensive actions avoid the obvious problems of the moral intuition cases: they do not ignore danger and the violation of rules justified by harm prevention (and promotion of the good). It is curious, though, that Haidt terms these actions *offensive yet harmless*. This description presupposes that offense does not count as harm. Yet since it is unpleasant to be offended, any offense actually taken, regardless of its justification, is bad qua pain. Even if one defines harm as bodily damage—which seems dubiously to discount severe psychological trauma as compared to modest physical pain—that would merely make the harmful fail to circumscribe the bad, according to any plausible theory of value.

Moreover, in order for Haidt to claim that people are dumbfounded in their response to these cases, as he expressly does, he must hold that criticism of these acts as disgusting or offensive does not count as providing reasons to judge them wrong. Surely no one who hears about the scenario where a person eats a chicken after using its carcass for masturbation is dumbfounded to the extent of being unable to say that this is perverted and disgusting. Recall that the second counter-argument given by the experimenter playing devil's advocate is that just because something is disgusting doesn't make it wrong. That is true, as far as it goes, but it doesn't go very far. It seems hard to deny that the offensiveness and disgustingness of some action count as reasons not to do it. Thus only by narrowly and contentiously limiting what count as *moral* reasons can the dumbfounders claim that "it's disgusting" and "it's offensive"—which were granted in the very description of the case—*do not even count as (moral) reasons.*[14] Recall that to be morally dumbfounded is not to have any supporting reason for one's judgment. The second argument given by the devil's advocate thus seems to grant that these actions are disgusting, on one hand, and then to take it back with the other. If so then those subjects who offered such reasons were not dumbfounded so much as persuaded by an authority figure on dubious grounds. This is a much less interesting experimental result, to say the least.

Once we recognize that even utilitarianism can adduce features of actions other than those included in the theory's *criterion* of right and wrong, it becomes evident that Haidt's secondary examples are all similarly flawed. These secondary cases come in two varieties: taboo violation tasks and offensive yet harmless actions. Consider first the tasks that Haidt and his collaborators include in the dumbfounding

---

[14] Moreover, Haidt calls the taboo-violation tasks "non-moral intuition tasks," presumably because the tasks subjects are asked to perform are (in the liberal view) self-regarding. Yet he insists, in later work, that it is a mistake of Western liberalism to limit the moral domain to the harmful and the unjust (Haidt and Bjorklund 2008). I cannot broach the complex issue of the distinction between moral and non-moral reasons here, except to note that the argument that people are dumbfounded with respect to what is wrong about the offensive yet harmless actions implicitly assumes a substantive position on this issue, and one that Haidt seems to reject in later work.

study (though they find much less evidence of dumbfounding): Roach and Soul. In Roach, the subject is offered a sip of water into which a sterilized cockroach has been dunked. One might think there is a perfectly obvious and satisfactory reason to turn down the offer: it is disgusting. It is hard to discern why Haidt (2000: 12) concludes that "[p]articipants were often clearly dumbfounded" by Roach and Soul, since the data don't seem to reflect this. Moreover, in order to claim that the subjects are dumbfounded, Haidt cannot allow the disgusting-ness of the roach-dunked water to count as a reason not to drink it. The question is why not.

There are two distinct senses of the term "disgusting": one sense is dispositional (roughly, causes disgust) and the other normative (merits disgust). I will by stipulation use "disgusting" in its normative sense. But let's focus first on actual disgust, before turning to fitting disgust, which is directed at what merits that response: the disgusting. Many people will be at least mildly disgusted by the prospect of drinking roach-water, whether or not it really is disgusting. For the utilitarian, this seems like an obviously good reason not to drink it: disgust is unpleasant, and unpleasant states of consciousness are intrinsically bad. How then can Haidt claim that people are dumbfounded by their aversion to drinking roach-water? Surely they are not unable to articulate their aversion; it cannot escape them that they are disgusted by the prospect. Yet the study seems to presuppose that the unpleasantness of disgust, like offense, doesn't count as a reason not to drink the roach-water. Although no explanation is given for why "I don't want to do something unpleasant" isn't a perfectly good reason not to perform the task, a hint is given in Haidt's terminology: he calls them *taboo-violation* tasks. If an aversion is wholly irrational, and there is no further reason beyond the unpleasantness of doing something irrationally aversive, then one might conclude that there are no reasons not to act. In this view, such aversions are mere taboos—nothing more than prejudice and superstition. And one might think that irrational preferences cannot provide reasons, although this conclusion requires argument and does not comport well with utilitarianism (or any other view on which all pain is intrinsic-ally bad).

It is easy enough to infer why Haidt and his collaborators think this aversion irrational. The reason they sterilize the cockroach is to ensure that it does not carry germs. If an unsterilized cockroach were dipped in one's water, they would surely grant that one had hygienic reasons not to drink it. Disgust is about contamination, they claim, and it is fitting only when directed at something that really is contaminated. Since the cockroach has been sterilized, it cannot contaminate the water; so the roach-dipped water is *not* actually disgusting (in the normative sense). Hence any disgust over drinking the water would be unfitting and should therefore be discounted as taboo.[15] The tacit and dubious assumption here lies in the adoption of what might be called the *germ theory of contamination*. According to this theory, to be contaminated just is for it to be germy. But what is and isn't disgusting is not a matter of prosaic fact; it is not a matter of how germy something is. One can perfectly well grant that the roach-water isn't full of germs and still think it disgusting. Indeed, this is my own view.

This is a first-order normative claim, which Haidt and his followers reject. It is equally coherent to hold, as they seem committed to claiming, that nothing sanitary is disgusting. But they imply further that to think otherwise is to succumb to magical thinking. On the contrary, I contend that their view leads to a *reductio ad absurdum*. Suppose that a properly embalmed corpse is less germy than a living human being. Would that show that it is mere prejudice and superstition to think that necrophilia is disgusting but normal sex is not? I am content to rest this aspect of my dispute with the dumbfounders on this question (though I could make the case even more gruesome for them). If I am right, then either disgust isn't solely about contamination or the germ theory of contamination is false as a substantive account of the disgusting. I grant that I have no *further* reason for the judgment that necrophilia is disgusting, but it seems misguided to hold that an argument is required. The disgusting is a quasi-perceptual evaluative concept, and if you can't "see" what is disgusting about having sex with a corpse then so much the worse for you.[16]

---

[15] See Rozin and Nemeroff (1990) on contagion as "sympathetic magic." This argument is made explicit and developed in Knapp (2003).

[16] It is sometimes objected that people have sincerely held that homosexuality or miscegenation is disgusting, falsely. But the fact that substantively false, or even morally pernicious, judgments of the disgusting are possible does not tell against my argument. I am not claiming that these judgments are infallible, only that it is untenable to deny that necrophilia really is disgusting (or to claim that nothing is disgusting in the normative sense, which has this implication *a fortiori*).

In the other taboo-violation task, Soul, the experimenter offers the subject two dollars for signing an explicitly non-binding "contract" that grants possession of the subject's soul after death to the experimenter. Here the one significant mark of dumbfounding was that some people made statements of dumbfounding: they said they wouldn't do it but couldn't say why. Again there is a perfectly adequate and obvious reason not to sign, however, which subjects might have felt but not been able to articulate—or perhaps were inhibited about articulating. Even pretending to sell your soul to someone is a *symbolic* act of subjection. The fact that the contract isn't binding does not erase this symbolism. Haidt's failure to acknowledge the symbolic and expressive aspects of action is strangely myopic. The dumbfounders seem to think that it is mere prejudice and superstition to. be sensitive to the symbolic aspects of one's action. But consider: would you use toilet paper imprinted with the picture of your beloved on it, if it were given to you for free (and otherwise just as good as your usual brand)? I confidently assume not. Hence, even if we grant that some undergraduates couldn't articulate their reason not to engage in purely symbolic self-degradation, why conclude that they are not responsive to it? It is a fine reason, albeit not a tremendously powerful one.[17]

The presentation of these task cases seems to ignore the fact that actions express attitudes independent of our motivation for performing them (which might be purely financial). When we repudiate the attitude that an action expresses, then we have a perfectly good reason not to engage in it. To deny this is to accept that any aversion to using the free toilet paper is mere irrationality. But that conclusion isn't forced upon us by any moral theory, since even the most simplistic hedonist consequentialism should hold that the aversion itself—or more precisely the pain associated with it—provides reason not to act. Moreover, it would take a substantial argument to show that there was something irrational

---

[17] But as with all these examples, there is little reason to perform the actions either. Speaking for myself, I would not sign some manipulative experimenter's bogus contract for my soul for $2, even though for $2000 I would laugh all the way to the bank. Consider an alternative scenario in which an eccentric millionaire offers you a menu of symbolically degrading acts for which he'll pay fees proportional to their repugnance. I would entertain such proposals, were the price non-negligible, and might well accept some of them. But it would be bizarre to deny that I have any reason not to debase myself for money—even if that reason is outweighed by the stack of cash. Yet Haidt seems committed to the stupefied claim that we have no such reasons.

about being averse to these admittedly offensive tasks; yet no argument at all is offered by the dumbfounders. It is a deep fact about human nature that we are symbol-making creatures, and that we imbue these symbols with meaning. Of course, humans are also prone to engage in magical thinking and even to believe in magic, but those tendencies involve holding false causal claims. No such factual error is implicated in our reluctance to debase a picture of a beloved or the symbol of a dearly held cause, let alone in our aversion to necrophilia and bestiality. No doubt these dispositions have various benefits, especially in terms of promoting social relations, as well as numerous costs. But to consider them mere prejudice and superstition—that is, taboo—is to alienate oneself from a significant aspect of human life. Moral psychologists should be wary of coming to this conclusion too quickly or without vivid awareness of what they thereby disparage or ignore.

The scenarios of eating the family pet, cleaning the toilet with the flag, and masturbating with a chicken carcass (let alone eating it afterwards) all suffer from this bizarre myopia about what can be counted as a good reason. If you love something, you will not want to perform actions that express indifference or contempt toward it. Admittedly this is symbolic, but there is nothing inherently irrational about being attracted to good symbolism and averse to bad symbolism. On the contrary, this deeply seated aspect of human nature seems, more plausibly, not to stand in need of further justification. The fact that you will turn down a small amount of money to perform the act doesn't show that you are in the grip of some taboo, since the very act of offering you money to symbolically betray something you care about is offensive. Indeed, Haidt *grants* it to be offensive: these are termed offensive yet harmless actions. But that very formulation shows that the notion of harm being used is a strangely narrow one, which must be systematically blind to expressive qualities of our action that are obvious to those who are not in the grip of a theory.

REFERENCES

Greene, Joshua (2008) "The Secret Joke of Kant's Soul." In Walter Sinnott-Armstrong (ed.), *Moral Psychology*, vol. 3 (Cambridge, MA: MIT Press), 35–80.

Haidt, Jonathan (2001) "The Emotional Dog and its Rational Tail," *Psychological Review* 108, 814–34.

——(2005) Interview in *The Believer*. August 2005. <http://www.believermag. com/issues/200508/?read=interview_haidt>.

——and Fredrik Bjorklund (2008) "Social Intuitionists Answer Six Questions About Moral Psychology." In Walter Sinnott-Armstrong (ed.), *Moral Psychology* (Cambridge, MA: MIT Press), 181–218.

——S. Koller, and M. Dias (1993) "Affect, Culture, and Morality, or Is it Wrong to Eat Your Dog?" *Journal of Personality and Social Psychology* 65, 613–28.

——Fredrik Bjorklund, and Scott Murphy (2000) "Moral Dumbfounding: When Intuition Finds No Reason." Unpublished manuscript.

Hare, R. M. (1981) *Moral Thinking* (New York: Oxford University Press).

Jacobson, Daniel (2000) "Mill on Liberty, Speech, and the Free Society," *Philosophy & Public Affairs* 29, 276–309.

——(2008) "Does Social Intuitionism Flatter Morality or Challenge It?" In Walter Sinnott-Armstrong (ed.), *Moral Psychology*, vol. 2 (Cambridge, MA: MIT Press).

Knapp, Christopher (2003) "De-moralizing Disgustingness," *Philosophy and Phenomenological Research* 66, 253–78.

Nisbett, Richard and Timothy DeCamp Wilson (1977) "Telling More Than We Can Know: Verbal Reports on Mental Processes," *Psychological Review* 84, 231–59.

Prichard, H. A. (1912) "Does Moral Philosophy Rest on a Mistake?" *Mind* 21, 21–37.

Rozin, P. and C. J. Nemeroff (1990) "The Laws of Sympathetic Magic: A Psychological Analysis of Similarity and Contagion." In J. Stigler, G. Herdt, and R. A. Shweder (eds.), *Cultural Psychology: Essays on Comparative Human Development* (Cambridge University Press), 205–32.

Singer, Peter (1972) "Famine, Affluence, and Morality," *Philosophy & Public Affairs* 1, 229–43.

——(2005) "Ethics and Intuitions," *The Journal of Ethics* 9, 331–52.

Stratton-Lake, Philip (2002) *Ethical Intuitionism: Re-evaluations* (Oxford: Clarendon Press).

Index